CD-ROM
INCLUDED

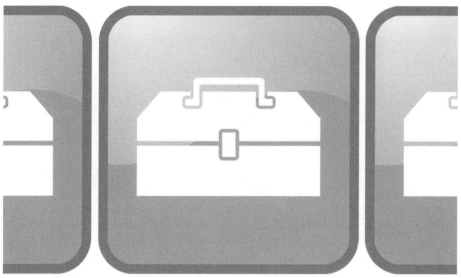

The complete
NEW
TESTAMENT
resource for
YOUTH
WORKERS
volume 1

Jack Crabtree, General Editor

ZONDERVAN®

ZONDERVAN.com/
AUTHORTRACKER
follow your favorite authors

youth
specialties

YOUTH SPECIALTIES

The Complete New Testament Resource for Youth Workers Volume 1
Copyright 2009 by Youth Specialties

Youth Specialties resources, 1890 Cordell Ct. Ste. 105, El Cajon, CA 92020 are published by Zondervan, 5300 Patterson Ave. SE, Grand Rapids, MI 49530.

ISBN 978-0-310-27335-6

Cover design by Toolbox Studios
Interior design by Brandi Etheredge Design

Printed in the United States of America

09 10 11 12 13 14 • 20 19 18 17 16 15 14 13 12 11 10 9 8 7 6 5 4 3 2 1

CONTENTS

INTRODUCTION

Welcome to *The Complete New Testament Resource for Youth Workers*, Volume 1.

In this volume are 107 complete lessons written by a team of 28 youth leaders from diverse backgrounds who teach the Bible to young people every week.

These lessons are *Bible-centered:* The goal is to bring the truth and its application to students. The majority of our young people are biblically illiterate and lack understanding of God's grace, what Jesus taught, and the lifestyle of someone who follows Christ. This volume will greatly enhance students' biblical knowledge and personal application. Each lesson is designed to make a Bible passage become alive and relevant to a young person.

As you can see, Volume 1 includes lessons for these New Testament books: Matthew, John, Romans, Galatians, Ephesians, Philippians, Colossians, 1 Timothy, 2 Timothy, Titus, Philemon, 1 John, 2 John, 3 John, and Jude. That's 107 chapters and, thus, 107 lessons. Volume 2, due to hit shelves February 2011, covers the rest of the New Testament books.

Each chapter's lesson comes complete with a comprehensive lesson plan easily accessible to busy youth workers. Each chapter lesson isn't the *only* theme, topic, or biblical principle in that chapter worth teaching—it's simply one good lesson.

Let me explain how these lessons work and how to use them in your ministry.

LESSON FORMAT

You'll quickly discover that the lessons follow this format:
- *Scripture* and *Topic*: The specific passage and direction of the lesson
- *Objective*: A statement of the desired outcomes for the lesson
- *Background/Overview*: Information to help put the passage in context

- *Game/Icebreaker*: An activity to enhance group chemistry and set the stage for the Bible teaching
- *Icebreaker Questions*: A transition from activity to Bible
- *Scripture*: The featured Bible passage, in the TNIV
- *Study Questions*: Serious interaction with the biblical text
- *Talking Points*: An expanded teaching outline
- *Real-life Connection*: An application point or activity
- *Media*: Options for adding video clips or other media to the lesson

USE

The ways to use this resource will be as varied and numerous as the users—each youth leader and group is unique. You may, for example, want to spend 28 weeks in Matthew, 16 weeks in Romans, or 1 week in Philemon. And you'll be able to do that, moving through your chosen book one chapter, one lesson at a time.

You may already be studying a book, say, Galatians, in your small group. You could access the lesson for the chapter of the next passage in your study and supplement (or replace) what you were planning.

Or you simply may use this volume as your emergency meeting plan. When you don't know what to do or don't have time to prepare, the work is already done for you. Scan the objectives and overview statements and find a timely lesson for your group. You can also mine this book for games, discussions, Bible studies, teachings, wrap-ups, or media ideas and use them wherever. The included CD-ROM makes this very easy.

WRITING PROCESS

These lessons were written by an experienced team of youth workers from Youth for Christ and various other churches and ministries. You can check the list of contributors for the true identities of the writers. The goal of all our planning, brainstorming, writing, and editing has been to assist you as you teach young people to understand and apply God's Word.

We tried hard to be attentive to the *real* teachings of Scripture—to be theologically sound and intensely practical as well. Certainly you'll need to adapt the lessons to the issues and needs of your students.

Thanks for buying this book and using its resources in your youth ministry. More importantly, thank you for your faithfulness to Christ and your commitment to reach kids for him.

Jack Crabtree,
Executive Director
Long Island Youth for Christ

CONTRIBUTORS

Jack Crabtree, Long Island Youth for Christ/Shelter Rock Church, Syosset, N.Y.

Dave Veerman, The Livingstone Corporation, Carol Stream, Ill.

Kevin Mahaffy, Smithtown Gospel Tabernacle, Smithtown, N.Y.

Craig Muller, Long Island Youth for Christ/Shelter Rock Church, Syosset, N.Y.

Ron Francis, New Life Community Church, Sayville, N.Y.

Jeremy and Laura Herr, Eastport Bible Church, Eastport, N.Y.

Christine Hong, Arumdaun Presbyterian Church, Bethpage, N.Y.

Stephanie Eggers, Long Island Youth for Christ/First Presbyterian Church, Babylon, N.Y.

Rachelle Ayala, Long Island Youth for Christ/Life Point Church, Huntington, N.Y.

Mark Ayala, Long Island Youth for Christ/Life Point Church, Huntington, N.Y.

Sam Sutter, Dix Hills Evangelical Free Church, Huntington Station, N.Y.

Matt Merker, Shelter Rock Church, Manhasset, N.Y.

Jill Laufenberg, Philadelphia Youth for Christ, Pa.

Joe Davis, Mobilepreacher.org, Sarasota, Fla.

Dimas Salaberrios, Infinity Church/Youth for Christ, Bronx, N.Y.

Kevin Mahaffy Sr., Franklin Park, Ill.

James Leon, Long Island Youth for Christ/Church of the Nazarene, Valley Stream, N.Y.

Dan O'Leary, Our Savior Lutheran Church, Centereach, N.Y.

Steve Kinsel, Long Island Youth for Christ/The Church at Farmingdale, Farmingdale, N.Y.

Jake Tyler, Eastern Region Youth for Christ

Seth Naicker, Bethel University, St. Paul, Minn.

Nina Edwards, Youth for Christ USA

Kerri Cataldo, Prodigal House Ministry, Port Jefferson Station, N.Y.

Oscar Rivera, Rivers Ministries YFC, McGuire Air Force Base, N.J.

Binu Thomas, Long Island Youth for Christ/Bethlehem Assembly of God, Valley Stream, N.Y.

David DeRosa, North Shore Community Church, Oyster Bay, N.Y.

Emilie Lamoureux, Long Island Youth for Christ/Dix Hills Evangelical Free Church, Huntington Station, N.Y.

Brian McGee, Young Life, Long Island, N.Y.

Jerry O'Sullivan, Shelter Rock Church, Syosset, N.Y.

MATTHEW

Matthew 1:18-25

TOPIC: Obeying God no matter what

OBJECTIVE: Students will be like Joseph and trust and obey God even when others don't understand their actions.

BACKGROUND/OVERVIEW: Mary and Joseph were asked to obey God even though everyone around them thought they were crazy. This passage teaches us that God's ways are much better than our ways, even if by following God's will we appear foolish.

GAME/ICEBREAKER: **Blindfolded obstacle course**
Items needed:

- Chairs
- Pillows
- Blindfold

Set up a fairly simple obstacle course. Use chairs, pillows, people—whatever you have that won't be dangerous for the students going through the course. Challenge a volunteer to make it through the course wearing a blindfold. Predictably she'll have a hard time doing it. Allow her to struggle and bump into things (while making sure she doesn't get hurt). Do it again with the same blindfolded volunteer, but offer the participant the opportunity to choose a partner—a trusted friend without a blindfold to verbally guide her through the course. It may take time, but the person will succeed with the help of the friend. Note: This game has many possible variations. For example, you could use competitive teams, and the team with the shortest time making it through the maze would win.

ICEBREAKER QUESTIONS:

- (To the competitor(s)): **As you went through the course blindfolded, what kind of pressure did you feel from yourself? From the people around you?**
- (To the competitor(s)): **In what ways did having a guide without a blindfold change how you felt about the game and going through the course?**
- (To the competitor(s)): **At what point in the course did you doubt what your partner was telling you to do? When did you trust your partner most?**
- (To the guide/partner): **What was frustrating about trying to get your blindfolded partner through the course?**

SCRIPTURE: **Matthew 1:18-25**
Read this aloud as students follow along in their Bibles.

[18] This is how the birth of Jesus the Messiah came about: His mother Mary was pledged to be married to Joseph, but before they came together, she was found to be pregnant through the Holy Spirit. [19] Because Joseph her husband was a righteous man and did not want to expose her to public disgrace, he had in mind to divorce her quietly.

[20] But after he had considered this, an angel of the Lord appeared to him in a dream and said, "Joseph son of David, do not be afraid to take Mary home as your wife, because what is conceived in her is from the Holy Spirit. [21] She will give birth to a son, and you are to give him the name Jesus, because he will save his people from their sins."

[22] All this took place to fulfill what the Lord had said through the prophet: [23] "The virgin will conceive and give birth to a son, and they will call him Immanuel" (which means "God with us").

[24] When Joseph woke up, he did what the angel of the Lord had

commanded him and took Mary home as his wife. [25] But he had no union with her until she gave birth to a son. And he gave him the name Jesus.

STUDY QUESTIONS:

- What would you say or do if your fiance (or, for the girls—if your brother's fiance) **told you she was pregnant but not by you** (or your brother)?
- What kind of pressure might Joseph have faced when he chose to follow God's instructions and marry Mary?
- What convinced Joseph to obey God's instructions?

TALKING POINTS:

Share the following points with your students:

Joseph's high-pressure situation

Joseph was faced with one of the most difficult situations one can imagine. His wife-to-be was pregnant, and he didn't do it. Can you imagine what he was feeling? Can you try to put yourself in his shoes and think of all the emotions he was feeling and all the thoughts he must have had? He must have been so confused, hurt, angry, and worried. Everyone who knew Mary and Joseph was going to think either Mary was unfaithful, or Joseph was with Mary before they were married.

God showed up and told them what to do

Then God showed up and told Joseph everything would be okay—that he, God, had a plan. God told Joseph that Mary did nothing wrong—she had the Messiah—the Savior of the world—in her womb, and Joseph was to take her as his wife. Joseph was to love her and be the earthly father of God's Son.

Joseph decided to obey God

Joseph responded and acted in complete obedience: He did exactly as God instructed. His obedience is remarkable because he could've reacted so differently. He could've used human wisdom to rationalize this situation. That can't be true. Women can't get pregnant by the Holy Spirit. Everyone will think I did something wrong. This can't be what is best for Mary, the baby, or me. Joseph said none of those things: Instead, he obeyed. Joseph's obedience was part of God's plan to bring his Son into the world to save all those who would believe in him.

Obedience without question

Bible teacher Donald Grey Barnhouse (1895-1960) told the following story: A young son of a missionary couple in Zaire was playing in the yard. Suddenly the voice of the boy's father rang out from the porch, "Philip, obey me instantly! Drop to your stomach!"

Immediately the youngster did as his father commanded.

"Now crawl toward me as fast as you can!"

The boy obeyed. After he crawled a short distance the father said, "Stand up and run to me!"

Philip responded without question and ran to his father's arms.

As the youngster turned to look at the tree by which he had been playing, he saw a large, deadly snake hanging from one of the branches. At the first command of his father, Philip could have hesitated and asked, "Why do you want me to do that?" Or he could have casually replied, "In a minute." Instead, he gave total obedience.

REAL-LIFE CONNECTION: God's ways are best

Spend some time discussing obedience with your students.

Ask—

In what situation have you found it difficult to obey God?

Say—

Maybe you have been tempted to cheat because it seems like everyone is doing it. You might think, *Nobody will know. I can't pass any other way.* Maybe you've been asked to share your faith with a friend. Do you ever tell yourself, "He'll think I'm weird?" or, "She won't want to be my friend anymore." Perhaps God is telling you to forgive someone who hurt you, and you need to bring yourself to forgive.

We need to be like Joseph and obey God's instructions—regardless of the circumstances. God's ways are best. We may not see what God is doing or where God is leading us, but when we obey, God takes us places we could have never thought of going. God's ways are always best for us. So trust God and obey God no matter what. Then watch what happens to you and the situation. God doesn't promise all conflicts will be resolved and all problems solved. In fact, obeying God may result in emotional or physical pain. But God promises he'll be with us in every circumstance, and he'll work in and through our difficulties to a greater good for us. We just need to trust him. It may get harder but you'll be in step with God and have his protection and peace. Let's pray right now and ask him to help us trust him tonight and this week.

MEDIA: He believed

Show a clip from *The Nativity Story*. Show the section where God speaks to Joseph in a dream about Mary having a baby. Joseph dreams about his community stoning Mary to death, and then the angel appears and tells him the real story of Jesus' conception. A scene follows in which Joseph tells Mary he believes her story and that they'll name the baby Jesus. This scene is found in chapter 12 (47:14). Part of this scene, titled "I Believe You" (1:17), is available at www.wingclips.com. Search for *nativity*.

Matthew 2:1-12

TOPIC: Wise Christmas gifts

OBJECTIVE: Students will know why we exchange gifts at Christmas, and each will give a meaningful gift to someone who needs it.

BACKGROUND/OVERVIEW: The wise men (magi) stopped their lives to seek out Jesus the King: They rearranged their entire lives to find him. These men who were very knowledgeable about the heavens noticed the new star in the sky, so they knew something historic was taking place. They followed the star and found the Savior.

GAME/ICEBREAKER: **That's a wrap**

Items needed:

- Bags of candy
- Boxes
- Wrapping materials

Divide into teams of five to 10 students, and give each team a bag of candy, a box, and a set of wrapping materials (tape, string, wrapping paper, newspaper in lieu of wrapping paper, etc.). Explain that at your signal, they'll have three minutes to wrap their gift (the bag of candy in the box) as tightly as possible, making it very difficult to open. They may use any or all of the materials. The gift should also be attractive. (Points will be awarded for wrapping aesthetics). Then give them a few minutes to strategize.

Give your signal and let the wrapping begin. After three minutes have the teams display their wrapped gifts. Judge the boxes for *beauty* and award points (1st—1000, 2nd—750, 3rd—500, etc., depending on the number of teams). Explain it's now time for round two. Have each team select a representative to participate. Seat him in front of the group (or have him stand behind a long table). Then place one of the gifts in front of each person, making sure no one has the gift from his or her team. Explain that at your signal, the contestants should work as quickly as possible to unwrap the gifts—points will be awarded. (Encourage teams to cheer for their contestants.) Give the signal and watch the chaos. Eventually the competitors will pull out the bags of candy and hold them high. Once again, award points (1st—2,000, 2nd—1,500, 3rd—1,000, etc.). Determine the overall winning team, and let the competitors share the bags of candy with their respective teams.

ICEBREAKER QUESTIONS:

- When have you anticipated a gift so much you couldn't wait to rip off the wrapping paper and open it?
- Did anyone think it was impossible to open the gift?
- Why do we enjoy receiving gifts? Why do we enjoy giving them?
- Why do we give gifts on Christmas?

SCRIPTURE: Matthew 2:1-12

Have five students read this aloud from their Bibles—each student should read one paragraph.

[1] After Jesus was born in Bethlehem in Judea, during the time of King Herod, Magi from the east came to Jerusalem [2] and asked, "Where is the one who has been born king of the Jews? We saw his star when it rose and have come to worship him."

[3] When King Herod heard this he was disturbed, and all Jerusalem with him. [4] When he had called together all the people's chief priests and teachers of the law, he asked them where the Messiah was to be born. [5] "In Bethlehem in Judea," they replied, "for this is what the prophet has written:

[6] "'But you, Bethlehem, in the land of Judah, are by no means least among the rulers of Judah; for out of you will come a rule rwho will shepherd my people Israel.'"

[7] Then Herod called the Magi secretly and found out from them the exact time the star had appeared. [8] He sent them to Bethlehem and said, "Go and make a careful search for the child. As soon as you find him, report to me, so that I too may go and worship him."

[9] After they had heard the king, they went on their way, and the star they had seen when it rose went ahead of them until it stopped over the place where the child was. [10] When they saw the star, they were overjoyed. [11] On coming to the house, they saw the child with his mother Mary, and they bowed down and worshiped him. Then they opened their treasures and presented him with gifts of gold, frankincense and myrrh. [12] And having been warned in a dream not to go back to Herod, they returned to their country by another route.

STUDY QUESTIONS:

- When did the wise men (magi) start their journey to find Jesus?
- Why was Herod so interested in the magi finding Jesus?
- Where were Mary and Jesus when the wise men finally found them?
- What were the three gifts they brought? Why were these good gifts for this baby?
- Why did the wise men return home a different way?
- What clue do you notice in this passage that shows Jesus wasn't a newborn when the wise men found him?

TALKING POINTS:
Share the following points with your students:

Big news
The birth of Jesus was huge. We get caught up in shopping, Santa, and self at Christmas and forget what a life-changing, earth-shattering event Jesus' birth was. It changed everything. While studying the stars and the sky, the magi noticed the new star that was shining, and they knew it meant that something awesome had occurred. So they traveled, following the path of a star across the night sky, to find the King of the Jews.

A long trip for three gifts
The magi left everything to find Jesus—this wasn't a short trip. The journey to find Jesus was long. We know this because the Bible explains they found Jesus in his house as a child, not a baby. They brought rare and expensive gifts to Jesus—gold, frankincense, and myrrh. Each gift held special meaning: Gold was a precious material that foretold Jesus as King; frankincense represented Jesus as a prophet; and myrrh was a burial spice, foretelling Jesus' death.

Christmas gifts
At Christmas we exchange gifts in remembrance of the magi giving Jesus gifts. This puts a whole new feeling to gift giving. We are practicing what the wise men did for Jesus. Our giving to others should represent and honor Jesus.

REAL-LIFE CONNECTION: Give a gift
Spend some time with your students discussing ways they can give to other people:

This year at Christmas think about the gift Jesus gave us. He died so we can have life eternally. With whom do you want to share Jesus' love this Christmas? Celebrating Christmas means sharing in the joy of God's love for his children. This year find someone who needs a gift. This could be a lonely kid at school, an elderly neighbor, or a child at church. Save some money and buy a gift for someone who needs to know he or she is loved. The gift doesn't have to be big, just a symbol of God's love to another person. And if you really want to have fun, give the gift anonymously, never letting the person know you were the giver.

MEDIA: Finding the star

The movie The Nativity Story has a clip (chapter 8—27:20) in which the wise men discuss the appearance of the star and what it means. Meanwhile, Mary is making her journey to her Aunt Elizabeth's house.

There is a second clip (chapter 18—1:18 to 1:21) where the wise men are following the star to Bethlehem while Mary is giving birth.

Either or both of these clips would be a great way to open up the discussion on who these men were.

Matthew 3:13-17

TOPIC: God is alive, talking, and pleased

OBJECTIVE: Students will learn God (Father, Son, and Spirit) is real and can be trusted.

BACKGROUND/OVERVIEW: Jesus came to John the Baptist to be baptized at the start of his earthly ministry. Immediately following the baptism God the Father declared with a voice from heaven, "This is my Son, whom I love; with him I am well pleased" (Matthew 3:17).

GAME/ICEBREAKER: Trust fall

Ask the group if they trust you and your staff. Then choose two or three of the students who said yes to come to the front. Station two of your strong and capable volunteers at one end of a sturdy chair or small table. Have one of the trusting students stand on the chair or table. Tell her this will be a test of her trust. Then have the student fall back into the arms of your strong and trustworthy volunteers. Repeat with the next student, etc. Ask if others would like to volunteer and repeat the process with them.

ICEBREAKER QUESTIONS:

- (To those who participated): **Why did you volunteer?**
- (To everyone else): **Why didn't you volunteer?**
- (To those who participated): **What questions were you thinking before you decided to lean back and fall?**
- (To those who participated): **How did you feel after you fell back and before you were caught?**
- What makes us willing to trust someone?
- What makes a person or an institution trustworthy?
- Why is it easier to believe in what you see rather than what can't be seen?

SCRIPTURE: Matthew 3:13-17

Read the passage aloud as students follow along in their Bibles.

13 Then Jesus came from Galilee to the Jordan to be baptized by John. 14 But John tried to deter him, saying, "I need to be baptized by you, and do you come to me?"

[15] Jesus replied, "Let it be so now; it is proper for us to do this to fulfill all righteousness." Then John consented.

[16] As soon as Jesus was baptized, he went up out of the water. At that moment heaven was opened, and he saw the Spirit of God descending like a dove and alighting on him. [17] And a voice from heaven said, "This is my Son, whom I love; with him I am well pleased."

STUDY QUESTIONS:

- **In this passage we have three appearances of God. What are they and how do they relate to each other?** (Answer: Jesus was being baptized; the Holy Spirit descended; the Father spoke from heaven.)
- **What did God the Father say about Jesus?**
- **If God spoke in an audible voice about you today, what do you think he'd say?**
- **Jesus pleased his Father. How are we able to please God?**

TALKING POINTS:
Share the following points with your students:

Heavenly endorsement
When Jesus came up from the water, the Holy Spirit descended upon him like a dove. This is the Holy Spirit's stamp of approval on Jesus. God was telling the world Jesus is the Messiah—God incarnate who had come to earth to rescue human beings.

If that weren't enough, God the Father spoke in a voice all could hear, declaring Jesus as his Son and his pleasure with him. God—three in one—declared to the world that nothing would ever be the same. God the Son has come with the power of the Holy Spirit and the approval of the Father to save the world.

Who is Jesus?
Ever wonder if Jesus was really God? Ever wish God would just tell you—just stick his head out of the clouds and tell you the truth? He did. Right here, when Jesus was baptized, what so many wish for actually happened: God spoke. Later Peter recalled this event and reminded his readers the account of the power and coming of Jesus Christ wasn't just a cleverly invented story. Peter and others were eyewitnesses of this incredible moment when the Holy Spirit descended on Jesus, and God spoke aloud so all could hear (2 Peter 1:16-18). And the event was recorded in Scripture for us to read.

At times we may wonder if God is real and Jesus is the Savior of the world. But this passage and many others provide evidence of God and his work.

REAL-LIFE CONNECTION: Godly confidence

Say to your students—

If you ever wonder about Jesus, who he is and if he can be trusted, remember eyewitnesses wrote the Bible. This week, review the evidence. Read the gospel of John and then the first chapter of 1 John.

During your prayer times, confess your lack of trust and ask God to give you confidence in him.

MEDIA: Faith

Show the clip "Faith in Evidence" (1:00) from *The Case for Christ* by Lee Strobel. This clip is available at Wing Clips. Search on www.wingclips.com with the words *faith in evidence*.

Matthew 4:1-11

TOPIC: Temptation

OBJECTIVE: Students will know how Jesus responded to three big temptations, and they'll follow his example when personally tempted.

BACKGROUND/OVERVIEW: Jesus was led by God into the wilderness to fast and pray for 40 days and nights. While he was there Satan came and tempted Jesus in three different ways. Jesus resisted each temptation. Through his example he shows us how to resist temptation.

GAME/ICEBREAKER: **What's Your Price?**

Items needed:

- Nine squares of paper (see below)
- Video camera or tape recorder
- One $1 bill
- One $50 bill

This is a staged sting operation dramatized in front of the group. The four people involved should be informed and prepared ahead of the meeting. They'll play their parts according to the scripted plan. At the end of the game, you'll tell the entire group the truth so they know these people were acting for the group.

Begin by selecting two students to leave the room and two students to supervise them while they're out of the room. They'll return individually to play a scaled-down *Deal or No Deal* type of game. Post nine squares of paper on the wall. Each square has a number from one to nine written on one side of the paper and an amount of money written on the other side hidden from the audience and contestants (No. 3 is $0; No. 9 is 5 cents; No. 8 is 10 cents; No. 2 is 25 cents; No. 1 is $1; No. 5 is $2; No. 4 is $5; No. 6 is $10; and No. 7 is $50). The contestants will each pick three squares to be turned over one at a time. They win the money from the square with the highest value. When the contestants are out of the room, tell the remaining group they'll be testing the contestant's ability to make good choices. When the first contestant returns to the room, he should pick No. 8, then No. 2, then No. 9. (This contestant would win $1.) The leader should then put all nine squares back up on the wall. The second contestant should come in and pick No. 8, then No. 3, then No. 7 to win the $50. But before the leader awards the money, one of the two supervisors who were outside should break into the conversation saying she has something everyone should see before the prize is awarded. She'll either play an audiotape or show a video of the other game supervisor making a deal with the second contestant to split the $50 prize if he gives him the winning number to pick. (This recording should be made while they're out of the room waiting to play the game—the supervisor should tempt the contestant with the answer if he'll give half the prize to him.)

When the leader hears about the tape of this plan, he'll stop giving the award to the student and talk with the group about what happened and what they should do about it.

ICEBREAKER QUESTIONS:

- What made this temptation to get the right number so attractive to our contestant?
- How would you have responded if you'd had the opportunity to cheat in order to win some money?
- How is your opinion about the contestants different after seeing/hearing the tape?

(Important: After the discussion tell the whole group the truth: All the participants played roles. No one cheated—it all was planned to look real.)

SCRIPTURE: Matthew 4:1-11
Read the following passage aloud to your students.

[1] Then Jesus was led by the Spirit into the wilderness to be tempted by the devil. [2] After fasting forty days and forty nights, he was hungry. [3] The tempter came to him and said, "If you are the Son of God, tell these stones to become bread."

[4] Jesus answered, "It is written: 'People do not live on bread alone, but on every word that comes from the mouth of God.'

[5] Then the devil took him to the holy city and had him stand on the highest point of the temple. [6] "If you are the Son of God," he said, "throw yourself down. For it is written:
"He will command his angels concerning you,
and they will lift you up in their hands,
so that you will not strike your foot against a stone.'"

[7] Jesus answered him, "It is also written: 'Do not put the Lord your God to the test.'"

[8] Again, the devil took him to a very high mountain and showed him all the kingdoms of the world and their splendor. [9] "All this I will give you," he said, "if you will bow down and worship me."

[10] Jesus said to him, "Away from me, Satan! For it is written: 'Worship the Lord your God, and serve him only.'"

[11] Then the devil left him, and angels came and attended him.

STUDY QUESTIONS:

- In what ways did Satan tempt Jesus?
- How did Jesus respond to Satan's enticing invitations and resist the temptations?
- When you're tempted to do wrong, how do you respond to the invitations of others or to the thoughts inside your head?
- What would Jesus tell us about temptation and how to resist it?

TALKING POINTS:

Share the following points with your students:

Jesus was tempted as we're tempted

Jesus went into the wilderness to seek God by fasting and praying. His desire was to neglect his physical needs in order to hear God better. Here we see the most obvious attack by temptation in all of Scripture: Satan appeared to Jesus and tempted him three times—first to give in to his physical desires; then to seek wealth and possessions; and finally to become powerful and famous. Physical gratification, money, prestige, and power are the three big areas of temptation we all face. John summarizes the nature of temptation in 1 John 2:15-17; there we see these three desires.

To each temptation Jesus responded by quoting Scripture. This certainly wasn't the only time Jesus was tempted. But every time he was tempted, he kept his focus on his identity and the Father's purpose. Knowing Satan's way would provide temporary pleasure but would ultimately lead to destruction, Jesus rejected the tempter's lies and made the right choices.

Jesus is our example when we face temptation

Sometimes we think Jesus can't possibly understand what it's like to live the life we live. After all, we think, we face temptations around every corner, and these desires can be so difficult to resist—but that line of thinking is false. The unfortunate truth is when we're tempted, we offer little resistance and give in easily. When Jesus was tempted he never gave in. He resisted even the strongest temptations. He did it by believing what God says, not in Satan's empty promise. He focused on God's promises. Are we going to believe God's Word is true all the time and in every circumstance, or are we going to believe the lies of the Enemy? I hope and pray each of us gets better at resisting the temptations of the Enemy by believing in God's promises. Remember, he promised never to leave us, to give us strength to resist temptation, and he promises us guidance in every situation.

REAL-LIFE CONNECTION: Stay strong in God's Word

Share the following with your students—have them write down the Bible verses they're to remember:

Since temptations will always be in our lives, we must get better at how we respond to them. Let's do what Jesus did—use God's Word, the Bible, to remind us that God's ways are best for us. Here are some examples to try this week:

- When you're tempted to lie, say— "Kings take pleasure in honest lips; they value a man who speaks the truth" (Proverbs 16:13).
- When you're tempted to gossip, say— "A gossip betrays a confidence, but a trustworthy man keeps a secret" (Proverbs 11:13).
- Remember God is on your side. First Corinthians 10:13 says, "No temptation has seized you except what is common to man. And God is faithful; he will not let you be tempted beyond what you can bear. But when you are tempted, he will also provide a way out so you can stand up under it."

MEDIA: Resist the temptation

Joshua Harris, author of *I Kissed Dating Goodbye* (Sisters, Oregon: Multnomah, 1997), speaks about how to resist temptation. He speaks about following Jesus' example when tempted.

This video (2:06) can be found on www.youtube.com. Type in either *Joshua Harris* or *how to resist temptation*. The Gospel Coalition produces this video.

Matthew 5:43-48

TOPIC: Loving your enemies

OBJECTIVE: Students will know the command of Jesus to love their enemies, and they'll identify difficult people in their life whom they're commanded to love.

BACKGROUND/OVERVIEW: As part of his Sermon on the Mount, Jesus redefined what real love is. The religious leaders had misinterpreted God's law, telling people only to love those who loved them and to hate their enemies. Jesus teaches us to love our enemies because God loves them.

GAME/ICEBREAKER: Do you love your neighbor?
Items needed:

- Chairs or seats for each player, minus one.

Set up the chairs in a circle facing inward. Choose someone to be *It*, and have that person stand in the center of the circle of chairs. Everyone else should take a seat. The person who is *It* stands in front of one of the seated people and asks, "Do you love your neighbor?" The person then chooses to say yes or no. If the person says yes, his two neighbors (the ones seated directly to the left and right) have to switch seats before he can steal one of their chairs. Whoever is left standing is *It*. If the person says no, they also says, "but I love people who _____." He fills in the blank with anything pertaining to one or more participants in the circle (e.g., have blond hair, are 15 years old, are wearing white socks, etc.). Those people in the circle who fit that description must leave their seat and try to find a new one before *It* steals their chair.

ICEBREAKER QUESTIONS:

- In what ways does that game relate to the Bible? (Answer: Jesus tells us to love our neighbors.)
- Who else does Jesus say we should love?
- What TV or movie character is most despicable to you?
- Why would it be hard to like that person (if he or she were a real person)? If you knew that person in real life, how would you deal with him or her?

- What big things do people do that make them enemies? What small things?
- Do you have people you consider enemies? What did they do that got them on your enemies list?

SCRIPTURE: Matthew 5:43-48

Read this passage aloud while students follow along in their Bibles. Jesus is speaking.

[43] "You have heard that it was said, 'Love your neighbor and hate your enemy.' [44] But I tell you, love your enemies and pray for those who persecute you, [45] that you may be children of your Father in heaven. He causes his sun to rise on the evil and the good, and sends rain on the righteous and the unrighteous. [46] If you love those who love you, what reward will you get? Are not even the tax collectors doing that? [47] And if you greet only your own people, what are you doing more than others? Do not even pagans do that? [48] Be perfect, therefore, as your heavenly Father is perfect."

STUDY QUESTIONS:

- What ancient rule of human relationships did Jesus challenge here? (Answer: Love your friends and hate your enemies.)
- How is Jesus' definition of real love different from what most people do?
- What is your test of real love? How do you know love is real?
- What is really difficult about loving our enemies?
- What specific actions could we take to love an enemy?

TALKING POINTS:

Share the following points with your students:

Who's your enemy?

Most of us have a list in our head of a few people we don't like—maybe even some people we hate. We think about all the things they've done to hurt us. We tell other people so they know how badly we've been treated. We plot and plan how we could repay them. Nothing would make us happier than seeing something bad happen to them. You know whom I'm talking about: You're thinking about that person right now.

A new response to our enemies

Jesus calls us to think and act quite differently toward these people we consider enemies. He tells us to love the people who hurt us. He commands us to love the people we love to hate. When someone gives us a hard time, Jesus tells us to pray for them; we're not to want bad things to happen to them. Jesus says God gives everyone the same love he gives us. Jesus said if we're children of God the Father, we should love the same people he loves—all people.

Real love personified

Love is one of the most misunderstood and misused words. What is real love? Jesus shook up the world because he described God's love so specifically. He said it wasn't loving just to be nice to those who treat us nice—real love is wanting the best for people we don't like, too. Jesus didn't just talk about this kind of love—he demonstrated this kind of love by getting involved with people others despised. Jesus says we can know we're part of God's family when we love the same people God loves. When we love this way, we glorify God and make his name famous. People know God is real when they see followers of Christ loving people who are hard to love. The power and motivation to love our enemies come from God. He loves us unconditionally, and we can love others the same way. We live in his forgiveness and stay connected to him. We should try every day to look and act like our heavenly Father.

REAL-LIFE CONNECTION: Tough love

Give your students the following instructions:

- Make a list of people in your life who are hard to love. Think about your history with these people. What would have to happen to your heart in order for you to be able to pray for them?
- Pray for those enemies—for God to change them and for your reconciliation and peace with them. Pick one person you dislike and pray for that person every day this week.
- Think of specific ways you can show love this week to someone on your list.
- Go against your normal human feelings and when you're with them, act like Jesus would.

MEDIA: **They loved their enemies**

These movie/video clips of real-life situations can be used to provoke discussion about loving your enemies. How did these people do this? What were the results?

Take a look at *End of the Spear*—"He Gave It" (2:56). Years after Mincayani killed Steve's missionary father, they end up together at the scene of the massacre, and Steve is given the chance to take revenge. Search for this clip with the words, *he gave it*.

You can also try *To End all Wars*—"Human Beings" (3:04). After being bombed by Allied troops, Ernest makes the choice to help the injured enemy soldiers. Search for this clip with the words, *human beings*.

Both these video clips are available from www.wingclips.com.

Matthew 6:31-34

TOPIC: Where's your faith?

OBJECTIVE: Students will know that God can and will provide all their needs.

BACKGROUND/OVERVIEW: This is part of the famous *Sermon on the Mount,* where Jesus was teaching his disciples, and the crowds were listening. Jesus said, "But seek first his kingdom and his righteousness, and all these things will be given to you" (Matthew 6:33). When we focus on God and seek him in every area of our lives, we'll naturally turn to him first for help. Jesus teaches that when we do this, God will meet all of our needs.

GAME/ICEBREAKER: **What would you do for candy?**
Items needed:

- Small prizes (candy or dollar bills)
- Jar of baby food or can of spinach
- Prune juice

Bring students to the front one at a time. Out of an envelope, have them draw a slip of paper on which a challenge has been written. Then have them perform the challenge. Give everyone who successfully meets the challenge a prize.

- Sing the national anthem in 15 seconds.
- Get five people to do the chicken dance with you.
- Eat a can of spinach or a jar of baby food in 15 seconds.
- Receive two wet willies from two different people.
- Scream as loud as you can for 10 seconds.
- Give 30 people a high five in 15 seconds.
- Drink a whole bottle of prune juice.
- Get six people to act like monkeys for 15 seconds.

ICEBREAKER QUESTIONS:

- (For the participants): **Was what you did worth the candy or dollar?**
- (For the people who did not participate): **Why did you choose** *not* **to do one of these challenges for the reward?**
- **In real life what risky things do you do to get rewards?**
- **How do you decide if the promised reward is worth the risk of doing something?**

SCRIPTURE: Matthew 6:31-34

Read the following passage aloud.

[31] So do not worry, saying, "What shall we eat?" or "What shall we drink?" or "What shall we wear?" [32] For the pagans run after all these things, and your heavenly Father knows that you need them. 33 But seek first his kingdom and his righteousness, and all these things will be given to you as well. [34] Therefore do not worry about tomorrow, for tomorrow will worry about itself. Each day has enough trouble of its own.

STUDY QUESTIONS:

- What are some of your worries?
- In what ways does worrying help you or hurt you?
- How can you stop worrying or reduce how much you worry?
- What does this passage promise about God and worry?
- How much confidence do you have that God will take care of you and provide everything you need?
- How have you seen God take care of you and the things you worry about?

TALKING POINTS:

Share the following points with your students:

Why we worry

Worry is normal for most of us. We don't know what is going to happen in the future, so we worry. Tomorrow could bring a disaster or a tragedy into our lives. When we start thinking about this possibility, we imagine all kinds of terrible events. We worry because we wonder if and when the bad things will happen to us. (Share with your students a personal example or two of your worries.)

Worry is negative faith

When we worry, we take our focus off God and put it on our problems. We believe the worst is bound to happen, not the best. Sometimes people say they don't have faith, or they can't believe in a God they can't see, or they can't trust his promises to take care of them. But when we worry, we're believing something that hasn't happened yet will happen. We think and act like it's true.

Life involves choices

Every day of our lives, the biggest choice we make is whether we believe God will take care of us. If we believe he's good, he cares for us, and he wants the best for us, then we'll give him first place—the top priority in all our other daily choices. We can be confident God will provide what we need and work out what we can't control. When worry starts pounding away in our head, we get to choose whether we'll believe the worst or believe what Jesus promises—that God will provide all we need.

REAL-LIFE CONNECTION: Case studies

Have your students break into groups of four and discuss these case studies (one at a time). Each member of the group should answer the questions. After 10 or 15 minutes, bring everyone together and debrief the answers from the small groups.

Case Study No. 1:

You have a big test to take at school in two weeks. You have to get an 80 percent to pass the class.

- How do you trust God in this situation? Or, do you worry about this test?
- How much of passing this test depends on what you do?
- How much depends on what God will do to help you?

Case Study No. 2:

You need to buy a car and get it insured. Right now you don't have any money for a car.

- **What do you do?**
- **How does trusting God help you get what you want or need?**

MEDIA: Doubt is the greatest weakness

Show the clip "Greatest Weakness of Man" (.56) from the film *The Great Debaters*.

In this clip James tells his father, Dr. Farmer, that he has made the debate team. His father asks "What is the greatest weakness of man?"

James replies, "Not believing. Doubt."

This clip is available from www.wingclips.com. Use the search words *greatest weakness of man*.

Matthew 7:24-29

TOPIC: Wisdom

OBJECTIVE: Students will learn that Jesus' teachings are everlasting and that building their lives on Jesus' words is essential.

BACKGROUND/OVERVIEW: Jesus warns against false teachers by telling his followers to listen to him to find wisdom and life.

GAME/ICEBREAKER: Gingerbread house
Items needed:

- Graham crackers
- Decorative candies (M&Ms, Twizzlers, marshmallows, etc.)
- Frosting
- Empty pint-sized milk cartons

Divide into teams and give each team a set of the same materials. Tell students they have 10 minutes to build a house. Afterward, have a panel of judges (staff members) pick the winning house.

ICEBREAKER QUESTIONS:

- What problems did you encounter in trying to build your house?
- If you had to build a real house, what are some issues you would have to consider?
- If you were building a house by the water, what would you do differently?
- If you needed help in your house-construction efforts, whose advice would you seek? What credentials would be important to you?

SCRIPTURE:
Matthew 7:24-29
Ask a student to read the passage aloud from her Bible. Explain to students that in this passage, Jesus is speaking.

> 24 "Therefore everyone who hears these words of mine and puts them into practice is like a wise man who built his house on the rock.
> 25 The rain came down, the streams rose, and the winds blew and beat

against that house; yet it did not fall, because it had its foundation on the rock. ²⁶ But everyone who hears these words of mine and does not put them into practice is like a foolish man who built his house on sand. ²⁷ The rain came down, the streams rose, and the winds blew and beat against that house, and it fell with a great crash."

²⁸ When Jesus had finished saying these things, the crowds were amazed at his teaching, ²⁹ because he taught as one who had authority, and not as their teachers of the law.

STUDY QUESTIONS:

- Why is the foundation of a house important?
- What does Jesus equate with real wisdom?
- What "sandy foundations" have you seen people build their lives on?
- What does Jesus think would be a strong foundation for a person's life?
- What can we do to build our lives on Christ?

TALKING POINTS:

Share the following points with your students:

Where do I build?
What kid doesn't love to build sandcastles? When building a sandcastle the key decision is choosing where to build one. If you build the castle too far from the water the sand is too dry, and you can't get enough wet sand to form anything. Build too close to the water, however, and all your hard work will soon be washed away by the waves. When building a real house by the water, choosing the location or foundation is even more important. Certainly a person would want to build his or her house on a foundation that will last.

Who's got wisdom?
Everyone wants wisdom—no one wants to be considered a fool. In this passage Jesus makes an incredible claim: He says if we do what he says, we'll be like a wise person who builds a house on a strong foundation. If we don't do what he says, however, we'll be like a fool who builds on shifting sands. Jesus says if we follow his instructions for life, we will have a lasting foundation: Building our lives on him is like building a house on a rock.

Jesus and his teachings will never fail us. They won't change. They'll never be less than what we need to build on.

Test it

You can test it if you like. Jesus himself claims that when the storms come, the results will prove whether or not you chose the right foundation. You can test this assertion, but the better choice is to believe Jesus and take him at his word. Let's choose to believe him and build on his foundation now, before the storm. When you build on something else and the storm comes, you'll lose everything. Build your beliefs, your attitudes, your ideas, your choices, your actions, and your very life on the foundation that will never fail—our Rock, Jesus.

REAL-LIFE CONNECTION:
What choices have you made?

Have your students each take a piece of paper and write down all the choices they remember making so far today (or go back five days if necessary).

- How many of those choices were pleasing to God and in agreement with what Jesus tells us to do?
- How many weren't? Circle the choices that went against God's advice.
- Did you just forget to ask God about these choices?
- Did you know it wasn't pleasing to God, but you did it anyway?

Say—

Bad choices put your foundation on sandy ground. Your disaster is coming. What choices will you make this week? Write down at least three.

- Write *Ask God* next to each choice.
- Write *Obey God* next to *Ask God*.

How many times have you trusted in something other than Jesus and fallen because of it? How many times are you willing to fall because you won't listen to Jesus? Right now reevaluate your foundation. Are you building your life on the Rock? Or are you building your life on whatever seems popular today? Don't be a fool. Don't let your house be destroyed. Build on the Rock. It may mean you need to change some things. You may need to think differently. You may need to read and study exactly what Jesus is saying. Do it. It is worth it. Let's pray and ask God for help.

MEDIA: Danger ahead

Play the "Swordfish" (0:53) clip from the movie *Get Smart*. In this clip, Maxwell Smart drives into all sorts of danger and ends up crashing into a swordfish, even though his boss is trying to point out all the apparent dangers. Often we hear Jesus' words of advice and ignore them, and we end up in big trouble. This clip is available on www.wingclips.com—use the search word *swordfish*.

You can also visit www.youtube.com and look for hurricane or tornado videos. These videos will show the power of a storm and the destruction it brings to those on sandy foundations.

Matthew 8:5-13

TOPIC: Don't worry—trust Jesus

OBJECTIVE: Students will identify their worries, and they'll know they can ask Jesus for help and trust him to respond to their needs.

BACKGROUND/OVERVIEW: Jesus entered Capernaum and was approached by a Roman centurion. This Roman Empire commander had heard about Jesus and believed Jesus could heal his servant who was deathly ill at home. Jesus agreed to go and heal the man's servant, but he saw a great act of faith. The Roman centurion said, "You don't have to come to my house. I understand the kind of authority you have. Just say the word and my servant will be healed." Jesus was moved by the trust and faith this man had and did exactly what the centurion knew he could do. Jesus healed the servant without going to his house.

GAME/ICEBREAKER: **Is there anything in here?**
Items needed:

- A small box
- A gift/prize to put in the box (candy, gift card, etc.)
- Wrapping paper or a few boxes that will fit inside each other
- A pair of dice

Place an item in the box (or a series of boxes) and wrap each layer securely with the wrapping paper—many layers of it. You want the participants to only be able to unwrap it one layer at a time. Tell the group—
This box contains something that you will be happy to find.
Then ask—
Do you have faith (or do you believe) that something is in this box? (Faith is something you hope for, but can't see.) Can you see what's in this box?
Then throw (or threaten to throw) the box in the trashcan and watch for their reactions.
Will we ever know what's in the box if I throw it away?
Have the group sit in a circle. Give one person a pair of dice and give the person next to her the box. The person with the box can try to unwrap it as fast as possible. The person with the dice must try to roll a three, a seven, or doubles. When that happens, the person unwrapping stops (her turn is over) and passes the box to someone else. The dice also get passed

to someone else. The unwrapping and dice-rolling start again. Repeat this until the box is unwrapped and someone gets the prize.

ICEBREAKER QUESTIONS:

- At what point in the game did you not believe a prize was in the box?
- When did you finally believe a prize was in the box? What changed your mind?
- In life are you more likely to believe bad things or good things will happen to you? Tell us an example.
- What promises do you find hard to believe from the adults in your life?
- Is it easy or difficult for you to believe Jesus can help you with your problems? Explain.

SCRIPTURE: Matthew 8:5-13
Have each person read this passage silently from her Bible.

[5] When Jesus had entered Capernaum, a centurion came to him, asking for help. [6] "Lord," he said, "my servant lies at home paralyzed, suffering terribly."

[7] Jesus said to him, "Shall I come and heal him?"

[8] The centurion replied, "Lord, I do not deserve to have you come under my roof. But just say the word, and my servant will be healed. [9] For I myself am a man under authority, with soldiers under me. I tell this one, 'Go,' and he goes; and that one, 'Come,' and he comes. I say to my servant, 'Do this,' and he does it."

[10] When Jesus heard this, he was amazed and said to those following him, "Truly I tell you, I have not found anyone in Israel with such great faith. [11] I say to you that many will come from the east and the west, and will take their places at the feast with Abraham, Isaac and Jacob in the kingdom of heaven. [12] But the subjects of the kingdom will be thrown outside, into the darkness, where there will be weeping and gnashing of teeth."

[13] Then Jesus said to the centurion, "Go! Let it be done just as you believed it would." And his servant was healed at that very hour.

STUDY QUESTIONS:

- How was Jesus using this situation to teach people about faith?
- What would you ask Jesus about faith?
- What are some of the things you worry about?
- If Jesus told you not to worry about those things but instead to have faith in him to help you work them out, what would you say? What would you think? What would you do?
- How can we increase our faith in God?

TALKING POINTS:

Share the following points with your students:

The unexpected example of faith

A Roman centurion was a man of war. He understood how authority worked. He had soldiers beneath him whom he expected to obey his every command without question. He also had officers above him, and he knew without hesitation he'd obey every one of their instructions.

The centurion understood if Jesus wanted to do something, it would be done. So he asked Jesus to heal his servant, fully confident it would be accomplished. The centurion's act of faith came from understanding Jesus was in control.

Do you believe Jesus is in control?

We may find it difficult to trust anyone because we've been let down too many times. Jesus is different than any of the people who have let you down. He has complete authority over everything. Can you trust him with your problems? If you find yourself worrying about things and don't believe Jesus can help you, maybe you just don't know him as well as you need to. Our faith increases when we understand Jesus better. He's in control. He loves us and wants the best for us.

REAL-LIFE CONNECTION:Jesus, help me!

Give your students the following instructions:

- Make a list of your major, persistent worries. What's on that list?
- Draw a cross next to any of your worries where you know Jesus has promised to help you.

Do you believe he'll help you? Can you trust him?

- At the top of your list write a new title for the page—Trust List.

- Next to each of your written worries write, Ask Jesus For Help.
- Carry this list with you every day this week. When you start to worry get it out and read it.

MEDIA: Don't worry

Play the song "Don't Worry Now" from the *Say It* album by Britt Nicole. Several versions of this song are on YouTube. (On www.youtube.com search for the song by the song title.) This song makes present-day application of the same type of faith the centurion showed when he believed and trusted Jesus for the healing of his servant. We don't have to worry—Jesus hears our prayers and knows what to do for us. Play this during "Real-Life Connection" when students are making their lists.

Matthew 9:9-13

TOPIC: We all need Jesus

OBJECTIVE: Students will understand that everyone is a sinner and in need of Jesus as Savior.

BACKGROUND/OVERVIEW: Jesus called Matthew, a tax collector, to be one of his disciples. Tax collectors were hated during this time because they were often cheats and liars who would extort money from taxpayers to make themselves rich. That Jesus called Matthew to be his disciple shocked people. Matthew, however, was delighted to follow Jesus, and he invited Jesus to come to dinner at his house. Many other tax collectors and sinners came and listened to Jesus at that dinner party. The religious leaders of the time were astonished that Jesus chose to eat with such people. Jesus, knowing their thoughts, answered them in a powerful way.

GAME/ICEBREAKER: Party quirks

Item needed:

- A small prize for the winner of the contest

Have one person leave the room—this person will be the *party host*. Next select three other students to be *party guests*. You can assign characters for them, or you can have the group make up characters. These characters could be caricatures of types of students (e.g., extreme jock, weird nerd, spaced-out partygoer, etc.). Or the characters could be celebrities from entertainment, politics, etc. (e.g., Oprah Winfrey, Jessica Simpson, Barack Obama, Simon Cowell), or from TV shows and movies (e.g., Jack Bauer, Bart Simpson, Liz Lemon). Have the host return and then, one at a time, have each guest come to the party acting like his character. The host must try to guess the characters the students are acting out. Repeat with another party host. Award a prize to the host who guesses correctly in the shortest amount of time.

ICEBREAKER QUESTIONS:

- (To the hosts): **How did you feel as the host?**
- (To the guests): **How did you feel as one of the guests?**
- (To the audience): **What did you think when you were watching this?**
- (To the audience): **How accurately did the guests portray their roles?**

- What's the point of parties?
- When have you felt totally left out at a party? Why?

SCRIPTURE: Matthew 9:9-13

Read this aloud while everyone follows along in his Bible.

⁹ As Jesus went on from there, he saw a man named Matthew sitting at the tax collector's booth. "Follow me," he told him, and Matthew got up and followed him.

¹⁰ While Jesus was having dinner at Matthew's house, many tax collectors and sinners came and ate with him and his disciples. ¹¹ When the Pharisees saw this, they asked his disciples, "Why does your teacher eat with tax collectors and sinners?"

¹² On hearing this, Jesus said, "It is not the healthy who need a doctor, but the sick. ¹³ But go and learn what this means: 'I desire mercy, not sacrifice.' For I have not come to call the righteous, but sinners."

STUDY QUESTIONS:

- Why do you think Jesus called Matthew to be a disciple?
- Why did Matthew invite Jesus to dinner?
- Why did Jesus eat with people with such bad reputations? How did that affect *his* reputation?
- What did the sinners and religious leaders get out of their time with Jesus? What did they learn about him?

TALKING POINTS:

Share the following points with your students.:

Jesus spent time with sinners

The religious leaders thought Jesus should not be hanging out with sinners and tax collectors, much less eating with them. They thought a rabbi like Jesus should be much more holy than that: He should be dining with more upright and righteous company. Jesus subtly reminded them of a profound truth: Everyone is a sinner, and everyone needs forgiveness and salvation.

Some religious people think they're better than others

The issue was the religious leaders thought they were righteous and didn't need any help. But the sinners knew they were in trouble—they knew they needed help. Jesus comes for anyone who will accept him. They know they need help and are willing to accept it.

The journey with God has several stages
First we must realize we need a Savior. When we turn from our sins (repent) and turn to Jesus (believe), he rescues us from the penalty and power of our sin. Then the process of becoming more like him begins. This involves training on how to protect ourselves from the Enemy, on how to hear and understand God's voice, and on how to obey God—living as he wants.

In the early stages especially, this means staying clear of situations that might pull us away from God. Eventually, when we're strong enough, it means going to those who are lost and telling them the truth. We need to point the lost to Jesus so he can help them. Jesus came to be a doctor to those who are sick—everyone needs Jesus.

REAL-LIFE CONNECTION: God puts people who need him in front of us

Read this personal testimony from Craig Muller, a youth ministry graduate from Nyack College, in Nyack, N.Y.:

I went to a Christian college, which I loved. Most people there loved Jesus and were trying to pursue God's plan for their lives. It was a great atmosphere to help young people on their journey with God. Many students, however, were in rebellion. Some because they had been confined for so long and this was their first taste of freedom. Others because they were so broken they were looking for an escape. Still others came to school curious or confused about Jesus being the way to God. Whatever the reason, they didn't know God and were running away from him fast. They needed to be loved. They needed someone to tell them the truth. They were longing for someone to be an example of the Jesus they so desperately needed. Unfortunately, many of the Christians at my school had forgotten that they too had been lost, rebellious, and enemies of the Savior they now longed to serve. They treated their lost fellow students as outcasts, untouchables who were hopeless and loveless and who could not be associated with. I became friends with a lot of those outcasts. I did my best to love them as Jesus would have, and I was privileged and honored to see God redeem many of them. I figured that if God could love a mess like me, well then he could love anyone. If God was willing to save me, then he was willing to save anyone. Never forget that we all need Jesus. No person is better than another. Never forget.

Ask—

God has put many people in your life. Which of them need friendship and love? How could you treat them this week that would show them Jesus?

MEDIA: I need you

Play "All I Need Is You" by Hillsong United: *The I Heart Revolution: With Hearts as One.* This song expresses worship and declaration of trust in Jesus, which is the center of our relationship with him.

Matthew 10:1, 5-10

TOPIC: Preparing to serve God

OBJECTIVE: Students will recognize opportunities in their lives preparing them to do God's work, and they'll identify individuals who can mentor and disciple them as they embark upon that work.

BACKGROUND/OVERVIEW: Jesus sent his disciples to preach the good news and to tell people about how the kingdom of heaven is near. He sent them with no coat, no money, and no extra clothes—nothing except the power of the living God, with which they could heal, cast out evil spirits, and know what to do and say. Jesus sent them out with empty hands, yet they had everything they needed.

GAME/ICEBREAKER: Ready, set, snowboard
Items needed:

- Three sets of clothing and equipment needed to go snowboarding (helmet, gloves, snow pants, jacket, thermals, boots, and snowboard)

Have three students in front of the group race to see who can get dressed to snowboard the fastest. The first one to get all the equipment on properly and pretend to ride down a mountain wins. Be sure to play some lively music while they're racing to get dressed.

Other options: Use skateboarding equipment (helmet, pads, T-shirt, etc.) or diving equipment (mask, snorkeling pipe, fins, wet suit, etc.).

ICEBREAKER QUESTIONS:

- How did you feel as you raced to put on all that clothing and equipment?
- What of that equipment is essential for you to be prepared for that sport?
- How important is the right equipment to enjoying or doing a sport well?
- What equipment do you think a person needs to succeed in life?

SCRIPTURE:
Matthew 10:1, 5-10
Ask a student to read the verses aloud from her Bible.

[1] Jesus called his twelve disciples to him and gave them authority to drive out evil spirits and to heal every disease and sickness.

[5] These twelve Jesus sent out with the following instructions: "Do not go among the Gentiles or enter any town of the Samaritans. [6] Go rather to the lost sheep of Israel. [7] As you go, proclaim this message: 'The kingdom of heaven has come near.' [8] Heal the sick, raise the dead, cleanse those who have leprosy, drive out demons. Freely you have received, freely give.

[9] Do not get any gold or silver or copper to take with you in your belts— [10] no bag for the journey or extra shirt or sandals or a staff, for workers are worth their keep."

STUDY QUESTIONS:

- What kind of equipment did Jesus give his disciples when he sent them out?
- What training and preparation did the disciples get from Jesus?
- What would you have thought or said if Jesus told you to take nothing when he sent you out to tell other people about God's kingdom?
- What equipment do you think God has given you to tell other people about him? What do you think you still need?
- What could you learn spending time with Jesus or one of his disciples that would help prepare you to do God's work?

TALKING POINTS:
Share the following points with your students:

More is *caught* than *taught*
Jesus ran a be-with training school. This school didn't involve taking tests, writing papers, or memorizing formulas. Instead the disciples spent time with Jesus, listening to him and watching him in action. He taught them how to love God with all their heart, soul, mind, and strength, and how to love others as they loved themselves. He showed them how to listen to the Father, how to pray, and how to know his will. Then Jesus sent them out on assignment with simple instructions: "Do what you have seen me do. Tell the world my story." Now, 2,000 years later, we still learn our most important lessons by watching others and hanging out with them—specifically mature Christians.

Jesus wants his disciples to depend on him
Jesus gave his disciples a huge job. He had good reason for not giving the disciples any tangible resources to carry as they went on assignment. He was

telling them, "You're ready. God with his wisdom and power is all you need for your ministry." Sometimes we think we need music, media, advertising, or celebrities to effectively deliver God's message. All those may be helpful, but people who know God and act like him do front line ministry person-to-person.

God puts people in your life
God puts the following people in your life:

> Someone to teach you: The Christian faith spreads person-to-person. It grows deep in mentor-discipling relationships. Every young Christian needs a mature believer to show him how to live out God's grace and truth (copying Jesus) as they walk together through life. Who is your mentor-discipler?
>
> Someone for you to teach: The Christian faith never stops spreading. Even as a young believer, God pushes you out of the nest and gives you opportunities to serve others and tell God's story. Someone is looking up to you and watching Jesus work in your life. You will bring hope, healing, and love to him.

REAL-LIFE CONNECTION:
Who are those people in your life?
Ask your students the following questions:

- Who is your mentor/discipler? Whose life are you watching and sharing?
- If you don't have one, who could be a teacher and example to you for the next few years of your life?

Say to your students—
Take time this week to identify someone you want to mentor you and help your walk with Jesus grow stronger. Think of someone who will challenge you to grow and take on big challenges that could only be accomplished with God's help. Ask them to push you as you develop the gifts God has given to you.

MEDIA: Do what you've been called to do
Check out *The Lord of the Rings* movie trilogy and find a scene where Gandalf is teaching/mentoring Pippin. In *Return of the King* (Extended Version: Disc 2, Chapter 49—36:16) during the battle of Minith Tirith, Gandalf talks about what's after death and encourages Pippin to do what he has been called to do.

Matthew 11:28-30

TOPIC: Yoked to Jesus

OBJECTIVE: Students will understand we're meant to live with Jesus. Being yoked to him will lead us to the life we're seeking.

BACKGROUND/OVERVIEW: After a harsh rebuke to those who had seen him and didn't repent, Jesus gave another offer of relationship with him. He invited them into a relationship greater than any other—one that offers rest and fulfillment.

GAME/ICEBREAKER: **Three-headed orange-eater**
Items needed:

- An orange for every three students

Have three students stand side-by-side and link arms. The two outer students should use their outside arm to hold the same orange. The student in the middle—without use of his own hands—must, with the help of his two partners, eat the orange. You can have teams of three compete to see who can do this the fastest.

ICEBREAKER QUESTIONS:

- How did it feel to compete by eating the orange when you were attached to two other people?
- What would have been the advantages or disadvantages of doing it alone?
- What if you had a disability that made it impossible to hold or peel an orange—how would that change how you would feel about doing this with someone else?
- Today we're talking about living with Jesus attached to us. What makes life easier or harder to live and do things with Jesus?

SCRIPTURE: Matthew 11:28-30

Read this short passage aloud, twice.

28 "Come to me, all you who are weary and burdened, and I will give you rest. 29 Take my yoke upon you and learn from me, for I am gentle and humble in heart, and you will find rest for your souls. 30 For my yoke is easy and my burden is light."

STUDY QUESTIONS:

- We're looking for some primitive agricultural information. What is a yoke?
- What does this illustration of us being hooked together with Jesus (like two bulls or horses pulling a plow) tell us about the kind of relationship he wants to have with us?
- If Jesus (either visible or invisible) was hooked side-by-side to you every day, how do you think your life would change?
- How would having Jesus hooked side-by-side with you make it more restful and peaceful for you?
- Jesus is suggesting this image of being hooked together. How is this possible in real life?

TALKING POINTS:

Share the following points with your students:

Come to me

Immediately after rebuking folks for not repenting, Jesus offers some of his most famous words: "Come to me...I will give you rest...my yoke is easy and my burden is light." Jesus offers us relationship we were created for. He knows we all have to be yoked to something. We are either yoked to Jesus or we're with the Enemy. By reminding us that he's humble and gentle, he's claiming to be the best option for yoking.

Take my yoke

A yoke was a piece of wood that joined two animals so they could plow a field together. Farmers would often take a young calf and put it with an experienced, strong bull so the younger could learn how to do what it was intended to do. Jesus gives the same offer to us: He says, You'll have to be yoked to something, so get yoked to me. I will take care of you. I will teach you how to live how you were intended to live. I will carry the burden for you. I will be what you need.

You will find rest

By being yoked to Jesus, your soul will find rest—his yoke is easy and his burden light. Choose Jesus to be yoked to. He'll carry your heavy burdens and teach you how to be strong. If you're tired of being burdened down, go to Jesus—you will find rest being yoked to him because of his strength.

(This is a great spot for a real-life testimony from a young leader about how giving her life to Christ brought her rest and peace.)

REAL-LIFE CONNECTION: Imitate Jesus

Use this at the end of the meeting to quietly, but confidently, suggest this is a night of commitment and change.

Say—

What has caused you to be tired? We all get weary. Maybe it's trying to keep up with the pressures you face. Maybe it's the fear your friends might discover who you really are. Could it be because the life you're living is the not the life you were made for? Or maybe you think you know how God wants you to live, and you're trying to do it in your own strength. Whatever it is, Jesus wants you to leave it and come to him. He doesn't care where you have been or what you have done. He wants you just the way you are. He wants to give you rest. He wants to give you the life you were made to live. This is an open invitation. *Come.* When you're tired and overburdened, go back to him and stay yoked to Christ. It may take a change of thinking. Try to find what he's doing—go where he is—imitate him. Let Jesus teach you his ways. That's what being yoked to Jesus means.

MEDIA: Conform to Jesus

Play the skit "Chapter 11 Conforming Cross" (:65) from a DVD of *One Time Blind* (a drama team based in Detroit). This skit shows how we should conform to Jesus rather than try to have him conform to us.

There is another One Time Blind drama on YouTube that fits this lesson by demonstrating how Jesus wants us to trust him, listen to him, obey him and depend on him as the basis of our relationship with him. Go to www.youtube.com and type in *One Time Blind* and *trust fall*. The time for this video is 7:38.

Mathew 12:1-8

TOPIC: What's really important

OBJECTIVE: Students will understand that caring for those you care about is more important than following any religious laws.

BACKGROUND/OVERVIEW: When Jesus and his disciples traveled, they didn't carry many supplies with them. On one journey, the disciples got hungry so they started picking the grain on the edge of the field near the road. This happened on the Sabbath, and the Pharisees were enraged at the disciples for breaking a law. They demanded Jesus do something.

GAME/ICEBREAKER: Simon Says

Play a version of this children's game. But be sure to add creative twists, such as—

- Simon says shake the hand of the person on your right.
- Simon says scratch the head of the person on your left.
- Snort like a pig.
- Simon says stop shaking.
- Stop scratching.
- Etc.

ICEBREAKER QUESTIONS:

- What are the rules for Simon Says?
- Which instructions were the most difficult to follow?
- Who is the most important person in the game? Why?

SCRIPTURE: Mathew 12:1-8

You might want to select students to act out this passage twice: First as it's written, then in a modern setting.

[1] At that time Jesus went through the grainfields on the Sabbath. His disciples were hungry and began to pick some heads of grain and eat them. [2] When the Pharisees saw this, they said to him, "Look! Your disciples are doing what is unlawful on the Sabbath."

[3] He answered, "Haven't you read what David did when he and his companions were hungry? [4] He entered the house of God, and he and his companions ate the consecrated bread—which was not

lawful for them to do, but only for the priests. [5] Or haven't you read in the Law that the priests on Sabbath duty in the temple desecrate the Sabbath and yet are innocent? [6] I tell you that one greater than the temple is here. [7] If you had known what these words mean, 'I desire mercy, not sacrifice,' you would not have condemned the innocent. [8] For the Son of Man is Lord of the Sabbath."

STUDY QUESTIONS:

- Why were the Pharisees so upset?
- Why would Jesus mention David and the "house of God"?
- What was his point about the priests on duty in the temple?
- What do you think Jesus is saying in verse seven?
- What do you think was more important to Jesus, the care of his disciples or following a Jewish law? Why?

TALKING POINTS:

In your own words, share the following points with your students:

What are your priorities?

Jesus brilliantly made his point to the Pharisees about what really matters when following God. He ignored tradition and made sure his hungry disciples had something to eat. He showed the Pharisees that love should outrank tradition. To bolster his case, Jesus used King David, one of the most revered humans according to Jewish law. David had broken the law to provide food for his soldiers. The well-being of his comrades was more important than keeping the Sabbath law forbidding harvesting grain.

Jesus explained that avoiding all work on the Sabbath would be impossible since the temple has to be guarded at all times—someone has to work on the Sabbath at some point. Jesus explained God's top priority by quoting Hosea 6:6—"For I desire mercy, not sacrifices, and acknowledgement of God rather than burnt offerings."

What are your motives?

Why do we do what we do? Do we come to church because our parents tell us to? Do we recite a little prayer to make us feel better before we eat or before we go to sleep? Do we think God loves us more because we don't smoke or drink? Jesus said what he did to the Pharisees because their motives were distorted. He wanted them to think about what truly matters—if we want to get our motives right, we have to get back to Jesus. Only by following him can we know what really matters. Jesus said he's Lord over the

Sabbath (Matthew 12:8), meaning he outranks tradition. If we compared our life to "Simon Says," Jesus is Simon and he has told everything we need to know.

REAL-LIFE CONNECTION: Rules are not your religion

On a flip chart or poster board, make a list of religious rules that, while good and important, are not the basis of our salvation and relationship with God. After writing the list, draw a big X over the whole sheet, declaring that following any of these rules won't erase our sins. Only Christ can do this for us. Draw a large cross the width and length of the page over the top of the list of rules.

Say—

Don't let a set of rules be your religion. God wants you to have a living relationship with him through Jesus Christ. Let's make a list of some of the rules people try to follow, thinking if they can keep these rules God will be pleased and give them eternal life.

(Note: Each person could also do this individually as the leader directs him. Students could take this home and post it in their rooms.)

MEDIA: Man-made rules

Show a clip from the movie *Fiddler on the Roof*—"Tradition!" You can use this clip as a transition from the game to the actual lesson. This song is about all the rules a community of Russian Jews has followed for generations. This is the foundation of their lives. It provides a good illustration of how we can allow tradition (or the way we've always done things) to dictate how we live. The daughters of Tevye, the father, will challenge these rules and traditions about life as they grow up and fall in love. This is a good lead-in for a discussion about how religious leaders and people felt when Jesus started preaching that following rules wasn't the way to know God. You can use this clip as a transition from the game to the actual lesson. You can find this song and movie clip on YouTube. Go to www.youtube.com and type *tradition—fiddler on the roof*.

From the movie *The Great Debaters*, show the clip "Righteous Mind" (0:45). It's available from www.wingclips.com—use the search words *righteous mind*. In this clip Melvin educates his students about a slave owner's method of controlling his slaves. His strategy was to "keep the slave physically strong but psychologically weak and dependent on the slave owner." This video illustration works if the man-made rules are compared to the slave owner. The rules-focused religion keeps people working hard but not secure in love from their God.

Matthew 13:44-46

TOPIC: Your most valuable possession

OBJECTIVE: Students will know their connection to God is a priceless treasure, and they'll feel the confidence their decision to follow Christ is worth more than any possession they could ever gain.

BACKGROUND/OVERVIEW: Jesus compared the kingdom of heaven to a priceless treasure and told of two men who sold everything they had to obtain it.

GAME/ICEBREAKER: **Bigger and better**
Items needed:

- Pencils
- (Optional) Interesting items to give to the students

Divide your group into teams and give each team a pencil. When you give the signal, the teams should head out into the neighborhood and go door-to-door, explaining that they're with a youth group and are playing a game called "Bigger and Better." They'd like to trade what they have (beginning with the pencil) for something bigger and better. When the trade is made, they move to the next home and so forth until the allotted time has expired. The team with the biggest and best item at the end wins.

Option: If leaving the building isn't practical, set up *houses* in six to eight different rooms with adult leaders acting as the residents of these *houses*. Stock these rooms with interesting items and have students trade for items in these rooms. Be sure to return whatever you take out of the rooms for this game.

ICEBREAKER QUESTIONS:

- How did you feel asking strangers to trade with you?
- It's easy to figure out what items are bigger, but how do you decide which ones are better?
- What did you have that was difficult to trade away?
- Which two possessions are most valuable to you?
- Which of your most valuable possessions would you trade for a lifetime connection with God? Why is it difficult to give up the stuff we have for what Jesus has to offer?

SCRIPTURE: Matthew 13:44-46
Explain that Jesus is speaking to the crowds. Then read the passage aloud.

44 "The kingdom of heaven is like treasure hidden in a field. When a man found it, he hid it again, and then in his joy went and sold all he had and bought that field.

45 "Again, the kingdom of heaven is like a merchant looking for fine pearls. 46 When he found one of great value, he went away and sold everything he had and bought it."

STUDY QUESTIONS:

- How is the value of something determined?
- What point was Jesus trying to make with this short story?
- How much is a personal faith in God worth?
- What do many people in our world today think is more valuable than a personal faith in God? Why do they believe this?
- How can a person show that his faith is more important and valuable than anything else?

TALKING POINTS:
Share the following with your students:

Nothing we have is worth more than what Jesus promises us
Do you believe that? Jesus tells this intriguing short story to take our eyes off all the wealth, fame, and selfishness of this world. Jesus asks you a pointed question: Is the kingdom of heaven worth all you have?

You can't play it both ways
Being a part of the kingdom of God is worth all we have. Jesus knows this. These parables challenge us to have only one priority in life. Many people live with competing priorities. We give God lip service, and we hold on to our personal agenda and pleasures. God doesn't demand everything to control us or to trick us into missing out on the fun of life. He doesn't actually need anything from us. Instead we need what he has and offers. The truth is whatever we have, nothing comes close to what Jesus has in store for us. The bad news is if we choose to hold on to what we have, we may never receive what God has for us.

Invest all you have in the kingdom of heaven

At times we may look at God's Word and feel as though God is always telling us what to do or not do. And we may think being a Christian means giving up a lot of stuff we really want—a boyfriend or girlfriend, certain favorite video games, talking the way we do, or something else. But Jesus is worth everything we have. The things we grasp tightly, thinking they'll make us happy, always disappoint us. They can't and won't bring us joy and fulfillment. Only a relationship with Jesus will give us what we're seeking. God's commands always protect what is best for us. He never wants to hurt us or deny us something we truly need or deserve. He always wants what is best for us. We can trust him.

REAL-LIFE CONNECTION:What do you need to give up?

Ask your students the following questions:

- What's in your life that rivals or undercuts your love, trust, and commitment to following Jesus Christ?
- What would be difficult for you to give up (or sell off) to make following Jesus your top goal?
- What changes and choices do you need to make in your life for your faith in Jesus Christ to be the number one priority in your life?
- What first steps toward those changes will you make this week?

MEDIA: Just out of reach

Use these two movie clips to have fun with the idea of the pursuit of possessions and treasures and the reward that is promised, but not received:

Ice Age: The Meltdown—"Acorn" (1:51). Skrat, the saber-toothed squirrel, chases the ever-elusive acorn. Use the search word *acorn*.

Ice Age: The Meltdown—"Acorn Heaven" (2:43). In a near-death experience, Skrat enters the gates of heaven and sees a bountiful supply of acorns. Use the search words *acorn heaven*.

These clips are available from www.wingclips.com.

Matthew 14:13-21

TOPIC: Your all is enough

OBJECTIVE: Students will know whatever they have to give is enough for Jesus to work his purposes out in their life.

BACKGROUND/OVERVIEW: Jesus fed more than 5,000 hungry people by getting his disciples involved in the miracle and using only a small lunch they found in the possession of a young boy.

GAME/ICEBREAKER: Picnic
Items needed:

- Bags filled with random foods to make weird sandwiches, such as baloney, cottage cheese, hot sauce, guacamole, barbeque sauce, raw vegetables, etc.

Divide the group into teams. Give each team a bag of random foods. Have each team make two sandwiches with the odd ingredients you provide (both teams get the same ingredients). Cut the sandwiches in half. Have the teams select four eaters (two male and two female) who will each eat a half a sandwich. Make the race like a relay with each eater racing to a table and sitting down to eat his half sandwich. A contestant must show a judge at the table his mouth is empty before standing up and returning the team and tagging the next eater to compete. Both teams should be seated and should watch the people eating at the table.

ICEBREAKER QUESTIONS:

- What is the hungriest you have ever been? How long have you ever gone without food?
- What's the grossest food you have ever eaten?
- If Jesus were to send you out to feed 5,000 people, what ideas would you have about how to get it done?
- In what ways has God provided for you and your family?

SCRIPTURE: Matthew 14:13-21
Have each person read this passage silently from his Bible.

[13] When Jesus heard what had happened, he withdrew by boat privately to a solitary place. Hearing of this, the crowds followed him on foot from the towns. [14] When Jesus landed and saw a large crowd, he had compassion on them and healed their sick.

[15] As evening approached, the disciples came to him and said, "This is a remote place, and it's already getting late. Send the crowds away, so they can go to the villages and buy themselves some food."

[16] Jesus replied, "They do not need to go away. You give them something to eat."

[17] "We have here only five loaves of bread and two fish," they answered.

[18] "Bring them here to me," he said. [19] And he directed the people to sit down on the grass. Taking the five loaves and the two fish and looking up to heaven, he gave thanks and broke the loaves. Then he gave them to the disciples, and the disciples gave them to the people. [20] They all ate and were satisfied, and the disciples picked up twelve basketfuls of broken pieces that were left over. [21] The number of those who ate was about five thousand men, besides women and children.

STUDY QUESTIONS:

- Why did Jesus ask the disciples to get them food when he could have done the miracle without their help?
- Why did Jesus decide to use the loaves and fishes from a boy's lunch?
- What miracle would you like to see God do in front of your whole school? What would you be willing to do to be part of it?
- In what ways does God want us involved in what he does?

TALKING POINTS:
Share some of the following points with your students:

Let's eat
These people had been with Jesus for at least a whole day, and in the late afternoon they were extremely hungry. Jesus' disciples asked what they should do to get food for the crowd. Jesus told them not to send the people away—instead, the disciples were to get food. The disciples obediently looked for food. They reported back to Jesus they could only find five loaves and two fishes from one young boy's lunch. But God has no *only*.

Our little is enough for God

The young boy and the disciples did exactly what Jesus told them to do. They gave all they had—one boy's lunch. Jesus didn't say, "You need to find more food." Nor did he say, "I don't want your tiny lunch", or "I can feed these people without you." Instead, he did the impossible by feeding all those people with what they had to give.

God will always give us what we need. The first step is giving God everything we have.

God wants us to be part of what he's doing

Give God what you have, and you will see what he'll do in you and around you. God wants the world to see his greatness and power. And he wants to do that *through us*. Our faith is tested when God asks us to do something, and we grow in faith when we see God do great things through us. You may think what you have is insignificant, but it may be the perfect ingredient for a miracle. Don't miss the opportunity to be involved in God's work. Give him all you have and look for ways you can be a witness for God's life-changing power.

What do you have to offer him? What's holding you back?

REAL-LIFE CONNECTION: Your gift to God

Items needed:

- Ribbon
- Blank paper
- Pens/pencils

Give everyone the following instructions:

- Take a blank sheet of paper and a 12-inch length of ribbon.
- Draw a circle in the middle of the paper.
- Write in the circle the gifts, talents, resources, and opportunities God has given you.
- Underline the gifts and talents you're willing to give to God for his use.
- Fold in the corners of the paper to the center like you're wrapping a present.
- Wrap the ribbon around the paper.
- Write a note to God on the outside of the wrapped paper—tell him this is your gift to him.

Have students, one by one, place their presents in a special offering plate. Pray for God to bless these gifts.

MEDIA: Surrender

Play the song "All I Can Say" from the *All I Can Say* album by David Crowder. Print out the words to use as you play the song or show a video of the song from www.youtube.com. This song expresses our complete dependence on God and our surrender to his will in our life.

Matthew 15:18-20

TOPIC: Matters of the heart

OBJECTIVE: Students will understand that what we focus on in our hearts and minds eventually comes out in our actions and words. They'll know that God is interested in changing their hearts as well as their outward behavior so they can reflect the changes he's making in them.

BACKGROUND/OVERVIEW: In this chapter Jesus spoke about inner purity. The Pharisees and religious rulers confronted Jesus, saying his disciples had not washed their hands before eating. This was a big deal because it was considered unclean. Jesus challenged the religious rulers, saying what matters most isn't what comes in and out of our bodies that is impure. We should be more concerned with what goes in and comes out of our hearts.

GAME/ICEBREAKER: What's inside?

Items needed:

- Different food items, two of every kind—one name brand and one generic brand with the labels obscured with duct tape or construction paper. (Food item ideas: Chocolate pudding, whipped cream, peanut butter, juice, soda, salsa, ice cream, and so forth.)

Recruit a student volunteer to taste the food and try to determine which food item is the name brand and which is the generic.

ICEBREAKER QUESTIONS:

- (To the volunteer who tasted the food): **Which items tasted almost the same?**
- (To the volunteer who tasted the food): **Which items could you tell weren't the real thing because they tasted different?**
- (To the volunteer who tasted the food): **What made it difficult or easy to tell the difference?**
- **In real life, how do you know when people are one thing on the outside and something else (mostly bad) on the inside?**

SCRIPTURE: Matthew 15:18-20

Have a student read the passage aloud from his Bible.

> [18] But the things that come out of the mouth come from the heart, and these defile you. [19] For out of the heart come evil thoughts, murder, adultery, sexual immorality, theft, false testimony, slander. [20] These are what defile you; but eating with unwashed hands does not defile you."

STUDY QUESTIONS:

- What does the Pharisees' concern about Jesus' disciples being unclean tell you about what was important to them? What was more important to Jesus?
- What are the outward behavior and appearance standards some churches emphasize? What outward behaviors are Christians not supposed to have?
- Jesus says that what we think about in our minds and hearts is just as important as what people see us do. What are some of those inner thoughts and desires Jesus wants to change in people who follow him?
- How do evil thoughts of anger, hatred, murder, adultery, and others get into our hearts?
- How can we clean these bad thoughts and desires out of our minds and hearts? What does God want us to do?

TALKING POINTS:

Share the following info with your students:

It's in our nature

Have you ever watched small children play together? They look so sweet and innocent from a distance. When you get up close and watch them play, you may see selfishness and anger when one doesn't want to share a toy with a playmate. They may fuss over the toy, and eventually one might smack the other in frustration. Where does that come from? It's a universal fact that perfect people don't exist. Have you met any? We can never get away from sin—we were born this way. It's in our human nature—we inherited it from Adam and Eve, who disobeyed God in the garden of Eden.

What are you like on the inside?

One good way for us to know what is going on inside our hearts is to look at our thoughts, words, and actions. What do your thoughts look like? Are they negative and depressing? Are you comparing yourself with others, looking down on some people and hating people who seem better than you? Are your thoughts loaded with fear about what other people think about you and whether you fit in? Is your heart full of lust or violence? When you talk ugly to others, does that come from your own insecurity? So much is going on inside you. Only you and God know what is happening under the surface.

God knows everything

This might scare you: God knows everything. You can't hide anything from him. The big surprise is—God still loves you and accepts you even with all those nasty thoughts and desires throbbing inside you. He didn't intend for you to live this way. The sin of Adam and Eve changed all of us. God could have wiped us out, but he loves us so much he doesn't want us to stay filled with all this fear and selfishness. He wants to see us cleaned up inside. God will start changing your heart and mind when you ask him to come and live inside you. But because your human nature is sinful, this is a lifelong struggle. You have to keep giving God permission to show you what needs to change and give you strength and courage to have your thoughts and actions transformed to be like Christ's. You may believe the lie that you're not worthy or good enough for God, but he paid the ultimate price for you when he allowed his Son Jesus to die on the cross for you. Nobody else loves you that much. Give him control of your life and your choices. That's the smartest move you can make.

Don't pretend you don't need to change

Jesus nailed these Pharisees and religious leaders because they pretended to be holy and good. They made up their own rules of what God wants from us and told everybody to act the way they did, and that would be good enough for God. They kept a lot of rules, but their hearts and minds were still filthy. Jesus loved them just as he loves us, but their pride and stubbornness kept them from admitting their need for a real change—starting on the inside. You can be a Christian forgiven by God and still make outward mistakes—it's what's inside your heart that matters. Do you want to do what pleases God? Will you take correction and guidance from the Holy Spirit about the heart-change God is constantly working on in you?

REAL-LIFE CONNECTION: Our dirty laundry

In your own words, share the following concepts with your students:

How many of you do your own laundry? Think of what life would be like if we didn't wash our clothes for two months. It would stink pretty badly in here! We'd need to learn we're responsible for taking our dirty clothes and putting them into the washing machine, putting in the detergent, and starting the machine. After we do our part, the washing machine does what it was made to do.

Like doing laundry, we have to take the dirty and smelly things in our hearts and bring them to God. We need to use prayer and reading the Bible like we use the detergent. When we put all that together, we can watch God clean our hearts and transform us. Just as often as we wash our clothing, we should ask God to change our hearts.

MEDIA: Transformed

Find a movie clip from any of the superhero movies—*Superman, Batman, Ironman*—in which a seemingly ordinary person changes into a superhero. There are plenty of dramatic transformational moments in these movies. Showing one of these at the beginning of the meeting sets the stage for the discussion of how God wants to transform us from the inside out. We'd like such an instantaneous change and superpowers but God changes us in a different way so we might do great work in this world.

Matthew 16:13-20

TOPIC: Who is Jesus to you?

OBJECTIVE: Students will know the true identity of Jesus as God's Son and the Savior of the world, and they'll be motivated to tell others who Jesus is.

BACKGROUND/OVERVIEW: A defining moment in life is when we accept that Jesus is God's Son and the Savior of the world. It is life-changing when we declare him *our* Savior and Lord.

GAME/ICEBREAKER: Name-draw showdown
Item needed:

• A large blanket

Divide your group in half. Have two people stand on chairs and hold a large blanket on either end so the blanket serves as a wall between the two groups. The blanket needs to be touching the floor and still be taller than any person in the groups so the students on either side of the blanket can't see each other. With the blanket held up between the groups, each group is to silently pick one person to stand an arm's length from the blanket. The leader should count to three, and the people holding the blanket then drop it. The two people facing each other are to shout the name of the person facing them. The first one to correctly say the name wins a point for the team. The blanket will go back up, and the teams should select a new person for the next showdown. Repeat numerous times. The participants can also kneel (if both sides do so). If the group isn't well acquainted, it will help to review names before introducing the game. If a person doesn't know the name of their opponent in the showdown, use that moment to declare that person's name to the whole group.

ICEBREAKER QUESTIONS

• What makes people freeze up when they're under pressure to say a person's name?
• Whose names were easiest for you to say? Which names were hardest?
• What embarrassing experiences have you had when you did not know or you forgot someone's name?
• How do you learn and remember a person's name?

• What's the difference between knowing a person's name and really knowing who that person is?

SCRIPTURE: Matthew 16:13-20

Have volunteers read the passage aloud from their Bibles. You may want to have students act this out.

13 When Jesus came to the region of Caesarea Philippi, he asked his disciples, "Who do people say the Son of Man is?"

14 They replied, "Some say John the Baptist; others say Elijah; and still others, Jeremiah or one of the prophets."

15 "But what about you?" he asked. "Who do you say I am?"

16 Simon Peter answered, "You are the Messiah, the Son of the living God."

17 Jesus replied, "Blessed are you, Simon son of Jonah, for this was not revealed to you by flesh and blood, but by my Father in heaven. 18 And I tell you that you are Peter, and on this rock I will build my church, and the gates of death will not overcome it. 19 I will give you the keys of the kingdom of heaven; whatever you bind on earth will be bound in heaven, and whatever you loose on earth will be loosed in heaven." 20 Then he ordered his disciples not to tell anyone that he was the Messiah.

STUDY QUESTIONS:

• What did Jesus want the disciples to tell him about his name?
• What did he want them to know about him that was more important than his name?
• Who did Peter say Jesus was? How did he know that?
• How do you think Peter's life was changed by really knowing who Jesus was?
• How has getting to know Jesus changed your life?

TALKING POINTS:

Have a conversation with your students, using the following points as a guide:

I know Jesus' name, but do I really know him?

Many people have heard about Jesus and know his name, but they don't really know him. A person can even go to church and know about Jesus and not really know him.

During his three years of ministry, Jesus gave people an opportunity to see who he really was and to know him (more than just his name). He wanted them to know he was God's Son, all-powerful yet living in a human body. He explained God and the purpose of our lives. He wanted his disciples to know he was the Messiah (the Savior) whom God had promised to send to the world to bring peace and freedom. Even his disciples didn't understand what he told them often about himself—how he'd willingly die to pay for the sins of the world—until it really happened.

On this day Peter realized Jesus was the Messiah from God and he shouted it aloud so everyone could hear.

Who do you think Jesus Christ is?

Many crazy ideas about Jesus are swirling about these days. The important question of your life is finding out who he is and getting to know the real Jesus.

The Bible says, "If you confess with your mouth, 'Jesus is Lord', and believe in your heart that God raised him from the dead, you will be saved" (Romans 10:9).

It's important to know his name, who he is, and what he has done for you.

REAL-LIFE CONNECTION: Do you know Jesus?

Ask your students the following question:

If someone asked you, "Who is Jesus?" how would you respond? Think about what you would say. What true facts and stories about his life could you tell your questioner? What would you tell the person about how you got to know Jesus, and what he means to you?

MEDIA: My king

Check out the YouTube video "That's My King" (3:33). This video can be downloaded from www.ignitermedia.com—use the search words *that's my king*. This video gives a visual of S. M. Lockridge's well-known declaration about the true identity of Jesus Christ.

Matthew 17:1-13

TOPIC: Seeing Jesus for who he really is

OBJECTIVE: Students will know the real Jesus and commit to follow him.

BACKGROUND/OVERVIEW: Jesus invites Peter, James, and John for a walk up a mountain. There they have an incredible experience when Jesus' true identity is revealed.

GAME/ICEBREAKER: Famous and funny people
Items needed:

- Small pieces of paper
- Pens/pencils

Have each person write down a secret name (this could be a famous person, a historical person, a cartoon character, or a character from a TV show or movie) on a small piece of paper and give it to you without telling anyone else. For example, someone might write LeBron James; someone else might write Kelly Clarkson; and someone else might write Batman. You should write down three additional names to add to the mix to make guessing at the end more difficult. Read aloud all the names twice for everyone to hear. Explain that you won't read them again. The youngest person in the room begins the contest by trying to guess the secret name of one person; i.e., who wrote a specific name. The guess might sound something like this: "Caleb, I think your secret name is Bono." If the person guesses correctly, he or she joins with the person just guessed to become a team and work together, guessing again. Every correct guess adds a new member to the team. When a wrong guess is made, the person who was asked if it was her secret name gets to make the next guess. As long as a team makes correct guesses, they gain new team members and continue to guess. If a person who is part of a team has his name guessed correctly, the whole team transfers to the new team. Continue this game until everyone is on one team.

ICEBREAKER QUESTIONS:

- That was crazy. How did you figure out the secret names of people?
- Whose secret name really fit them for who they are? How did you figure it out?

- Who really fooled us?
- Whose secret name was the one you least suspected?
- We are going to talk about seeing someone for who they really are. What are some personal characteristics we don't see in people when we first get to know them?
- How do you get to know someone for who he is?

SCRIPTURE:
Matthew 17:1-13
Have students read this silently from their Bibles.

1 After six days Jesus took with him Peter, James and John the brother of James, and led them up a high mountain by themselves. 2 There he was transfigured before them. His face shone like the sun, and his clothes became as white as the light. 3 Just then there appeared before them Moses and Elijah, talking with Jesus.

4 Peter said to Jesus, "Lord, it is good for us to be here. If you wish, I will put up three shelters—one for you, one for Moses and one for Elijah."

5 While he was still speaking, a bright cloud covered them, and a voice from the cloud said, "This is my Son, whom I love; with him I am well pleased. Listen to him!"

6 When the disciples heard this, they fell facedown to the ground, terrified. 7 But Jesus came and touched them. "Get up," he said. "Don't be afraid." 8 When they looked up, they saw no one except Jesus.

9 As they were coming down the mountain, Jesus instructed them, "Don't tell anyone what you have seen, until the Son of Man has been raised from the dead."

10 The disciples asked him, "Why then do the teachers of the law say that Elijah must come first?"

11 Jesus replied, "To be sure, Elijah comes and will restore all things. 12 But I tell you, Elijah has already come, and they did not recognize him, but have done to him everything they wished. In the same way the Son of Man is going to suffer at their hands." 13 Then the disciples understood that he was talking to them about John the Baptist.

STUDY QUESTIONS:

- Why did Peter propose to build the three shelters?
- What was wrong with that?
- What was significant about the message out of the cloud?
- How would you react if you had been with Jesus for the transfiguration?
- What was the most significant thing the three disciples learned about Jesus that day?
- In what situations and experiences does God reveal himself today?
- In what ways has your knowledge and understanding of Jesus changed?

TALKING POINTS:

Share with your students some or all of the following points:

Unexpected visit

Imagine what this experience must have been like. Three very normal people who had been following Jesus saw him transformed before their eyes into a glorified state. Moses and Elijah showed up and talked to Jesus. God the Father spoke from the heavens and declared, "This is my son" (verse 5). Wow! Most of us would probably have responded the same way they did—falling to the ground terrified.

God in a body

These three disciples saw Jesus for who he really is. Because of what they witnessed and heard, they knew Jesus is the Son of God, the Messiah. They understood Jesus is whom the Scriptures point to—God himself come to earth to rescue humans from their sin. God the Father let them see this so they could understand who he is. This is exactly what God wants all of us to know about Jesus.

Inside information

Once the three disciples saw Jesus' true identity, Jesus told them what would happen in the future. He gave them the plan of what's to come. Isn't that what we all want? We want to know God's plan. But what they heard isn't at all what they expected. Jesus said he would suffer just like John the Baptist did—shocking news, since John the Baptist had been beheaded by King Herod. This isn't the plan they had in mind. They wanted Jesus to set up a kingdom on earth for them—they didn't want to die like John did. But God's plan isn't to establish an earthly kingdom, but rather a heavenly kingdom that will last forever.

See Jesus—follow his plan

God wants us to know his plan for our lives—but we must know him first. Then we'll be able to trust him and be confident his plan is best. Too often we get caught up in looking for the details. What should I do? Where should I go? The truth is, God is more interested in us knowing him. Once we see God for who he is, he'll start to give us the details we need. Seek him first, and he'll tell you all need to know.

REAL-LIFE CONNECTION: Why do you trust Jesus?

Hand out sheets of paper and pens. Ask everyone to write everything they know about Jesus. Tell them to write as many sentences as they can. They should begin every sentence with the same two words: Jesus is...

At the bottom of their sheets, they should complete this sentence: "I trust Jesus with my life because..."

MEDIA: God will reveal himself

Show a clip from the movie *Amistad*—the scene in which the slaves are in jail during their trial (Chapter 13—1:35 to 1:41). A slave who cannot read is looking at a Bible, and he's able to understand the gospel by looking at the pictures. In this scene we also see as the men walk to the courthouse, people are praying for them. This illustrates how God uses his Word, as well as the prayers and actions of people, to reveal himself when normal communication isn't possible.

Matthew 18:10-14

TOPIC: Jesus will never give up on you

OBJECTIVE: Students will know they're valuable and loved by Jesus. They'll feel valuable and loved when they believe Jesus is their loving Shepherd.

BACKGROUND/OVERVIEW: Jesus explained how important each individual is to God.

GAME/ICEBREAKER: Sardines

You'll need a big meeting space for this activity. Have one student hide. Then have the rest of the students search for the hidden one. Whoever finds this person must quietly hide in the same place with her. The game continues until everyone is hiding together—jammed into the same space, like sardines. The last person to find the hiding students is the first one to hide in the next round.

ICEBREAKER QUESTIONS:

- How would you feel if you hid and no one came looking for you? How would that influence your opinion about being part of this group?
- What makes a person good at finding people who are hiding?
- If one of your friends were missing for a day what would you do to find him?

TRANSITION:

Ask—

If you were in a disaster situation and were missing, who do you think would come looking for you?

Say—

Jesus talked to his disciples about scary moments when you might think your life is over or no one cares about you. Listen to what he says.

SCRIPTURE: Matthew 18:10-14

Have a student read this passage aloud from his Bible.

10-11 "See that you do not despise one of these little ones. For I tell you that their angels in heaven always see the face of my Father in heaven.

[12] "What do you think? If a man owns a hundred sheep, and one of them wanders away, will he not leave the ninety-nine on the hills and go to look for the one that wandered off? [13] And if he finds it, truly I tell you, he is happier about that one sheep than about the ninety-nine that did not wander off. [14] In the same way your Father in heaven is not willing that any of these little ones should perish.

STUDY QUESTIONS:

- What would you think if you were one of the 99 and the shepherd left to go looking for the lost one?
- What would you think if you were the lost one?
- When Jesus tells this story, what is he trying to tell us about God? About us?
- When have you been like a lost sheep?
- How has Jesus been like a good Shepherd looking for you?

TALKING POINTS:

Here are some important ideas to share with your students:

A shepherd and the sheep enjoy a special relationship

Jesus describes himself as a Shepherd and his followers as sheep. Being a shepherd is much more than a menial job: Shepherds love their sheep for many reasons and will risk their lives for them. A lamb is one of the most helpless animals, completely dependent on the shepherd. A lost lamb will probably die. So the shepherd does everything possible to find it—he doesn't just wait and hope the lost sheep will come home. He goes after it and brings the animal back from danger.

Jesus is our Shepherd

Jesus loves each of us in that way. He knows we need him; we're helpless on our own. So if we become lost, he does all he can to find us to bring us back to safety. Jesus won't give up searching until he finds us when we're lost. The greatest example of search-and-rescue is when Jesus came to Earth to save us. He knew if he didn't come and rescue us, our death—eternal death—was certain. Jesus loves you so much that even if you were the only person lost, he'd still have died on the cross to rescue you from sin and death.

Jesus is looking for you

If you feel lost and it seems like no one is coming to get you, remember the truth: God is your Shepherd—you belong to him. You could never stray away without Jesus coming after you. You're most important to him, and he'll do anything to rescue you—even die for you. If you're lost, stop running and start listening. Jesus is calling your name—he's coming for you. When he finds you, he'll bring you home and restore you to the place you were meant to be. Stop running and just let him rescue you.

REAL-LIFE CONNECTION: Your rescue story
Ask—

- Do you have a rescue story? Were you ever lost and alone? How did the police or your parents find you?
- Do you have a spiritual rescue story? How did you get lost and separated from God? How has Jesus come looking for you and brought you back from danger?
- Write down your stories, or record them on audio or video.
- Share your story with friends. Let people know how much God cares for you and them.

MEDIA: He won't abandon us
Show your students the video clip "I will come for you" (2:40) from *The Day after Tomorrow*. Trapped in a flooded New York City library during a massive global weather crisis, Sam makes contact with his father, who vows to find and rescue him. This clip is available from www.wingclips.com (search using the words *come for you*), or a local video outlet.

Matthew 19:16-30

TOPIC: What's more important?

OBJECTIVE: Students will identify what is most important to them and surrender it to God.

BACKGROUND/OVERVIEW: Jesus attracted all types of people who wanted guidance and direction for their lives. These people asked questions and wanted help from this powerful man of God. One day a successful young man came to Jesus asking how to please God and be rewarded with eternal life. He walked away from Jesus after getting a response he did not expect.

GAME/ICEBREAKER: Label blitz

Items needed:

- Sheets of 10 blank labels—one sheet for each student
- Small prizes

Give everyone a sheet of 10 blank mailing labels. With everyone standing up and moving around, instruct the group to stick all their labels on other people. The idea is to have few or no labels on themselves and lots of labels on everyone else. They can't drop the labels on the floor or put them on an object—they can only stick them on another person in the game. Play some loud, lively music and give prizes to the people with the least and most labels stuck to them.

ICEBREAKER QUESTIONS:

- This game is about giving and receiving. What did you excel in—giving or receiving?
- Take three labels off yourself (or someone else if you have fewer than three labels on you) and write on each something you have that is most important to you. It could be a material object, an ability, a relationship, an activity you enjoy, or anything that is a very big part of your life right now. (Allow a minute or two for this.)
- Stick those labels to the front of you. Each label should have something important to you written on it.
- Let's do a little survey. One at a time call out what someone next to you has on their three labels. Let's find out what is important to us.

SCRIPTURE:
Matthew 19:16-30
Have two adults read this passage aloud—one should read the role of the man.

16 Just then a man came up to Jesus and asked, "Teacher, what good thing must I do to get eternal life?"

17 "Why do you ask me about what is good?" Jesus replied. "There is only One who is good. If you want to enter life, keep the commandments."

18 "Which ones?" he inquired.

Jesus replied, "'You shall not murder, you shall not commit adultery, you shall not steal, you shall not give false testimony, 19 honor your father and mother,' and 'love your neighbor as yourself.'"

20 "All these I have kept," the young man said. "What do I still lack?"

21 Jesus answered, "If you want to be perfect, go, sell your possessions and give to the poor, and you will have treasure in heaven. Then come, follow me."

22 When the young man heard this, he went away sad, because he had great wealth.

23 Then Jesus said to his disciples, "Truly I tell you, it is hard for the rich to enter the kingdom of heaven. 24 Again I tell you, it is easier for a camel to go through the eye of a needle than for the rich to enter the kingdom of God."

25 When the disciples heard this, they were greatly astonished and asked, "Who then can be saved?" 26 Jesus looked at them and said, "With human beings this is impossible, but with God all things are possible."

27 Peter answered him, "We have left everything to follow you! What then will there be for us?"

28 Jesus said to them, "Truly I tell you, at the renewal of all things, when the Son of Man sits on his glorious throne, you who have followed me will also sit on twelve thrones, judging the twelve tribes of Israel. 29 And everyone who has left houses or brothers or sisters or

father or mother or wife or children or fields for my sake will receive a hundred times as much and will inherit eternal life. [30] But many who are first will be last, and many who are last will be first.

STUDY QUESTIONS:

- Which is more dangerous—being very rich or very poor? Explain.
- When this young man said he had kept all the commandments perfectly, do you think this statement was true, or do you think he was blind to his sins?
- What point was Jesus making with this young man?
- So many other people followed Jesus, why didn't this young man?
- What would be difficult for you to give up in order to follow Jesus?
- How do you know if you do give up what you love most to follow Jesus it will be better for you?
- Jesus says being rich makes it tough to get into heaven. Why is that true?

TALKING POINTS:

Have a conversation with your students using the following points as a guide:

He asked all the right questions

This young man's desire was to find purpose and meaning for his life. He had success, wealth, and reputation. He wanted to please God and find eternal life. His priorities and goals were good: He was thinking and asking about how his life could be blessed by God.

He knew all the right answers

This young man knew the law of Moses and had followed it carefully. He told Jesus he had kept the commandments about his relationships with other people perfectly. He seemed confident and open to discuss any aspect of his personal and moral life. Compared with others his moral life met the highest standards.

He failed the final exam

Jesus' response must have shocked the man. Jesus said he needed one more thing to be perfect. The man should sell his possessions and give the money to the poor—then he should follow Jesus. The young man walked away because he was very wealthy. The watching disciples were shocked. If this young man couldn't follow Jesus, then who would be qualified to be a disciple? The challenge Jesus gave the young man hit him where it hurt most. Apparently his wealth was a key part of his self-worth—it was most important to him. Jesus wasn't telling everyone to sell everything and give it to the poor. He was testing this young man to see what was the boss of his life. In gaining eternal life, two steps were required: The man had to give up everything important to him and follow. Jesus asked him to obey and relinquish control of what was most important to him. That question forced him to admit he loved his money more than he loved God. He couldn't step away from his wealth and step toward Jesus.

What does Jesus want you to put on eBay?
What's more important to you than God? If you want to follow Jesus, at some point he'll ask you to give up the things important to you so you can follow him. Nothing is wrong with having possessions and loving certain people, but any thing or person that hinders us from obeying Jesus puts Jesus in second place. The big question that rattles our brain is: Can I trust God to give me what I need when I surrender to Jesus everything I have?

REAL-LIFE CONNECTION: Label reminder
Items needed:

- A half sheet of paper or a large index card
- Pens/pencils

Give the following instructions:

- Transfer the three labels from your clothes to your paper/card.
- These three labels may identify something in your life you might be tempted to love more than God. Take a good look at the labels.
- Imagine Jesus looking us in the eye, telling us to surrender what is so important to us.
- Write your answer to him at the bottom of your paper. Fold it up and stick it in your pocket. Carry that paper with you everywhere you go this week. Think about what you have to do to make Jesus Christ number one in your life.

MEDIA: Biblical Monopoly
Play "One Thing" (:50), a reading of the story of the rich young ruler, over a fast-moving game of Monopoly. It's available through YouTube or Sermonspice. (Go to www.sermonspice.com or www.youtube.com and search using the words *one thing revolutionEYES*.)

Matthew 20:29-34

TOPIC: Pray like you mean it

OBJECTIVE: Students will feel God's care for them when they read about Jesus helping the blind men, and they'll begin to express their needs, desires, and hopes to God in prayer.

BACKGROUND/OVERVIEW: As Jesus walked by two blind men, they shouted out their need for help. Jesus knew their needs, but he asked these men to say exactly what they wanted him to do for them.

GAME/ICEBREAKER: **Guess your present**
Items needed:

- 20 pieces of paper, each with an item your students might like to receive written on it (e.g., iPhone, flat-screen TV, surfboard, and so forth). Fold the papers so the item is obscured.

Divide the group into two teams. Have two students—one from each team—face each other. One student draws one of the folded papers, silently reads it, and shows it to his or her team. Then, the student from the other team asks 10 questions of the opposing student to try to figure out what the item is. After the 10th question the student must make a guess. A correct guess is worth 1,000 points for the team. Students then switch roles and repeat. Play with 10 pairs of students opposing each other. Move this along quickly—don't let it drag.

ICEBREAKER QUESTIONS:

- What was the most difficult present to guess? What made it the hardest?
- What was the easiest item to guess in the game?
- What was the best strategy? Which questions were most helpful in making correct identifications?
- What in your life would you better understand or receive if you asked the right questions?

SCRIPTURE: **Matthew 20:29-34**
Read aloud the following passage. Or have a few students act it out (be sure to prepare beforehand).

[29] As Jesus and his disciples were leaving Jericho, a large crowd followed him. [30] Two blind men were sitting by the roadside, and when they heard that Jesus was going by, they shouted, "Lord, Son of David, have mercy on us!"

[31] The crowd rebuked them and told them to be quiet, but they shouted all the louder, "Lord, Son of David, have mercy on us!"

[32] Jesus stopped and called them. "What do you want me to do for you?" he asked.

[33] "Lord," they answered, "we want our sight."

[34] Jesus had compassion on them and touched their eyes. Immediately they received their sight and followed him.

STUDY QUESTIONS:

- If Jesus is all-knowing, why do you think he asked the blind men what they wanted?
- Why did the crowd rebuke the men, trying to keep them quiet and away from Jesus?
- Today, how do people try to keep others away from Jesus?
- What might make people hold back from telling Jesus what they need?
- What are your needs, problems, and struggles?
- What would you like Jesus to do for you?

TALKING POINTS:
Share the following points with your students:

Did these blind men change Jesus' plans?
Were these men looking for Jesus, or was Jesus looking for them? Jesus showed his compassion for these blind men. Their disability had forced them into a life of poverty and begging, but Jesus took time to speak with them and hear their needs.

God cares about us, and he sees the problems that twist our lives away from him. Don't hesitate to seek God with determination, knowing God is also looking for you. You're on his schedule. He wants to communicate with you.

Why not ask God for what you need?
Many people think they don't have to tell God what they need, want, or

desire because he already knows. Some think God doesn't care or can't do anything anyway. But Jesus wants us to come to him, speaking and confessing our needs. Blind men in the Bible were outcasts of the society, yet Jesus heard their cries and healed them. "If our hearts do not condemn us we have confidence before God and receive from him anything we ask, because we keep his command and do what pleases him" (1 John 3:21-22). Through Christ, we can come to God and tell him our requests.

Don't let anyone or anything silence your requests to God

Sometimes when we need to speak to God about our desires, certain obstacles can get in the way—like the unruly crowd blocking the blind men. One obstacle could be a friend telling you it's stupid to think God cares. At times our own doubts can lead us to believe God is far away and not listening. Or our pride can make us think we can solve our own problems without God's help. But we have a choice. In this passage, Jesus demonstrates that God cares and wants us to pursue him. He waits for us to ask him to change us, heal us, or bless us so we can serve others. What do you let silence you or keep you from praying to God?

REAL-LIFE CONNECTION: If I pray my requests to God and nothing changes, what's wrong?

Share the following with your students:

When you make your request to God, be ready for an answer, but here's a word of wisdom and caution: You might not get the answer you want or expect. Our prayers are not to an ATM or vending machine. God cares about our growth and character more than he cares about our comfort. Sometimes the answer God gives his children is no or not now as well as yes. When we don't get the answers we want, often that's because God is using the challenges we face to help us get stronger. God cares about us and wants to be with us in our struggle. Many people say they grow closer to God when life is hard rather than when life is easy. Either way God is at work in us for our best.

MEDIA: Tell him what you need

Show your students the YouTube video "Cry Out to Jesus" from the *Wherever You Are* album by Third Day. This song highlights the importance of telling the Lord our needs. Go to www.youtube.com and use the search words *cry out to Jesus third day*

Matthew 21:12-16

TOPIC: A house that pleases God

OBJECTIVE: Students will commit to living God-honoring lives marked by purity, prayer, power, and praise.

BACKGROUND/OVERVIEW: Jesus' cleansing of the temple showed just how corrupt the sacrificial system of worship had become. More significantly, his actions fulfilled messianic prophecy and expectation, which included purification of the temple (Ezekiel 40—47; Zechariah 6:12-13).

GAME/ICEBREAKER: Bible Balderdash
Items needed:

- Dictionary
- Small pieces of paper
- Pens/pencils

This game is played with the regular rules of the popular game Balderdash. Use a dictionary to find the definition of obscure and outrageous words and names from the Bible. Break the group into teams of five to six people. Read and spell the word so each group can write it down. Give the teams a few minutes to write a phony (but believable) definition for the word. They should write it down and give the paper to you. Then you will shuffle the papers and read aloud all the definitions including the correct one, which you will have written down on a small piece of paper. By raising their hands, the students will vote for the correct definition. (Each team will have one vote—they should decide as a team which definition they believe to be the correct one.) Award one point to each team that guesses the correct definition and three points to each team that got other people to vote for their phony definition. That motivates teams to try and fool others by writing very convincing wrong definitions. Here are several examples of good Bible words you can use: Praetorium (Matthew 27:27), Ehud (Judges 3:15-30), Nimrim (Jeremiah 48:34), and Sanballat (Nehemiah 4:1-7).

ICEBREAKER QUESTIONS:

- Which of your phony definitions fooled the most people?
- (To the people who got the definitions correct): **How did you know what was correct?**

- How do people in real life trick people using words that mean something different than what they think it means?
- In our Bible reading we'll learn about people who redefined what God's temple was to be used for. In what ways do people misunderstand the real purpose of going to a church or temple?
- What bad things do people do that confuse others about what it really means to be a Christian or go to a church?

SCRIPTURE: Matthew 21:12-16
Read aloud the passage.

12 Jesus entered the temple courts and drove out all who were buying and selling there. He overturned the tables of the money changers and the benches of those selling doves. 13 "It is written," he said to them, "'My house will be called a house of prayer,' but you are making it 'a den of robbers.'"

14 The blind and the lame came to him at the temple, and he healed them. 15 But when the chief priests and the teachers of the law saw the wonderful things he did and the children shouting in the temple courts, "Hosanna to the Son of David," they were indignant.

16 "Do you hear what these children are saying?" they asked him.

"Yes," replied Jesus, "have you never read,

"'From the lips of children and infants

you have ordained praise'?"

STUDY QUESTIONS:

- What was it that made Jesus so upset when he entered the temple?
- Did Jesus sin? Explain your answer.
- What made the chief priests and the teachers of the law so upset?
- What did Jesus want to see happening in the temple?

TALKING POINTS:
Share some or all of the following points with your students:

Did Jesus sin?
What a confusing picture of Jesus we have in this story. In virtually all of the

Jesus films, we see a sweet, tender Jesus walking around in a shiny white robe caring for people. He doesn't seem as though he'd hurt a fly. But now we read about him apparently losing it and going off on people. What happened? Did Jesus sin? Did he slip up and go against God's will? Today we want to get a clearer understanding of what drove Jesus to do what he did that day in the temple and discover what he was looking for—and is looking for in each of us.

Understanding the scene

In Jesus' day the people were to bring a yearly tithe (10 percent) of all their goods to a designated place to offer to the Lord in accordance with his command. God made a provision, however, to accommodate those who lived a great distance from the place where the tithe was to be offered, or for those whose tithe was so large it was impractical to transport. This provision is spelled out in Deuteronomy 14:22-26. In such cases a person could sell their tithe to someone in their town and take the money from the sale with them on their journey. Once they reached the location where the sacrifice was to be made (by the time of Jesus this was the temple), they'd exchange their money for an equivalent amount of grain and animals they had sold back home, and they'd then offer their sacrifices to the Lord according to the established ways.

The real deal

It wasn't the money changers and other merchants themselves who infuriated Jesus. The problem was these people were fraudulent in their transactions. They were ripping people off! The entire sacrificial system God had established had been corrupted and turned into big business. Rather than facilitating worship, the business transactions were getting in the way. Instead of joyfully celebrating the goodness of God, vendors were celebrating making big money, and customers were feeling bitter. All focus on God had been lost. Far from sinning, Jesus manifested a righteous anger that revealed God's heart (Ephesians 4:26). Jesus' actions showed God's passion for justice and true worship while fulfilling the prophecy of Malachi 3:1-4.

Incredible contrast

Interestingly, Jesus wasn't the only one to get upset that day. The chief priests and the teachers of the law also got upset. While they weren't disturbed by the injustice and the corruption of the sacrificial system, they were highly disturbed when they saw Jesus healing people and heard children singing praise to God. The contrast is incredible and shows us just how out of whack the values of the religious leaders had become.

A house that pleases God
This story deals with the physical temple, but we're now the temples in which God lives (1 Corinthians 6:19). The truth of this passage, including Jesus' passion for the physical temple, applies to us. God wants to live in houses pleasing to him. In this story we can see four things God truly wants and should characterize our lives.

1. A house of purity (Matthew 21:12).
2. A house of prayer (verse 13).
3. A house of power (verse 14).
4. A house of perfected praise (verses 15-16).

REAL-LIFE CONNECTION: Keep your focus on Jesus
Ask your students the following questions:

• If Jesus were to come to your spiritual house today, what would he find that pleases him? What would he have to start tossing because they're defrauding him of his rightful place in your life?
• What can you can do to help fight injustice in the world?
• Who are the people or what are the things on God's heart he wants you to begin praying for?
• What can you do to keep your focus on Jesus when you're in a difficult or hostile situation?

MEDIA: God's house
Show the video clip "God's House is a House of Prayer" (1:31). This video can be purchased from Sermonspice—go to www.sermonspice.com and use the search words *house of prayer*. This video features an inspiring sound track and scenes of people praying.

Matthew 22:34-40

TOPIC: The greatest commandment

OBJECTIVE: Students will learn the two greatest commandments, and they'll know how to love God and love their neighbor.

BACKGROUND/OVERVIEW: The Pharisees (religious leaders) were trying to trap Jesus with questions about the most important commandment so they could discredit him as a teacher from God. People were still trying to figure out God and come up with new formulas on how to please him. Jesus clearly explained God's expectations of us and gave us practical ways to fulfill them.

GAME/ICEBREAKER: Now you make the rules

Items needed:

- Blank pieces of paper cut to look like the stone tablets Moses carried down from his meeting with God on Mount Sinai
- Pens/pencils

Divide your students into groups of six. Have some groups equally mixed by gender. Have some groups all one gender. Give each group a blank sheet of paper cut to look like the stone tablets Moses carried down from his meeting with God on Mount Sinai. Tell the groups they get to pretend they're the new leaders of the country. All the old government leadership and laws are gone. All the churches are now out of business. Definite proof has been presented that God doesn't exist. (Don't explain how you know—this is a role-play. Their job is to come up with the major laws (if any) for this new society and write them on the paper. Give them seven minutes to work on their new laws.

Ask five of the small groups to present and explain their new laws to the whole group. Ask each group to identify the one or two laws that are the most important for people to obey.

ICEBREAKER QUESTIONS:

- How did you decide what laws were needed for your new society?
- What was your reason for the laws you chose to put on people?
- What will you do if people don't follow your new rules?
- What will you do to convince people your laws are right and good for them and everyone?

• How many of our rules are similar to the commands God gave us 5,000 years ago?

SCRIPTURE: Matthew 22:34-40
Ask a student to read the passage aloud from his Bible.

³⁴ Hearing that Jesus had silenced the Sadducees, the Pharisees got together. ³⁵ One of them, an expert in the law, tested him with this question: ³⁶ "Teacher, which is the greatest commandment in the Law?"

³⁷ Jesus replied: "'Love the Lord your God with all your heart and with all your soul and with all your mind.' ³⁸ This is the first and greatest commandment. ³⁹ And the second is like it: 'Love your neighbor as yourself.' ⁴⁰ All the Law and the Prophets hang on these two commandments."

STUDY QUESTIONS:

• Why did the Pharisees want to test Jesus?
• What two commandments did Jesus say were most important?
• What does it mean to "Love God with all your heart and with all your soul and with all your mind"? How do you do it?
• What do you do when you love someone as you love yourself?
• What did Jesus mean when he said, "All the Law and the Prophets hang on these two commandments"?

TALKING POINTS:
Share the following points with your students:

Is being a Christian about having a bunch of rules to follow?
Have you ever heard students or adults say, "The church and Christianity are nothing but a bunch of rules that take all the fun out of life"? Are they right? Do you ever measure your relationship with God on how much you go to church activities or how well you avoid bad behavior?

The Pharisees felt as if they were the godliest people because of the group they belonged to and because of what they did for God when everyone was watching. Jesus and his honest preaching threatened their popularity and authority with the people. They wanted to discredit him as a rabbi, so they asked him which commandment was the most important. Their motive was to get Jesus to choose one of the Ten Commandments as the most important and then smear him for making the other commandments less important. They wanted to make Jesus look bad.

How do you love someone?

Jesus knew their motives and gave them an answer they didn't expect. Jesus said the most important thing a person should do is to "love God" with all her heart, mind and soul (verse 37).

What does loving God, or anyone else, for that matter, really mean?

When you love someone you usually do some or all of the following:

- Think about that person all the time.
- Find out what he or she likes and doesn't like.
- Spend a lot of time with him or her.
- Talk to the person about little and big things.
- Do favors for that person and receive them, too.
- Give him or her gifts.

Jesus was telling the Pharisees (and us) that love isn't just following a bunch of rules in a book. Loving others starts with learning to love God and using what we learn from God's example to love others: Listening, caring, giving, and so forth. We were created to communicate with God as often as possible—seeing what pleases and displeases him and telling him about the big and little issues in our life. A good starting place is agreeing with God about our disobedience and pride so we can ask for his forgiveness. Jesus' statement tells us our relationship with God is most important.

What about the second great commandment?

Jesus said we're to love our neighbors as we love ourselves. This is nearly as important as loving God. Have you seen a sibling or child behave in a way that is just like their older sibling or parent? When we learn to love God daily, we start sounding and looking like him. By loving our neighbors (people we like and those we dislike), we show people God's love for them. They get to see God's love through us.

More than following rules

Jesus also said, "All the Law and the Prophets hang on these two commandments" (verse 40). When you love someone and you get to know her, you want to do things that make that person happy because when she's happy, you're happy. When you start talking to God and build the relationship with him, you naturally will want to follow what God asks you to do because it makes sense and because it will make others happy, too.

Going to church, doing Christian things, and calling yourself a believer is easy. But we can do all that and never know who God is or love others like God loves us. God wants to be in us and working through us.

REAL-LIFE CONNECTION: Get to know God
Ask your students the following questions and give them the following instructions:

- Jesus says knowing and loving God is most important. What are you doing to make this knowledge and love stronger and better?
- Start learning to love God by just talking to him everyday. Tell him what you think about him. Thank him for who he is and his love and forgiveness to you. Ask him to help you, but this week try to spend more time praising God than asking him for solutions to your problems.
- Read the Bible every day this week. Get to know God better through spending time with him, listening to him.
- Go out of your way this week to love someone as God would love her. Ask God to help you learn to love people, especially those who get under your skin. Love them as you love yourself. Let God show you people who need help with physical or spiritual needs.

MEDIA: Worship music
Using a video from www.youtube.com (or musicians from your own group), sing and worship together as a group with a song like "How Great Is Our God" from the *Arriving* album by Chris Tomlin, or any other good worship song that declares love for God.

Or have your group write a new song. Get a background music track of a popular song most of your group would recognize. Have small groups (two to four people) write new lyrics that focus on loving God and loving others. Sing or speak the new lyrics to the music.

Matthew 23:1-12

TOPIC: Keeping rules and losing God

OBJECTIVE: Students will know that God wants us to worship him in a relationship, not by fulfilling a required list of religious obligations.

BACKGROUND/OVERVIEW: Pharisees were men who wanted to live by rules of the Bible, which for them was the law of Moses (the Torah). Most of them had memorized it. In addition their rabbis had set it out in 613 rules they thought must be obeyed to please God. You can imagine this was very burdensome for ordinary people. What Jesus offered was a wonderful way of freedom by the Holy Spirit. Rather than trying to obey rules, we can let the Holy Spirit create in our hearts both love for God and love for neighbors.

GAME/ICEBREAKER: Make your own religion

Divide into groups of three and give them 10 minutes to create, design, and describe a new religion. Tell them to be creative and to give it a name. They should list rules, holidays, rituals, beliefs, and leaders. Have someone in each group ready to present the new religion to everyone else.

After 10-12 minutes have the groups report on their new religions. Laugh and have fun hearing all the crazy ideas. As a group select the top new religion.

ICEBREAKER QUESTIONS:

- What was the most fun or the most interesting part of making this new religion?
- What was the best idea of any of these "religions" you heard described?
- In general, how did most of these *religions* tell us to connect with God?
- What would you think if someone took *your religion* and changed the rules?
- What did Jesus think of what the Jewish religious leaders, the Pharisees, had done to the commandments and instructions God had given to Moses and the prophets?

SCRIPTURE: Matthew 23:1-12

Read the passage aloud, emphasizing Jesus' statements about and to the Pharisees.

¹ Then Jesus said to the crowds and to his disciples: ² "The teachers of the law and the Pharisees sit in Moses' seat. ³ So you must be careful to do everything they tell you. But do not do what they do, for they do not practice what they preach. ⁴ They tie up heavy, cumbersome loads and put them on other people's shoulders, but they themselves are not willing to lift a finger to move them.

⁵ "Everything they do is done for people to see: They make their phylacteries wide and the tassels on their garments long; ⁶ they love the place of honor at banquets and the most important seats in the synagogues; ⁷ they love to be greeted with respect in the market-places and to have people call them 'Rabbi.'

⁸ "But you are not to be called 'Rabbi,' for you have only one Master and you are all brothers. ⁹ And do not call anyone on earth 'father,' for you have one Father, and he is in heaven. ¹⁰ Nor are you to be called 'teacher,' for you have one Teacher, the Messiah. ¹¹ The greatest among you will be your servant. ¹² For those who exalt themselves will be humbled, and those who humble themselves will be exalted."

(Note: If you have time, have someone else read 23:13-39. Otherwise, just refer to these statements by Jesus that blast the Pharisees.)

¹³⁻¹⁴ "Woe to you, teachers of the law and Pharisees, you hypocrites! You shut the door of the kingdom of heaven in people's faces. You yourselves do not enter, nor will you let those enter who are trying to.

¹⁵ "Woe to you, teachers of the law and Pharisees, you hypocrites! You travel over land and sea to win a single convert, and then you make that convert twice as much a child of hell as you are.

¹⁶ "Woe to you, blind guides! You say, 'If anyone swears by the temple, it means nothing; but whoever swears by the gold of the temple is bound by the oath.' ¹⁷ You blind fools! Which is greater: the gold, or the temple that makes the gold sacred? ¹⁸ You also say, 'If anyone swears by the altar, it means nothing; but whoever swears by the gift on the altar is bound by the oath.' ¹⁹ You blind men! Which is greater: the gift, or the altar that makes the gift sacred? ²⁰ Therefore, anyone who swears by the altar swears by it and by everything on it. ²¹ And anyone who swears by the temple swears by it and by the one who dwells in it. ²² And anyone who swears by heaven swears by God's throne and by the one who sits on it.

23 "Woe to you, teachers of the law and Pharisees, you hypocrites! You give a tenth of your spices—mint, dill and cumin. But you have neglected the more important matters of the law—justice, mercy and faithfulness. You should have practiced the latter, without neglecting the former. 24 You blind guides! You strain out a gnat but swallow a camel.

25 "Woe to you, teachers of the law and Pharisees, you hypocrites! You clean the outside of the cup and dish, but inside they are full of greed and self-indulgence. 26 Blind Pharisee! First clean the inside of the cup and dish, and then the outside also will be clean.

27 "Woe to you, teachers of the law and Pharisees, you hypocrites! You are like whitewashed tombs, which look beautiful on the outside but on the inside are full of the bones of the dead and everything unclean. 28 In the same way, on the outside you appear to people as righteous but on the inside you are full of hypocrisy and wickedness.

29 "Woe to you, teachers of the law and Pharisees, you hypocrites! You build tombs for the prophets and decorate the graves of the righteous. 30 And you say, 'If we had lived in the days of our ancestors, we would not have taken part with them in shedding the blood of the prophets.' 31 So you testify against yourselves that you are the descendants of those who murdered the prophets. 32 Fill up, then, the measure of the sin of your ancestors!

33 "You snakes! You brood of vipers! How will you escape being condemned to hell? 34 Therefore I am sending you prophets and sages and teachers. Some of them you will kill and crucify; others you will flog in your synagogues and pursue from town to town. 35 And so upon you will come all the righteous blood that has been shed on earth, from the blood of righteous Abel to the blood of Zechariah son of Berekiah, whom you murdered between the temple and the altar. 36 Truly I tell you, all this will come on this generation.

37 "Jerusalem, Jerusalem, you who kill the prophets and stone those sent to you, how often I have longed to gather your children together, as a hen gathers her chicks under her wings, and you were not willing. 38 Look, your house is left to you desolate. 39 For I tell you, you will not see me again until you say, 'Blessed is he who comes in the name of the Lord.'"

STUDY QUESTIONS:

- For what reasons did Jesus so strongly condemn these religious leaders, the Pharisees?
- What motivated the Pharisees to live and behave like they did?
- In what ways did the Pharisees twist God's law into a lifestyle Jesus condemns?
- What temptations are faced by people who are good at following religious rules?
- What does Jesus say happens to people who act like big shots?
- What character traits make a great leader?

TALKING POINTS:

Share the following information with your students:

The Pharisees created a new religion Jesus condemned

The Pharisees were good people who wanted to live by rules of the Bible, which for them was the law of Moses (the Torah). Most of them had memorized it. And their rabbis had expanded it into 613 rules they thought must be obeyed to please God. Jesus condemned them for twisting faith in God into a contest of egos and appearances.

They made faith a burden

Instead of finding freedom, the Pharisees taught people that pleasing God was built on obligation. "They tie up heavy, cumbersome loads and put them on other people's shoulders." (verse 4). Jesus said, "My yoke is easy and my burden is light" (Matthew 11:30). Don't let your faith become a list of rules.

They lived to impress others

Jesus called them out. "They do all their deeds to be seen by others" (verse 5). They did good deeds so others would see them and give them recognition.

We need to think about why we help others or give. If our self-worth is based on what others think about us, we're susceptible to doing what will impress others instead of doing God's will.

What you see isn't what you get

The Pharisees' religion had lots of talk about God, but it really was all about them. They professed giving glory to God, but they wanted the glory for themselves—the praying and giving was all for show. Jesus promised that although they puffed themselves up to gain admiration, God would deflate them. God's way is the humble way. Jesus promises that God will exalt the humble and reward those who do what pleases God without selfish ambitions. The outward expression Jesus seems to delight in is "the greatest among you will be your servant" (verse 11).

Christianity isn't a religion

Religion has been defined as "man's search for God." In other words, all religions have this fact in common: They are attempts by human beings to connect with the divine. This may be defined as trying to gain salvation, eternal life, oneness with God, etc., but it's a very serious attempt to find God. That's what we saw in all the religions we created earlier. And it certainly describes what the Pharisees were doing. But true Christianity isn't a religion—it's a relationship. Christianity says we can't get to God on our own—it's impossible. But he can come to us—and he did, in Christ. So by trusting in him—in his work on the cross—we gain eternal life. It's not a matter of doing stuff but of knowing him.

Pharisee religion is very contagious—be careful

We can easily spot hypocrisy and self-centeredness in others, but often overlook our own issues. So here's the question to ask: Do you have a religion or a relationship? In other words: Are you trying to please God by keeping rules and doing religious activities? Are you comparing yourself with others to justify your actions? Are you proud of your righteous lifestyle? Whom are you really worshipping, and what is your motivation? Are you doing good works to please God or to impress others?

These are interior issues—only you know the answers. God wants you to trust him, to worship him alone, and to receive the grace he gives to everyone who puts his faith in Jesus Christ.

REAL-LIFE CONNECTION: Religion or relationship?
Items needed:

- Index cards, key chains, packs of dental floss, wristbands, or anything people will see every day

Have the following conversation with your students:

Do you have a religion or a relationship? Do you want a list of rules to follow or a relationship with the almighty God who created you and loves you? One way to remember the difference is to daily remind yourself of the gospel message. John Newton said, "I know two things: That I am a great sinner, and Christ is a great Savior" (quoted in the film *Amazing Grace* and in the biography of John Newton, *John Newton: From Disgrace to Amaz-*

ing Grace by Jonathan Aitken [Wheaton, Illinois: Crossway Books, 2007]). And that about sums it up. Keep the focus on you (not others), admit your problem, receive God's help, and praise God always. That's a long way from being a Pharisee.

Take this simple reminder home with you. Read it every day as you love God and love others.

(Note: The reminder is simply that statement—"I am a great sinner, and Christ is a great Savior." You can attach this reminder to index cards, key chains, packs of dental floss, wristbands, or anything people will see every day. Prepare these prior to the meeting and distribute them as the meeting ends.)

MEDIA: Inside or outside?

Show a video clip from Sermonspice: "Clean the Cup" (2:46). (Go to www. sermonspice.com and use the search words *clean cup*.) This clip takes place in a coffee shop and discusses whether we're more concerned about the cleanliness of the outside of the cup versus the inside of the cup. The final question asks if we're more concerned about what God thinks of us, or what other people think about us.

Matthew 24:45-51

TOPIC: Get ready—be ready

OBJECTIVE: Students will have a clear idea of what it means to be ready for the return of Jesus.

BACKGROUND/OVERVIEW: Jesus gives insight to his second coming and explains that believers should be ready and waiting for his return.

GAME/ICEBREAKER: Whack-a-Foot
Item needed:

- A rolled-up newspaper

Have your group sit in a circle with their feet out toward the middle of the circle. Let each student tell everyone in the group his name. Pick someone to be *It*. The leader will call out a name. The person who is *It* must try to whack that person in the foot with a rolled-up newspaper before that person can say his name and the name of someone else in the circle. The person who is *It* must try to whack the new person mentioned until he can get someone before another name is called.

ICEBREAKER QUESTIONS:

- How did it feel when your name was called? Were you surprised, nervous, afraid?
- What did you do to get ready for your name being called?
- Whose name did you have prepared to say?
- When have you felt totally unprepared for something big that happened?

SCRIPTURE: Matthew 24:45-51
Have a student read the passage aloud from her Bible. Explain that Jesus is speaking.

45 "Who then is the faithful and wise servant, whom the master has put in charge of the servants in his household to give them their food at the proper time? 46 It will be good for that servant whose master finds him doing so when he returns. 47 I tell you truly, he will put him in charge of all his possessions. 48 But suppose that servant is wicked

and says to himself, 'My master is staying away a long time,' [49] and he then begins to beat his fellow servants and to eat and drink with drunkards. [50] The master of that servant will come on a day when he does not expect him and at an hour he is not aware of. [51] He will cut him to pieces and assign him a place with the hypocrites, where there will be weeping and gnashing of teeth."

STUDY QUESTIONS:

- Imagine you're a parent and you hired a house sitter/caretaker to watch your home and children, left on a weeklong vacation, and returned a day early to find your caretaker had neglected your kids, destroyed your property, and ignored all your instructions. How would you feel? What do you do?
- What do you think it means to be watchful?
- If you knew a thief would try to burglarize your house tonight, what would you do today?
- When someone says Jesus is coming back soon, what do you think about?
- What does it mean to be ready for the Christ's return?

TALKING POINTS:
Have a conversation with your students—use the following points as a guide:

Don't be afraid
The idea of the end times often puts fear into most of us, mostly because we're afraid of the unknown. We read about events that will happen at the end of time, and we start to think that sounds a lot like today. But really we have nothing to fear because Christ will return. Instead of making us fearful, these reports should make us want to be ready.

(Read Matthew 24:45-51 aloud again.) Jesus is assuring his disciples that the second coming will happen. We should be ready every day. We don't know when Christ will return, but we shouldn't let the wait make us unprepared.

Be ready
What Jesus tells his disciples is like the classic movie scenario where the parents go away and the kids are left home alone. They have a choice to make: Will they behave like responsible young adults—feed the cat, water the plants, take out the garbage, keep the house clean, etc., so when their parents return, they gain their trust and more freedom and responsibility? Or will they ignore their responsibilities and think of themselves only—maybe throw a party or break into their parents' liquor cabinet. You know how it goes: The

parents always come home during the out-of-control party, and all trust is broken and lost.

Jesus gives us a much-needed reminder: He's coming back. We won't know when, but we do know his return is guaranteed. This event will be marvelous for all who believe. Belief isn't just something we say—it's something we do. We need to live all the time as though we're ready for Christ's return—like we want him to return and are excitedly anticipating the day we see him face to face.

Are you ready?

Jesus is coming back—are you ready? Are you living in a way that will please him? Thinking about this can be scary—we wonder what will happen. If we're honest, we have to admit to enjoying many earthly things. We don't want Jesus to come back—at least not right now. We want to get married first, have kids, get a good job, and grow old. None of those desires is bad; however, nothing compares to being with Jesus. Evaluate yourself. Does your heart desire to be with Jesus more than anything? If it does, the end times and the return of Christ won't scare you. It will be the greatest experience of your life.

REAL-LIFE CONNECTION: Seven days of prep

Share with your students the following challenge for seven days of preparation:

I challenge you to live the next seven days with the absolute conviction that Jesus is coming back sometime very soon. How will your behavior and language change? How will you treat your family? How about your friends? Tell me how your prayer time and Bible study will be different this week. Will you be motivated to resolve some situations where you have not forgiven?

Don't blow off school or empty your bank account. This isn't a call to complete your bucket list, doing things for yourself during the next week. Jesus doesn't tell us to go and wait somewhere for him to return. He tells us to be busy doing what he has called us to do. Then, when he comes, he'll find us hard at work doing his work and carrying out what he gave us to do. Nothing we learn or do will be wasted. Let Jesus find you faithful.

With Jesus' return in mind, keep a list of what you do this week.

MEDIA: Be prepared

Show the clip "Camp Kids Montage" (1:04) from the movie, *Daddy Day Camp*. (On the DVD this is chapter 11—29:35 to 31:25. This clip is also available from www.wingclips.com—search using the words *camp kids*.) This quick montage shows how kids loaded up on sugar go crazy under the care of their day care run by two unemployed fathers. It demonstrates how bad things can get when you choose pleasure over discipline. This helps connect the warning to live ready for the return of Christ.

Matthew 25:31-46

TOPIC: When did we see you?

OBJECTIVE: Students will learn that following Jesus means our focus should be on caring for the needy, not just pleasing ourselves.

BACKGROUND/OVERVIEW: Jesus used parables and figures of speech to teach his disciples what judgment day will be like when he returns as King and Judge of the world.

GAME/ICEBREAKER: **Least of These** (experiential Bible study)
Items needed:

- Fish-shaped crackers
- Cups of water
- Strips of colored cloth (three inches wide, and three to four feet long)
- Bandages
- Boxes with locks and keys
- Small pieces of paper
- Pens/pencils
- Magic markers
- Posterboard

Students will move through five different stations where they learn about loving and caring for people in need. Group students into pairs (same gender) and release them into the room with five stations set up around the perimeter of the room. Lower the lights. Play some quiet music to set the atmosphere. Spread the pairs out over the five stations and tell them they must visit all of them in the 20 minutes allotted.

Station No. 1: Set up cups of fish-shaped crackers and cups of water (one each for each person in the group). Have a sign at the station that says on the top: I WAS HUNGRY AND YOU GAVE ME SOME-THING TO EAT . I WAS THIRSTY AND YOU GAVE ME SOMETHING TO DRINK. At the bottom of the sign write: FEED YOUR PARTNER AND GIVE HIM OR HER A CUP TO DRINK.

Station No. 2: Hang strips of colored cloth (three inches wide and three to four feet long) with photos of people who look different or weird. On the top of the sign write: I WAS A STRANGER AND YOU

WELCOMED ME. I WAS NAKED AND YOU CLOTHED ME. At the bottom of the sign write: PUT A CLOTH AROUND YOUR PARTNER'S NECK LIKE A SCARF.

Station No. 3: Have at least two bandages for each person. On the top of the sign write: I WAS SICK AND YOU TOOK CARE OF ME. On the bottom, write: PUT TWO BANDAGES ON YOUR PARTNER'S FACE.

Station No. 4: Have several boxes with locks and keys. Provide some pencils and small sheets of paper. Write on the top of the sign: I WAS IN PRISON AND YOU VISITED ME. On the bottom of the sign write: ON A SMALL PIECE OF PAPER, WRITE ONE OR MORE THINGS THAT CAN IMPRISON A PERSON OR HOLD HIM CAPTIVE. PUT YOUR PIECE OF PAPER IN THE LOCKED BOX.

Station No. 5: Have several magic markers and a large blank poster-board. On another poster, write: TRULY WHATEVER YOU DID FOR THE LEAST OF THESE, YOU DID IT FOR ME. At the bottom, write: THINK OF SOMEONE IN YOUR WORLD WHO NEEDS HELP FROM YOU OR OTHERS. WRITE THE PERSON'S INITIALS ON THE BLANK POSTER BOARD AND PRAY FOR HIM OR HER.

At the end of 20 minutes bring the pairs back to the large group to discuss the following questions.

ICEBREAKER QUESTIONS:

- What station of activity was most memorable and helpful to you?
- Why does God want us associating with the poor, needy, and outcast?
- What stereotypes do you need to overcome to effectively work with needy people?

SCRIPTURE: Matthew 25:31-46

Explain that Jesus is speaking. Then read the passage aloud while students follow along in their Bibles.

[31] "When the Son of Man comes in his glory, and all the angels with him, he will sit on his glorious throne. [32] All the nations will be gathered before him, and he will separate the people one from another as a shepherd separates the sheep from the goats. [33] He will put the sheep on his right and the goats on his left.

³⁴ "Then the King will say to those on his right, 'Come, you who are blessed by my Father; take your inheritance, the kingdom prepared for you since the creation of the world. ³⁵ For I was hungry and you gave me something to eat, I was thirsty and you gave me something to drink, I was a stranger and you invited me in, ³⁶ I needed clothes and you clothed me, I was sick and you looked after me, I was in prison and you came to visit me.'

³⁷ "Then the righteous will answer him, 'Lord, when did we see you hungry and feed you, or thirsty and give you something to drink? ³⁸ When did we see you a stranger and invite you in, or needing clothes and clothe you? ³⁹ When did we see you sick or in prison and go to visit you?'

⁴⁰ "The King will reply, 'Truly I tell you, whatever you did for one of the least of these brothers and sisters of mine, you did for me.'

⁴¹ Then he will say to those on his left, 'Depart from me, you who are cursed, into the eternal fire prepared for the devil and his angels. ⁴² For I was hungry and you gave me nothing to eat, I was thirsty and you gave me nothing to drink, ⁴³ I was a stranger and you did not invite me in, I needed clothes and you did not clothe me, I was sick and in prison and you did not look after me.'

⁴⁴ "They also will answer, 'Lord, when did we see you hungry or thirsty or a stranger or needing clothes or sick or in prison, and did not help you?'

⁴⁵ "He will reply, 'Truly I tell you, whatever you did not do for one of the least of these, you did not do for me.'

⁴⁶ "Then they will go away to eternal punishment, but the righteous to eternal life."

STUDY QUESTIONS:

- Based on this story, how will the people of the earth be divided when Christ returns?
- How can we know from this story if we're sheep or goats? What will Jesus say to us if we're a goat or a sheep?
- What is the major difference between being a sheep and a goat?
- How would your life change if you treated each person in your life as if she were, in fact, Jesus?

TALKING POINTS:
Share the following points with your students:

Sheep and goats
Using a metaphor that would be very familiar to the nomadic people of his time, Jesus described what would happen at the judgment. The sheep are the people who took care of him when he was in need, and the goats are the people who didn't. He said the sheep will receive their inheritance and blessing from God while the goats will be punished and separated from God forever.

Follow like sheep
Does this mean the way to heaven is though good works? Absolutely not. The key is in the analogy: Sheep are animals that live with a flock mentality, which means they stay together and follow the shepherd. They do this to stay safe and cared for. They know their shepherd's voice and follow him always. This is exactly what Christians are to be like. We are to be like sheep, with Jesus as our Shepherd. We follow him so we stay safe, cared for, and joyful. The people referred to as sheep are people who follow Jesus. They know his voice and stay close to him, doing what he does. That is why they were able to care for the needy and not even know it—they were simply following their Shepherd.

Don't be a goat
Goats, however, are much more independent and stubborn. They go their own way and don't like to follow. The people referred to as goats lived lives independent of Jesus—doing things on their own, choosing not to believe in Jesus as the Savior. That is why they didn't notice when Jesus wanted them to care for the needy. They chose not to follow the Shepherd while they lived, so they were sent away for eternal punishment.

Follow Jesus
Jesus wants us to look after the needy. He made it clear that when we care for the very least, we're caring for him. The only way to know what to do is to follow Jesus the way sheep follow a shepherd. God's sheep are the ones who will receive the reward. Believing in what Jesus did for us and following him always is the only way to heaven.

REAL-LIFE CONNECTION Care for the needy
Ask your students the following questions:

- Who are the needy people around you?

- What resources do you have available to serve the needs of others?
- What act of kindness or mercy toward the needy can you do today?

As a group, research the service opportunities available in your community and participate as a group, helping meet needs for the needy. Look for opportunities for students to care for the needs of peers in their schools who are socially or developmentally challenged.

MEDIA: God will tell us how to help
Show a clip from *Millions* (Chapter 4—15:47 to 20:10). When Damian finds a bag of money, he struggles with what to do with it. Damian meets St. Patrick, who tells him to help the poor. This can open a good discussion on what we'd do if we found a million dollars.

- What would God want us to do with the money?
- What does he want us to do with the money and resources we have right now?
- How do we listen for instructions from God and do his will?

Matthew 26:36-44

TOPIC: Accepting God's will

OBJECTIVE: As a result of this lesson, students will know not everything God wants us to go through will be easy, but his plan is always best.

BACKGROUND/OVERVIEW: Jesus asked his disciples to come and pray with him. Although Jesus knew God's plan was for him to die on the cross, he asked his father if there was another way—but he was committed to doing his Father's will.

GAME/ICEBREAKER: Happy Meal Shake

Items needed:

- A kid's meal from McDonald's or Burger King
- Small prizes

Put everything from the kid's meal into a blender and blend everything together. See who will drink a cup of the Happy Meal Shake. Then give prizes to those who do.

ICEBREAKER QUESTIONS:

- How did it taste? How many stars would you give it?
- Pretend you're on a commercial for the new Happy Meal Shake. What would you say? Freeze the smile or look on your face for the end of the commercial. (Option: Videotape students making their commercial and show it to the group.)
- How would you feel about doing that again?
- Why did you drink it?

SCRIPTURE: Matthew 26:36-44

Have students read the passage silently from their Bibles:

[36] Then Jesus went with his disciples to a place called Gethsemane, and he said to them, "Sit here while I go over there and pray." [37] He took Peter and the two sons of Zebedee along with him, and he began to be sorrowful and troubled. [38] Then he said to them, "My soul is

overwhelmed with sorrow to the point of death. Stay here and keep watch with me."

[39] Going a little farther, he fell with his face to the ground and prayed, "My Father, if it is possible, may this cup be taken from me. Yet not as I will, but as you will."

[40] Then he returned to his disciples and found them sleeping. "Couldn't you men keep watch with me for one hour?" he asked Peter. [41] "Watch and pray so that you will not fall into temptation. The spirit is willing, but the flesh is weak."

[42] He went away a second time and prayed, "My Father, if it is not possible for this cup to be taken away unless I drink it, may your will be done."

[43] When he came back, he again found them sleeping, because their eyes were heavy. [44] So he left them and went away once more and prayed the third time, saying the same thing.

STUDY QUESTIONS:

- Imagine what Jesus felt like at this moment. He knew what would happen to him in the next hours. Is there anything that has happened in your life that has given you a similar feeling?
- How would you pray about something God wanted you to do that you knew would be difficult and painful? What would you say to God?
- Why do we find taking to God as honestly as Jesus did so difficult?
- What would it take for you to be willing to do something for God you really don't want to do?
- When Jesus says he'll do God's will, how does that impact your life?

TALKING POINTS:

Have the following conversation with your students:

Is there any other way?
Knowing his death on the cross was just hours away, Jesus prayed to God in great distress. Who can blame him? He knew the pain and horror he was about to experience: The sin of the whole world was about to land solely on Jesus. He asked his Father three times to let this cup pass from him. He called God Abba, which means "daddy." This is the most intimate name

used for *father*. "Daddy, please don't let me go through this. But if it is your will, then I want what you want."

Is this any way to pray?

If Jesus could talk to his Father that honestly, don't you think it's okay for you to pray openly, too? God wants his children (that's us) to ask for what they want. Jesus didn't want to have to die the way he did, taking the punishment for sin and being separated from his Father. Yet he did because he wanted most of all to obey God. He wanted to fulfill his Father's plan to save the entire world from the penalty of sin. So he submitted his will to his Daddy's will. He drank the cup he earlier begged would not be given to him.

How should we pray?

What does that mean for how we should pray? Jesus shows us it's all right to ask God difficult questions. God is our Father, and he wants us to talk openly and honestly with him. As God's children we need to grow and come to the understanding that we should obey God above everything else we do. For the moment it may seem God is giving us much more than we can possibly handle, but God knows best. With God all things are possible, and his plan is better than any choice we can make.

Choose to live out God's will

Like Jesus we must be willing to drink the cup God has for us. We struggle with the choice: Is living out God's will more important than choosing to follow our own will and desires? Imagine if Jesus had cared more about his will than God's. What would have happened to the world and all of us? Imagine what God might have in store for your life if you listen to him like Jesus did.

REAL-LIFE CONNECTION: Drink the cup

Set up a table with a clear pitcher of grape juice and some clear plastic cups. Invite students to come to the table to symbolize their desire to do God's will in the choices of their life.

Ask—

- What cup is God asking you to drink? What is something big or small he wants you to do? Are you struggling to say, "Yes, I will do your will"?
- Is it something you want but are afraid of what it will cost you?
- Is it something you don't think you can handle? Will you trust God? Will you bend your will to the Father's will? Ask God to show

you what he wants you to do. Ask him to give you everything you need to be obedient, to drink the cup he has for you. Get excited about what good works God has planned for your life.

Say—

- Hold up your cup.
- As a sign of your willingness to obey God, ask for your cup to be filled.
- Tell God: Not my will, but your will be done.

Have everyone drink the juice in his cup. Then end by singing a song of commitment together.

MEDIA: Gethsemane

Play a clip from the movie *The Passion of the Christ*. Show the first 9:20 of the movie (chapters 1-3). In this opening scene Jesus is praying in the garden of Gethsemane before his arrest. He's agonizing over what awaits him and fighting temptation by Satan to disobey God the Father. End the clip when Jesus stomps on the head of the serpent. This clip opens a good discussion about how Jesus was obedient to lay down his life for all the people of the world.

Matthew 27:15-17, 21-22

TOPIC: Choose Jesus

OBJECTIVE: Students will be encouraged to choose Jesus in each of the daily choices in their lives.

BACKGROUND/OVERVIEW: Jesus had been betrayed and was being tried. Pilate didn't think Jesus had done anything to deserve punishment, but the crowd wanted Jesus to be put to death. Pilate made the crowd choose between releasing Jesus or a notorious criminal, Barabbas. The crowd chose Barabbas and shouted for Jesus to be crucified.

GAME/ICEBREAKER: **Let's Make a Deal**
Items needed:

- Gifts with various values (money, candy, DVD, potato, empty can, old shoe, etc.)
- (Optional) Video camera

This is the classic game of blind choice. Choose one student at a time to play *Let's Make a Deal*. Before the meeting place gifts with various values around the room. You could put these in wrapped boxes, behind a door, in a cabinet, or in your pocket. These gifts could be good (e.g., money, candy, a DVD—anything they'd be happy to receive). Some could be bad (e.g., a potato, an empty can, an old shoe—anything they would be less than thrilled to receive).

Offer the first player a choice between two of your hidden gifts. When the player chooses one, explain that before finding out what the gift is, she may choose to keep this gift or she may choose another gift behind the door or in your pocket. Make it seem as though whatever is being offered is better than what the player already has. Have fun with it. This works best with students who are indecisive or anxious about making choices. You can jazz it up by making it like a TV show. Having a video cameraman moving around and getting their reactions up close will add more fun.

ICEBREAKER QUESTIONS:

- How did it feel knowing you were going to have to a choice?
- How did you feel having to choose, not knowing what you were going to receive?

- When have you had to choose something with out really knowing what you would get? What happened?
- What's the difference between choosing something you're told will be really great but you don't get it right away versus choosing something that is just okay but you can see it and have it right now? How do you know what to choose?

SCRIPTURE: Matthew 27:15-17, 21-22

Have a student read this aloud, dramatically.

15 Now it was the governor's custom at the Festival to release a prisoner chosen by the crowd. 16 At that time they had a well-known prisoner whose name was Jesus Barabbas. 17 So when the crowd had gathered, Pilate asked them, "Which one do you want me to release to you: Jesus Barabbas, or Jesus who is called the Messiah?"

21 "Which of the two do you want me to release to you?" asked the governor. "Barabbas," they answered. 22 "What shall I do, then, with Jesus who is called the Messiah?" Pilate asked. They all answered, "Crucify him!"

STUDY QUESTIONS:

- What influenced the crowd to choose to free Barabbas instead of Jesus?
- What or who influences the choices you make?
- What choices in your life have brought bad consequences for you?
- How could choosing Jesus change your life?
- What makes it difficult to submit to God's plan and choose to do what he wants?

TALKING POINTS:

Share the following with your students:

The plan

The same crowd who shouted for Jesus to be crucified had, one week prior, shouted praises to him as he was entering Jerusalem. They had seen Jesus perform miracles and had hoped he was going to be their king, but when events didn't happen the way they expected, they turned on him. They wanted Jesus to be an earthly king, but Jesus' plan was to set up an eternal kingdom—to conquer Satan and to rescue human beings from the penalty of sin. The crowd's plan was different from God's plan.

The turn

When Jesus didn't fulfill the expectations they had of him, the crowd turned on him. In their ignorance, they turned so fast and so hard they blindly would have picked anyone to save other than Jesus. That's exactly what they did. When Jesus was arrested, Pilate gave the crowd a choice to have a prisoner released: Either Jesus, a known rabbi who had taught in the temple, healed the sick, and cast out demons—or Barabbas, a well-known murderer and revolutionary. It seems insane that anyone would choose Barabbas over Jesus, much less a whole crowd of people. But the alternative didn't matter. They didn't want Jesus anymore because he wasn't going to do what they wanted.

The choice

Every person is given the same choice: We can either choose to follow Jesus, or not. When we choose Jesus, we choose to do things his way, to follow his plan. Jesus' way is always the best way. When we don't choose Jesus because we don't like his plan, we automatically get the alternative. Some people can't stand the idea of submitting to God—they end up choosing an alternative that will lead to destruction. They never really examine the other choice. They just get so wrapped up in not following God that, like the crowd, they end up allowing something very dangerous into their lives.

Have you ever expected something from Jesus that wasn't part of his plan for your life? What was your response? Did you reject his plan and reject him? You must believe Jesus knows best and choose to follow his way. A real enemy out there wants to destroy you. When you reject Jesus, you choose the Enemy. There is no neutral choice. Either you choose God, who has the perfect plan for your life, or you end up with the Enemy, who has a plan to destroy you. This week examine your choices and why you have made them. Make the best choice there is to make: Choose Jesus.

REAL-LIFE CONNECTION: Every choice is important

Items needed:

- A small 2"x 4" notepad for each student (available at stationery and business stores)

Give students their notepads with the following instructions:

Keep track of all your choices this week—from the mundane to the important.

Jot down the small—but important choices—(e.g., brush my teeth before school, get online versus reading school book, what clothes to wear, etc.) as well as the big, life-shaping choices.

Carry the notepad all week and review daily what choices reflected a commitment to follow Jesus and what choices were taking you away from God's plan for your life.

Sit down a week later with students and ask them to tell you the funny and serious choices they made. Show them your notepad and the choices you made. You will learn a lot from each other.

MEDIA: Choose God

Show the clip "Gift for Creasy" (1:32) from the movie *Man on Fire*. Because of his relationship with Pita, Creasy chooses to read his Bible instead of hit the bottle. This is a clear picture of how we all have a choice to follow God—but we must choose one path or another. This clip is available at www.wingclips.com—search using the words *for Creasy*. Or, you can view this clip on the DVD, chapter 10-11—45:00 to 45:44.

Matthew 28:18-20

TOPIC: The Great Commission

OBJECTIVE: Students will gain deeper insight into Jesus' post-resurrection charge and discover ways to live as Great Commission Christians.

BACKGROUND/OVERVIEW: Jesus had just risen from the dead and appeared to his disciples. They gathered on a mountain in Galilee to hear from him. In this passage he gave them what has come to be known as the Great Commission.

GAME/ICEBREAKER: Leadership test

Type up a test like the one below, leaving space for answers where needed. If possible have the test take up the whole sheet of paper, with question 10 appearing right at the bottom of the sheet.

Hand out the test. Tell everyone to begin at your signal and that they have just five minutes to finish.

<u>LEADERSHIP TEST</u>

Directions: Answer each question in sequence. If you do not know an answer, go on to the next one. Read through the entire test before answering questions.

1. Print your complete name in upper left-hand corner.
2. Print your address here:
3. Underline the correct answer in each of the following statements:
   - A good leader must be: Dogmatic, restrictive, dedicated.
   - The best kind of leadership is: Authoritative, socialistic, democratic.
   - The best way to get something done is: Form a committee, do it yourself, have others do it.
4. Put your age in the upper right-hand corner.
5. Raise your left hand until the instructor recognizes you.
6. True or False: Circle the correct answer for each of the following statements:
   - A good leader always has an answer. It is a sign of weakness not to have an answer. T F
   - A good leader should know how to follow directions. T F
   - A good leader gets things done quickly. T F
   - It is better to do a job right rather than to do it quickly. T F
7. Underline the words that follow *directions* in the question above.
8. Stand up until you're recognized.

9. Define a leader (approximately 50 words) on the back of this page.
10. If you have read through this entire test as you were instructed to do, you don't have to take it. Just sign your name in the upper right-hand corner and wait until the time is up. Do not answer questions 1 through 9.

ICEBREAKER QUESTIONS:

- For those of you who ignored the directions and just tried to race through, how did you feel when you read question 10?
- When have you or your parents tried to take a shortcut while driving somewhere and it either ended up taking longer to get there or you ended up lost? What happened?
- When have you tried to bake or cook without following the directions? How did the food turn out?

TRANSITION:
Say—

Sometimes we're tempted to take shortcuts and not follow the directions. But when we do that, we often sell ourselves short. We get lost. We end up eating something that doesn't taste the way it's supposed to. We end up doing something that could have been beautiful but has caused pain because we disobeyed. We forfeit the best for something that seemed good at the time. In a moment we're going to hear about a time Jesus was tempted to take a shortcut, but because he refused the shortcut, he was able to speak these words to his disciples—words that carry just as much weight for us today as they did back then.

SCRIPTURE: Matthew 28:18-20
Ask a student to read the passage aloud from his Bible.

[18] Then Jesus came to them and said, "All authority in heaven and on earth has been given to me. [19] Therefore go and make disciples of all nations, baptizing them in the name of the Father and of the Son and of the Holy Spirit, [20] and teaching them to obey everything I have commanded you. And surely I am with you always, to the very end of the age."

STUDY QUESTIONS:

- What does the word authority mean to you?
- Who is an authority figure in your life? What gives that person his or her authority?
- What does Jesus mean when he says "making disciples"?
- How do you think the disciples felt seeing their Lord risen from the dead, and hearing him promise to be with them forever?
- What do you think they were thinking and feeling as they watched Jesus ascend into the sky and leave them shortly after giving them this challenge (Acts 1:1-11)?

TALKING POINTS:
Share the following points with your students:

The Great Commission
Jesus' words to his disciples in this passage are well known and often quoted among Christians. This post-resurrection statement is known as The Great Commission. More than a catchy slogan to inspire people to go on mission trips, it tells us what Jesus wants us to do until he returns.

On his behalf
Jesus told his disciples to act on his behalf. He gave them the authority to speak and act for him. That would be like having the power of attorney for someone. Now here's what he wants his disciples to do:

As you go
Jesus didn't give the disciples a detailed travel itinerary or a road map. He told them to do his work wherever they went. Remember this deep saying: "Wherever we go, there we are"? In Jesus terms that means wherever we find ourselves is where we're to be about the business of making disciples for Jesus.

Make disciples
Our job is to make disciples—followers or apprentices of Jesus. We must show people who Jesus is and how he wants to work in their lives. We must help them understand what that means, call them to make a decision to embrace Christ personally, and teach them how to walk out their decision and to grow in maturity.

Baptizing them
Baptism is important because it identifies us publicly with the Christian community through Christ's death, burial, and resurrection (Romans 6:4).

Teach them to obey
The disciples took over Jesus' role as teacher. They began to pass on to others what Jesus had done and had taught them. The goal of teaching is transformation—helping people discover and live out the teachings of Jesus and the Bible.

Everywhere
Jesus makes clear that his call to discipleship is an invitation to every tribe, nation, and people. God's call is for all people to be saved (1 Timothy 2:3-4).

The promise
Jesus left his disciples with a promise: "I am with you always, to the very end of the age." He promised to be with them. He had also said that when two or three would be gathered in his name, he'd be among them (Matthew 18:20). Jesus wasn't abandoning them—he had equipped them, he had empowered them. Now He was entrusting them with the mission of continuing his redemptive work in the world until the end of the age.

REAL-LIFE CONNECTION: How do you live out the Great Commission?
Ask your students the following questions:

- In what ways are you actively making disciples as you go through life?
- If you've been water-baptized, describe the journey that led you to that moment and what your baptism was like—what it means to you.
- What kinds of practices do you engage in to ensure you're constantly soaked with the reality of God's presence?
- Jesus gave his disciples the assurance of his presence as they went forth to fulfill his purposes. How do you sense his presence with you as you seek to be a Great Commission Christian?

MEDIA: Evangelism
Show the Sermonspice video "Evangelism" (7:00). (This video can be purchased from www.sermonspice.com—use the search word *hijacked*). This hysterical video by the Skit Guys deals with the simple command of Jesus to go into the world and spread his message of love. Sometimes this command gets misunderstood and misinterpreted. Sometimes it gets outright hijacked for selfish purposes.

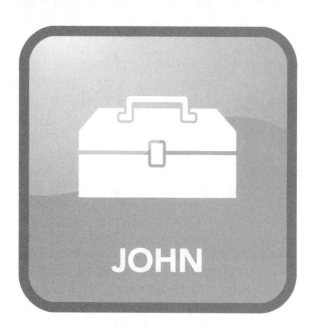

John 1:1-5

TOPIC: Light in the darkness

OBJECTIVE: Students will learn that God, who the Bible tells us is light, sent his Son, Jesus, to be the light in a dark world and the light shining in our lives.

BACKGROUND/OVERVIEW: John 1 begins the story of Jesus and his coming as a light into the world. The story really starts before the world was created. Jesus was alive before time existed. John calls Jesus the *Word* and uses the Greek word *logos*. In both the Jewish concept and the Greek, the word *logos* was associated with beginnings. So John is saying that Jesus, as God the Creator, has always existed. This same Word is the Savior we know as Jesus Christ. The Word became flesh so all the world may see the light and turn away from the darkness.

GAME/ICEBREAKER: The blindfolded agent
Item needed:

- Blindfold

Choose an *agent* and a *captive*. Blindfold the agent. Then place the captive in one corner of the room, surrounded by many. When you give the signal, the blindfolded agent should try to find the captive without peeking. During the search the whole group should yell and give false directions, creating a chaotic situation. After a few minutes quiet the group, remove the blindfold, and give the agent 10 seconds to scan the room. (He probably will be able to spot the captive.) Then blindfold the agent and let the search resume along with the yelling. The agent should find the captive easily this time, even with all the noise.

ICEBREAKER QUESTIONS:

- (To the agent): Why was it easier to find the captive the second time?
- In what areas of our lives do we act as though we're wearing blindfolds?
- What is happening in our world that could be described as darkness?
- When darkness and light come in contact with each other, what happens?

SCRIPTURE: John 1:1-5
Read the passage aloud, slowly and with emphasis.

[1] In the beginning was the Word, and the Word was with God, and the Word was God. [2] He was with God in the beginning. [3] Through him all things were made; without him nothing was made that has been made. [4] In him was life, and that life was the light of all people. [5] The light shines in the darkness, and the darkness has not overcome it.

STUDY QUESTIONS:

- When John describes Jesus as "the Word" and "the light," what is he trying to tell the world about Jesus?
- How could Jesus be there in the beginning when the world was created?
- What does this statement mean: "In him was life, and that life was the light of all people"?
- What are some of the dark parts of our world and our own lives where Jesus' light is needed?
- What can a person do to shine the Light into his or her life?

TALKING POINTS:
Share the following points with your students:

The Light helps us see what is good and what is bad

When God said, "Let there be light" (Genesis 1:3), he meant for it to allow us to see the created world with our eyes. When God sent the Light of the World (Jesus), he did it so we could see God with our hearts and souls. We can also see good and bad in our world and in our lives because the Light shines in the darkness.

Darkness can't overcome the Light

Verse 5 points out that darkness cannot overcome the Light. This means no matter what Satan and the world try to do, we can't be defeated if we're on Jesus' side. The Light is so evident that no matter how dark the world is, no matter how much anybody tries to hide in sin, the Light exposes the bad and always overcomes the dark parts of our lives.

Darkness can't understand the Light

When we live apart from God, we don't see we're living in sin. We don't understand what is so wrong. We go about our lives wanting nothing to do with the Light because we have adjusted our eyes to the darkness and think it's normal. We like the darkness because it gives us more places to hide. We can't understand why anybody would want to follow Jesus. When the Light takes over and invades our hearts, however, we see everything clearly. We can't understand how we once lived without him.

REAL-LIFE CONNECTION: The Light of the World

Tell your students:

Today I want you to go home and find a flashlight. Make sure it works. Take it to your room and turn off all the lights. Sit in the darkness for a few minutes and think about some of the ways you're living in darkness and not following God. Think about God's offer to forgive your sins and give you eternal life. Ask God to shed light on the areas of your life you don't want overcome. Turn on the flashlight and point it toward the ceiling. See what a difference that little light makes in your room. Point the flashlight at specific parts of your room and talk to God about the light of Christ coming into those parts of your life. Pray your way around your room and ask Christ to take over each part of your life. We live in the light now, so let us walk in the light.

MEDIA: Light

After the icebreaker, light a candle in the center of the room and shut off all the lights. As everyone looks at the candle in the room, read this poem or have a different student read each section of the poem. In both cases the reader(s) should practice reading the poem aloud prior to the meeting.

"Light" by Dan O'Leary

The phenomenon known as light is extremely unexplainable, and glorious in its mystery. When light appears darkness (light's nemesis) cannot extinguish it, or even fathom it.

If both darkness and light were people, darkness would be confused when light showed up.

Darkness would wonder why this light was so intruding, and he would be annoyed and blown away by this inconceivable ideal.

Light, in its purest sense, cuts through darkness, destroying the blindness, the confusion, the fear, and the ability to hide.

Not even darkness itself has the ability to hide from light's revelation.

Darkness can never overcome light, and it could never understand its power.

When light is introduced to darkness, the darkness is destroyed.

A small light in an enveloping drapery of darkness still shines through, piercing the dark so that people may see.

No amount of darkness can cover light, because darkness is merely the absence of light. Wherever there is light, darkness disappears, confused and defenseless.

The presence of the mystery known as light dismantles the dark, forcing submission.

Light has come into the world, but the darkness has not understood it.

You can also use "How Great is Our God" from the *Arriving* album by Chris Tomlin—print out the words and have the group sing them together or watch the song on video. Use the title to search www.youtube.com for the song.

John 2:1-11

TOPIC: Risk and reward

OBJECTIVE: Students will realize that God works through ordinary people who are willing to take risks for Jesus.

BACKGROUND/OVERVIEW: This is the story of Jesus' first public miracle. In the book of John it marks both the beginning of Jesus' public ministry and the middle of his search for disciples. The story takes place at a wedding. Ancient Middle Eastern weddings typically lasted for seven days. Jesus' family probably were close friends of the wedding family since Jesus' mother was informed of the crisis and spoke to the servants as someone who had connections. Wine at a feast in ancient Israel was both a symbol of joy *and* a source of joy. Running out of wine at an ancient wedding would be like running out of food at a contemporary wedding after only half the guests had been served—the host family would be very embarrassed and maybe have some angry guests.

GAME/ICEBREAKER: Wall of trust

This is a good jump start to trust-building. One of its advantages is it's based on forward movement; another is that it allows individual contact, rather than using the group en masse. Trust will develop through the feeling of safety a participant has each time he's caught by the safety nets, so in the end members feel safe even when running (slowly).

Have the whole group form a line facing a wall about 10-15 feet away. Choose two people to act as safety nets. They should stand near the wall, opposite the line. The person at the front of the line walks, eyes closed, toward the wall. The safety nets are to catch each person before he hits the wall. (Note: You want these two people to be physically capable of catching the people in the group.)

The key to this exercise is the willingness of the participants to keep their eyes closed while approaching the wall. Blindfolds can be used, but personal commitment to keeping eyes closed is a big part of the trust experience.

After each person has had a turn at a walking pace, the pace is sped up on each turn, until group members are running at a reasonable and safe speed. Be sure to give the signal each time for when participants should begin moving toward the wall.

ICEBREAKER QUESTIONS:

- What were you thinking when I told you I wanted you to walk into a wall with your eyes closed?
- What does it feel like when you're moving toward the wall (before you get caught)?
- Did you worry or doubt the safety net person would let you walk into the wall?

TRANSITION:

Say—

Sometimes we feel like what we're doing for Jesus is foolish or will cause us great harm, but Jesus is trustworthy. We can trust him to keep us safe. In fact, after Jesus has proven himself to us, our faith increases.

SCRIPTURE:

John 2:1-11

Use students to act this out as they read it. You'll need people to play the following characters: Narrator, Jesus' mother, Jesus, servants, and the master of the banquet.

[1] On the third day a wedding took place at Cana in Galilee. Jesus' mother was there, [2] and Jesus and his disciples had also been invited to the wedding. [3] When the wine was gone, Jesus' mother said to him, "They have no more wine."

[4] "Woman, why do you involve me?" Jesus replied. "My hour has not yet come."

[5] His mother said to the servants, "Do whatever he tells you."

[6] Nearby stood six stone water jars, the kind used by the Jews for ceremonial washing, each holding from twenty to thirty gallons.

[7] Jesus said to the servants, "Fill the jars with water"; so they filled them to the brim.

[8] Then he told them, "Now draw some out and take it to the master of the banquet."

They did so, [9] and the master of the banquet tasted the water that had been turned into wine. He did not realize where it had come from, though the servants who had drawn the water knew. Then he called the bridegroom aside [10] and said, "Everyone brings out the choice wine first and then the cheaper wine after the guests have had too much to drink; but you have saved the best till now."

[11] What Jesus did here in Cana of Galilee was the first of the signs through which he revealed his glory; and his disciples put their faith in him.

STUDY QUESTIONS:

- Why did Mary go to Jesus and tell him about the problem of the wine?
- Why do you think Jesus would tell his mother he couldn't help?
- How might Jesus' idea of the type of glory he was going to reveal differ from Mary's idea of what was going to happen?
- Who in the story could see what Jesus did?
- What would you have done if Jesus had told you to pour in the water and then taste it? If he told you it was going to be wine, what do you think you would have said?
- What do you suppose happened to the servants who did what Jesus asked when they took the new drinks into the party? What risks were they taking serving people drinks out of the pots they filled earlier?

TALKING POINTS:
Have a conversation with your students using the following points:

The servants obeyed
Focus on the servants. Imagine them as busboys at a banquet hall at the bottom of the waitstaff food chain in a big restaurant. All they know about Jesus is that Mary told them to obey her son.

Jesus told them to do something that seemed crazy. They filled up the equivalent of five garbage cans with water. Jesus then told them to do something quite risky. He told them to take this water and give it to the master of the banquet—their boss' boss' boss. This was a great risk. They were risking shame, money, employment, and their trustworthiness as employees or friends based on what Jesus asked them to do.

Jesus came through

They risked a lot to obey Jesus, but Jesus delivered. Imagine the negative reaction the servants may have expected from their master. Imagine how happy they were when the master was thrilled to serve this high-quality wine to his guests.

The servants became disciples

The only ones to completely see this first sign were the first of Jesus' disciples and the servants who obeyed Jesus in faith. Quite possibly these servants became disciples and followers of Jesus.

The big question: What is Jesus asking you to do or be that seems to defy logic and is a huge risk?

REAL-LIFE CONNECTION: Risks and rewards

Divide into discussion groups. Get students to tell stories about the difficulties and rewards of being followers of Christ in their schools and neighborhoods. Then ask—

- What are some of your stories where you took risks for Jesus? What happened?
- What seems toughest about following Jesus?
- What are some of the rewards of being a Christ-follower?

MEDIA: Leap of faith

Show the video clip "Team Training" (1:05) from the movie *Bolt*. (You can find this clip at www.wingclips.com—search using the title of the clip.) Thinking he has the superpowers of his TV character, Bolt tries a daring jump onto a moving train with Rhino and Mittens. Use this clip to make a point about the servants at the party who did what Jesus told them to do. These servants might have doubted that any wine would come out of the jars they filled with water, but they were bold and did what he said anyway. When we follow Jesus we have to be daring and willing to do what seems impossible.

John 3:1-15

TOPIC: Born—again?

OBJECTIVE: Students will realize that when we choose to accept Jesus into our life, we start living the life we were truly created for.

BACKGROUND/OVERVIEW: Nicodemus was one of the Pharisees. He was enamored with Jesus and knew there was truth in what Jesus taught. Nicodemus knew if he met with Jesus during the day he'd get into trouble. The other Jewish leaders might even punish him. So he visited Jesus by night to learn what he could from him.

GAME/ICEBREAKER: Clay house
Item needed:

- Enough clay for every four people to have a lump of it

Divide into teams of four and give each team an equal amount of clay. Have each team use the clay to make a creative and elaborate house. You and your volunteers will judge the final product.

ICEBREAKER QUESTIONS:

- Tell us about the house you made. What are its special features?
- What did you have in mind to do when you built your house, and how did you reach your goal?
- What was the difference or similarity in the lumps of clay the groups had before we started making the houses?
- How is your house similar to the houses other groups made?
- What Bible passage does this contest remind you of?

SCRIPTURE: John 3:1-8
Read the passage aloud for the group:

[1] Now there was a Pharisee, a man named Nicodemus who was a member of the Jewish ruling council. [2] He came to Jesus at night and said, "Rabbi, we know that you are a teacher who has come from God. For no one could perform the signs you are doing if God were not with him."

³ Jesus replied, "Very truly I tell you, no one can see the kingdom of God without being born again."

⁴ "How can anyone be born when they are old?" Nicodemus asked. "Surely they cannot enter a second time into their mother's womb to be born!"

⁵ Jesus answered, "Very truly I tell you, no one can enter the kingdom of God without being born of water and the Spirit. ⁶ Flesh gives birth to flesh, but the Spirit gives birth to spirit. ⁷ You should not be surprised at my saying, 'You must be born again.' ⁸ The wind blows wherever it pleases. You hear its sound, but you cannot tell where it comes from or where it is going. So it is with everyone born of the Spirit."

STUDY QUESTIONS AND TALKING POINTS:
Have a conversation with your students. Use the following points and questions to get started:

Wasn't I born already?
Jesus got right to the point with Nicodemus. He knew Nicodemus was searching for truth, so Jesus told him exactly what he needed to know in a very simple sentence. Nicodemus couldn't grasp this idea at first.

- Why would it be difficult to understand being "born again"?
- When you try to explain what it means to be born again what do you say?

Jesus doesn't expect us to understand these things because we have limited, finite minds—Jesus lets us know this very bluntly in verse 8. He has seen these things, and God gave him this knowledge. If Jesus is given this knowledge, we can learn about spiritual things from him. Just like Nicodemus, we need to ask Jesus. We need to look at what he said about this.

SCRIPTURE: John 3:9-15
Read this passage aloud:

⁹ "How can this be?" Nicodemus asked.

¹⁰ "You are Israel's teacher," said Jesus, "and do you not understand these things? ¹¹ Very truly I tell you, we speak of what we know, and we testify to what we have seen, but still you people do not

accept our testimony. [12] I have spoken to you of earthly things and you do not believe; how then will you believe if I speak of heavenly things? [13] No one has ever gone into heaven except the one who came from heaven—the Son of Man. [14] Just as Moses lifted up the snake in the wilderness, so the Son of Man must be lifted up, [15] that everyone who believes may have eternal life in him."

STUDY QUESTIONS AND TALKING POINTS:

- To go forward with this discussion, let's take a quick side step. In your own words, tell us what it means to be alive.
- Now tell us what makes something dead?
- What didn't Nicodemus understand?
- How is Jesus trying to help him understand?

From a lump of clay

In verses 3-6 Jesus stated we're already born in the flesh as human beings. He said we must also be born of the Spirit—our moms couldn't do that for us. The only way we can be born in the Spirit is if we allow the Holy Spirit in our life. When you were given the task of making the house, you started with simple lumps of clay. Nothing special there—just lumps. But once you put your work into it, you started designing what you wanted that lump to be, and you formed a house. You turned a nothing into something.

Jesus is teaching Christianity 101 in the verses we just read. When we're born from our mothers, we're just like that lump of clay. All we know is the human body perspective. All we can understand is how the human body works. We have no spiritual life in us—we wouldn't even know we needed it. That's why God gave us Jesus, to let us know we can be and need to be connected to God. We can only do that by believing in Jesus, the Son of God. When we do this, God gives us the Holy Spirit to guide our lives. He opens our eyes to a new way of living. Jesus calls it being "born again" because we're really living a different life than we were before.

When we follow Jesus we're remade from physical lumps into physical houses for the Holy Spirit. We're recreated from something dead to something truly alive. Jesus mentions this again in John 10:10:"I have come that they may have life, and have it to the full."

The best way you can live is following Jesus. Anything else is just being a lump of clay—not truly living. Invite Jesus to put his hands on you and bring you to life.

REAL-LIFE CONNECTION: John 3:16

Say to your students—

John 3:16 is called the most famous verse in the Bible. Let's all say it together. If you don't know it by memory repeat after me:

> For God so loved the world that he gave his one and only Son that whoever believes in him shall not perish but have eternal life.

God invites you and promises you eternal life if you believe in his Son, Jesus. If you have never done this, this meeting is your opportunity to respond to God's invitation.

MEDIA: God's grace

Show the "Grace" (2:18) clip from *The Case for Faith*. (This clip is available on Wing Clips—search www.wingclips.com using the words *case for faith*.) Lee Strobel explains how God's grace is one of the areas in which Christianity differentiates itself from other religions.

Also recommended is the clip "The Tree" (4:38). With a pencil and paper, artist Matt Yocum uses a picture of a tree to illustrate creation, the fall, and atonement through Christ. This clip is available from www.sermonspice. com—search with the words *the tree Matt*. This can lead directly into or summarize the talking points of the lesson.

John 4:7-29

TOPIC: Acceptance before evangelism

OBJECTIVE: Students will know they should tell everyone about Jesus, and they'll use practical ways to do so.

BACKGROUND/OVERVIEW: Jesus took time to talk to a Samaritan woman. She then told everyone about Jesus and how he knew everything about her.

GAME/ICEBREAKER: Twenty trifles
Item needed:

- A "20 Questions" handout you prepare ahead of time

Pair kids up with someone they don't know well. Distribute copies of a handout with 20 questions on it (e.g., *What's your shoe size? What's your favorite time of year? What's the name of your gym teacher?*) Tell kids to discover from one another the obscure facts asked for on the sheet. Players should write down their partner's responses.

ICEBREAKER QUESTIONS:

- What was something you discovered about your partner that surprised you?
- Why does knowing some silly and random facts about a person make us feel more comfortable talking to them?
- Why is it difficult to talk to people we don't know and ask them questions about themselves?
- What could you ask a person that might start a good conversation?

SCRIPTURE: John 4:7-29
Distribute copies of this passage and have everyone read it and look for hints about Jesus' approach to evangelism. Or you could have students act out the story.

[7] When a Samaritan woman came to draw water, Jesus said to her, "Will you give me a drink?" [8] (His disciples had gone into the town to buy food.)

⁹ The Samaritan woman said to him, "You are a Jew and I am a Samaritan woman. How can you ask me for a drink?" (For Jews do not associate with Samaritans.)

¹⁰ Jesus answered her, "If you knew the gift of God and who it is that asks you for a drink, you would have asked him and he would have given you living water."

¹¹ "Sir," the woman said, "you have nothing to draw with and the well is deep. Where can you get this living water? ¹² Are you greater than our father Jacob, who gave us the well and drank from it himself, as did also his sons and his flocks and herds?"

¹³ Jesus answered, "Everyone who drinks this water will be thirsty again, ¹⁴ but those who drink the water I give them will never thirst. Indeed, the water I give them will become in them a spring of water welling up to eternal life."

¹⁵ The woman said to him, "Sir, give me this water so that I won't get thirsty and have to keep coming here to draw water."

¹⁶ He told her, "Go, call your husband and come back."

¹⁷ "I have no husband," she replied.

Jesus said to her, "You are right when you say you have no husband. ¹⁸ The fact is, you have had five husbands, and the man you now have is not your husband. What you have just said is quite true." ¹⁹ "Sir," the woman said, "I can see that you are a prophet. ²⁰ Our ancestors worshiped on this mountain, but you Jews claim that the place where we must worship is in Jerusalem."

²¹ "Woman," Jesus replied, "believe me, a time is coming when you will worship the Father neither on this mountain nor in Jerusalem. ²² You Samaritans worship what you do not know; we worship what we do know, for salvation is from the Jews. ²³ Yet a time is coming and has now come when the true worshipers will worship the Father in the Spirit and in truth, for they are the kind of worshipers the Father seeks. ²⁴ God is spirit, and his worshipers must worship in the Spirit and in truth."

²⁵ The woman said, "I know that Messiah" (called Christ) "is coming. When he comes, he will explain everything to us."

[26] Then Jesus declared, "I, the one speaking to you—I am he."

[27] Just then his disciples returned and were surprised to find him talking with a woman. But no one asked, "What do you want?" or "Why are you talking with her?"

[28] Then, leaving her water jar, the woman went back to the town and said to the people, [29] "Come, see a man who told me everything I ever did. Could this be the Messiah?"

STUDY QUESTIONS:

- What hints did you pick up about Jesus' approach to evangelism?
- The Samaritan woman was surprised Jesus asked her for a drink. What could you do to someone that would surprise her and make her want to talk to you?
- What good conversations have you had with people you never thought you would want to talk with?
- What was the woman looking for, and what did Jesus offer to her?
- What was the reaction of the Samaritan woman after she understood Jesus was talking about more than drinking water?
- What did the Samaritan woman get from Jesus that she had to tell everyone about?

TALKING POINTS:

Share some, or all, of the following points with your students:

Jesus broke the social rules

Jesus took time to talk to a woman to whom he wasn't supposed to talk, according to the social codes of the time. Samaritans and Jews didn't associate with each other. Think of it as the two complete opposite cliques in your school—the two types of people talking with one another was taboo. Jesus, however, took the time to talk to this woman. He wanted to share with her the truth about living water—eternal life with him, the Messiah. Jesus spoke with this woman about water because it related to her, and he used water as an example so she could understand what he was trying to tell her.

The woman couldn't stop talking

Later in this chapter the Bible tells us many Samaritans went on to listen to Jesus' message and believed because this woman told them about him. Jesus satisfied her deep, lifelong need—she was overflowing with joy and couldn't keep quiet about it. This is how God's message spreads best—person to person.

Two Jesus lessons

Jesus didn't preach at this woman; instead, he engaged in a good conversation. Jesus gave the woman his full attention. One of the best ways to love someone is to listen to what's going on in the person's life. Jesus responded to the woman's questions and answered her concerns. She probably was used to being ignored or ridiculed by the people in her town, but Jesus was different. He wasn't afraid of people who were social outcasts who were hurting physically and emotionally—he took the time to spend with them.

Second, Jesus spoke with the woman on her level. When he met this woman, she was getting water for her house, so he used water as an example to help her understand his message. He didn't talk down to her or over her head. His words made sense to her.

REAL-LIFE CONNECTION: Prayer connection

Hand out a small piece of paper for each student and a pen or pencil. Then say—

We know many people we don't identify with. We know some people with whom making a connection is tough because we don't have anything in common, or because they have a bad reputation. Neither of those factors stopped Jesus.

On this piece of paper, write the name of someone you think needs to hear the message of Jesus, but you just don't know how to connect with her. Make a commitment to pray for this person and for God to use you to connect with her during the next week. Ask God to open a way for you to have a conversation with this person and maybe even a way for you to get to know her. Look for an opportunity where you could do something helpful or kind for this person. This will open the door for you to share God's story with her.

MEDIA: Reach out

Show the clip "Don't Go" (3:02) from the movie *Edward Scissorhands*. When door-to-door Avon saleswoman Peg stumbles upon a towering Gothic mansion, she meets Edward and decides to take him home with her. This clip illustrates what Jesus did with the woman at the well: He accepted her and talked to her even though she was different. Students can discuss how willing they are to interact with people who are different or even a little weird. (This clip is available on Wing Clips. Go to www.wingclips.com—search using the word *scissorhands*.)

You can also use the clip "One Chance" (1:34) from the movie *End of the Spear*. This film tells the story of a team of missionaries who try to bring the message of Jesus to a violent tribe of natives in South America. The young missionaries discuss the new opportunities to reach the notoriously violent Waodani tribe. This is a visual example of what Jesus did when he took his Jewish disciples into Samaria and initiated contact with the woman at the well. (Visit www.wingclips.com and type *end of the spear*.)

John 5: 1-9

TOPIC: Do you want to get well?

OBJECTIVE: Students will realize Jesus wants them to express their desires to him. They'll begin to take their needs to him.

BACKGROUND/OVERVIEW: Jesus asks a man if he wants to get well, giving the man the option to respond. The man reflects his problem onto others, but Jesus brings the solution back to the man's heart.

GAME/ICEBREAKER: Guided tour
Items needed:

- Blindfold
- Pitcher with water
- Glass
- Pillows to construct a maze

Have students pair up. One will put on a blindfold and the other will guide the blind partner through a maze or tasks (such as pouring a glass of water). You can have varying levels of difficulty. The guide can touch the person or simply use vocal commands. Or you may want to use vocals only, then touch only, and finish with using both (if time allows.) Switch positions and repeat.

ICEBREAKER QUESTIONS:

- What was most difficult about being blindfolded?
- What was the most difficult part in being the guide?
- When do you feel as though you're blind?
- In what parts of your life do you need help or someone to guide you?
- Who gives you instructions? How do you respond to those instructions?

SCRIPTURE: John 5:1-9
Read this aloud, or have students act it out, with you serving as the narrator:

¹ Some time later, Jesus went up to Jerusalem for one of the Jewish festivals. ² Now there is in Jerusalem near the Sheep Gate a pool, which in Aramaic is called Bethesda and which is surrounded by five

covered colonnades. [3-4] Here a great number of disabled people used to lie—the blind, the lame, the paralyzed. [5] One who was there had been an invalid for thirty-eight years.

[6] When Jesus saw him lying there and learned that he had been in this condition for a long time, he asked him, "Do you want to get well?"

[7] "Sir," the invalid replied, "I have no one to help me into the pool when the water is stirred. While I am trying to get in, someone else goes down ahead of me."

[8] Then Jesus said to him, "Get up! Pick up your mat and walk." [9] At once the man was cured; he picked up his mat and walked.

STUDY QUESTIONS:

- Why did Jesus ask the man if he wanted to get well?
- What was this man's problem? Why couldn't he just get better on his own?
- Who or what did the man blame for not being able to get rid of his condition?
- What do you notice about the man's reaction to Jesus' command? How would you have responded to what Jesus said?

TALKING POINTS:
Have a conversation with your students, using the following points as a guide:

We all need healing
No one is perfect—no one has life all figured out. In some way, shape, or form, we're all damaged. We were made for something great, but we aren't living that way. We are trapped by bad habits and bad attitudes that keep us from getting the help we need. Deep on the inside, we think we can fix the problems in our lives; in reality we need someone to do it for us.

Jesus heals and gives life
The crippled man was as good as dead. He was just lying there, waiting for an answer or some stroke of good luck to drop out of the sky. He blamed the system for his problems. On his own this man was losing his life day by day, but Jesus brought life to him and gave him a radical change. The man stood to walk for the first time in many years—this was the start of a new life. What kind of new life would you like Jesus to give you?

Do you want to get well?
We have to ask ourselves, Do I want to get well? Do I want to change? What would it take to make you feel really alive and excited about every day and challenge? What are you willing to do to get the help you need? If you do want to get well and be the person you were created to be, Jesus is the only solution. Place your faith in him and take your first step to living the way God intended for you.

REAL-LIFE CONNECTION: Freedom and Healing

Ask everyone to lie down on the floor (not touching anyone else), and have them close their eyes. Tell them to think of all the bad things that have happened to them as if they are heavy weights on top of them. Tell them to think about all the negative influences they have from others and have them imagine their legs being wrapped together on the floor with duct tape. Ask them to imagine all the bad influences and habits in their lives right now are like ropes tying their arms tightly against their torso. Ask them to imagine the worst headache possible as they think about all their fears about the future. Challenge them to really feel all this.

Now have the conversation with them that Jesus had with the man by the pool. Ask them if they want to get well. Tell them to stand up and throw off all the junk from the past, the negative influences and habits. Tell them to jump up and down and stretch their hands and arms up to the sky. They should really feel how it is to be free.

Pray with the group, asking God to give each person freedom and healing. Invite people participating to talk to an adult leader about finding lasting freedom in Christ.

MEDIA: Freedom

Show the scene from the movie *Forrest Gump* (on the DVD, chapter 3—15:00 to 18:00) where Forrest has to run away from the bullies. As he runs the braces that constrict his legs fall off. This illustrates how Jesus challenged a man who had been paralyzed 38 years—he told him to stand up and walk home. When he tried to stand Jesus' healing power gave him strength in his legs.

John 6:1-13

TOPIC: Give what you have

OBJECTIVE: Students will know God does great things with whatever they give him.

BACKGROUND/OVERVIEW: After Jesus had performed miraculous healings, a huge crowd followed him while he was attempting to get some rest. He knew the people following him did not have anything to eat and he felt compassion for them.

GAME/ICEBREAKER: Invention convention
Items needed:

- Have your staff and parents collect a bunch of their old junk (empty cans, broken appliances, boxes, empty toilet paper tubes, etc.). Just make sure everything is clean and not dangerous (no sharp edges).
- Duct tape
- Craft paint
- Small prize

Divide into teams and give each group a little bit of trash, one roll of duct tape, and some paint. Explain they have 10 to 15 minutes to create the weirdest, funniest, most artistic invention out of the junk. Tell them to create something that will make the world a better place. Each team should give their new invention a name and explain its purpose. Have a panel of judges choose the winning team and award them a prize.

ICEBREAKER QUESTIONS:

- When you first saw what we gave you as raw materials for your artistic invention, what were you thinking?
- Did you think anything beautiful or helpful could come out of this junk? Why or why not?
- Who could make something valuable or useful out of this junk?
- How does God use people who don't appear to have much talent?
- How could God even use the bad things that happen in your life to help you and help others?

SCRIPTURE: John 6:1-13

Choose students to read the passage aloud from their Bibles—one paragraph per student.

[1] Some time after this, Jesus crossed to the far shore of the Sea of Galilee (that is, the Sea of Tiberias), [2] and a great crowd of people followed him because they saw the signs he had performed by healing the sick. [3] Then Jesus went up on a mountainside and sat down with his disciples. [4] The Jewish Passover Festival was near.

[5] When Jesus looked up and saw a great crowd coming toward him, he said to Philip, "Where shall we buy bread for these people to eat?" [6] He asked this only to test him, for he already had in mind what he was going to do.

[7] Philip answered him, "It would take almost a year's wages to buy enough bread for each one to have a bite!"

[8] Another of his disciples, Andrew, Simon Peter's brother, spoke up, [9] "Here is a boy with five small barley loaves and two small fish, but how far will they go among so many?"

[10] Jesus said, "Have the people sit down." There was plenty of grass in that place, and they sat down (about five thousand men were there). [11] Jesus then took the loaves, gave thanks, and distributed to those who were seated as much as they wanted. He did the same with the fish.

[12] When they had all had enough to eat, he said to his disciples, "Gather the pieces that are left over. Let nothing be wasted." [13] So they gathered them and filled twelve baskets with the pieces of the five barley loaves left over by those who had eaten.

STUDY QUESTIONS:

- How would you have answered Jesus' question about feeding the crowd?
- Why would something impossible for us be very possible for Jesus?
- What are some talents the people in this group have? What do you do well?
- Tell me about someone you think has used his talents in an awesome way to help others or to please God.
- How can God use people who feel very ordinary and untalented?

TALKING POINTS:
Share the following points with your students:

Jesus doesn't see problems the way we do
As humans we're limited by how we think about things—our human nature has us only believing in what we see in front of us. It takes so much effort for us to take chances and try new ways of doing something we haven't done before. The disciples were so used to doing things a certain way. These men had been brought up with the idea that they had the full responsibility for providing food for their family or guests, so they felt responsible for feeding the hungry crowd. They thought about how much money they had, which was far less than what was needed. After some scrambling, all they could find was a young boy with a small lunch. His contribution looked like a drop in the bucket compared with what they needed. Jesus, however, saw the perfect solution.

Give what you have
Jesus says all God requires is that we put our faith in God's Son. If we believe and act on that belief, Jesus can take us places we have never dreamed of. He shows us the true potential we have when we believe in him—he shows us he has no limits on how he can use us for the good of the kingdom. To be used we have to give ourselves with the same faith the boy had when he gave his small lunch.

That little boy probably didn't think he had much to offer when he gave his bread and fish to Jesus. Nevertheless he gave it and watched what Jesus did with it. Jesus took what that boy had and multiplied it beyond the disciples' wildest dreams. Because that boy was willing to give, Jesus was willing to use it.

REAL-LIFE CONNECTION: Dreams and talents
Items needed:

- Paper
- Pens/pencils

Give the following instructions to your students:
- Take a sheet of paper and fold it in half vertically.
- On the left side of the fold, write what you want God to do through you. List several dreams you have.
- On the right side of the fold, write what you're doing now and the

interests you have. List several of the raw gifts and talents God is developing in you.

• Unfold the paper and look at both sides—what you want to see happen and what you're doing now—and draw any lines of connection between the two columns. Can you see the gifts and talents that match up with your dreams?

MEDIA: You've got skills

This would be good to use after reading the Bible passage—before the study questions. Show the clip from the film *Napoleon Dynamite*—"Great Skills" (1:40). Napoleon laments to Pedro no girl will go to the dance with him because he has no great skills. The clip is available from www.wingclips.com—search using the words *great skills*.

John 7:37-39

TOPIC: The promise of the Holy Spirit

OBJECTIVE: Students will have a deeper understanding of the Holy Spirit and be challenged to receive this wonderful gift promised by Jesus. With the power of the Holy Spirit, we will be empowered to fulfill God's purposes in the world.

BACKGROUND/OVERVIEW: The featured incident took place during the Feast of Tabernacles, a joyous celebration in which the priests would bring water (symbolic of the water supplied from the rock in Exodus 17) to the temple. The water would then be poured out on the altar as an offering to God while the people cheered and sang. Jesus was the fulfillment of all that the ceremony typified. Jesus not only satisfies our individual thirst for fulfillment, but also desires for us to bring refreshment to others through living lives filled with the Holy Spirit.

GAME/ICEBREAKER: Shaving-cream sculptures
Items needed:

- Plastic sheets or a card table for each team
- Cans of shaving cream
- Towels
- Small prize

Do this activity with individual competitors or in teams. Be sure to control the use of the shaving cream after the contest, or you're likely to have an impromptu shaving-cream fight.

Assign competitors each a place on a long table (or on a plastic sheet on a hard floor), or give each competitor a card table. Give each team/contestant a can of shaving cream. Explain that at your signal, they're to make a sculpture of a famous building or monument—in five minutes. Tell them to use all the shaving cream available to them. When they're done the sculptures will be judged on creativity and realism. After you give instructions, give teams a minute to decide on their strategy and on which building they'll sculpt—then give the signal to begin.

Afterward give the competitors towels for cleaning their hands and move everyone away from the sculptures. The judges should try to guess what buildings or monuments have been sculpted. They'll determine the best sculpture according to your criteria of creativity and realism. Award a prize to the winner.

ICEBREAKER QUESTIONS:

- (To the competitors): How did you decide what building to sculpt? What was your strategy?
- (To everyone): Were you surprised by how much shaving cream was in such a small can?
- How might this illustrate a person's relationship with God? What are the parallels?
- The Bible talks about being "filled with the Holy Spirit"—how does that work?
- Where does this illustration fall short of the work of the Holy Spirit in our lives?

TRANSITION:

Say—

God has called us to carry out his work in our world. This can be a daunting and overwhelming task. In fact, more than intimidating, it's actually impossible for us to accomplish on our own. That's why Jesus supplied us with the gift of the Holy Spirit—we're empowered to fulfill his will.

SCRIPTURE: John 7:37-39

Tell your students about the context of this passage, then read it aloud.

[37] On the last and greatest day of the Festival, Jesus stood and said in a loud voice, "Let anyone who is thirsty come to me and drink. [38] Whoever believes in me, as Scripture has said, rivers of living water will flow from within them." [39] By this he meant the Spirit, whom those who believed in him were later to receive. Up to that time the Spirit had not been given, since Jesus had not yet been glorified.

STUDY QUESTIONS:

- Who are the people in the story? Who is in the crowd?
- Put yourself in the scene that day. What do you imagine the people were thinking when they heard Jesus' words?
- Who would those people be today?
- Which type of person would you be in that story?
- What would you have thought when Jesus stood up and shouted what he did?
- What is the difference between a spring (of water) and a river?
- What goes through your mind when you hear "the Holy Spirit"?
- What is the purpose of the Holy Spirit?

TALKING POINTS:
Share the following information with your students:

Springs versus rivers
In John 4 we read about Jesus' conversation with a Samaritan woman he meets by a well. He tells her, "Everyone who drinks this water will be thirsty again, but those who drink the water I give them will never thirst. Indeed, the water I give them will become in them a spring of water welling up to eternal life" (4:13-14). Using the picture of a spring or a fountain, Jesus explains he's the source of true, everlasting satisfaction that cannot be found in this world.

In today's passage Jesus uses a similar picture to communicate a spiritual truth. He says if we embrace him as the Messiah—the Savior of the world—not only will we have a fountain of water, but also he'll fill us with his Holy Spirit and rivers of living water will flow out of us.

Jesus not only offers us satisfaction for our own spiritual thirst, he also desires for us to be channels of blessing and refreshment for others. The spring referred to by Jesus in John 4 refers to our salvation. The rivers mentioned in John 7 refer to the Holy Spirit, whom Jesus gives us as a gift to empower us to be agents of his love in the world.

John points out the fulfillment of the promise of the Holy Spirit had to await the completion of Christ's work on earth. The Holy Spirit has always been—he did not come into existence when Jesus finished his work on earth. Rather, when Christ's work was complete, we were able to experience his personal work in our lives in a new way: When the work of Christ was accomplished, he unleashed the river of the Holy Spirit so we could carry out his work on the earth. The Spirit empowers us to live as rivers of love, joy, peace, and power. Just like with our shaving cream cans, the Spirit flows out of us. But, unlike the cans, the Spirit never runs out.

Key ingredients for being filled
The Spirit-filled life is God's desire for every believer. While there is no magic formula for being filled, the Bible does give us some key ingredients for those who desire to be filled.

First we need to recognize our need. If we don't know we're thirsty, we won't look for something to drink. Before we can be filled, we need to recognize something is missing, that our lives are lacking and incomplete.

Second, we need to respond by believing Jesus is who he says he is. The Holy Spirit is given to us through Christ. In order to receive the Holy Spirit, we need to believe in Jesus and his finished work that paved the way for the outpouring of the Holy Spirit.

Thirdl we need to remember the Holy Spirit is a gift. In his sovereignty God has given himself to us to empower us to do his work on the earth. We haven't earned it. We can't earn it. We don't deserve it. It's simply a mysterious part of his amazing grace.

Third, we must receive the gift of the Holy Spirit. Some people freak out about the idea of the Holy Spirit. They like God the Father—Jesus is good, too—but the Holy Spirit is a little too weird and mysterious. However, when we remember God gives us the Holy Spirit as a gift through Jesus, our fears should be alleviated. God is good and would never give us anything that would harm us. Receive the Holy Spirit with gratitude and hope.

REAL-LIFE CONNECTION: The role of the Holy Spirit

Have students look up and read aloud the following verses concerning the Holy Spirit. Then discuss his function in our lives:

- Mark 13:11
- John 14:26
- John 16:13
- 1 Corinthians 12:1-11
- 2 Corinthians 1:22; 5:5

Share with your students:

In our western version of Christianity, a lot of emphasis is placed on a personal relationship with God through Jesus. Jesus isn't just about quenching a person's spiritual thirst—he wants to flow through us to bring water to others.

Take some time to pray for one another to be filled afresh with the Holy Spirit, to be empowered to carry out God's work on the earth.

MEDIA: We are sailing

Show this short video clip available for purchase from www.sermonspice. com—"Sailing: Filled with the Holy Spirit" (2:17). Use the search words *sailing Holy Spirit*.

This excellent video uses the metaphor of sailing to illustrate the importance of being filled with the Holy Spirit.

John 8:1-11

TOPIC: Forgiveness

OBJECTIVE: Students will know Jesus forgives the big sins in our lives and gives us new directions for life.

BACKGROUND/OVERVIEW: A group of religious leaders brought to Jesus a woman who'd been caught in the act of adultery. Those men were trying to trap Jesus into violating Moses' command, but Jesus surprised them with his response. This passage illustrates our human tendency to condemn and Jesus' willingness to forgive.

GAME/ICEBREAKER: **Caught in the middle**
To play this game you'll need a group of at least 15. Seat students in a circle. Pick three guys and two girls to play. When the music starts, the guys each have to grab the hand of a girl seated in the circle and pull the girl into the middle. Then the guy should take the girl's seat in the circle. While the guys are doing this, the girls in the middle will also each take the hand of a guy sitting in the circle and pull him into the middle. Then each girl will take the boy's seat in the circle. Students should continue to do this until the music stops. Once the music stops, whoever is left standing in the middle must perform a consequence chosen by students of the opposite sex. Have a bunch of consequences ready (e.g., quack like a duck for 10 seconds, do 15 push-ups, imitate an *American Idol* contestant, etc.).

Note: If the group is very unbalanced in genders, you can play the game without the gender factor.

ICEBREAKER QUESTIONS:

- (To those who were caught in the middle): **How did you feel once you were caught?**
- (To those who chose the consequences): **How did it feel giving someone a punishment?**
- **This game allows everyone playing the equal chance to have the power to punish her friends, but at the same time everyone is susceptible to the same punishment. Which did you enjoy most?**
- **For what sins do people tend to get punished or rejected by other people?**

SCRIPTURE: John 8:1-11

Read the passage aloud for the group as everyone follows along in their Bibles.

[1] Jesus went to the Mount of Olives.

[2] At dawn he appeared again in the temple courts, where all the people gathered around him, and he sat down to teach them. [3] The teachers of the law and the Pharisees brought in a woman caught in adultery. They made her stand before the group [4] and said to Jesus, "Teacher, this woman was caught in the act of adultery. [5] In the Law Moses commanded us to stone such women. Now what do you say?" [6] They were using this question as a trap, in order to have a basis for accusing him.

But Jesus bent down and started to write on the ground with his finger. [7] When they kept on questioning him, he straightened up and said to them, "Let any one of you who is without sin be the first to throw a stone at her." [8] Again he stooped down and wrote on the ground.

[9] At this, those who heard began to go away one at a time, the older ones first, until only Jesus was left, with the woman still standing there. [10] Jesus straightened up and asked her, "Woman, where are they? Has no one condemned you?"

[11] "No one, sir," she said.
"Then neither do I condemn you," Jesus declared. "Go now and leave your life of sin."

DISCUSSION QUESTIONS:

- How do you feel about what Jesus did with this woman?
- What do you think different groups of people thought about Jesus after this happened?
- Do some creative thinking: How do you think this woman lived after her encounter with Jesus? Why?
- What are the toughest situations for you to forgive people for what they have done?

TALKING POINTS:

Share the following points with your students:

A trap for Jesus

The teachers of the law and Pharisees brought this guilty woman to Jesus to see if he'd agree with the law of Moses by saying the woman should be stoned for committing adultery. If he said no, they'd label him a heretic and lawbreaker. If he said yes, they'd hand him over to the Roman authorities. (They weren't allowed to kill anyone under Roman law.) Jesus saw right through the trap.

Jesus set everyone straight

Jesus had every right to call out these leaders on their error and embarrass them. He had every opportunity to show them they were distorting the law of Moses, which they held in high esteem. Jesus could have even, with some effort, turned the stoning toward these men for making such a mockery of the Law. But he didn't.

Jesus caught the religious leaders in their error, and the crowd was ready to throw stones at somebody. There stood Jesus with every right to punish everyone in the crowd. But Jesus diffused the situation by stating what should be called the primary rule of forgiveness: "'Let any one of you who is without sin be the first to throw a stone...'"

Think about it

Ideas are powerful. What if everyone forgave when someone did wrong by him? What if everyone you have wronged has forgiven you? What would the world look like?

Colossians 3:13 says, "Bear with each other and forgive one another if any of you has a grievance against someone. Forgive as the Lord forgave you."

This is the kind of life Jesus wants us to live. He hasn't called us to throw stones at anyone, but to live a life of love, mercy, and forgiveness because he forgave us first.

REAL-LIFE CONNECTION: Throwing the stones away

Items needed:

- Index cards
- Pens/pencils

Share with your students—

At some time in our lives we'll have either wronged someone, or someone will wrong us. Either we'll throw stones or get them thrown at us. But Jesus illustrates the beauty of forgiveness—in this case it saved a woman's life. Jesus had every right to punish her, but he chose to forgive because he loves that much.

Give everyone a small card and a pencil. Ask them to write on this card a brief description of a sin someone has committed against them. Then have them ask Jesus to help them forgive this person completely. Challenge them, when they're ready and willing to forgive, to tear the card into tiny pieces and throw it away.

MEDIA: What it means to forgive

Show a clip from *Antwone Fisher*—"Find Your Family" (2:35). (It's available from www.wingclips.com—use the title of the clip to search.) In this clip Antwone Fisher finds love and forgiveness when he goes looking for his family. Use this clip to illustrate the power of forgiveness.

John 9:13-34

TOPIC: It's enough to make a blind man cry

OBJECTIVE: Students will know Jesus has the power to heal and change lives.

BACKGROUND/OVERVIEW: Jesus performed many miracles during his time of ministry. No one could explain how he did everything. The Jewish leaders argued about the source of Jesus' power, but no one could deny something miraculous and wonderful had occurred.

GAME/ICEBREAKER: **Three truths and one lie**
This game has three variations:

Variation No. 1: Have four volunteers sit up front. Each one should tell a story of something extraordinary that has happened to him—all but one should be telling the truth. The group will vote on which person isn't telling the truth.

Variation No. 2: Have four volunteers sit up front. Beforehand they should've chosen one wild thing that has happened to one of them. Then all of them should pretend it happened to them (e.g., everyone could say, in turn, *When I was younger I broke my leg skateboarding behind a car*). The group gets to ask each person three questions (details about the statement, etc.) to help them determine who is telling the truth. Afterward, have the group vote on who they think is telling the truth.

Variation No. 3: Have everyone in your group sit in a circle. Each person should come up with two things they've actually done and one thing they haven't. Go around the circle and have each person share his three things. After each person shares the group should vote on which story was the lie. Each person will earn points based on how many people believe the lie—award one point per person who votes that a true story is the lie, and five points per person who votes that the lie is a true story.

ICEBREAKER QUESTIONS:

• Who was the most convincing liar?
• How did you know what was true?

- How can you tell if someone is telling you the truth or a lie?
- If someone told you Jesus healed him from an illness, would you believe him or think there was another explanation for what happened? Explain how you would know what to believe.

SCRIPTURE: John 9:13-34

Consider having students act out this story while everyone else follows along in their Bibles.

13 They brought to the Pharisees the man who had been blind. 14 Now the day on which Jesus had made the mud and opened the man's eyes was a Sabbath. 15 Therefore the Pharisees also asked him how he had received his sight. "He put mud on my eyes," the man replied, "and I washed, and now I see."

16 Some of the Pharisees said, "This man is not from God, for he does not keep the Sabbath."

But others asked, "How can a sinner perform such signs?" So they were divided.

17 Then they turned again to the blind man, "What have you to say about him? It was your eyes he opened."

The man replied, "He is a prophet."

18 They still did not believe that he had been blind and had received his sight until they sent for the man's parents. 19 "Is this your son?" they asked. "Is this the one you say was born blind? How is it that now he can see?"

20 "We know he is our son," the parents answered, "and we know he was born blind. 21 But how he can see now, or who opened his eyes, we don't know. Ask him. He is of age; he will speak for himself." 22 His parents said this because they were afraid of the Jewish leaders, who already had decided that anyone who acknowledged that Jesus was the Messiah would be put out of the synagogue. 23 That was why his parents said, "He is of age; ask him."

24 A second time they summoned the man who had been blind. "Give glory to God and tell the truth," they said. "We know this man is a sinner."

25 He replied, "Whether he is a sinner or not, I don't know. One thing I do know. I was blind but now I see!"

26 Then they asked him, "What did he do to you? How did he open your eyes?"

27 He answered, "I have told you already and you did not listen. Why do you want to hear it again? Do you want to become his disciples too?"

28 Then they hurled insults at him and said, "You are this fellow's disciple! We are disciples of Moses! 29 We know that God spoke to Moses, but as for this fellow, we don't even know where he comes from."

30 The man answered, "Now that is remarkable! You don't know where he comes from, yet he opened my eyes. 31 We know that God does not listen to sinners. He listens to the godly person who does his will. 32 Nobody has ever heard of opening the eyes of a man born blind. 33 If this man were not from God, he could do nothing."

34 To this they replied, "You were steeped in sin at birth; how dare you lecture us!" And they threw him out.

DISCUSSION QUESTIONS:

- When have you ever had someone not believe you when you told her some great news? Tell us about what happened.
- What miracle or unexpected action have you seen happen? What have you heard about from someone else? Which do you find easier to believe: What you hear or what you see?
- If someone told you that you were lying about God healing or helping you, how would you respond?
- What made the Pharisees so skeptical about Jesus and about the blind man's story?
-

TALKING POINTS:
Talk with your students using some of the following points:

Some events can't be explained
Some events we can't really explain—even though we see them happen before our very eyes. A baseball player hitting a 90 mph fastball is a scientific miracle. The time it takes to process thoughts isn't enough time to properly measure distance, ready the swing, and then actually hit the ball with enough force to send it flying. Scientists still debate how this task is actually

accomplished, but we can't deny it happens—it happens all the time. We see it with our own eyes.

Don't be afraid to share what you see

Think about the blind man's parents for a minute. We don't really know the man's age, but we know he was born blind. The man's parents couldn't explain how their son received his sight, but they knew their son wasn't blind anymore. The once-blind man couldn't deny that something beautiful and miraculous had occurred. He wasn't a religious leader or legal scholar, but he knew these kinds of great things could only come from God. If you know about something God has done, don't let anything or anyone keep you quiet—give God credit and without fear declare his greatness.

Don't fear the skeptics

The Pharisees were the God-police of the land. People were afraid of them because of their authority and power. The Pharisees refused to believe Jesus was the Son of God—they didn't want to give up their position and privilege as the God-experts. They attacked Jesus because he was a threat to them and their beliefs. Plenty of people will argue against God existing, and even more people don't believe Jesus' claims to be the Messiah and the only way to heaven. They ridicule and reject people who believe Jesus is Savior and Lord. Maybe they haven't heard the clear evidence about Jesus and his life. God calls people to humble themselves and receive what Christ has done for them. Skeptics learn how to do that from watching Christians live humble, faithful, serving lives dominated by self-sacrificing love—few skeptics come to Christ because they lost a debate to a Christian.

Think about it

This man had some guts—he wasn't intimidated. He just told his story: Once he was blind, and now he could see. You have a story, too. It may not be as dramatic as physical blindness, but perhaps it's a different type of blindness, or a big change in life. Let people know Jesus changed (and still is changing) you. If you know for a fact something happened, why not stick up for what you see?

REAL-LIFE CONNECTION: Real-life testimonies

Items needed:

- Flip chart or whiteboard
- Markers

Use the flip chart or whiteboard and make a list. In the left column, have students list people they know about (alive or dead) from whom they have heard how Jesus Christ changed their lives. In the right column ask students to list people they know personally who have seen God change their lives.

If the list is short, send students home with an assignment to find five people for each column. If the list is sufficient, ask a couple of students to briefly tell the story of a person on the list. Or you could have several people from the group share the story about how Christ changed *their* lives. Encourage everyone to this week tell someone a story they heard about how Christ has changed a person's life.

MEDIA: Faith

Show the clip from the DVD of Lee Strobel's *The Case for Christ*—"Faith in Evidence" (1:00). At the end of the presentation, Lee summarizes all of his research about Jesus Christ. Go to www.wingclips.com and search using the words *faith in evidence*.

John 10:1-18

TOPIC: Following the Good Shepherd

OBJECTIVE: Students will know Jesus is the one who brings life to them by laying his life down. They'll decide to learn how to recognize and listen for Jesus' voice.

BACKGROUND/OVERVIEW: Jesus had just finished giving a blind man sight on the Sabbath. The Pharisees didn't believe the man was really healed by Jesus, but the healed man came back to Jesus and expressed his belief in who Jesus is. In this passage Jesus tells the people and the watching Pharisees the purpose of his ministry.

GAME/ICEBREAKER: **Spot the phony**
Items needed:

- Answer sheet for tests
- Pens/pencils
- Real and phony items (see below)

Beforehand, prepare a series of tests, each of which features something true/real and something phony. Give everyone an answer sheet and a pen/pencil. Bring out the tests one at a time, with each pair labeled A and B. Challenge each person to write on his answer sheet the letter of the item he thinks is true—the real deal. Note: With a small group, you can allow more interaction with the items (e.g., touching, smelling, looking closely—but no tasting). Use the following pairs of items as your test subjects:

- Two glasses of clear liquid—one is water (the phony), and one is lemon-lime soda
- Two glasses of brown liquid—one is watered-down prune juice (phony), and one is cola
- Two cooked burgers—one is tofu (phony), and one is beef
- Two "designer" clothing articles—one is a knockoff, and one is the real deal
- Two celebrity autographs—one is fake, and one is real (or you could feature the signature of the pastor, one of their teachers, or a youth staff member)
- End with a pair (or two) of individuals making the same claim (e.g., *I am related to royalty;, I weighed less than 3 lbs. at birth; I can play my*

nose). Note: To make sure this works, use kids from outside the group or adults from the church. No one in the group should know the truth about these people before you reveal it. For this test, allow students to ask the individuals a few questions related to their claims.

After you have done all the tests, reveal the correct answers—the real deals. See who got the most right and award a prize.

ICEBREAKER QUESTIONS:

- What was difficult about spotting the phony product?
- What would have been most helpful to you in determining which autograph was the real one?
- (To the winner): How did you do so well? What was your secret?
- What made the stories of phony people seem believable?
- How did you finally know who was really telling the truth?

SCRIPTURE: John 10:1-18

Distribute copies of the passage and pens/pencils. Tell students to write on the back of the sheet the differences between the good shepherd and anyone else entering the sheep pen.

[1] "Very truly I tell you Pharisees, anyone who does not enter the sheep pen by the gate, but climbs in by some other way, is a thief and a robber. [2] The one who enters by the gate is the shepherd of his sheep. [3] The gatekeeper opens the gate for him, and the sheep listen to his voice. He calls his own sheep by name and leads them out. [4] When he has brought out all his own, he goes on ahead of them, and his sheep follow him because they know his voice. [5] But they will never follow a stranger; in fact, they will run away from him because they do not recognize a stranger's voice." [6] Jesus used this figure of speech, but the Pharisees did not understand what he was telling them.

7 Therefore Jesus said again, "Very truly I tell you, I am the gate for the sheep. [8] All who have come before me are thieves and robbers, but the sheep have not listened to them. [9] I am the gate; whoever enters through me will be saved. They will come in and go out, and find pasture. [10] The thief comes only to steal and kill and destroy; I have come that they may have life, and have it to the full.

[11] "I am the good shepherd. The good shepherd lays down his life for the sheep. [12] The hired hand is not the shepherd and does not

own the sheep. So when he sees the wolf coming, he abandons the sheep and runs away. Then the wolf attacks the flock and scatters it. [13] The man runs away because he is a hired hand and cares nothing for the sheep.

[14] "I am the good shepherd; I know my sheep and my sheep know me— [15] just as the Father knows me and I know the Father—and I lay down my life for the sheep. [16] I have other sheep that are not of this sheep pen. I must bring them also. They too will listen to my voice, and there shall be one flock and one shepherd. [17] The reason my Father loves me is that I lay down my life—only to take it up again. [18] No one takes it from me, but I lay it down of my own accord. I have authority to lay it down and authority to take it up again. This command I received from my Father."

STUDY QUESTIONS:

- What differences did you find between the good shepherd and anyone else entering the sheep pen?
- Jesus says his sheep will never follow a stranger's voice. What is Jesus telling us about how we follow him?
- In Jesus' shepherd and sheep illustration, are you in the flock with Jesus, or have you wandered away? Are you looking at Jesus from a distance, wishing you were with him?
- Who might be some modern phony shepherds?
- When Jesus mentions "the thief," whom do you think he's talking about? What does the thief do to the sheep?
- Who might be some modern thieves? What do they hope to accomplish?
- As the Good Shepherd, what does Jesus say he does of his own free will for the sheep? Why does he do that?
- How would you describe your relationship with Jesus the Good Shepherd?

TALKING POINTS:
Share with your students the following points:

Jesus is God, the true and Good Shepherd
Jesus says he's the "good shepherd." He makes a contrast between himself and all other people we could follow. He says when troubles come, all the phony shepherds won't be available or able to see us through and protect us. Jesus makes it clear he does everything he can to protect his "sheep."

Choose the voice of life
Why should we choose to follow Jesus' voice? Jesus says he knows us so well he calls each of us by name—he guides and leads his sheep where they need to go. When we choose to listen to Jesus' voice, we choose to let our lives be protected and guarded by the One who really cares and loves us. When we choose to listen to and follow any other voice, we walk into danger and rough times.

Know how much he loves you
Sometimes we claim to love a person so much we'd die for her. But would we really? Here's a test. Think of your most prized possession. Would you be willing to sell that possession and use the money to send someone to an event, retreat, or meeting where God may speak to her? That would be tough to do. Jesus said his Father didn't force him to give up his life—he willingly gave up his life to protect us and bring us home. Jesus isn't just a shepherd—he's the Good Shepherd.

REAL-LIFE CONNECTION: The loudest voices
Give your students the following instructions:
Take out a piece of paper. Write out what a typical week looks like when you're not in school. Write down everything you do and for how long. Include extracurricular activities, visits to friends' homes or fast-food places, and hobbies. For example, if you watch certain TV shows, write down the name of each show, what time you watch it, and for how long.

When you're done, switch papers with someone. Take turns trying to figure out what voices are louder in your life. Usually the areas where we spend the most time are the voices we listen to the most.

What can you do to hear God's voice? What changes should you make in your schedule or activities to do that better?

MEDIA: Protection
Show the clip "The Hulk Protects Betty" (0:44) from the *Incredible Hulk*. This is where the Hulk protects Betty with his own body when an airstrike comes for him. (You can download this video from www.wingclips.com—search using the word *Betty*).This could serve as a discussion starter about someone giving his life for someone else, leading into the Scripture about the Good Shepherd giving his life for the sheep.

John 11:1-44

TOPIC: Seeing with faith, from God's point of view

OBJECTIVE: Students will understand the importance of walking by faith and trusting the word of the Lord—even when it doesn't seem to make any sense.

BACKGROUND/OVERVIEW:

Lazarus was dying, and his sisters Mary and Martha sent word to their friend Jesus, notifying him of Lazarus' condition. They fully expected Jesus to drop everything and come immediately. But by the time Jesus arrived, Lazarus had been dead four days. Jesus then performed a remarkable miracle, raising Lazarus from the dead, manifesting the glory of God for all to see.

GAME/ICEBREAKER: Perspective

Items needed:

- Video presentation (see below)
- DVD/tape player

Put together a video presentation featuring a series of scenes that begin either as a close-up or focused on one small part of the picture. Then the camera should pull back to reveal the full picture and make clear the scene being taped. At the beginning of each new scene, pause the tape/DVD and ask what the students think the big picture will be. Then continue to reveal the correct answer. Here are some possible scenes:

- A close-up of part of the door to the church or high school. The film continues with the camera moving back and revealing the whole building.
- The center of a car hubcap—then moving back to reveal the whole car.
- A beach scene that turns out to be a picture in a magazine.
- An out-of-focus blur of colors that, when it comes into focus, is a bouquet of flowers.
- An extreme close-up of a flake of cereal that turns out to be outside the bowl on a counter with a full breakfast.
- A scary-looking inside view of a fun attraction at an amusement park.
- An empty and dark room that is suddenly filled with party guests yelling, "Surprise!"

- A menacing-looking flame that is revealed to be at the tip of a candle in a church.
- (Use your imagination and add others.)

ICEBREAKER QUESTIONS:

- That activity was called *Perspective*—why do you think it was called that?
- In what ways was your perspective (point of view) limited in those early shots of each scene? (Answers: Distance—either too close or too far; seeing only part of the picture)
- In life what limits our perspective in our experiences? (Answers: Proximity to the event, lack of knowledge, lack of life experience, blocked vision, etc.)
- When have you made a decision or judgment based on poor perspective?

TRANSITION:

Say—

Perspective makes all the difference. Today we're going to read a story about a family who, through a dramatic turn of events, learned to see life from God's point of view.

SCRIPTURE: John 11:1-44

Summarize part of the story and have students read the key passages aloud. Or read the whole passage with students following along in their Bibles.

[1] Now a man named Lazarus was sick. He was from Bethany, the village of Mary and her sister Martha. [2] (This Mary, whose brother Lazarus now lay sick, was the same one who poured perfume on the Lord and wiped his feet with her hair.) [3] So the sisters sent word to Jesus, "Lord, the one you love is sick."

[4] When he heard this, Jesus said, "This sickness will not end in death. No, it is for God's glory so that God's Son may be glorified through it." [5] Now Jesus loved Martha and her sister and Lazarus. [6] So when he heard that Lazarus was sick, he stayed where he was two more days, [7] and then he said to his disciples, "Let us go back to Judea."

[8] "But Rabbi," they said, "a short while ago the Jews there tried to stone you, and yet you are going back?"

[9] Jesus answered, "Are there not twelve hours of daylight? Those who walk in the daytime will not stumble, for they see by this world's light. [10] It is when people walk at night that they stumble, for they have no light."

[11] After he had said this, he went on to tell them, "Our friend Lazarus has fallen asleep; but I am going there to wake him up."

[12] His disciples replied, "Lord, if he sleeps, he will get better." [13] Jesus had been speaking of his death, but his disciples thought he meant natural sleep.

[14] So then he told them plainly, "Lazarus is dead, [15] and for your sake I am glad I was not there, so that you may believe. But let us go to him."

[16] Then Thomas (also known as Didymus) said to the rest of the disciples, "Let us also go, that we may die with him."

[17] On his arrival, Jesus found that Lazarus had already been in the tomb for four days. [18] Now Bethany was less than two miles from Jerusalem, [19] and many Jews had come to Martha and Mary to comfort them in the loss of their brother. [20] When Martha heard that Jesus was coming, she went out to meet him, but Mary stayed at home.

[21] "Lord," Martha said to Jesus, "if you had been here, my brother would not have died. [22] But I know that even now God will give you whatever you ask."

[23] Jesus said to her, "Your brother will rise again." [24] Martha answered, "I know he will rise again in the resurrection at the last day."

[25] Jesus said to her, "I am the resurrection and the life. Anyone who believes in me will live, even though they die; [26] and whoever lives by believing in me will never die. Do you believe this?"

[27] "Yes, Lord," she told him, "I believe that you are the Messiah, the Son of God, who was to come into the world."

[28] After she had said this, she went back and called her sister Mary aside. "The Teacher is here," she said, "and is asking for you." [29] When Mary heard this, she got up quickly and went to him. [30] Now Jesus had not yet entered the village, but was still at the place where Martha had met him. [31] When the Jews who had been with Mary in the house,

comforting her, noticed how quickly she got up and went out, they followed her, supposing she was going to the tomb to mourn there.

³² When Mary reached the place where Jesus was and saw him, she fell at his feet and said, "Lord, if you had been here, my brother would not have died."

³³ When Jesus saw her weeping, and the Jews who had come along with her also weeping, he was deeply moved in spirit and troubled. ³⁴ "Where have you laid him?" he asked.

"Come and see, Lord," they replied.

³⁵ Jesus wept.

³⁶ Then the Jews said, "See how he loved him!"

³⁷ But some of them said, "Could not he who opened the eyes of the blind man have kept this man from dying?"

³⁸ Jesus, once more deeply moved, came to the tomb. It was a cave with a stone laid across the entrance. ³⁹ "Take away the stone," he said.

"But, Lord," said Martha, the sister of the dead man, "by this time there is a bad odor, for he has been there four days."

⁴⁰ Then Jesus said, "Did I not tell you that if you believe, you will see the glory of God?"

⁴¹ So they took away the stone. Then Jesus looked up and said, "Father, I thank you that you have heard me. ⁴² I knew that you always hear me, but I said this for the benefit of the people standing here, that they may believe that you sent me."

⁴³ When he had said this, Jesus called in a loud voice, "Lazarus, come out!" ⁴⁴ The dead man came out, his hands and feet wrapped with strips of linen, and a cloth around his face.

Jesus said to them, "Take off the grave clothes and let him go."

STUDY QUESTIONS:

- What indication do we have that the disciples' perspective was limited? (Answer: They didn't realize Lazarus had died; they tried to dissuade Jesus from going to Jerusalem.)
- What emotions would you have had if your friend Jesus seemed

to ignore your plea to come and see your loved one on his death-bed—and your friend ended up dying? How would you have felt? What would you have wanted to say when you saw Jesus?

- What indication do we have that the perspective of Mary and Martha was limited? (Answer: They were upset with Jesus for letting their brother die.)
- What did the people in the crowd think about Jesus? Who did they think he was and what did they think he could do before he raised Lazarus from the dead? How about afterward?
- If you've lost a loved one, and it's not too painful to share, what was it like to lose someone who was close to you?
- When have you been confused, frustrated, or even angry because of how Jesus apparently did or did not act in a situation?
- What hinders our perspective when we confront personal loss?

TALKING POINTS:
Have a conversation with your students using the following points as a guide:

Just this once
If ever there were a time when people could have been considered justifiably upset with Jesus, this was probably it. Mary and Martha were very close with Jesus. They had been with him on many occasions when he ministered to other people. And he had spent time in their house. Jesus had helped so many other people; surely he'd be there for them when their brother Lazarus became deathly sick. Yet Jesus seemed to brush off the news and waited for two days before deciding to pay Lazarus a visit. He came too late.

Have you ever felt this way? Have you ever approached Jesus with great urgency about something only to have him seemingly ignore you? Then, when he did show up, it seemed to be too late. Your hope had already been lost.

"Jesus, I've been faithful to you," you say. "I've spent lots of time learning from you. I've told people about you. I've stood against injustice. I've stood up for what was right, even when it was difficult. I've prayed for people who were sick and seen you touch them. Now, Lord, my mom is sick with cancer, and I need you to heal her. Lord, my friend has been in a car accident and is in a coma. Lord, I've seen you do it for others. Please do it for me—just this once."

Silence. All you get is silence.

Three considerations
Let's consider three important factors that give us perspective during these times. Knowing these three factors won't necessarily answer all of our questions, but they'll give us something to consider during those times of confu-

sion, frustration, and downright anger with God.

God's will: First, let's remember God is accomplishing something in the world and in our lives. He's forming us into the image of his Son so we can fulfill his purposes in the world.

God's ways: Second, we need to remember God has different ways to accomplish his will. Just because God worked a certain way in someone else's life doesn't mean he'll act the same way in our circumstances. God refines each person according to a personalized growth plan unique to that person. We need to remember God's thoughts are not our thoughts, nor are his ways our ways (Isaiah 55:8).

God's timing: Finally we need to remember God has a timetable for accomplishing his will. This often is the aspect most difficult for us to accept. We live in a culture of instant gratification. We don't like to wait for anything, but God isn't in a hurry as we are. He patiently sculpts us—molds us into the image of his Son.

It's all about perspective—seeing life from God's point of view.

REAL-LIFE CONNECTION: We all need prayer

Have everyone get into groups of four. Use these questions as a small-group talkback time:

- Share about a time when you felt as if God owed you one. Why did you think that?
- Share about a time when you tried to cut a deal with God (e.g., *Lord, if you do this, I promise I will...*). Why do we do that?
- Which is the hardest for you: Discovering God's will? Understanding God's ways? Or waiting on God's timing?
- Share about something you're going through right now for which you need prayer.

MEDIA: Jesus raised him from the dead

Show the video clip "Lazarus" (3:44). It's available for purchase from www.sermonspice.com—search using the word *Lazarus*. This is a dramatic reading of the Lazarus story from John 11.

John 12:37-43

TOPIC: Not afraid to take a stand

OBJECTIVE: Students will know the importance of having strong beliefs, and they'll know how to stand up for what they believe.

BACKGROUND/OVERVIEW: Everywhere Jesus went and spoke about God, people reacted strongly. Some reactions were positive and some were negative. Some people believed Jesus and wanted to follow him but didn't because they were afraid their religious leaders would attack them if they did so.

GAME/ICEBREAKER: Would You...?
Explain that you have an imaginary scale (one to 10) across the front of the room. One represents *Absolutely Not*, and 10 on the other side of the room represents *Yes, Definitely*. Tell students that as you read each situation aloud, they should move to the appropriate place on the imaginary scale to indicate what they'd do in each situation. If they're not sure, they should stand in the middle (5 on the invisible scale). Read the statements one at a time and let students respond.

- I would yell at a referee or umpire while watching a game.
- I would sneak into the movies if I knew I wouldn't get caught.
- I would tell my friend he has bad breath.
- I would tell my date (on our first date) she has bad breath.
- I would cry while watching a movie.
- I would be embarrassed to talk about sex with my parents or my grandparents.
- I would go out on a blind date with someone I was told wasn't attractive.
- I would stop and ask for directions if I was lost.
- I would tell the store clerk if he made a $20 mistake in my favor on my purchase.
- I would have cosmetic surgery.
- I would lie about my age.
- I would crash a wedding reception.
- I would lie about having an accident with my parents' car.
- I would get drunk on spring break.
- I would raise my hand in class if the teacher asked who believed in Jesus Christ.
- (Add statements that fit your group.)

ICEBREAKER QUESTIONS:

- How many times did you look at where others were standing before you decided where you were going to stand?
- What is the toughest part about taking a stand for what you believe when you think the people you're with will disagree with you?
- How do you feel when you're not sure what to do?
- What strong beliefs do you have that you won't compromise?

SCRIPTURE: John 12:37-43

Ask a couple of students to read the passage aloud from their Bibles, alternating verses.

[37] Even after Jesus had performed so many signs in their presence, they still would not believe in him. [38] This was to fulfill the word of Isaiah the prophet:
"Lord, who has believed our message
and to whom has the arm of the Lord been revealed?"

[39] For this reason they could not believe, because, as Isaiah says elsewhere:
[40] "He has blinded their eyes
and hardened their hearts,
so they can neither see with their eyes,
nor understand with their hearts,
nor turn—and I would heal them."

[41] Isaiah said this because he saw Jesus' glory and spoke about him.

[42] Yet at the same time many even among the leaders believed in him. But because of the Pharisees they'd not openly acknowledge their faith for fear they would be put out of the synagogue; [43] for they loved human glory more than the glory of God.

STUDY QUESTIONS:

- Why were some people afraid to stand up for (or publicly follow) Jesus?
- What social and relational stresses do we encounter because of our faith?
- When is it good or bad to want people to like you?
- What are the dangers of wanting to be accepted?

• Why is it helpful to have some close friends who share your belief in and commitment to Christ?

TALKING POINTS:

Share the following points with your students:

Stand up for what you believe

Many of us are afraid of the opinions of other people. We feel stress when we're invited to do something we know isn't right for us or not right any time. We know we should say no, but the pressure gets to us. It's not so much the other people pressuring us—it's something inside us pressuring us not to risk losing respect of or friendship with the people around us. We can easily criticize others who compromise their beliefs, but how do we know we'll stand our ground when we're tested. Here are some suggestions for developing strong convictions:

The Bible helps: Reading God's commands and plan for life from the printed page makes it clear what pleases God. Reading the Bible defines the big issues and gives us a sense of God's will for the smaller issues. Studying it helps us see the *why* behind God's commands. It gives us encouragement when we read about the real people whose stories fill the Bible.

Christian friends help us stand strong: At times we know right and wrong but we just need the confirming words from a good friend encouraging us to go the right way. We can help each other remember our commitments and the ultimate goal and reward out in our future.

Take action to avoid temptation: Recovering substance abusers know they have to stay away from the old people, places, and things from the old life. That's true for us, too, and it means filling our lives with other positive activities and influences. We need to stay away from tempting situations and remember our goal and what is best for us long-term—not just in the moment of temptation.

Don't underestimate the desire to be accepted: Everyone wants to be liked by others, but that natural desire can control us if we don't ask God to help us control it. We need to learn to recognize that feeling—when it comes, we should ask God to help us focus on wanting to please him more than pleasing other people.

REAL-LIFE CONNECTION: Temptation drama

Break into small groups of four. Ask the groups to identify a tempting situation common for people in their school. Tell them to be creative and plan out a short drama they can show to the whole group to depict what happens when temptation comes. Explain that they should stop the drama just before the tempted person makes the decision to resist or give in to the temptation. At that point, they should let the audience decide what they think the person will do.

Give them five minutes to plan their drama. Select several to show to the whole group. At each stopping point in the drama, ask the audience what they think the tempted person will do. Take a few moments to talk specifically what he could have done to avoid the temptation or making the wrong decision.

MEDIA: The danger of temptation

From the movie *The Lion, the Witch, and the Wardrobe*, show the clip of Edmund accepting the Turkish Delight from the White Witch and what happens as a result (2:19). This clip can be found on www.wingclips.com. Search using the words *turkish delight*.

Or from the movie *Igor*, show the clip "One Act of Evil" (0:43). Igor attempts to make Eva, his monstrous creation, perform one act of evil. This clip can also be found on www.wingclips.com—search using the title of the clip.

These clips demonstrate the power and the danger of temptation.

John 13:1-17

TOPIC: Humility and service

OBJECTIVE: Students will feel the extent of Jesus' loving service and will embrace Jesus' call to follow his example by sacrificially serving others.

BACKGROUND/OVERVIEW: Jesus and his disciples are sitting down for the Passover meal when Jesus assumes the role of a servant and washes the disciples' feet. Not only was this a humble act of service, but it also was a very dirty task—considering the sandaled feet and the dirty roads. Jesus was teaching his closest followers a profound lesson about how to live and how to relate to each other.

GAME/ICEBREAKER: Feet meeting

Items needed:

- Felt-tip pen
- Lemon
- Markers

Choose a couple of these games to play with your group:

Foot Signing: Kids take off their shoes and socks and receive a felt-tip pen (the kind that will wash off). On your signal the group has one minute to see how many signatures they can get on the bottom of their feet.

Foot Wrestling: Kids pair off and sit down with right feet together. They lock big toes. On your signal they try to pin the other person's foot (as in arm wrestling).

Feet-by-the-Foot: Teams line up with their feet in a single file line (heel-to-toe) to see which team has the most footage. Longest line wins.

Lemon Pass: Teams remove shoes and try to pass a lemon down the line without using their hands—only feet. The lemon can't drop, or teams have to start over.

Foot Drawing: Each team chooses some object in the room. Using only feet for patterns, they trace parts of the feet on paper to create that object. Other teams must then try to guess what the object is.

ICEBREAKER QUESTIONS:

- What was it like to have to have your feet touched by other people?
- What was it like to touch everyone else's feet?
- If you could pay somebody to do something you can't stand doing, what job would you give her?
- What job do you hope you never have to do on a missions trip or elsewhere?

TRANSITION:

Say—

The games we just played were pretty gross. Now let's think about what it would have been like to play these games before people wore socks and shoes—back when they wore sandals and walked everywhere on dirt roads. While people in the Bible probably didn't play games with their feet, we do find a story about some pretty disgusting feet and an incredible feat performed by Jesus.

SCRIPTURE: John 13:1-17

Distribute copies of this passage. Have students read it silently—highlighting the interesting parts with a pencil or pen.

[1] It was just before the Passover Festival. Jesus knew that the hour had come for him to leave this world and go to the Father. Having loved his own who were in the world, he loved them to the end.

[2] The evening meal was in progress, and the devil had already prompted Judas, the son of Simon Iscariot, to betray Jesus. [3] Jesus knew that the Father had put all things under his power, and that he had come from God and was returning to God; [4] so he got up from the meal, took off his outer clothing, and wrapped a towel around his waist. [5] After that, he poured water into a basin and began to wash his disciples' feet, drying them with the towel that was wrapped around him.

[6] He came to Simon Peter, who said to him, "Lord, are you going to wash my feet?"

[7] Jesus replied, "You do not realize now what I am doing, but later you will understand."

[8] "No," said Peter, "you shall never wash my feet."

Jesus answered, "Unless I wash you, you have no part with me."

[9] "Then, Lord," Simon Peter replied, "not just my feet but my hands and my head as well!"

[10] Jesus answered, "Those who have had a bath need only to wash their feet; their whole body is clean. And you are clean, though not every one of you." [11] For he knew who was going to betray him, and that was why he said not every one was clean.

[12] When he had finished washing their feet, he put on his clothes and returned to his place. "Do you understand what I have done for you?" he asked them. [13] "You call me 'Teacher' and 'Lord,' and rightly so, for that is what I am. [14] Now that I, your Lord and Teacher, have washed your feet, you also should wash one another's feet. [15] I have set you an example that you should do as I have done for you. [16] Very truly I tell you, servants are not greater than their master, nor are messengers greater than the one who sent them. [17] Now that you know these things, you will be blessed if you do them."

STUDY QUESTIONS:

- What parts of the passage did you underline? Why?
- Close your eyes and picture yourself back in this time. Picture yourself walking down the roads the disciples had been traveling on. Given the culture in which Jesus did this, what would the disciples' feet have looked like? Smelled like? Felt like?
- Why do you think Jesus chose to wash the disciples' feet?
- Why was Peter so confused by what Jesus was doing?
- What must it have been like for Jesus to wash the feet of the man who was going to betray him (Judas Iscariot)? The feet of one of his best friends who was going to deny even knowing him (Peter)? The feet of the rest of his closest friends who were going to abandon him during the most difficult moment of his life?
- What were some of the characteristics Jesus needed in order to perform this task?

TALKING POINTS:

Have a conversation with your students using the following information:

P-U!

Have you ever been watching television when a family member or friend walked in and kicked off their shoes causing the entire room to reek? Have you ever been that person who caused the room to smell? Feet can get pretty rank!

Imagine living in a time and place where virtually everyone walked everywhere. No one had socks or shoes. Bare feet or sandals were the only options. There were no paved roads or sidewalks, only dirt when it was dry and mud when it rained. Oh, and by the way, everywhere you went, the streets were shared by all kinds of animals pulling carts, livestock being herded to market, and other animals looking for whatever food they can find or seeking a convenient spot to relieve themselves. No litter boxes, newspapers, or private animal restrooms? That's okay—the middle of the road worked just fine. How would your feet smell after a day walking on these streets? That's the kind of streets the disciples had been walking on that day before joining Jesus for supper.

Not me!

Given the conditions in which people traveled, it was understandably customary when you went to a friend's house for a meal, someone would wash your feet before you ate. This highly prized job was usually reserved for the household servants—and not just any servants, but the servants of the lowest rank. Washing feet caked in dust, mud, and feces was one of the most demeaning tasks any servant could do.

As far as we can tell from what the Bible says, when Jesus and his disciples arrived at the home in which they were going to eat, no servant was available to wash their feet. That meant someone from the group would have to do it. But who? Certainly not Peter, John, or James! They'd obviously achieved special status with Jesus, even going on special getaways with him (Matthew 17:1). It would have to be one of the others—one of the lesser disciples. Yet even they weren't the ones asked to do such a lowly task.

I'll do it!

In a move that must have stunned the disciples and left everyone but the group spokesman, Peter, speechless, Jesus—their master, their leader—got up, put aside his garments, and put on the apron of a slave. This couldn't be happening! But it was. Jesus got down on his hands and knees and began to wash the filthy feet of the 12 men he had been leading for three years along those dirt roads.

Follow my example

Upon completing his task, Jesus told his disciples he'd given them a pattern they should follow. He wasn't establishing the act of foot washing as a time less practice, but rather instilling in his followers the revolutionary attitude of humility that becomes visible in acts of service.

Nothing and no one is below a Christ-follower
If we as Christians don't follow the example of Jesus in humbling ourselves to meet the needs of others, we're walking in pride and essentially saying we're better than Jesus himself. But Jesus said, "A servant is not greater than his master" (v. 16). Just as Jesus wasn't too good to get down on his hands and knees and wash his disciples' disgusting feet, we need to recognize that nothing and no one is below us as followers of Christ. Whether this means cleaning toilets in a shack in a third-world country, helping dementia-afflicted patients in a nursing home, or walking across the lunchroom to sit with the kid everyone makes fun of, people deserve to know the love of Jesus through us, his followers.

REAL-LIFE CONNECTION: Walking the way of the cross
Items needed:

- A large paper cross to tape to the floor
- Colored poster paints
- Pans
- Towels
- Soap

Ask your students the following questions:

- What would it be like to know that everyone in the room feels as if they're better than you—that nobody wants to do what you're doing?
- What if Jesus asked you to do the job you despise most? And what if he asked you to do this job for the rest of your life?
- What gets in the way of you serving others?
- What obstacles do you need to overcome in order to serve others—even those who have hurt you?
- As an exercise in breaking pride and embracing humility, prayerfully write down an act of service you will do this week you really don't want to do.

Following the lesson gather the group around a large paper cross that has been taped to the floor. Place pans of colored poster paint around it. Use a different color in each pan. Then talk about what it means to be a part of the cross—to be willing to walk as a servant in the same way Christ did. Invite the kids to choose a color and (one at a time) dip their feet and walk across the paper, leaving their footprints on the cross. This can be done as an indication of their decision to follow in the way of the cross.

Next you can conduct a foot-washing ceremony, as kids wash the paint off each other's feet. Provide pans, towels, and soap.

MEDIA: Serve as Jesus served

Show the Sermonspice video—"iServe" (1:45). This video can be purchased from www.sermonspice.com. Search using the title of the clip. This is a *Mac vs. PC* parody that shows the difference between serving and not serving in the church.

John 14:5-11

TOPIC: Is Jesus the only way?

OBJECTIVE: Students will hear Jesus' claim to be the only way to God the Father and will respond to his claim by putting their faith in him.

BACKGROUND/OVERVIEW: Jesus had an extended teaching time with his disciples before his death (John 13-17) where he reemphasized what he'd been showing and telling them regarding his identity and how he wanted them to believe and act. They were filled with questions. Jesus explained that he's the only way to God. If they'd seen him, they'd seen God the Father.

GAME/ICEBREAKER: Not our baby
Items needed:

- Doctor costume
- Baby doll wrapped up in a blanket

This skit is adapted from an analogy written by Lee Strobel. (From the article "Are There Many Paths to God? There is only one way to heaven, and that is through Jesus Christ" [PreachingToday.com, Christianity Today International].)

You will need three actors for the parts of a doctor (get a white jacket and stethoscope, etc.), a father, and a mother (with a baby doll wrapped up in a blanket). Skits always work best when the actors express (and overexpress) the emotions of the moment. Ham it up.

Doctor: Congratulations on the birth of your new baby. I have some important news you need to know. She has jaundice. It's a liver disorder that causes her skin and the whites of her eyes to turn yellow.

Parents: Are you talking about our baby? She looks okay to us. If fact she looks beautiful. (Together they ooh and aah as they look at the baby). If we take her home and give her a lot of love, I'm sure the problem will go away.

Doctor: She is beautiful but this is a potentially devastating disease. If we don't do something she'll have a lot of trouble.

Parents: (Now panicking.) Oh, no! What are we going to do? (Now screaming.) We need help! Doctor, doctor you've got to help us. What do we do?

Doctor: I have good news. This potentially devastating disease is easily treated. All we have to do is put the baby under a special light for a while. This will stimulate her liver to start working properly and she'll be all right.

Mother: (Very skeptical.) That doesn't sound good. My mother and grandmother always told me not to shine a bright light on a baby—that will hurt the baby. I'm not doing that.

Doctor: There is nothing to worry about. The light will help her liver and remove this yellow hue from her skin.

Mother: (Increasingly skeptical.) I don't see how sitting under a light will remove her yellow—that's too easy. How about instead if we scrubbed her with soap and dipped her in bleach? If we worked hard enough, I'm sure we could get her normal coloring back.

Doctor: You seem like a very concerned parent, but scrubbing and dipping won't solve this problem. And using bleach on a human could cause injury or death! There's only one way to treat this. Get your baby under the light, and she'll get healthy.

Father: (Smug and confident.) I agree with my wife—that sounds too easy. If we just relax and let her grow up naturally everything will turn out okay.

Doctor: Let me be clear about this. Your baby has jaundice and needs help right now.

Father: (Anger rising.) I don't like your tone, Doc. You're getting a little pushy with this light-treatment thing. You say jaundice is real. Maybe for you, but we don't see it that way. We go by what we see and believe and if we sincerely believe that, things will work out for the best.

Doctor: You're going to jeopardize your baby if you do that. Look, there's only one way to cure her. You hesitate because it sounds too easy, but look at the credentials hanging on my wall. I've studied at medical school, and I've used what I've learned to cure countless babies like yours. Trust me!

Mother: (Angry and emotional.) I don't like it when you say you know how to fix this problem. Maybe there are other ways to handle this. I think *you* are very narrow-minded to push this light-treatment thing on *us* and *our* baby.

Doctor: I am telling you this because I want to save your baby. This is the best and only way we know to treat jaundice in newborn babies. I want to cure your little girl. This isn't narrow-minded—it's the only rational choice in accordance with the evidence.

Father: (Angry and emphatic.) My parents taught me to be skeptical of people who act like they have all the answers. Who can know everything? I think we're done here.

(Parents turn and leave.) THE END

ICEBREAKER QUESTIONS:

- What's happening here? What is the doctor trying to do?
- What do you think about the response of the parents?
- What's keeping these parents from receiving the help the doctor is offering?
- Who is being responsible and rational, and who is being arrogant and narrow-minded?
- Today we're going to talk about Jesus Christ being the solution to our problems and the only way to really knowing God. If we replayed this skit and talked about Jesus, what would the doctor say about Jesus being the answer?
- What would the parents say expressing their disbelief?
- Why is Jesus being the only way to God such a highly charged argument?

SCRIPTURE: John 14:5-11

Read the passage aloud. Tell your students to listen to what Jesus said to his disciples about who he is.

[5] Thomas said to him, "Lord, we don't know where you are going, so how can we know the way?"

[6] Jesus answered, "I am the way and the truth and the life. No one comes to the Father except through me. [7] If you really know me, you will know my Father as well. From now on, you do know him and have seen him."

⁸ Philip said, "Lord, show us the Father and that will be enough for us."

⁹ Jesus answered: "Don't you know me, Philip, even after I have been among you such a long time? Anyone who has seen me has seen the Father. How can you say, 'Show us the Father'? ¹⁰ Don't you believe that I am in the Father, and that the Father is in me? The words I say to you I do not speak on my own authority. Rather, it is the Father, living in me, who is doing his work. ¹¹ Believe me when I say that I am in the Father and the Father is in me; or at least believe on the evidence of the works themselves.

STUDY QUESTIONS:

- What did Thomas ask Jesus? What response did he receive?
- How did Jesus describe his relationship with the Father?
- What evidence did Jesus suggest to prove his relationship with the Father?
- In what ways is faith in Jesus Christ exclusive or narrow?
- How do people who don't believe Jesus is the only way to God describe who Jesus was?
- What do you think about Jesus' claim to be "the way and the truth and the life"?

TALKING POINTS:
Share some of the following points with your students:

The way to God
These are life's biggest questions: Where did we come from, and what is our purpose? All the evidence around us in the world and the complexity of our own bodies tell us we were designed by an intelligent and omnipotent higher power. The Bible tells us God who loves us and wants to be connected to us created us. The Bible records how God revealed himself and spoke to us through prophets, telling us about a time when God himself would come to earth. For many years people looked for this special Messiah who would come from God to earth.

Jesus' outrageous claim
When we read John 14, you heard Jesus' response to Thomas, asserting no one could come to the Father except through him (v. 6) and anyone who had seen him had seen the Father (v. 9). Jesus clearly claimed to be the Messiah whom the prophets promised. The religious leaders who arranged

the arrest of Jesus later that night were motivated to act and charge him with blasphemy—he claimed to be God.

Backing up his claim

Jesus is unique and dramatically different from the key religious figures. They claimed to help people find the way to God, but Jesus said he is the Way. Many religious leaders have made outrageous claims, but they're ultimately judged by their ability to back up those claims. The recorded history of Jesus' life reveals his miraculous birth, his sinless life, his power to heal and perform physical miracles, and even his ability to bring dead people back to life, culminating with his own bodily resurrection three days after being brutally killed in public view. More than 500 witnesses saw Jesus alive after his resurrection. Jesus' life was filled with moments when ancient prophecies were fulfilled far beyond what could be humanly manipulated. Jesus Christ stands alone in history as God come to earth to provide by his sacrificial death a way to God for anyone who believes.

Narrow-minded?

This frequent, popular criticism of Jesus and the Christian faith overlooks the wide-open door Jesus made for everyone to be reconciled to God and be given eternal life. Most people agree the world is messed up and no one is perfect—we're all distant from God and certainly not doing what God wants us to do. All religions try to address this and bring us to a connection with God—but they can't all be right. When Jesus says he's the only way to God, is that narrow? Most certainly. But truth is always narrow. For example, your teachers don't grade on sincerity—if you put the wrong answer on the test, it's wrong. Period. And in our skit earlier, we saw those parents were wrong, even if they sincerely believed their way was right.

What Christ has done for the world opens the door for everyone to come to God. This isn't narrow at all. Instead of saying, Why did God only give us one way to him?, we need to say, Thank you, God, for making a way! Jesus Christ is the only way to God for the good people and the bad, the religious and nonreligious, the rich and the poor, the educated and uneducated—Christ covers all the human divisions of the world.

REAL-LIFE CONNECTION: How will you respond?

Say to your students—

The most important person who needs to know Jesus Christ is the only way to God is you. Some people argue and worry about how the masses of people worldwide will find Jesus Christ if he's the only way. God is fair and just, and that situation won't catch him by surprise. Instead, we should be thankful God has provided Jesus, the Way, and that we can take it.

How do you respond to Jesus when he says, "I am the way and the truth and the life. No one comes to the Father except through me"? These are the most important words ever spoken—and they point to eternal life.

Jesus is saying that to you. How will you respond? He'd like to hear you say something like this: *Lord Jesus, I do believe you are the Son of God and that you died on the cross to pay the penalty for my sin. Please come into my life, forgive my sin, and make me a member of your family. I want to turn from going my own way. I want you to be the center of my life. Thank you for giving your life to make a way for me to come to you, to know you, and to receive the gift of eternal life. I say and ask all of this in your name. Amen.*

If those words reflect what you want to say to Jesus, repeat them or respond to Jesus with your own words. This is a big moment in your life. Talk to a leader before you leave and tell her you responded to Jesus and asked him to come into your life.

MEDIA: Jesus is the Way

Show the clip from the DVD, *The Case for Christ* by Lee Strobel, "Fulfilling Prophecies" (1:35). Lee explains the chances of Jesus randomly fulfilling the messianic prophecies was one out of a trillion, trillion, trillion....

This clip is available at www.wingclips.com. Search for the clip using the word *prophecies*.

John 15:1-8

TOPIC: Don't just believe, *connect*

OBJECTIVE: Students will learn the importance of being connected to Jesus and how it affects their lives. They'll understand the difference between just believing in God and being truly connected to him.

BACKGROUND/OVERVIEW: Jesus was with his disciples speaking in parables and metaphors. Here Jesus relates our relationship and life with him to a vine and its branches.

GAME/ICEBREAKER: Chain tag

Pick one to three people to be *It*. They run by themselves trying to tag people. Once a person gets tagged, he becomes *It* with the person who made the tag and must link onto that person by holding hands or linking arms. The *Its* will continue until they're chasing one person—that person is the winner.

ICEBREAKER QUESTIONS:

- What made it difficult for the people who were It to catch others?
- In what ways did the game change as the It line got longer?
- Why is getting the It line to work and move together so difficult?
- How does being connected help a Christian grow and be like Christ?

SCRIPTURE: John 15:1-8

Have a staff person read the passage aloud while everyone follows along in the Bible. Explain that Jesus is speaking.

[1] "I am the true vine, and my Father is the gardener. [2] He cuts off every branch in me that bears no fruit, while every branch that does bear fruit he prunes so that it will be even more fruitful. [3] You are already clean because of the word I have spoken to you. 4 Remain in me, as I also remain in you. No branch can bear fruit by itself; it must remain in the vine. Neither can you bear fruit unless you remain in me.

[5] "I am the vine; you are the branches. If you remain in me and I in you, you will bear much fruit; apart from me you can do nothing. [6] If you do not remain in me, you are like a branch that is thrown away and withers; such branches are picked up, thrown into the fire and

burned. [7] If you remain in me and my words remain in you, ask whatever you wish, and it will be done for you. [8] This is to my Father's glory, that you bear much fruit, showing yourselves to be my disciples.

STUDY QUESTIONS:

- Why did Jesus talk to his disciples about vines and branches?
- What happens if a branch breaks away from the vine?
- What does Jesus mean when he says, "No branch can bear fruit by itself"?
- What is the fruit Jesus is talking about?
- What are the consequences of a Christian not being connected to Jesus?
- When is it difficult for a Christian to be connected to Jesus?

TALKING POINTS:

Have a conversation with your students using the following points as a guide:

Know the source of life and love
Jesus said he's the true Vine. What does that mean? Well, look at a vine. The fruit of the vine comes off of the branches, right? But the branches aren't the source of the fruit. We know that because, if a branch was ripped off the vine, it could no longer make that fruit. In fact the branch would soon dry up and die. The vine is where the branch gets all its nutrients that enable the branch to make fruit. When Jesus says he's the Vine, he's saying he's the Source of all the nutrients we need to produce fruit.

Staying connected fulfills your purpose
When a branch produces fruit, it's doing what it was always intended to do. When a branch can't produce fruit, it's not doing what it's supposed to be doing. When we aren't connected to Jesus, we can't find our purpose—we aren't doing what we were always made to do. Thus we might feel very dry and out of place. But when we're connected to Jesus, our lives are rich and filled with everything we need to produce good things.

Religion isn't enough
If a branch could think and talk and was broken off the vine, it would probably still know the vine's exact location. But just because it knows where it is doesn't mean the branch will still live. Just believing God exists or going to church isn't enough. Jesus said to remain in him—to stay connected to him.

Being connected means all the nutrients are yours, making you strong. When you're disconnected, you're alone and soon dry out.

Make it real

Say to your students—

Many people want to know their purpose in life, but they don't know where to find it. Jesus says those who are connected to him get everything they need to do what they were made to do. So how can you make this real for you?

First, make sure you have made that connection to Christ—that you have give your life to him.

Second, talk to God often, not just when you need something big—all the time, just as you would with a close friend.

Then make sure you have godly people in your life with whom you can share your questions and concerns.

Finally, listen for God to speak to you while you pray and read the Word. When God does speak, do what he says.

MEDIA: Vines

Show the video clip "I am the Vine" (1:57). It's available for purchase from www.sermonspice.com. The clip features an overgrown plot with lots of vegetation and the Scripture from John 15.

Or you can show the video clip "Vine and Branches" (1:22). It's available on YouTube. This edgy video asks what type of leaves and fruit a Christian is producing. Search www.youtube.com using the words vine and branches muddy river media.

John 16:33

TOPIC: Who's in charge here?

OBJECTIVE: Students will gain security knowing that God is in control even when they experience pain and trials.

BACKGROUND/OVERVIEW: Jesus was preparing his disciples for his death and departure from the world. They wanted to know what would happen to them when Jesus wasn't there to protect them. He gave them some bad news with a great promise.

GAME/ICEBREAKER: The worst that can happen
Items needed:

- Paper
- Pens/pencils

Hand out paper and pencils to everyone. Ask them to write a list of the five worst things that can happen to them between the time their alarm rings in the morning and the time they eat lunch on a school day. Tell them not to put their names on the papers. Read their answers (without names) to the group. You can either laugh or cry together as they are read.

ICEBREAKER QUESTIONS:

- How many of those worst things have actually happened to anybody here?
- What problems have you been though in your life that you can laugh about now?
- What problems have you had that you would not wish on your worst enemy?
- When people have unexpected problems, how often do you hear them use God's name in a bad way?
- How often do they call out to God in a good way?

SCRIPTURE: John 16:33

Put the passage in context, explaining that Jesus is speaking. Then have someone read the verse aloud from her Bible—two or three times for emphasis.

[33]"I have told you these things, so that in me you may have peace. In this world you will have trouble. But take heart! I have overcome the world."

STUDY QUESTIONS:

- If you were there with Jesus, how would you have responded to his promise of trouble ahead and being there for you?
- What trouble do the followers of Jesus have in the world today?
- How does Jesus overcoming the world help or encourage you?
- What problems or trouble has God turned into good for you?

TALKING POINTS:

Share the following points with your students:

Expect problems

Jesus reminds us the world is out of step with God. We can expect a steady flow of selfish anger, greed, tension, violence, lying, betrayal, and so forth from people who don't know God. Sometimes it will be directed at us, causing pain and suffering.

Take courage

Despite all the trouble and problems, Jesus promises to be with us and never leave us alone. We can expect our relationship with Christ to bring us peace and comfort in the middle of our difficulties and trials.

God is in control

Sometimes we go through problems we caused because we made dumb choices. Sometimes we get hurt because of other people's actions. The world is fallen and sin-scarred. Still, everything—every person and situation—is under God's control.

Someday pain will end

God promises to eliminate all pain and all evil (Revelation 21:4). We'd like it to happen today, but God has a different schedule than what we want. Still, we can be confident God will keep his promise both to bring an end to pain and evil and to be with us while it's still going on.

REAL-LIFE CONNECTION: Baking a cake

Items needed:

- The ingredients for a cake
- Small pieces of cake for people to sample

Pass around the ingredients for a cake in separate containers. Have everyone dip a finger and taste each ingredient (salt, sugar, baking powder, vanilla, cocoa, flour, butter, and oil). As they're sampling, ask how the different ingredients taste. Now pass around small pieces of cake for everyone to sample. Contrast the taste of the individual ingredients with the taste of the cake. Alone, some of the ingredients are bitter and not desirable, but mixed together and heated up, the results taste good.

Say to your students—

God takes all the things that happen to us and uses them to make something good happen in our lives. He's in control, making you mature, complete, and good-tasting.

MEDIA: Cooking how-to

Record a cooking show (or get a cooking DVD at a library or video store) and show a clip where they're using varied ingredients to make something delicious. The process of mixing ingredients to produce a wonderful dish illustrates how God mixes our life experiences (even trials and troubles) to produce a great result. During the "egg-breaking and flour-pouring" phase we can wonder what's going on. But God knows the end result and what the ingredients will produce.

John 17:1-26

TOPIC: The Lord's Real Prayer

OBJECTIVE: Students will know Jesus wants believers to be unified and to love each other.

BACKGROUND/OVERVIEW: Jesus wrapped up his teaching ministry by telling his disciples about his impending departure. He then turned his attention in prayer toward heaven and to the climactic fulfillment of his priestly ministry. His prayer is threefold: For himself, for his disciples, and for those who will come to believe as a result of the ministry of his disciples.

GAME/ICEBREAKER: Final prayer
Items needed:

- Sheets of paper
- Pens/pencils

Give each student a sheet of paper and a pen. Tell them to imagine they have just hours left to live. Then give them five minutes to write out one final prayer to God.

Afterward ask for volunteers to read aloud their prayers. Don't press for this—it's okay if no one volunteers.

ICEBREAKER QUESTIONS:

- What was it like thinking of the end of your life?
- As you look at your prayer, what is important to you? What do you value?
- Who or what did you pray for? Why?

TRANSITION:
Say—

Jesus was really experiencing the situation we just pretended to be in—he knew he was close to the end of his life on earth. After talking to his disciples one last time, he turned his attention toward heaven and lifted a prayer to his Father. Let's read that prayer.

SCRIPTURE: **Read John 17:1-26**

Make sure everyone has access to a copy of the passage. Then take turns reading it aloud, one person per verse.

¹ After Jesus said this, he looked toward heaven and prayed:

"Father, the hour has come. Glorify your Son, that your Son may glorify you. ² For you granted him authority over all people that he might give eternal life to all those you have given him. ³ Now this is eternal life: that they know you, the only true God, and Jesus Christ, whom you have sent. ⁴ I have brought you glory on earth by finishing the work you gave me to do. ⁵ And now, Father, glorify me in your presence with the glory I had with you before the world began.

⁶ "I have revealed you to those whom you gave me out of the world. They were yours; you gave them to me and they have obeyed your word. ⁷ Now they know that everything you have given me comes from you. ⁸ For I gave them the words you gave me and they accepted them. They knew with certainty that I came from you, and they believed that you sent me. ⁹ I pray for them. I am not praying for the world, but for those you have given me, for they are yours. ¹⁰ All I have is yours, and all you have is mine. And glory has come to me through them. ¹¹ I will remain in the world no longer, but they are still in the world, and I am coming to you. Holy Father, protect them by the power of your name, the name you gave me, so that they may be one as we are one. ¹² While I was with them, I protected them and kept them safe by that name you gave me. None has been lost except the one doomed to destruction so that Scripture would be fulfilled.

¹³ "I am coming to you now, but I say these things while I am still in the world, so that they may have the full measure of my joy within them. ¹⁴ I have given them your word and the world has hated them, for they are not of the world any more than I am of the world. ¹⁵ My prayer is not that you take them out of the world but that you protect them from the evil one. ¹⁶ They are not of the world, even as I am not of it. ¹⁷ Sanctify them by the truth; your word is truth. ¹⁸ As you sent me into the world, I have sent them into the world. ¹⁹ For them I sanctify myself, that they too may be truly sanctified.

²⁰ "My prayer is not for them alone. I pray also for those who will believe in me through their message, ²¹ that all of them may be one, Father, just as you are in me and I am in you. May they also be in us

so that the world may believe that you have sent me. [22] I have given them the glory that you gave me, that they may be one as we are one— [23] I in them and you in me—so that they may be brought to complete unity. Then the world will know that you sent me and have loved them even as you have loved me.

[24] "Father, I want those you have given me to be with me where I am, and to see my glory, the glory you have given me because you loved me before the creation of the world.

[25] "Righteous Father, though the world does not know you, I know you, and they know that you have sent me. [26] I have made you known to them, and will continue to make you known in order that the love you have for me may be in them and that I myself may be in them."

STUDY QUESTIONS:

- **For whom did Jesus pray in his prayer?** (Answer: Himself, his disciples, all future believers.)
- **What did he ask God to do for him?** (Answer: To glorify him.)
- **Do you think Jesus' prayer for himself is selfish? Why or why not?**
- **What did he ask God to do for the disciples?** (Answer: To make them one, to protect them from the world, to sanctify them, and to know his true identity, to see his glory.)
- **Where are you in Jesus' prayer?** (Answer: "I pray also for those who will believe in me through their message," v. 20.)
- **What is Jesus' request for those future believers?** (Answer: That they may be one, unified and that the world will see God in them.)
- **How do you feel knowing that Jesus prayed for you in his last prayer?**

TALKING POINTS:

Use these points as a guideline for what to share with your students:

The Lord's Real Prayer

We often refer to Jesus' instruction on prayer in Matthew 6:9-13 as The Lord's Prayer, and John 17 would probably be accurately described as The Lord's Real Prayer. It's the longest prayer of Jesus found in the Bible, and it truly shows us how Jesus prayed. This prayer by Jesus, commonly referred to as his high priestly prayer, is broken down into three sections:

- The first section (vv. 1-5) contains Jesus' prayer for himself. While it might seem selfish for Jesus to pray for himself, the emphasis of his prayer makes it clear this isn't the case. Jesus' prayer for himself was that he might bring honor and glory to the Father.

- The second section (vv.6-19) contains Jesus' prayer for his disciples. He prayed they would be unified and protected from the evil one as they embraced the ministry of truth he called them to and carried out their work in the world.
- The third section (vv.20-26) contains Jesus' prayer for those who would become his followers through the generations as a result of the ministry of his original disciples. If you're a follower of Jesus today, this section of Jesus' prayer extends to you more than 2,000 years later!

Two main themes
While a number of points emerge in this prayer, two themes stand out that are of particular importance:

1. Unity: Jesus prayed we would follow the intimate unity he demonstrated in his relationship with his Father. Though there is great diversity in the body of Christ in terms of gifts, personality, and function; oneness of heart, mind, purpose, and mission is absolutely essential if the church is to fulfill her calling of revealing God to the world (1 Corinthians 12:12-27). Paul writes in Romans 15:5-6, "May the God who gives endurance and encouragement give you same attitude of mind toward each other that Christ Jesus had, so that with one mind and one voice you may glorify the God and Father of our Lord Jesus Christ." Where God finds the unity he desires, he releases his blessing and unleashes his favor (Psalm 133).

2. Love: Jesus also prayed that the love that marked his relationship with the Father, which he modeled before his disciples, would characterize the lives of his followers throughout all time as well. The love Jesus referred to was agape love—a love marked by service and sacrifice. In John 13:34-35 Jesus said, "A new command I give you: Love one another. As I have loved you, so you must love one another. By this everyone will know that you are my disciples, if you love one another."

We glorify God through our unity of purpose and our sacrificial love. Living in unity and walking in love will allow the world to observe the very real presence of Jesus in our lives and cause them to consider the claims of Jesus as the Son of God and the Savior of the world.

REAL-LIFE CONNECTION: Where's the love?

Break the group in groups of three and discuss these questions together:

- Of all the things Jesus could have prayed for us, why do you think he focused on unity and love?
- Where do you see Christians living in unity and love? What would increase the unity and love in the church?
- What is required for people to live in unity?
- How can you be a more loving person?

MEDIA: Jesus' prayer

Show this Sermonspice video: "John 17" (3:51). Search for this video on www.sermonspice.com using the search terms *prayers John 17*. Pray along with Jesus as he expresses his heart and the Father's heart toward us.

John 18:15-18, 25-27

TOPIC: Ashamed of Jesus?

OBJECTIVE: Students will know the story of Peter denying he was a follower of Jesus, and they'll decide to let people in their world know of their relationship with Jesus.

BACKGROUND/OVERVIEW: Peter promised Jesus he'd never deny him when they had their last supper together, but Jesus warned that Peter would deny him three times before the rooster would crow in the morning. Later, while Peter was standing outside the courtyard where Jesus was being held, Peter did just that: He denied three times he knew Jesus.

GAME/ICEBREAKER: **True identities**
Items needed:

- Paper
- Pens/pencils

Beforehand, write names of celebrities on slips of paper. Be sure to have enough for every member of your group. Use celebrities who could be identified by the way they act or speak. These celebrities may be living or dead, real or cartoon, and from every arena: Music, movies, radio, sports, politics, fiction, etc. You could include characters such as Abraham Lincoln, Sarah Palin, the Joker, Harry Potter, Aslan, John F. Kennedy, Britney Spears, Tiger Woods, Billy Graham, Beyoncé, Mickey Mouse, your pastor, Barack Obama, Ariel, Marge Simpson, Nancy Pelosi, Ryan Seacrest, Benjamin Franklin, Usain Bolt, Peyton Manning, you.... Use your imagination.

Give everyone an answer sheet and a pen. Explain they're to act as much as possible as their character—even in speech, if possible. At the same time they should be trying to ascertain the identities of everyone else in the group. On their sheets they should write a person's real name and the role they think that person is playing. They may ask each other questions but should stay in character when they ask as well as answer the questions.

After a few minutes reveal the identities one person at a time and see who guessed the most correctly.

ICEBREAKER QUESTIONS:

- Who did a really good job of acting in that game?
- (To those people): What was your secret?
- (To everyone): How did you feel as you acted out your new identity?
- When might someone be tempted to pretend to be someone different than he or she is?
- When might you be tempted to hide your true identity?
- If you were at a party and someone asked you point blank, "Are you a follower of Christ? Do you love Jesus?" how would you feel? What do you think you would say?

SCRIPTURE: John 18:15-18, 25-27

Have a few students—preferably good actors from the icebreaker—read the passage aloud, taking these parts: Narrator, Peter, servant girl, official at the fire, and priest's servant.

[15] Simon Peter and another disciple were following Jesus. Because this disciple was known to the high priest, he went with Jesus into the high priest's courtyard, [16] but Peter had to wait outside at the door. The other disciple, who was known to the high priest, came back, spoke to the servant girl on duty there and brought Peter in.

[17] "You aren't one of this man's disciples too, are you?" she asked Peter.
He replied, "I am not."

[18] It was cold, and the servants and officials stood around a fire they had made to keep warm. Peter also was standing with them, warming himself.

[25] Meanwhile, Simon Peter was still standing there warming himself. So they asked him, "You aren't one of his disciples too, are you?"
He denied it, saying, "I am not."

[26] One of the high priest's servants, a relative of the man whose ear Peter had cut off, challenged him, "Didn't I see you with him in the garden?" [27] Again Peter denied it, and at that moment a rooster began to crow.

STUDY QUESTIONS:

- What do you imagine Peter was thinking when these people started questioning him?
- Why do you think Peter denied knowing Jesus when just a couple of hours earlier he had promised Jesus to never deny him?
- When and where is it hard for you to openly acknowledge your relationship with Christ?
- Under what circumstances might you be tempted to deny knowing or following Jesus?
- In what ways can a person deny knowing Jesus by his or her actions?
- If you know someone for a long time and they never ask you about Jesus and you never talk about Jesus, is that being ashamed of him? Explain.

TALKING POINTS:

Use the following points as a jumping-off-point for discussion with your students:

Jesus is controversial

The name of Jesus is powerful. We're told to pray using his name. The Bible says Jesus is the only name by which people can be saved. Some people will talk about God or pray saying God or the Almighty, but they won't say the name of Jesus. They think the name Jesus is offensive to people. But when it comes to cursing, lots of people use the name Jesus Christ, almost to the point of wearing it out. When have you been afraid to speak about Jesus in a positive way? If you won an Oscar or a Grammy, would you thank God? Would you thank Jesus? Or would you not say anything about God and Jesus? How about an award at your school—whom would you thank? When you talk about your faith with people who don't go to church, do you talk about God more than you talk about Jesus? Try this: When you're out with some friends, ask them what they think about Jesus, or tell them about talking to Jesus when you were at church. What will happen in the minutes after you say that? Maybe we do know how Peter felt that night.

We can be afraid of what others think

How many of us have admitted to being afraid to speak about Jesus at some point in our lives? Admit it—it's real. I think many of us are afraid of what others think about us. Our fear of other people can shut us up about God or Jesus. If you were in a freshman college class and the professor were to ask in a condescending tone if anyone in the class believes in Jesus, would you raise your hand? Would you speak up? What might identification with Jesus cost you? Do you think people might laugh at you or leave you out of their social plans? Would the professor pick on you or give you a religious nickname for the rest of the semester? Jesus knew the pressure Peter would face that night. He warned him about what would happen. He knew Peter was afraid. Jesus knows about *our* fears, too.

Making promises in church is easy

Talking about Jesus in church carries no risk—we sing Jesus songs and read Jesus stories. That makes sense here because most people at church agree with and support our faith. But what kind of Jesus follower are you when you're with people who seem uninterested or hostile toward him? Where in your life are you hiding Jesus right now? In what places do you need to live openly as his follower?

A big mistake isn't the end

Peter really blew it and disgraced himself that night in the courtyard. But that wasn't the end of his story. If you read ahead to John 21, we see Jesus inviting Peter to breakfast by the lake and speaking to him. None of us have made a mistake Jesus can't forgive. Nobody loves us as he loves us. That's why we shouldn't be afraid to let others know who loves us most and whom we love most. The big turnaround for Peter began that morning at the lake and exploded like fireworks a couple of months later when he told the story of Jesus to thousands in Jerusalem on Pentecost. When you mess up, Jesus comes close to you and gives you forgiveness and courage for your next opportunity to do or say what pleases him. It's the beginning, not the end.

REAL-LIFE CONNECTION: An outward symbol of an inward faith

Give everyone an opportunity to make a public statement about Jesus. Challenge them to write Jesus' name on something they'll wear or on their visible skin with a marker or temporary tattoo. Can they wear it for the next 48 hours? Ask them to report to the group how it made them feel being so associated with Jesus. What comments or responses did they get from others who saw it on them?

MEDIA: Not ashamed of Jesus

Play one of these songs or show the YouTube version: "I'm Not Ashamed" from the *Shine* album by the Newsboys, or "Jesus Freak" by DC Talk and Toby Mac on the *Welcome to the Freak Show* album.

John 19:28-37

TOPIC: Jesus died for you

OBJECTIVE: Students will know why Jesus Christ died on the cross and how they're involved with his death.

BACKGROUND/OVERVIEW: After three years of public ministry where he often spoke about his suffering and death, Jesus was arrested, beaten, and crucified until he died. This was the worst day for his family and disciples, but it was a day God had planned since the creation of the world.

GAME/ICEBREAKER: Sacrifice simulation
Items needed:

- Playing cards from multiple decks—cards numbered one through10
- Candy prizes

This group exercise takes some pre-meeting preparation. The goal is to simulate how Jesus voluntarily took the punishment for our sins against God.

For this game you will need decks of playing cards, but you will only use the cards numbered one through 10. You will need enough of the numbered cards so each person in the group can have five cards. Remove from the decks all the face cards and all but nine of the No. 10 cards. Prior to the meeting give five of the No. 10 cards to a pre-selected student who is to play the role of Jesus. This student needs to be prepared about what to do prior to the meeting.

Start by shuffling the cards (remember all the cards in your hands must be numbered from one to nine and just four No. 10 cards). Give every person five cards. The goal is for them to get a numerical total of 50 with their five cards. They're to exchange cards with each other trying to improve the numerical value of their five cards. (Note: Make sure it's impossible for anyone to get 50). A person can only have five cards in his or her hand.

Tell them those with the highest numerical totals will receive prizes, but those who do not get 50 will receive the punishment of a shaving cream pie in the face. No exceptions.

After five minutes of trading, you will hear the frustration building about not getting 50. Encourage them to do their best to get the prizes. At that five-minute mark release the *Jesus* person quietly into the group—but he should not tell anyone he's *Jesus.* Give him five No. 10 cards to show to others but not to trade with anyone. Tell *Jesus* to go to people individually and ask them to give him all their cards and link up to him and stay connected as they move around the room. He should tell them if they give him all their cards he'll take the pie in the face for them. Expect some confusion with varying degrees of people understanding what is going on and some arguing about what can and can't be done. At 10 or 15 minutes have *Jesus* make a loud appeal to everyone. Have a countdown to the end of the exercise. Ask everyone to sit down where they are, and start the debriefing and questions.

ICEBREAKER QUESTIONS:

- **Your goal was to get 50 with your cards. Who got 50?** (Should be no one.)
- **Well, there are prizes for the high totals! Who got 40 or more?** (Distribute candy prizes.)
- **Enjoy the candy, but the rules said if you didn't get 50 you got a pie in the face, so let's get started.** (Get out a pie pan and a can of shaving cream.) **Who's going first?** (Don't do it to anyone; just talk about it.)
- **I notice some of you don't have cards. Did you follow the rules? Where are your cards?** (Someone should tell about giving cards to this one person who said he would take the pie for them.)
- **Who took the cards of all these people?** (Ask *Jesus* directly.) **Are you going to take the pie for these people? Who are the people you're doing this for? Let's do this.** (Bring *Jesus* up to the front. Have the people who gave him their cards stand around him. Give the pie in the face to *Jesus*.) **Now all the rest of you holding cards and not having 50, this is going to happen to you.**

TRANSITION:

Speak to the whole group—

Before we do that let's talk about what happened here.

Debrief how this Jesus person invited them to believe and follow him and how they gave all their cards to him. Talk about this person having five No. 10 cards and being the only one in the room who didn't deserve the pie. Talk about why people didn't respond to his offer and kept their cards.

Explain you aren't going to give all of them a pie in the face, but you want them to remember Jesus taking the pie here with the group, so they'll understand they don't want to live their real lives holding all their own cards and facing God's judgment.

Then say—

Let's look at the real story of what happened when Jesus came to take our punishment.

SCRIPTURE: John 19:28-37
Read the passage slowly and with feeling.

²⁸ Later, knowing that everything had now been finished, and so that Scripture would be fulfilled, Jesus said, "I am thirsty." ²⁹ A jar of wine vinegar was there, so they soaked a sponge in it, put the sponge on a stalk of the hyssop plant, and lifted it to Jesus' lips. ³⁰ When he had received the drink, Jesus said, "It is finished." With that, he bowed his head and gave up his spirit.

³¹ Now it was the day of Preparation, and the next day was to be a special Sabbath. Because the Jewish leaders did not want the bodies left on the crosses during the Sabbath, they asked Pilate to have the legs broken and the bodies taken down. ³² The soldiers therefore came and broke the legs of the first man who had been crucified with Jesus, and then those of the other. ³³ But when they came to Jesus and found that he was already dead, they did not break his legs. ³⁴ Instead, one of the soldiers pierced Jesus' side with a spear, bringing a sudden flow of blood and water. ³⁵ The man who saw it has given testimony, and his testimony is true. He knows that he tells the truth, and he testifies so that you also may believe. ³⁶ These things happened so that the scripture would be fulfilled: "Not one of his bones will be broken," ³⁷ and, as another scripture says, "They will look on the one they have pierced."

STUDY QUESTIONS:

- How does reading or hearing this description of Jesus' death make you feel?
- What does Jesus' death mean to Christians?
- What did Jesus mean when he said, "It is finished"?
- How is Jesus' death on the cross connected to the forgiveness of our sins?
- Why did John write down all the details about Jesus dying on the cross?

TALKING POINTS:
Share the following information with your students:

Jesus lived to die
From a human point of view, putting Jesus on the cross was a miscarriage of justice. He spoke to his disciples often about his coming suffering and death. When he prayed in the garden, Jesus knew what was going to happen. It wasn't

going to be easy, but he chose to obey his heavenly Father because this was the reason for his life as a human on earth. From the foundation of time, God had planned to send a gift to his created world that would reconcile all people to him. When the angel told Mary and Joseph to name their baby Jesus, it was because he would save his people from their sins.

His death was a promised sacrifice

John makes special notes in this chapter to remind us of all the details about Jesus' death that were foretold by the prophets hundreds of years before Jesus was born. Jesus' death was the ultimate sacrifice in the sacrificial system God gave to Moses and the Jewish people as their means of being forgiven for their sins. That sacrificial system wasn't an end in itself but a foreshadowing of God paying the price for our sins and buying us back as redeemed people. Jesus with his sinless life was the perfect unblemished lamb laid on the altar as God's own sacrifice for his people.

There are no bystanders at the cross

Someone correctly said the crucifixion had no uninvolved observers. Everyone there was involved in what happened more than they ever realized. The Roman soldiers, the religious Pharisees, the other criminals, Jesus' mother and friends, and everyone watching were equally responsible for his death. Sound strange? Jesus died to pay for the sins of the world. All those people and all of us are sinners in God's sight and are alienated from him. Jesus died to satisfy God's righteous requirement and set us free from the penalty and power of sin. While our sins made the cross necessary, it was Jesus' never-ending unconditional love that put him willingly on that cross to die. His death is the unsurpassed definition of real love from God to us—that's you and me. We cannot stand and watch this crucifixion passively. That's our Savior doing for us what we can't do for ourselves—paying the debt for our sins and reconciling us with God our Creator and Father. God wants to have a personal encounter with us. Every time you see a picture of the crucifixion or even see a cross, think about it: He wants to remind you how much he loves you and how much he paid to give you eternal life.

Are you getting God's message?

REAL-LIFE CONNECTION: Playing-card prayers

Items needed:

- Playing card
- Pens/Markers

Give everyone a playing card from the earlier game plus a pen or marker.

Then say—

On the card draw a cross and write something you don't ever want to forget about Jesus dying on the cross for you.

MEDIA: He died on the cross for us

The Passion of the Christ movie presents a graphic, visual portrayal of what happened to Jesus as he died on the cross. Show chapter 28, 1:41:00—1:45:55. Stop the clip when Jesus says to the thief on the cross, "Today you will be with me in paradise." This image of Jesus is very bloody and painful to view, but it communicates what Jesus experienced. Ask your students to give special attention to the people in the clip who are watching Jesus on the cross. This ties into the Talking Points about no uninvolved bystanders at the cross. Talk about the reactions of different people to Jesus as he hung on the cross. Ask your group to put themselves in the scene and describe what they're seeing and feeling.

John 20:24-30

TOPIC: Redemption/love

OBJECTIVE: Students will know Jesus loves them so much that he went to the cross for them.

BACKGROUND/OVERVIEW: Thomas was absent when the disciples saw Jesus after the resurrection. Later, Thomas encountered Jesus and made his confession. Jesus blessed Thomas for seeing and believing.

GAME/ICEBREAKER: Show your scars

Ask students to tell about a scar they have, show it (if they can), and tell the story that goes with it. Warning: Keep this under control. Don't let it get too graphic or inappropriate or embarrassing for anyone. Also students may want to go on forever in a *Can you top this?* mode. Keep in mind the purpose.

ICEBREAKER QUESTIONS:

- What lesson did you learn in the acquisition of your scar?
- If you could, would you turn back the clock and change things so you didn't have the scar? Why?
- How does your scar influence what people think about you?
- How does it shape how you feel about yourself?

SCRIPTURE: John 20:24-30

Read the passage aloud while students follow along in their Bibles. Or you could have some students act out the encounter between Jesus and Thomas.

24 Now Thomas (also known as Didymus), one of the Twelve, was not with the disciples when Jesus came. 25 So the other disciples told him, "We have seen the Lord!"

But he said to them, "Unless I see the nail marks in his hands and put my finger where the nails were, and put my hand into his side, I will not believe."

26 A week later his disciples were in the house again, and Thomas was with them. Though the doors were locked, Jesus came and stood among them and said, "Peace be with you!" 27 Then he said to Thomas, "Put your finger here; see my hands. Reach out your hand and put

it into my side. Stop doubting and believe."

²⁸ Thomas said to him, "My Lord and my God!"

²⁹ Then Jesus told him, "Because you have seen me, you have believed; blessed are those who have not seen and yet have believed."

³⁰ Jesus performed many other signs in the presence of his disciples, which are not recorded in this book.

STUDY QUESTIONS:

- What do you think Thomas thought when he heard the reports from the disciples about seeing Jesus alive? How would you have responded?
- What do you think the other disciples thought about him?
- What do you think Thomas thought and felt when he saw Jesus? How would you have felt?
- What was Jesus doing to Thomas and all the observers?
- Why do you think God allowed this incident to happen? Why is it in the Bible?
- When have you asked God to show you something so you could believe? What happened?

TALKING POINTS:

Share the following points with your students:

Jesus' scars tell the story of authenticity/historicity
When Jesus showed Thomas his hands and side, the scars proved he was the one who had endured the cross. No one could deny Jesus had died and had risen again. Thomas and the others saw and touched their resurrected Savior.

Jesus' scars tell the story of redemption
When Jesus showed Thomas his hands and side, the scars proved that he, as the sinless Sacrifice, had accomplished salvation for humankind. Thomas and the others had seen Jesus die, and seeing the scars reinforced that truth—it had not been a dream or an illusion. Jesus had, indeed, been sacrificed, had given his life for them.

Jesus' scars tell the story of love
When Jesus showed Thomas his hands and side, the scars proved he loved ultimately (Romans 5:8). Seeing the scars, Thomas and the others knew

Jesus had died for them, in their place. And there he was with them again—amazing love.

REAL-LIFE CONNECTION: Remember the scars

Say to your students—

When you begin to doubt whether Jesus is real, remember eyewitness and historical accounts prove his authenticity. Thomas saw the scars in Jesus' hands and believed.

When you begin to doubt whether Jesus could save you, remember his perfect life and return from death prove he's able.

When you begin to doubt Jesus' love for you or even your own worth, remember Jesus' scars in his hands and side are proof of his infinite, limitless love for you.

MEDIA: The scars are proof

Have someone read aloud "The Orphan Girl" from *More Hot Illustrations for Youth Talks: 100 more attention-getting stories, parables, and anecdotes* by Wayne Rice (Grand Rapids, MI: Youth Specialties/Zondervan, 1995).

"The Orphan Girl" tells of a little girl rescued from a fire by a mysterious stranger who disappears into the night. The girl's grandmother is killed in the fire and she has no other living relatives, so a judge must appoint a guardian for her. After many qualified candidates offer to take her in, a burned and scarred man stands up at the back of the courtroom. The little girl runs to him and cries, "This is the man who saved me!" Because he saved her life, the judge decides the scarred man is the most qualified person to care for her. This story illustrates that Jesus is the One in whom we should put our trust because he bears the scars of our salvation.

John 21:15-17

TOPIC: The love factor

OBJECTIVE: Students will understand God loves them unconditionally. They'll realize the personal implications of his love.

BACKGROUND/OVERVIEW: After the resurrection, the disciples returned to fishing. Jesus met them on the beach and asked Peter three times (parallel to the three denials) about Peter's love for him.

GAME/ICEBREAKER: *Love Factor*
Items needed:

- Letters spelling love in several different languages
- Supplies for painting
- Props and dress-up clothes
- Digital camera

Divide into teams of five to 10. Explain that the game of *Love Factor* is about to begin. Explain that each team should come up with a name and a song together with movements to their song, which would serve as their group's team song. The song should highlight their understanding of love. Points will be given to each group for enthusiasm, creativity, good dance movements, and vocals. After a few minutes of preparation, have the teams perform.

If you have the time, then, have the teams continue the competition at the following stations:

Station One: The team is given a bag containing letters spelling *love* in several languages (Spanish, German, English, French). Their task is to unscramble the letters and form the love words.

Station Two: The team is given provisions for painting (posterboard, paint, brushes, color markers, rulers, etc.). Their task is to come up with a creative piece of art focusing on love and a slogan highlighted in the artwork.

Station Three: The team is given some props and dress clothes for a *family picture*. Their task is to pose for a photograph that displays a loving family. Be sure to have a photographer there to snap the picture.

ICEBREAKER QUESTIONS:

- What did you learn about love by playing *Love Factor*?
- What do you think might be wrong with love in the world today?
- Who has taught you the most about genuine love?
- How can you find and experience true love?

SCRIPTURE: John 21:15-17

Read the Scripture aloud to your students.

[15] When they had finished eating, Jesus said to Simon Peter, "Simon son of John, do you truly love me more than these?"
"Yes, Lord," he said, "you know that I love you."
Jesus said, "Feed my lambs."
[16] Again Jesus said, "Simon son of John, do you love me?"
He answered, "Yes, Lord, you know that I love you."
Jesus said, "Take care of my sheep."
[17] The third time he said to him, "Simon son of John, do you love me?"
Peter was hurt because Jesus asked him the third time, "Do you love me?" He said, "Lord, you know all things; you know that I love you."
Jesus said, "Feed my sheep."

STUDY QUESTIONS:

- Jesus asks Peter, "Do you love me?" Not once, not twice, but three times. Why do you think Jesus asks Peter the questions three times?
- Imagine yourself in Peter's place—how do you think you would respond?
- What did it mean for Peter to feed and take care of Jesus' lambs and sheep?
- What would that mean for you?
- What would you do for love?
- Where might love lead you?

TALKING POINTS:

Have a conversation with your students, using the following points as a guide:

Moving to a new stage

Love takes us to a new experience and stage in our walk with and service to God. Each time Peter professed to love Jesus, Jesus asked Peter to respond—specifically to feed his lambs, take care of his sheep, and feed his sheep. Each time an action was expected to flow out of the professed love. What is love if it isn't expressed or demonstrated? Every time we profess our love for Jesus Christ, is it just a love in words or do actions follow?

God moves you through the ranks

The imagery of the shepherd has been spoken of much in regard to David, who started out as a shepherd boy. We have become accustomed to hearing about Jesus as the Good Shepherd. There's a song that says "When others see a shepherd boy, God may see a king." Even though your life seems filled with ordinary activities and events, in just a moment God may touch you and change everything. Others may see a shepherd boy, but God will see a king.

Others may have seen Peter as the one who had denied Jesus. But Jesus stepped into the scene and moved Peter from the fallen to the sanctified. Even though Peter may have been grieved by the pressurized questioning of Jesus, it provided Peter with questions that drove him forward toward becoming the rock upon whom the Church would be founded. People watched the transformation from Peter the sellout, to Peter the rock of the Church.

REAL-LIFE CONNECTION: Feed the sheep

Encourage the group to put their love into action by *feeding sheep*—volunteering to do a significant chore for someone in their family or their neighborhood. This could be as simple as making breakfast, but whatever is selected must cost the individual, either in time or in money. Each youth group member is welcomed to report his love factor experience putting the love of Jesus Christ into action.

MEDIA: Love

Play the audio or video of the Black Eyed Peas song, "Where Is the Love?"— BET version. Search for this on www.youtube.com using the search words *love BET version*. Discuss with your group the love factor:

- In our culture, where is love missing?
- How can we bring love back into our lives and our culture?
- What difference will the love of Jesus coming through our lives make to change the world?

Romans 1:18-32

TOPIC: God's way made clear

OBJECTIVE: Students will know how abandoning God's intention for them leads into a downward spiral of sin and increasing depravity.

BACKGROUND/OVERVIEW: The apostle Paul was an evangelist and a theologian. He was able to explain the gospel of Jesus Christ in terms people could understand—in this letter to the Roman Christians, he explains the terrible results of sin. When we abandon the design God has for each of us the only way to go is down. Only through Jesus can we be sheltered from the wrath of God.

GAME/ICEBREAKER: Bedlam

This game requires four teams of equal size. Each team will take one corner of the room or playing field. The play area can be either square or rectangular. On a signal, each team should attempt to move as quickly as possible to the corner directly across from their corner (diagonally) performing an announced activity (that is, you tell them what to do and then give the signal to go) as they go. The first team to get all its members into its new corner wins that particular round. The first round can be simply running to the opposite corner. Afterward, mix it up with any number of possibilities: Walking backward, wheelbarrow racing (one person is the wheelbarrow), piggyback-ing, rolling somersaults, hopping on one foot, skipping, crab walking, and so forth. Mass bedlam will ensue in the center as all four teams crisscross.

ICEBREAKER QUESTIONS:

- Which of the crossing rounds was most difficult and frustrating?
- Which was the easiest of the rounds to perform? (Probable an-swer: The first round—walking.)
- What makes walking across the floor the easiest way to get across? (Probable answer: They could see where they were going, and walking was natural.)
- What in life seems as though it's more difficult than it should be or not what God intended?
- What gets in our way of doing what is right?

SCRIPTURE: Romans 1:18-32

Distribute copies of this passage and pens/pencils. Have everyone read it silently, underlining every sinful action recorded.

[18] The wrath of God is being revealed from heaven against all the godlessness and wickedness of human beings who suppress the truth by their wickedness, [19] since what may be known about God is plain to them, because God has made it plain to them. [20] For since the creation of the world God's invisible qualities—his eternal power and divine nature—have been clearly seen, being understood from what has been made, so that people are without excuse.

[21] For although they knew God, they neither glorified him as God nor gave thanks to him, but their thinking became futile and their foolish hearts were darkened. [22] Although they claimed to be wise, they became fools [23] and exchanged the glory of the immortal God for images made to look like mortal human beings and birds and animals and reptiles.

[24] Therefore God gave them over in the sinful desires of their hearts to sexual impurity for the degrading of their bodies with one another. [25] They exchanged the truth about God for a lie, and worshiped and served created things rather than the Creator—who is forever praised. Amen.

[26] Because of this, God gave them over to shameful lusts. Even their women exchanged natural sexual relations for unnatural ones.

[27]In the same way the men also abandoned natural relations with women and were inflamed with lust for one another. Men committed shameful acts with other men, and received in themselves the due penalty for their error.

[28] Furthermore, just as they did not think it worthwhile to retain the knowledge of God, so God gave them over to a depraved mind, so that they do what ought not to be done. [29] They have become filled with every kind of wickedness, evil, greed and depravity. They are full of envy, murder, strife, deceit and malice. They are gossips, [30] slanderers, God-haters, insolent, arrogant and boastful; they invent ways of doing evil; they disobey their parents; [31] they have no understanding, no fidelity, no love, no mercy. [32] Although they know God's righteous decree that those who do such things deserve death, they not only continue to do these very things but also approve of those who practice them.

STUDY QUESTIONS:

- What did you underline in the passage?
- What is God's response to the people who ignore and disobey him (v. 18)?
- How does God reveal himself to people (v. 19-20)?
- Why do you think God lets people have their own way?
- What is Paul saying happens to the hearts and minds of people who reject God?
- How are our attitudes about sexuality affected when we ignore and deny God (v. 24, 26-27)?
- When we push God out of our thinking, what evil attitudes and actions increase (v. 28-31)?

TALKING POINTS:

Share the following points with your students:

Doing things God's way

Paul leaves little doubt about how important it is to do things God's way. In fact, most Bibles title this section in Romans as "The Wrath of God" or "God's Wrath against Humankind." Many people today are very accepting of actions in direct opposition to God's Word. It's popular to accept these godless activities as acts of tolerance and ways of not being judgmental. Paul didn't believe in mincing words—he came right out and said God is against those who do things against the natural order. This is blunt and straightforward. We can't ignore it.

Look what's on the big list of sins

Paul condemns idolatry (v. 22-23), homosexuality (v. 26-27), atheism (the belief that there is no God, v. 28), wickedness, greed, envy, murder, gossip, slander, being senseless, faithless, heartless, ruthless, and more. Paul wasn't kidding around when he condemned sin and sinful actions.

One that made the list was being disobedient to parents (v. 30). What? How could Paul lump in parental disobedience with the likes of idolatry, atheism, and murder? That's because all of these things go against God's original intent for humans. God intended for people to worship only him, not things made by human hands. God made sex for one man and one woman—in marriage. God wants us to love each other and not envy, gossip, or slander. He created life and wants it honored, not taken at the hands of another person. God established family, giving parents the responsibility of rearing their children.

Why God hates sin but still loves us

God is angry. He will not—cannot—tolerate sin. Sin cuts us off from God. That is why God's wrath—his anger—is against those who embrace sin and reject the way God intended the world to be. He's *angry* at sin and how it has deceived so many when he has made it very plain what is the right way to act.

God loves us so much he tolerates our sinful choices. He continues to speak to us even when we don't want to listen—he speaks through our consciences. He reminds us of things we have read in the Bible or heard a pastor say. He shows us the glory and splendor of nature to show he cares for us even when we don't do what he created us to do.

While God is ticked off at sin, he loves sinners. Paul wrote these condemning words under the inspiration of the Holy Spirit. Early Christians experienced the same pressures to sin as you and I do today, but as Christians we have the power to live lives pleasing to God. That is precisely why Jesus left the world when he did. He said he'd send the Holy Spirit as our Advocate (see John 14:15-17), and he'd guide us into the truth.

If you want to please God and avoid his wrath, embrace God's grace and start living a life pleasing to him.

REAL-LIFE CONNECTION: Changes for life

Take a moment at the end of the meeting for some quiet reflection. Use any or all of these questions to challenge your students. Ask them to talk to another mature adult Christian this week about the changes they want to make in their lives. Then close in prayer.

- What in your life last week would convince someone watching you that you love God and are paying attention to what he wants you to do?
- What are some attitudes and actions you need in order to realign your life now that you understand how important it is to do what pleases God?
- What do you love more than God? When do you catch yourself ignoring God?
- Based on what you now know about the wrath of God against sin and the love of God for all people, how can you be a positive influence on your friends who don't know Jesus?

MEDIA: God loves us

Check out the www.visualscripture.com video "Romans 1:20" (1:19). Search using the title of the video.

Or you could use this video from Sermonspice: "Father's Love Letter" (6:00). This video paraphrases 57 Scriptures that show God's love for each of us. It offers a good balance to the Romans 1 study showing God's wrath toward sin. Go to www.sermonspice.com and use the search words *father heart love letter*.

Romans 2:17-29

TOPIC: The mark of a Christian

OBJECTIVE: Students will understand being a Christian is more than going to church, attending summer camp, or saying grace before a meal. Being a Christian, a true follower of Christ, is a heart matter, and it's all about faith.

BACKGROUND/OVERVIEW: The apostle Paul wrote Romans as a reasoned defense of Christianity. Many people embraced Christ, but struggled with the traditions of their Jewish faith and upbringing. *If Jesus was the Messiah, should I continue with my Jewish religious traditions?* was probably on the minds of many converts to Christianity. Also on their minds was the belief that non-Jews who converted to Christianity should follow Jewish tradition and become marked as Jews through circumcision. What they failed to realize was Jesus came as the supreme sacrifice required by Jewish law. His sacrifice removed the distinctions between Jewish Christians and Gentile Christians. One isn't a Christian because of some physical marking, but by a heart marked by Christ.

GAME/ICEBREAKER: **If you were under the old covenant law**
Read Leviticus 1 aloud or have students read a couple verses each until the chapter is finished.

> [1] The LORD called to Moses and spoke to him from the tent of meeting. He said, [2] "Speak to the Israelites and say to them: 'When you bring an offering to the LORD, bring as your offering an animal from either the herd or the flock.
>
> [3] "'If the offering is a burnt offering from the herd, you are to offer a male without defect. You must present it at the entrance to the tent of meeting so that you may be acceptable to the LORD. [4] You are to lay your hand on the head of the burnt offering, and it will be accepted on your behalf to make atonement for you. [5] You are to slaughter the young bull before the LORD, and then Aaron's sons the priests shall bring the blood and splash it against the sides of the altar at the entrance to the tent of meeting. [6] You are to skin the burnt offering and cut it into pieces. [7] The sons of Aaron the priest are to put fire on the altar and arrange wood on the fire. [8] Then Aaron's sons the priests shall arrange the pieces, including the head and the fat, on the wood that is burning on the altar. [9] You are to wash the internal

organs and the legs with water, and the priest is to burn all of it on the altar. It is a burnt offering, a food offering, an aroma pleasing to the LORD.

[10] "'If the offering is a burnt offering from the flock, from either the sheep or the goats, you are to offer a male without defect. [11] You are to slaughter it at the north side of the altar before the LORD, and Aaron's sons the priests shall splash its blood against the sides of the altar. [12] You are to cut it into pieces, and the priest shall arrange them, including the head and the fat, on the wood that is burning on the altar. [13] You are to wash the internal organs and the legs with water, and the priest is to bring all of them and burn them on the altar. It is a burnt offering, a food offering, an aroma pleasing to the LORD.

[14] "'If the offering to the LORD is a burnt offering of birds, you are to offer a dove or a young pigeon. [15] The priest shall bring it to the altar, wring off the head and burn it on the altar; its blood shall be drained out on the side of the altar. [16] He is to remove the crop and the feathers and throw them down east of the altar where the ashes are. [17] He shall tear it open by the wings, not dividing it completely, and then the priest shall burn it on the wood that is burning on the altar. It is a burnt offering, a food offering, an aroma pleasing to the LORD.

The object is to get the students to realize what a Jewish person had to go through to gain a *covering* for their sin under the Old Testament covenant. Use your imagination for effects or similar experiences, but be careful not to lose the students in the *grossness* of the moment!

ICEBREAKER QUESTIONS:

- **Why did God insist on animals without a blemish or mark on them?** (Answer: They were to be perfect in appearance—spotless—sinless, if you will.)
- **How do you think the person felt who had sinned and needed to present an animal for sacrifice?** (Answer: Glad to not be the one being killed for his or her sins. The sacrifice of animals was a temporary substitute to cover the person of his sin in God's eyes. Every Jew knew God had promised a supreme sacrifice that one day would totally wipe away their sins, not just cover them.)

- **How do you think the animal felt?** (Answer: Nothing, since it had no idea what was going on.)
- **How would you feel about committing a sin if you knew one of your pets would have to die because of your actions?** (Note: The objective is to get the students to realize their acts would cause suffering and death to an innocent animal.)

TRANSITION:

Say to your students—

Aren't you glad you're no longer under the old covenant where you had to bring specific sacrifices to a specific area to cover your sins? Jesus came as the final sacrifice and took our sins upon himself. Our sins are no longer simply covered, but completely removed. All we have to do is accept the work accomplished on the cross. Some, however, claim to be Christians but cling to their old ways. Let's look at a portion of Scripture that addresses this in detail.

SCRIPTURE: Romans 2:17-29

Have everyone read this passage from their Bibles.

[17] Now you, if you call yourself a Jew; if you rely on the law and boast in God; [18] if you know his will and approve of what is superior because you are instructed by the law; [19] if you are convinced that you are a guide for the blind, a light for those who are in the dark, [20] an instructor of the foolish, a teacher of infants, because you have in the law the embodiment of knowledge and truth— [21] you, then, who teach others, do you not teach yourself? You who preach against stealing, do you steal? [22] You who say that people should not commit adultery, do you commit adultery? You who abhor idols, do you rob temples? [23] You who boast in the law, do you dishonor God by breaking the law? [24] As it is written: "God's name is blasphemed among the Gentiles because of you."

[25] Circumcision has value if you observe the law, but if you break the law, you have become as though you had not been circumcised. [26] If those who are not circumcised keep the law's requirements, will they not be regarded as though they were circumcised? [27] The one who is not circumcised physically and yet obeys the law will condemn you who, even though you have the written code and circumcision, are a lawbreaker.

[28] A person is not a Jew who is one only outwardly, nor is circumcision merely outward and physical. [29] No, a person is a Jew who is one

inwardly; and circumcision is circumcision of the heart, by the Spirit, not by the written code. Such a person's praise is not from other people, but from God.

STUDY QUESTIONS:

- Verses 17-24 talk about Jews who bragged about being in a relationship with God, but did the very things they taught people not to do. What is a common word for people like this? (Answer: *Hypocrite*—"one who pretends to be what he or she is not.")
- Verse 24 uses the word "blasphemed." What are some other words for blasphemed? (Answer: *Blaspheme*—"To speak of [God or a sacred entity] in an irreverent, impious manner." Other words/ thoughts include: curse, cuss, swear, talk of or about God negatively, and act in a way that reflects negatively upon God.)
- Why was circumcision such a big deal in the Bible? (Answer: Read Genesis 17:1-14 for the first reference. It was a sign that the circumcised Jew was in covenant with God.)

TALKING POINTS:
Have a conversation with your students, using the following points as a guide:

Rules, rules, rules
At the time of Jesus, the actual sacrifice of animals was no longer a general practice. Plenty of religious laws, however, dictated how a real Jew was to act. So many of these laws had been written that no one could ever really measure up or fulfill all of them. They even dictated how many steps you could take on the Sabbath! (Sorry, Mom—can't go to church today. Cat got out and I used up all my allotted steps chasing her down the street.)

In the years following Jesus' death on the cross, many Jews turned to Christianity believing Jesus was indeed the promised Messiah—God's perfect sacrificial Lamb. Many of these Jews, however, resented the fact the Gentile Christians weren't circumcised, or marked in accordance with the Abrahamic covenant. These Jewish Christians believed that to be a true Christian, a person had to prove it through circumcision.

True believers
Paul was a Jew. In fact, he was a Jew who was hyperzealous for his beliefs (see Acts 22:1-10). But Paul realized that his faith in Jesus wasn't because of who he was or what he had done but because of who Christ Jesus is and what he

has done (Romans 6:1-14). Attending church faithfully does not make someone a Christian any more than eating a banana makes a person a monkey. Becoming a Christian is a work, done by the Holy Spirit. When God changes someone on the inside, that person dies to her old sinful ways and takes up the life of Christ, heart, soul, mind, and strength. The new believer's heart becomes circumcised, or marked, for God. People should be able to observe our lives and know we're Christ-followers just by the way we walk, talk, and act.

Walk matching the talk

The challenge is to search deep in our own hearts and determine if the way we walk with God is in name only, or if our lives are marked and changed as a result of dying to self. As Paul said in Romans 2:29, "... such a person's praise is not from other people, but from God." Don't live as a superficial Christian—one who says the right things and goes to church to impress people—live as if the only one watching you is God himself.

Not perfect, just forgiven

Are we perfect now that we've given our hearts to Christ? No, that won't happen until we die and go to heaven; however, we can do our best to live in such a way as to please God. Jesus came as the ultimate sacrificial Lamb to die for our sins. Now, instead of having to drag a goat to church for sacrifice every Sunday, all we need to do is repent of our sins and ask God for forgiveness. This is because the blood of Jesus cleanses us from all sin (Ephesians 2:13; Hebrews 12:24; 13:20; 1 John 1:7). We are free from the penalty of death.

REAL-LIFE CONNECTION: They'll know we're Christians
Ask your students the following questions:

- Think of a time when your actions didn't match your profession as a Christian. How could you have acted or reacted differently?
- Do the TV shows and movies you watch, the music you listen to, the text messages you send communicate to others you're a Christ-follower? If not, what should you do to change?
- How can you begin to change your actions so people know you're a Christian?
- What are some specific ways we can show others we're marked as Christ-ones?

MEDIA: **He died for us**

Consider watching all or parts of the movie *The Passion of the Christ*. (Make sure you secure parental permission due to the graphic nature and rating of this film.) Discuss with your students the impact the movie has on them since they know Jesus was the final sacrifice for sins. Read passages such as Isaiah 53:4-10, 52:13-14; Mark 15:16-19; Matthew 26:67; 27:26-31 showing what Jesus went through at the time of his crucifixion.

Check out the Sermonspice video "The One" (1:38). This fast-action video shows who Christ is. (Search for this video on www.sermonspice.com—use the search words *veracity project one*.)

Or you could check out the Sermonspice video "What Are Christians Known For?" (1:36). This clip asks people on the street what Christians are known for. (Search using the title of the video.)

Also take a look at this Nooma video: "*Name*" (11:00). Rob Bell talks about being our true selves. The DVD can be purchased at www.nooma.com.

Romans 3:20-28

TOPIC: The way to heaven

OBJECTIVE: Students will know that God makes the only way to heaven available to all people—through faith in his Son Jesus Christ.

BACKGROUND/OVERVIEW: Paul is writing to two audiences about how to find eternal life with God: The Gentiles who follow pagan rituals or superstitions, and the Jews, who believe keeping the law of Moses makes them righteous. Paul explains that God is providing a new way foretold by the prophets, which declares not guilty everyone who trusts in Jesus to take away their sins. Paul explains how God made this way available.

GAME/ICEBREAKER: **Cahoots**

Prepare beforehand with a student leader or adult leader. You will work together (pretending to use ESP or mental telepathy) to identify people in the room secretly selected by the group.

Introduce your associate (the person you have selected and prepared ahead of time) as someone with unusual powers of ESP. Then send this person out of the room. Next, have the group select one of their number as the *chosen one*. Bring your associate with ESP back into the room and explain that her task is to correctly identify the person chosen by the group.

This is very important: Begin by telling the group to be totally silent so your mind and your associate's can meld—so she can read your mind. Just before they get silent, ask your associate, "Are we in cahoots?" She'll answer, "No." That's when you should insist on complete silence. When it becomes quiet, look your associate in the eyes and dramatically rub your temples. During this process, some student will probably make a comment, clear his throat, or make another noise of some kind. When that happens, and you're sure your associate has the same person in mind, ask, "Are we in cahoots?" If your associate and you are on the same page concerning the noisemaking individual, she should answer yes. If not, repeat the process until you both are sure you have the same student in mind. Then you can begin. That student is the key, and your associate knows you will point to the *chosen one* two students after pointing to your key, the noisemaker.

Next, you should point at various students, one at a time (using a stance or hand motion the group may think is a signal to your associate), asking each time, "Is this the chosen one?" Your associate will answer no each time. Eventually, you point to the key person and ask, "Is this the chosen one?" The answer—no. You then point to another person and ask, "Is this the chosen one?" The answer—no. Then you point to the correct student (the second one after pointing to the key) and ask, "Is this the chosen one?" Answer—*Yes!*

Everyone will be amazed. Repeat the process. This time, of course, as you ask everyone to be quiet, someone else will make a noise and be your key—if you truly are *in cahoots.* (Note: You may also want to have a prearranged signal if the group insists you point to the *chosen one* first. This signal could be rubbing your chin, crossing your arms, or something similar.)

Do this a few times and keep them guessing and amazed. They probably won't be able to guess your secret, but they'll try.

ICEBREAKER QUESTIONS:

- What different ideas did you have about how this was working that were proved wrong?
- What was frustrating about not knowing the secret?
- In what other situations have you seen certain people chosen for an award, a team, or a specific assignment, and you can't figure out why they were chosen?
- What are some ideas people have about how God chooses those who get to go to heaven? How do we know which one is right?
- Some people say many different ways of believing or living lead to heaven. Why do you agree or disagree with that statement?

SCRIPTURE: **Romans 3:20-28**

Tell everyone to listen carefully as you read the passage aloud. They should be listening for answers to the question about how a person can get to heaven—and what won't work.

[20] Therefore no one will be declared righteous in God's sight by observing the law; rather, through the law we become conscious of our sin.

[21] But now apart from the law the righteousness of God has been made known, to which the Law and the Prophets testify. [22] This righteousness is given through faith in Jesus Christ to all who believe. There is no difference between Jew and Gentile, [23] for all have sinned and fall short of the glory of God, [24] and all are justified freely by his grace through the redemption that came by Christ Jesus. [25] God presented Christ as a sacrifice of atonement, through the shedding of his blood—to be received by faith. He did this to demonstrate his justice, because in his forbearance he had left the sins committed beforehand unpunished— [26] he did it to demonstrate his justice at the present time, so as to be just and the one who justifies those who have faith in Jesus.

²⁷ Where, then, is boasting? It is excluded. Because of what law? The law that requires works? No, because of the "law" that requires faith. ²⁸ For we maintain that a person is justified by faith apart from observing the law.

STUDY QUESTIONS:

- What is the bad news Paul writes in the passage we just read?
- What doesn't work as far as getting into heaven is concerned?
- What is the good news?
- What does the Bible say is the only way we can receive forgiveness from God?
- What makes it so difficult for many people to believe we can gain God's forgiveness by faith in Christ alone?
- Why does God offer his forgiveness and righteousness free to every person?
- What does it mean for someone to put her faith and trust in Jesus Christ?

TALKING POINTS:

Share the following points with your students:

First the bad news
Everyone has broken God's law—no one is righteous in God's eyes. Verse 23 says we're all doomed. That hits us hard. Most of us don't think we're too bad because we use the comparison method to judge ourselves: Compared with others we're better than average—surely God will give us a passing grade. Those of us who go to church and do good works for other people are the most surprised by this offer of free mercy and forgiveness. We think the reason we're doing all this church stuff is to win God's approval. Verse 22 says even the Jewish people who follow God's law so carefully are guilty, too. The message is clear: We're all doomed.

Now the good news
But verses 21-22 give us the best news ever—everyone who puts his faith and trust in Jesus Christ is declared not guilty and is forgiven. This is available to anyone, no matter what she has done. God sent his Son Jesus to take the punishment for our sins. He saves us from eternal judgment and punishment when we believe and put our faith in what Jesus did for us when he died on the cross. God's love and forgiveness are available for everyone. It cannot be purchased or earned—it's a free gift to those who believe.

The unopened gift

You would think the whole world would come running to receive this good news of forgiveness and eternal life from a loving God who paid for our sins with the life of his own Son. But people have a hard time believing this is true. This offends some self-righteous church people because God is offering forgiveness to bad people. Other nonreligious people resist God's offer because they're too proud to receive what God wants to give them. Either they don't believe they need any help, or they think they don't deserve the help after all the mistakes they have made. God's offer is waiting for them but they ignore it. What about you? How are you going to respond to God's offer?

REAL-LIFE CONNECTION: Response to God

Items needed:

- Paper
- Pens/pencils

Give the following instructions to your students:

How have you responded to God's gift? This is the biggest decision of your life. How you connect with the God who created you determines your life now and what happens to you when you leave this earth. What's your response to what he has done for you and what he offers you?

Take a piece of paper and write a response to God. It could be as short as one sentence or as long as a whole page. Tell God if you will put your trust and faith in Jesus or if you're choosing to go another way. Write your thoughts and questions to God.

Share your letter with a leader before you leave the meeting, or make a plan to show it to them sometime this week.

MEDIA: Triumph over evil

Show a scene from *The Chronicles of Narnia—The Lion, the Witch, and the Wardrobe.*

Show the end section where Aslan allows himself to be executed by the evil witch and then comes back to life and triumphs over the witch and all evil. (Chapters 17-20—1:37:50 to1:54:55.)

Or you could show the clip "Grace" (2:18) from the DVD *Case for Faith* by Lee Strobel. This clip can be found on www.wingclips.com. Search using the word *grace.*

Romans 4:1-5, 16-17, 23-25

TOPIC: Rituals or relationship?

OBJECTIVE: Students will know their salvation is based entirely on God's grace and not on good behavior.

BACKGROUND/OVERVIEW: Paul was delivering some very upsetting news to the religious Jews, who believed following the law of Moses would earn God's approval. He put Abraham on display as the prime example of being justified by faith.

GAME/ICEBREAKER: Grace-full competition
Items needed:

* Small prizes for each participant

Play three or four games with your group (relay races, push-up contest, television show trivia quiz, etc.) and award points to those who win rounds and games. When you've finished the games, total and announce the scores. But then give the same prizes to everyone who participates (no prizes to nonparticipants).

ICEBREAKER QUESTIONS:

* What was different about the games we played today?
* How did you feel about the way the prizes were awarded?
* If you did more or finished faster than someone else who tried their best, how should your prize differ from what they were awarded?
* How does God's love for someone who prays a lot differ from his love for someone who never prays?
* What role do people's actions play in determining how God rewards or punishes them?

SCRIPTURE: Romans 4:1-5, 16-17, 23-25
Choose three students to read these passages aloud from their Bibles, one student per passage.

[1] What then shall we say that Abraham, the forefather of us Jews, discovered in this matter? [2] If, in fact, Abraham was justified by works,

he had something to boast about—but not before God. [3] What does Scripture say? "Abraham believed God, and it was credited to him as righteousness."

[4] Now to anyone who works, their wages are not credited to them as a gift, but as an obligation. [5] However, to anyone who does not work but trusts God who justifies the ungodly, their faith is credited as righteousness.

[16] Therefore, the promise comes by faith, so that it may be by grace and may be guaranteed to all Abraham's offspring—not only to those who are of the law but also to those who have the faith of Abraham. He is the father of us all. [17] As it is written: "I have made you a father of many nations." He is our father in the sight of God, in whom he believed—the God who gives life to the dead and calls into being things that were not.

[23] The words "it was credited to him" were written not for him alone, [24] but also for us, to whom God will credit righteousness—for us who believe in him who raised Jesus our Lord from the dead. [25] He was delivered over to death for our sins and was raised to life for our justification.

STUDY QUESTIONS:

- What did Abraham do to have God declare him righteous?
- What does the average person think is the way to get God's approval?
- What religious rules are thought to be what God requires us to do?
- Why would faithful, religious Jews reading or hearing about being justified by faith be shocked, angry, or strongly opposed to Paul's message?
- Which nation or race are God's people?
- What makes it possible for a person to be forgiven and declared *not guilty* by God?

TALKING POINTS:

Share the following points with your students:

Nobody earns God's acceptance

God's declaration that faith makes a person righteous and accepted by God goes against what every major religion believes. That should include many Christian church attendees as well who think their church attendance, their financial giving, and their good deeds make them right in God's sight. Paul wrote this to his Jewish readers in the Roman church who believed their faithful practice of Jewish rituals and the law of Moses made them better and godlier than Gentiles (non-Jewish people). Paul started with the most revered father of the Jewish people—Abraham—who had found favor with God because he *believed* God. This message upset a lot of strongly religious people and smashed their religious ritual system.

Everyone can come to God by faith
The next earth-shaking declaration by Paul is that God wants every person to come to him by faith. This means God loves all cultures, races, and tribes equally. No people group is second-class in God's world. This was hard for traditional religious Jews to accept because they based their righteousness on their strict adherence to the extensive Jewish law. People misunderstand what God wants from us. He has always desired to bring salvation by faith to people of all nations.

We come only through Christ
Many people like to argue that we can please God and get to heaven many different ways. They strongly disagree that faith in Jesus is the only way or even that the Bible teaches salvation comes only by faith in Jesus Christ. Verses 23 through 25 tell us clearly that Abraham himself was saved only by faith and that God will accept us in the same way when we believe Jesus died for our sins and rose again to make us right with God.

REAL-LIFE CONNECTION: Believe the truth
Items needed:

- Paper
- Pens/pencils

Share with your students—
The idea that we earn our relationship with God and salvation by our good behavior is deeply imbedded in most of us. Write down these two statements:

- God cannot love you any more or any less because of your good or bad behavior. You're loved completely by God right now.
- God has given you everything when Jesus died for you. You have no reason to negotiate with God or hold back from putting your full faith in Jesus Christ.

After you have written these statements, find a friend and read them to him. Before you leave, trade your written copy with that person and ask him to read it at least five times a day this week—not to make you better for God, but to remind you to believe the truth.

MEDIA: Saved by grace

Show "Changes—Tim Curran" (2:44). One of the sport's most prolific surfers talks about how he came to know the Lord. Search for this clip on www.wingclips.com using the search words *Tim Curran*.

You can also go to YouTube and find a video version of a soloist or group singing "Were It Not for Grace," a powerful song by Larnelle Harris. Distribute the lyrics and have everyone follow along as you play the song.

Romans 5:1-5

TOPIC: Problems are good

OBJECTIVE: Students will understand that going through pain and hardship can build Christ-like character in them as they trust God and his work in their lives.

BACKGROUND/OVERVIEW: Paul was reminding the Roman church that following Jesus doesn't guarantee a protected, stress-free life. He taught that faith and Christian character develop best during hard times.

GAME/ICEBREAKER: Cup-stacker challenge
Items needed:

- Paper and plastic cup
- A computer to show a YouTube video

This is a race to stack plastic or paper cups—either by time, or in head-to-head competition. The first race is to stack 15 cups in a pyramid with five cups in a straight line on the bottom row; four on the next row; then three, two, and one. The race can be to stack them or to stack and then unstack and return them to the original position.

Another would be to see who can stack the highest tower within a time limit, with only one cup on the bottom. The cups must be stacked one on top of another.

At the end of the competition, show a video from the Internet about cup-stacking to see how it's done in serious competition. Go to www.youtube.com and type in *cup stacking competition*.

ICEBREAKER QUESTIONS:

- What's so hard about stacking cups?
- What's the secret to doing this fast?
- How did those little kids on the video get so good at something we did so slowly?
- How many failures do you think they experienced before becoming expert at cup-stacking?
- At what time in your life did you feel as though everything was falling apart? How did you get through it all?

- How does going through troubles get you stronger and more confident to face problems in the future?

SCRIPTURE: Romans 5:1-5

Have a student read the passage aloud from her Bible.

[1] Therefore, since we have been justified through faith, we have peace with God through our Lord Jesus Christ, [2] through whom we have gained access by faith into this grace in which we now stand. And we boast in the hope of the glory of God. [3] Not only so, but we also glory in our sufferings, because we know that suffering produces perseverance; [4] perseverance, character; and character, hope. [5] And hope does not put us to shame, because God's love has been poured out into our hearts through the Holy Spirit, who has been given to us.

STUDY QUESTIONS:

- In what ways can suffering, pain, and hard times produce positive results rather than negative results?
- How does God help Christians when they have problems?
- What can keep us positive and even full of joy when we're going through challenges and conflicts?
- Verses 3 and 4 say suffering produces perseverance; perseverance produces character; character produces hope. What is hope?
- How does not having hope affect a person?
- How does a person find hope?
- What is the greatest gift God has given to us?

TALKING POINTS:

Share with your students:

God's personal development plan

Knowing God isn't just about getting to heaven when you die. God forgives us and makes peace with us so he can be close to us and show us how to get the most out of life. Christ's presence in our life changes us. We start becoming like Christ, and we learn from him. And what we learn from Christ changes the world for the better. God lets us experience many problems to bring us closer to him and to help us become more like Christ.

Good problems

When we struggle and suffer, God is building patience in us. It's like building muscles—that only comes from working those muscles, by lifting weights, other exercises, and hard work. As the sign on many locker rooms reads, *"No pain—no gain"*. The problem is most of us want to avoid pain at all costs. We're also very impatient—we want what we want now! We can't stand to wait or go through pain without complaining. Being able to handle pain (to endure) is a sign of character, being strong on the inside. Having strong character means not giving up or losing our composure when bad things happen. We trust God, and our faith grows. As we live through the pain, we can be confident God is at work in us and through us and he'll work it out for the best no matter how long it takes.

Strength and confidence

This strength progression is a big part of our spiritual maturity. Our confidence in God and doing what is right grows with every life experience. It's like climbing a mountain or riding a bicycle up a hill. At first the climb seems so difficult we want to quit. But if we keep on going even though the pain is intense, we eventually get to the top. Then, when the next difficult hill comes, we're sure we can make it. Eventually we have confidence to climb longer and higher because we've experienced the positive results. When we learn to trust God, we get stronger and more confident to face our future struggles.

REAL-LIFE CONNECTION: Hope over pain

Items needed:

- Paper
- Pens/pencils
- Markers

Hand out sheets of paper and pens/pencils. Tell the group to write down the problems, pains, hard times, challenges, and struggles they have in their lives right now. When they have finished, throw out some markers and instruct them to write over top their list of problems, etc., in the largest letters possible to fill up the page. They should write *Thank You, I Trust God,* and *Give Me Hope.*

Pray together as a group about the challenges and the hope God is building in them.

MEDIA: Life struggles

Show the clip "Stay Alive" (3:02) from the movie *Cast Away*. Rescued after being stranded four years, Chuck communicates the need to survive all of life's battles. This clip is available through www.wingclips.com. Search using the words *stay alive*.

Or you could show the clip "One Day" (1:18) from the movie *We Are Marshall*. For the first time in Jack's coaching career, he realizes winning and losing don't matter, it only matters that they keep playing the game. This video clip is available through www.wingclips.com. Search using the title of the movie.

Romans 6:12-18, 23

TOPIC: Who's your master?

OBJECTIVE: Students will choose whom they'll serve, and they'll know this choice has eternal consequences.

BACKGROUND/OVERVIEW: Paul used the illustration of slavery and freedom to describe how faith in Christ can change our lives. Our sin leads us to death, but God's gift of Jesus Christ leads us to eternal life.

GAME/ICEBREAKER: It's out of my hands
Items needed:

- Four large jackets (or XXL sweatshirts with the back cut open)
- Nerf ball
- A package of 10 socks
- Children's blocks
- Oranges
- Bananas

Choose four pairs of competitors. Two of the pairs will be on one team and two on the other. The taller person in each pair will be the *head* and the shorter of the two the *hands*. Bring out four large jackets (or you could use XXL sweatshirts that have been cut open in the back). Explain that the *head* of each pair will wear a jacket backwards but without putting his arms in the sleeves—the jacket will just be buttoned or pinned around the person's neck. Then the *hands* person in each pair will stand behind his partner and put his arms through the jacket's sleeves. Bring out two card tables and place them side by side, with a little bit of room between them, each one in the diamond formation—with one corner toward the audience. Then place the competing pairs each on one side of a table, facing the audience. So table one will have one team of two pairs, half facing each other and half facing the crowd—the same with table two.

After everyone is set, explain that you have a series of tasks for them to complete. The team that completes a task first will receive 1,000 points. At the end of all the tasks, the team with the most points wins. Note: The *heads* may give instructions because the *hands* won't be able to see the table. But the *hands* must do all the handling of items. Each team of two pairs should work together.

Here are some tasks for the competing teams to complete:

- Play catch with a Nerf ball. Each person must catch the ball three times.
- Working with a stack of 10 socks, one person must sort them into the correct pairs, and the other person must roll up each pair.
- Using children's blocks, the team must build a tower in one minute—the tallest tower wins.
- Peel two oranges, eat the oranges, and make a smiley face out of the peels.
- Peel and feed each other a banana.
- (Add others if you need to and have time.)

ICEBREAKER QUESTIONS:

- (To the crowd): What made this competition funny?
- (To the *hands*): What was the most difficult task? Why? What made these tasks difficult to accomplish?
- (To the *heads*): What was the most frustrating part of this competition? How did you feel having to let someone else do the tasks while you could only watch and give instructions?
- (To everyone): What was the secret of success for the winning team?

TRANSITION:
Say—

In many ways, our little competition was an exercise in submission. The pairs of competitors had to trust and submit to each other. And, as we might expect, that could be especially frustrating for the heads who had to let the hands work and not interfere or help with their own. Submission is a choice. And Paul talks about that choice in today's passage.

SCRIPTURE: Romans 6:12-18, 23
Tell everyone to listen carefully for any words or phrases that relate to making choices or to submitting. Then read the passage aloud.

[12] Therefore do not let sin reign in your mortal body so that you obey its evil desires. [13] Do not offer any part of yourself to sin as an instrument of wickedness, but rather offer yourselves to God as those who have been brought from death to life; and offer everypart of yourself to him as an instrument of righteousness. [14] For sin shall no longer be your master, because you are not under the law, but under grace.

[15] What then? Shall we sin because we are not under the law but under grace? By no means! [16] Don't you know that when you offer yourselves to someone as obedient slaves, you are slaves of the one you obey—whether you are slaves to sin, which leads to death, or to obedience, which leads to righteousness? [17] But thanks be to God that, though you used to be slaves to sin, you have come to obey from your heart the pattern of teaching that has now claimed your allegiance. [18] You have been set free from sin and have become slaves to righteousness.

[23] For the wages of sin is death, but the gift of God is eternal life in Christ Jesus our Lord.

STUDY QUESTIONS:

- What *choosing* or *submission* words did you hear? (Note: List these on the board as they're given. You may want to read the passage aloud again and point these out: *Let, obey, offer, instruments, offer, offer, instruments, master, offer, obey, slaves, slaves, obey, slaves, obedience, slaves, obeyed, set free, slaves.*)
- Who or what determines what influences or controls a person's life?
- What choices do we have about what will be most important to us?
- What important choices does someone your age make during a year's time that strongly set the course of that person's life?
- Why is it so much easier to choose sin and doing wrong rather than following God?
- In what ways does sin and doing what is wrong destroy a person's life?
- What changes happen in people who decide to follow Christ and do what he says?

TALKING POINTS:
Have a conversation with your students using the following points as a guide:

Choosing our master
We get to decide what is most important to us—God gave us the ability to think and choose. While strong forces in the world can influence us either toward good or evil, we ultimately get to pick our own master—what we'll pursue and serve. Before Jesus came, all people were slaves to their selfish, sinful natures, but Christ's death on the cross broke the power of sin in the world.

Making the choice

Now we have the choice to embrace Christ and not let sin control our bodies and minds. Instead, we can be active and alert, seeking God in everything we do. Some people like to think no one controls them. They're their own masters. The Bible says if we think we're our own masters, we're really being controlled by sin. Without Christ we naturally follow self-centered habits and worship ourselves instead of worshipping God who created us and can bring us the fulfillment we desire.

Think about what you want your life to be. We all have dreams we want to achieve, but our laziness, procrastination, fears, greed, and selfishness can take over and make us settle for so much less. Christ in us gives us the power we need to overcome our old lifestyles and do what he wants us to do. Jesus Christ becomes our master, our boss. We submit to his leadership, his control, and do what pleases him. What pleases him is the best choice for us.

Experiencing the consequences

Our choices of whom we follow and what we do have serious consequences. Our eternal future is determined by whom we choose to serve. Verse 23 states, "For the wages of sin is death, but the gift of God is eternal life in Christ Jesus our Lord." Our choices are a life and death matter. That's no exaggeration. Don't be deceived. Now is the time to make your choice and decide who will be your master. Your life is the product of your choices starting right now. Let Jesus Christ set you free and lead you to life and freedom.

REAL-LIFE CONNECTION: Who will be your master?

Items needed:

- A sheet of paper per person
- A pencil per person
- Trashcan

Say to your students—

Divide the paper in half with a line. On one side of the line, draw symbols or write words that represent the bad choices, influences, and actions in your life right now. On the other side of the line, draw a symbol or picture of Jesus—however you think of him.

Draw yourself or write your initials on the paper where you want to be and who you want to be your master. Fold the paper on the line and tear off the half you don't want to be your master. Scrunch up the part of your life you don't want to control you and throw it away in the trash basket in the center of the room. Fold up your remaining paper and put it in your pocket to remind you of what you want most and who you want to be your master. Pray with a friend about what you want most in your life.

MEDIA: Whom will you serve?

Show the trailer for *Spider-Man 3* (1:37). Peter Parker must try to maintain his relationship with Mary Jane while battling an evil force that appears to be consuming him. Peter must choose whom he'll serve. (This clip is available on www.wingclips.com—search using the title of the movie.) This scene would be effective to use before—or as part of—the talking points. Make a point about the consequences of the choices we make regarding who or what will be our master.

Romans 7:15-19, 24-25

TOPIC: Spiritual dyslexia

OBJECTIVE: Students will understand Christians still struggle with sin, and following Christ is a lifelong process.

BACKGROUND/OVERVIEW: Paul wrote this letter to the Christians in Rome to encourage them in their personal relationship with God. We may feel like failures when we sin, but Paul explains all Christians struggle with sin, and victory over sin is available through the power of Christ.

GAME/ICEBREAKER: Extreme Simon Says

Follow the rules of Simon Says. (Everyone has to do what the leader says, but only if he or she prefaces the instruction by saying "Simon Says". Whoever does an action without that preface is eliminated.) But make the game extreme by saying the commands much faster and making them more complicated. You could say, for example, "Simon says raise your right hand while scratching your stomach with your left hand—Simon says stop scratching and hop on one foot while singing the National Anthem—Quack like a duck!—etc".

ICEBREAKER QUESTIONS:

- What makes winning at Simon Says difficult when the pressure is turned up?
- In Simon Says everyone found it difficult not to do the actions when Simon didn't say. Just like in the game, sometimes we have a hard time doing what God tells us to do. How does this game relate to you and your walk with God?
- When have you seen someone who knew what was right make the wrong choice? How did it hurt that person and others?

SCRIPTURE: Romans 7:15-19, 24-25

Have a volunteer read the passage aloud from his Bible.

[15] I do not understand what I do. For what I want to do I do not do, but what I hate I do. [16] And if I do what I do not want to do, I agree that the law is good. [17] As it is, it is no longer I myself who do it, but it is sin living in me. [18] I know that good itself does not dwell in me, that is, in my sinful nature. For I have the desire to do what is good,

but I cannot carry it out. [19] For I do not do the good I want to do, but the evil I do not want to do—this I keep on doing.

[24] What a wretched man I am! Who will rescue me from this body of death? [25] Thanks be to God, who delivers me through Jesus Christ our Lord!

So then, I myself in my mind am a slave to God's law, but in my sinful nature a slave to the law of sin.

STUDY QUESTIONS:

- According to this passage what is Paul's struggle?
- With which statements do you most identify?
- Why do Christians still struggle with sin in their lives?
- What can we do to overcome our sinful natures?
- Think of someone you know who really changed—what caused the change?
- How do you feel when you make a promise to God or tell everyone you're going to change something in your life and a short time later you're doing what you said you weren't going to do?
- What will have to happen for you to change and stop doing the things that are against God and the things that are hurting you?

TALKING POINTS:
Share the following points with your students:

Now we know
Before we came to know Christ we may have done many bad things without knowing they were wrong because everyone else did them, too. Now with Christ in our lives, we struggle because the Holy Spirit reminds us what is wrong and needs to be changed. We want to, but many times we fall back into our old habits and attitudes. Many of us have experienced that feeling of regret and shame after we have sinned.

We want to change
Sometimes that shame and regret aren't only because of the sin we've committed, but because deep down, we really didn't want to sin in the first place. Although we love God and our heart's desire is to honor him, we must also realize we all have a sinful nature. We're human beings and we're imperfect. Sometimes our physical bodies and emotions will override our

spiritual convictions. In those moments we can identify with Paul when he wrote, "For what I want to do I do not do, but what I hate I do."

We can change with Christ's help

Becoming a Christian doesn't mean we'll be perfect and never make mistakes again. Becoming like Christ is a lifelong process. And we can't become like Jesus on our own—by simply trying harder. It's impossible because sin will always get in the way. True change only comes through Christ in us; so we need to submit to him and ask him for the strength and knowledge to get through those tough times. Paul confessed his failures as a Christian and cried out for someone to rescue him and change his life. Then he exclaimed, "Thanks be to God who delivers me through Jesus Christ our Lord!"

REAL-LIFE CONNECTION: Accountable through prayer

Have everyone be quiet for a moment. Tell them to reflect on the things they seem to struggle with the most; to think of the one or two actions they keep doing that they shouldn't. Have them spend time in prayer, talking to God about those matters.

Encourage everyone to share this struggle with someone, a person who will pray for and with him and also help keep him accountable.

MEDIA: Do what is right

Show a clip from the movie *Liar, Liar* with Jim Carrey. YouTube has a good clip. Jim Carrey is Fletcher, a lawyer who gets through life by being a compulsive liar—much to his loved ones' frustrations. So on his son's birthday the boy wishes for his father to tell the truth for 24 hours. Show the clip where Fletcher tries to speak in court as a lawyer without lying. This movie is funny and illustrates Romans 7 in an opposite light. He's being forced to do what is right and fighting against it. (Caution: This movie also has some suggestive scenes. Be sure to carefully preview the scene you show.)

Romans 8:31-39

TOPIC: God's everlasting love

OBJECTIVE: As a result of this lesson, students will understand the extent of God's love for them and the security they'll have when they trust him with their lives.

BACKGROUND/OVERVIEW: When Paul wrote this letter, he hadn't yet been to Rome. So he presents a sort of theological treatise—a presentation of his understanding of God and God's plan, including the work of Christ and how believers should live. In this passage Paul assures readers of God's love and of their security in Christ.

GAME/ICEBREAKER: If you love me
Someone who has been chosen to be *It* walks up to someone else in the room and says, "If you love me, honey, smile." The second person replies, "I love you, honey, but I just can't smile" and tries to keep a straight face. If, however, that person smiles while responding, he or she becomes *It* and the process continues. *It* isn't allowed to touch the other person but can do almost anything else to get a smile (make faces, dance, etc.).

ICEBREAKER QUESTIONS:

- What are the best ways to make people in this group smile or laugh?
- How do you know if someone truly loves you?
- What are some characteristics of true love?
- When someone genuinely loves you, how does it change how you feel about yourself or your future?

TRANSITION:
Share with your students—

In our culture the word *love* gets thrown around a lot. We love swimming. We love TV shows. We love our parents. Sometimes we love our brothers and sisters. We love our pets. We love when someone does something funny. To be honest, the word has been cheapened. When the Bible talks about God's love for us, what exactly does that mean?

SCRIPTURE: Romans 8:31-39
Have four students read the passage aloud in these segments: 1—verses 31-32; 2—33-34; 3—35-37; 4—38-39.

[31] What, then, shall we say in response to these things? If God is for us, who can be against us? [32] He who did not spare his own Son, but gave him up for us all—how will he not also, along with him, graciously give us all things? [33] Who will bring any charge against those whom God has chosen? It is God who justifies. [34] Who then can condemn? No one. Christ Jesus who died—more than that, who was raised to life—is at the right hand of God and is also interceding for us. [35] Who shall separate us from the love of Christ? Shall trouble or hardship or persecution or famine or nakedness or danger or sword? [36] As it is written:

"For your sake we face death all day long;
    we are considered as sheep to be slaughtered."

[37] No, in all these things we are more than conquerors through him who loved us. [38] For I am convinced that neither death nor life, neither angels nor demons, neither the present nor the future, nor any powers, [39] neither height nor depth, nor anything else in all creation, will be able to separate us from the love of God that is in Christ Jesus our Lord.

STUDY QUESTIONS:

- What causes you to question or doubt God's love for you?
- What do you think the word *justifies* means in this passage (v. 33)? What does it mean for God to justify someone?
- In verse 36 Paul talks about facing the frightening possibilities of death, yet in verse 37 he says in all these things we're more than conquerors. How could we be more than conquerors over death?
- How do you feel when you read in verse 38 that nothing will be able to separate you from God and his love?

TALKING POINTS:

Share the following with your students:

All have fallen short

Have you ever felt like you did something that put you beyond the reach of God's love—messed up so badly you thought there was no way he could forgive you or ever love you again? Most people have felt this way! We've all fallen short of God's standards (Romans 3:23). In addition to our feeling guilty, Satan likes to get in our ear and remind us of all the bad things we have done (see Revelation 12:10).

In these climactic verses of Romans 8, Paul asks a series of rhetorical questions and offers positive responses to assure us of God's love for us and remind us of who we are in Christ.

Here are five truths from this passage God wants you to hear today:

1. <u>God is for you</u>: No matter who or what is against you, God is for you. As a follower of Christ, you will face hardships. There is no doubt about it. Jesus told his disciples following him would mean they'd face the same kind of hostile treatment he faced (John 15:18-21). Today, you can know for certain no matter what you face for the sake of Christ, God is for you. He's in your corner. He's cheering for you today.

2. <u>God has justified you</u>: When Satan accuses you and you feel condemned, remember God has declared you innocent. The word *justification* means "to declare or make righteous." Someone has said justified means just-as-if-I'd never done it. In spite of the charges brought against you by the prosecutor (Satan), the Judge (God) has handed down his judgment: Innocent. You can leave the court a free person with a clean record. Justified.

3. <u>Christ is your defense</u>: All of this is possible because when you stood in God's courtroom, you had the best defense attorney the world has ever known—Jesus. Satan brought all of his evidence into court and stacked it against you. Based on his evidence, you were guilty as charged. But the court case wasn't over yet! In a stunning move that rocked the courtroom, Jesus submitted the piece of evidence that Satan had not counted on. While the crime had indeed been committed, Jesus entered into evidence a receipt that showed the penalty for the crime had already been paid. Someone had already done the time for your crime. And that person was the lawyer himself, Jesus. You were guilty. But Jesus paid the price. He died in your place. Seeing that the mandatory sentence of death had already been carried out, God the Judge had no other choice but to set you free.

4. <u>Nothing can separate you from God's love</u>: Stunned and trying to take all of this in, we can easily be so overwhelmed that we can't believe what has happened—that we have been freed from sin. During these times Satan comes and tries to get us to doubt it is actually true. But Paul goes to great lengths to assure us that indeed it's true! And just like double jeopardy, you cannot be tried again. The decision cannot be reversed. You have been found innocent and are free because of the unending, unchanging love of God revealed in Christ Jesus. Nothing you can do, nothing you can experience, no enemy,

no circumstance, and no problem can separate you from God's love. His love even overcomes the power of death. No matter what you go through, nothing can separate you from the eternal love of the eternal God.

5. <u>You're more than a conqueror</u>: By virtue of the work of Jesus, Paul declares boldly and triumphantly you're more than a conqueror. While, at times, you will struggle and stumble and feel separated from God, at those moments you can declare the truth: Jesus has already won and made you the victor! When you fall, get up and continue to walk in his victory. You're on his side, and you're more than a conqueror. Remember the words of Paul in verse 1: "Therefore, there is now no condemnation for those who are in Christ Jesus." When Satan reminds you of your past, remind him of Jesus' work on the cross, remind him of God's judgment, and remind him of his future. He's defeated. You're more than a conqueror. Stay focused on this truth.

REAL-LIFE CONNECTION: Know the truth and live for Christ
Ask your students the following questions:

- Share a difficulty you're currently experiencing. What truth would God say to you about what you're experiencing?
- God has already won the ultimate victory, so why is life so difficult for us when we try to live for Christ?
- Think of a friend who is going through a tough time. What are some ways you can encourage her and speak God's truth into your friend's life?

MEDIA: The truth about love
Show the Sermonspice video "Love 101" (1:46). What is love? Entertain your students with this hilarious video that shows kids' perspectives on love. Search for this video on www.sermonspice.com using the words *flashlight love 101*.

Another option is the Sermonspice video "What is Love?" (:42). America answers the age-old question, What is love? Search for this video on www.sermonspice.com using the words *desert love*.

Or you can use the Sermonspice video "God's Love" (2:44). This is *God's Love Letter*—an excellent reminder of what God's love really looks like and the model of love we're to show one another. Search for this video using the words *seek first love letter*.

Romans 9:14-18, 30-32a

TOPIC: Beware of *Christianese*

OBJECTIVE: With compassion students will share the Gospel.

BACKGROUND/OVERVIEW: Paul begins this chapter by expressing his angst for his own race (the Jewish people), who were rejecting him because of his conversion to Christianity. "I have great sorrow and unceasing anguish in my heart," he says (Romans 9:2). Paul digs deeper as to why their rejection is so hard to accept: He cares deeply about them and wants them to know the love of God. Paul goes on to say he'd sacrifice his own salvation if it meant those around him could be saved (v. 3). One doesn't need to be Jewish to relate to this issue—many Christians struggle with their family and friends who reject the One they have committed their lives to. The difficult part is communicating the gospel in a way they can understand, but also in a way that speaks directly to their hearts.

GAME/ICEBREAKER: **The sun rises in the East**
Choose three people (with positive self-image and social confidence) and have them taken from the room. When they reenter, they should try to repeat the phrase "the sun rises in the East" *exactly* as each member of the group does. The catch is that everyone (except the three outsiders) will know exactly how to repeat the phrase, since you will inform them how to do so while the three are out of the room. They should say the phrase as they rise slightly from where they're sitting. To confuse the three outsiders, however, each person should add a motion different than everyone else's.

While the three are out of the room, seat everyone else in a circle, leaving three empty chairs for the outsiders. Make sure everyone understands the key motion (rising from their chair) and that they each have a way of performing it. For example: The first person could say, "The sun rises in the East," while leaning forward off his chair and drawing a circle on the ground. The second person could say, "The sun rises in the East," while sitting up and pointing across the room. The third person could say, "The sun rises in the East," while lifting both arms and rising off his chair.

When one of the outsiders has a turn, she'll repeat the phrase while trying to do the correct motion (slightly rising from their chair). If the person doesn't properly do it, the rest of the group responds, "No, it doesn't!" If the person does it correctly, everyone responds, "Yes, it does!" Continue going around in a circle until they all catch on (or you get tired of this).

ICEBREAKER QUESTIONS:

- How did you feel as an outsider, not knowing what was happening?
- Where in real life have you felt like an outsider?
- How might a visitor or non-Christian feel coming to this group?
- What might make him feel like an outsider?
- What *in* words, phrases, and expressions do we use that might make a visitor feel left out?
- Why do we use *Christianese*?

SCRIPTURE: Romans 9:14-18

Have a staff member read the passage aloud.

14 What then shall we say? Is God unjust? Not at all! 15 For he says to Moses,

> "I will have mercy on whom I have mercy,
> and I will have compassion on whom I have compassion."

16 It does not, therefore, depend on human desire or effort, but on God's mercy. 17 For Scripture says to Pharaoh: "I raised you up for this very purpose, that I might display my power in you and that my name might be proclaimed in all the earth." 18 Therefore God has mercy on whom he wants to have mercy, and he hardens whom he wants to harden.

STUDY QUESTIONS:

- Some people were accusing God of being unjust in his treatment of people. What is justice? How did Paul defend what God is doing?
- Justice is definitely a concept we learn over time and that Paul addresses in verse 14. How do you know when something is just or unjust?
- On what does salvation depend? Look at verse 16. (Answer: God's mercy.) What does that mean?

TALKING POINTS:

Share the following with your students:

Why so many questions?

Notice this particular passage starts with a question. The book of Romans has questions throughout, much like the challenging questions in chapter nine: "Shall what is formed say to him who formed it, 'Why did you make me this way?'" (v. 20) and "Who is able to resist his will?" This was a style of teaching Jesus used, and it was also effective for many rabbis. Paul was trained with this type of rabbinical teaching. It is effective because questions usually get our attention, and we're forced to think and come up with an answer.

What everyone wants
No matter what religion someone follows, every person looking for God wants compassion. But Christianity is the only religion in the world where a person doesn't have to do anything to earn it. Mercy, compassion, and our salvation are not received after doing good deeds or by checking off a list of spiritual disciplines. God is just because he offers mercy unconditionally to anyone who chooses to accept it.

No outsiders here
It's important we're aware of the way we communicate God's love to those around us. An unbeliever can become frustrated feeling like everyone around them is speaking Christianese, a language only Christians speak. We need to be careful our words and our actions reflect the mercy and compassion of God when sharing the gospel. It's not about saying the right lines or quoting the correct Scriptures, but simply about sharing the good news of Jesus Christ. Ask questions. Wait to hear what they have to say. And then simply tell them about God's love for them and all that they need to do is accept his mercy.

REAL-LIFE CONNECTION: Light your candle
Items needed:

- Glass tea-light/votive holders (one per student)
- Permanent marker
- Tea-lights (one per student)
- Index cards or paper
- Pens/pencils

Purchase glass tea-light/votive holders from your local dollar store and have your students write the name or initials of non-Christian on the outside of the glass with permanent marker. Hand out tea-lights/votive candles to the students and encourage them to light their candle each night as they pray. Challenge them to continue praying for this person daily, until the candle dies out.

Or, give each person two index cards or two slips of paper. Have each person think of someone they know who isn't a Christian and write their name or initials twice—once on each card.

Tape one card on a wall in your meeting space you will call the *Wall of Prayer*. If kids want the names to remain confidential, ask them to tape the card, name side down, against the wall. The names will come down when your students feel they've had a positive breakthrough with their person—that is, they talked with them about God; the person came to a Christian event; he or she or responded to the Lord. Keep your *Wall of Prayer* up for a month as a reminder.

The other card is for them to take home. Challenge students to pray for that person each day for the next week.

MEDIA: What language is that?
Watch a hysterical video on Christianese (2:48) on www.youtube.com. Use the search words *BADD christianese*.

Romans 10:9-13

TOPIC: Trusting God

OBJECTIVE: Students will recognize where they have been disappointed with God and why they should trust him anyway.

BACKGROUND/OVERVIEW: God made a number of promises to the Israelites in the Old Testament. The Israelites, however, failed to live up to their end of the covenant. Certainly the Jews must have wondered if God would negate his promises because of their sin. In this chapter, Paul addressed this issue, highlighting God's sovereignty and consistency and linking the past to the present and into the future. Just as God has been faithful in the past, he's faithful in the present and will be faithful in the future.

GAME/ICEBREAKER: **What's your preference?**
Items needed:

- A selection of baby food
- Spoons

Set-up: Purchase baby food and peel the labels off of each one, position them on a table, each with a designated number. Provide individual spoons for students to taste the samples.

Divide the group into *test-teams*. Explain you're conducting a survey and you want each test-team to collectively decide which baby food tastes the worst. Every person on the *team must* taste each of the samples. After everyone has made their taste tests, gather the group together and have them report their decisions.

ICEBREAKER QUESTIONS:

- Who found it difficult to participate? Why?
- How did you decide which food tasted the worst?
- What food do you now like to eat you preferred not to eat when you were younger?
- What in your life have you been forced to do that you did not like, but you now know was good for your growth and development?

SCRIPTURE: **Romans 10:9-13**

Have a student read the passage aloud from her Bible.

⁹ If you declare with your mouth, "Jesus is Lord," and believe in your heart that God raised him from the dead, you will be saved. ¹⁰ For it is with your heart that you believe and are justified, and it is with your mouth that you profess your faith and are saved. ¹¹ As Scripture says, "Anyone who believes in him will never be put to shame." ¹² For there is no difference between Jew and Gentile—the same Lord is Lord of all and richly blesses all who call on him, ¹³ for, "Everyone who calls on the name of the Lord will be saved."

STUDY QUESTIONS:

- What does the phrase "Jesus is Lord" mean? *Lord* over what?
- Why is it important to believe Jesus was raised from the dead? What difference does it make if he had been raised or not raised?
- How did God bless his people, the Jews, in the past?
- Why would this record of God keeping his promises to the Jews be good news to Gentile believers?
- Why do you think verses 12 and 13 would bring unity to the Jews and the new (Gentile) believers in Jesus? How do these verses relate and apply to you?
- When have you been disappointed with God?
- How would this Scripture help someone when experiencing trials?
- What does verse 11 promise in addition to salvation?

TALKING POINTS:

Use the following points to begin a conversation with your students:

More than a preference

Many think choosing a religion is like a taste test—people can try out a few and then choose one they think tastes the best. That may be the way people operate, but it misses the truth. Christianity isn't just one religious option among many—it's the truth. So becoming a Christian is much deeper than simply preferring one religion to another—it involves *belief* (see verse 9). The word *believe* in Greek isn't merely a way of thinking—it involves action. Other ways to describe its true meaning are "to trust in, rely on, adhere to, and obey." Even the word trust is deeper than how we use it day-to-day. It means having an unwavering confidence in what God has done for us.

Trustworthy

People fail us—promises get broken, commitments get canceled, and secrets get told. As we become accustomed to these types of failures, we can question God as well—we wonder if he'll let us down, too. When things don't turn out the way we expect and life seems to throw us curveballs, we wonder why and may doubt God's goodness. But God's love goes beyond our human understanding. He doesn't fail us as humans do and he always keeps his promises, especially the promise of salvation. God promises, "Anyone who believes in him will never be put to shame" (verse 11)—in other words, God will never let us down. Just as he faithfully kept his promises to the Israelites (see the Old Testament), he'll keep his promises to us.

REAL-LIFE CONNECTION: Call upon the Lord

Say to your students—

We experience simple pleasures daily that we trust will work for us. For instance, we turn on the shower and trust it to get warm; we turn the key and trust the engine to run in the car; when the traffic light turns red, we trust the cars will stop. When God promises us "anyone who calls upon the Lord will be saved," we trust him.

Pick a daily ritual you do (take a shower, eat breakfast, wash your hands, etc.) and commit to "calling upon the Lord" during that time for a week. You'll be amazed at all the extra time you have for prayer.

MEDIA: Faith

Get the DVD *The Case for Faith* by Lee Strobel. Select the chapters "Why Does a Good God Allow Suffering?" and "Is Jesus the Only Way?" on the main menu.

Romans 11:17-24

TOPIC: The other side

OBJECTIVE: Students will learn we're all connected to one another. When sharing the gospel we need to remember we're not better than anyone else—there is always another perspective.

BACKGROUND/OVERVIEW: In the two chapters leading up to chapter 11, Paul described his struggle with the fact that the Jews weren't accepting Christ. Paul reminded the Jews of their history and had them reflect on God's faithfulness to them, generation after generation. Did the Lord ever give up on them? No. They just needed to look at life from a different perspective.

GAME/ICEBREAKER: **Shuffle your buns**

Create a circle of chairs that matches the number of people in your group. Select a student to stand in the middle of the circle, leaving his chair empty, while everyone else remains seated. At your signal, the person in the middle will try to sit in the empty chair, while those seated try to prevent that by shuffling from seat to seat (clockwise) quite quickly. (Note: Students are not allowed to lock arms.) When the person in the middle succeeds in sitting down, the person to his right must go into the middle. You can add interest to this by yelling "switch" every now and then to signal a change in the direction of the shuffling. With a large group, place two people in the middle, and leave two chairs empty.

ICEBREAKER QUESTIONS:

- What does it feel like to be the person in the *middle?*
- What did you have to do to get a seat?
- When have you felt left out in a social situation or conversation? What did you have to do to be heard?
- When did you think you were right about something and had to push until people agreed or could, at least, see your point?
- When did that happen in reverse—that is, you were thinking one way and someone convinced you to look at it differently?
- How might pride get in the way of someone changing her mind, resolving an issue, or making a decision?

SCRIPTURE: Romans 11:17-24

Make sure everyone has a copy of this passage and have them read it individually. Tell them to underline any confusing passages.

[17] If some of the branches have been broken off, and you, though a wild olive shoot, have been grafted in among the others and now share in the nourishing sap from the olive root, [18] do not consider yourself to be superior to those other branches. If you do, consider this: You do not support the root, but the root supports you. [19] You will say then, "Branches were broken off so that I could be grafted in." [20] Granted. But they were broken off because of unbelief, and you stand by faith. Do not be arrogant, but tremble. [21] For if God did not spare the natural branches, he will not spare you either.

[22] Consider therefore the kindness and sternness of God: sternness to those who fell, but kindness to you, provided that you continue in his kindness. Otherwise, you also will be cut off. [23] And if they do not persist in unbelief, they will be grafted in, for God is able to graft them in again. [24] After all, if you were cut out of an olive tree that is wild by nature, and contrary to nature were grafted into a cultivated olive tree, how much more readily will these, the natural branches, be grafted into their own olive tree!

STUDY QUESTIONS: Begin by having students read the passages they underlined. Then explain them, using a commentary or study Bible (e.g., *Life Application Study Bible*) as a resource.

- As a child, who was your hero? Why that person or character? How did your desire to be like that person change you or help you grow?
- Who is one of your Bible heroes? In what ways does that person's example/story affect your life?
- Paul was dealing with the converted Jews who thought they were better than the Gentile Christians (people who weren't born Jews). How does the idea of grafting a branch onto a tree affect their thinking about accepting people different than they are?
- When do Christians think they're better than others?
- When has stubbornness or pride interfered with one of your relationships? (Give a personal example.)
- In what ways can stubbornness and pride harm our witness to unbelievers?

TALKING POINTS:
Share the following points with your students:

We are all connected
Grafting is a technique used by orchard farmers to help increase a tree's potential in bearing more fruit. Botanists may also use grafting to produce more flowers on a plant. In this process the farmer or florist attaches the branch from one plant to another. It is most commonly used for the propagation of trees and shrubs grown commercially. In most cases, one plant is selected for its roots, and this is called the *stock*. The other plant is selected for its stems, leaves, flowers, or fruits.

Paul uses grafting as an analogy to new Christians being connected to the Jewish faith/history with the Lord Jesus Christ as the root.

Growing in our faith
We talk openly about what we enjoy and appreciate—our friends, our recent vacation, the latest song, movie, TV show, sporting event...We also continue to tell people about personal interests and influences—hobbies, courses of study, career plans...As we grow and mature, so do those topics—consider the difference in the interests of a fourth-grader from a high school senior. Talking about our personal faith is a lot like sharing about our interests and what we like. At least, it should be. Because our faith is real, it should be growing. Not simply a one-time experience, our faith should be changing and growing over time. An important part of that growth is trust. Trusting the Lord gives meaning to our past, a purpose to our present, and a hope for the future.

Being overzealous when sharing the gospel
The best thing we can do is to love non-Christians the way Paul did. Paul didn't push the idea of Jesus being the Messiah on his Jewish colleagues but spoke to them with familiar stories referring to their personal faith—he showed them the ways they were already connected to Christ. He didn't push his beliefs on them. He talked about it so enthusiastically they wanted to know why it was important to him.

REAL-LIFE CONNECTION: A penny for your faith
Items needed:

- A penny for each student

Give each student a penny and remind them there are two sides to the coin. Both sides are very different, but they have something in common—they're part of the same coin. That is how we are with people. All of us are created by God, for God, and we all need God. We should never consider ourselves greater than others.

MEDIA: Don't do it that way!

Show "Bad Evangelism" or "10 Ways Not to Evangelize" on www.youtube. com. Search for these using the titles of the videos.

Romans 12:1-2

TOPIC: Don't conform...transform

OBJECTIVE: Students will be able to understand they have a choice to actively conform to the world or transform with the power of Christ. They'll begin to grasp what it means to renew one's mind and will reach out for God's help as they do this.

BACKGROUND/OVERVIEW: Paul is writing to those living in Roman society who are having trouble letting go of Greco-Roman traditions and living a new life in Christ. Paul encourages them in this chapter to take a stand, make a choice, and be utterly changed through God's power and personal conviction.

GAME/ICEBREAKER: Freestyle poem

Send around two different sheets of paper. On one write TO TRANSFORM IS TO... and on the other write TO CONFORM IS TO.... Pass the papers around in opposite directions so eventually each student will receive both pieces of paper. Ask a student to write a freestyle line of poetry (doesn't have to rhyme!) underneath the line you have already written. Then have them fold the paper so only the line they have written is visible—the one you have written should now be concealed. Have each student write an additional line and refold the paper in the same way so each person only views the line above theirs before adding their own. After both papers have gone around the room, have one student unfold both of them and read them out loud. This is a fun and interesting way to gain insight into what your students feel about what it means to conform or transform.

ICEBREAKER QUESTIONS:

- What was the most interesting line of poetry you heard?
- According to the poetry everyone wrote, what are some feelings we have about conforming and transforming?
- What in this world do we conform to that is negative and hurts us?

SCRIPTURE: Romans 12:1-2

Have three or four students read this aloud from their Bibles, one person after another.

¹ Therefore, I urge you, brothers and sisters, in view of God's mercy, to offer your bodies as a living sacrifice, holy and pleasing to God—this is true worship. ² Do not conform to the pattern of this world, but be transformed by the renewing of your mind. Then you will be able to test and approve what God's will is—his good, pleasing and perfect will.

STUDY QUESTIONS:

- In your own words, what does it mean to conform or transform? Which is easier? Why?
- What does Paul's statement "renewing of your mind" have to do with being transformed?
- Many Christians attempt to worship God and live for God while conforming to the secular standards of their culture. How do you think the Roman community was doing this? How do we do this?
- Why is it worthwhile to be transformed in Christ?
- How can a person be *transformed?* (Answer: By staying close to God, submitting to his Lordship and leadership, choosing to live his way [obeying], and living in community with other believers [church, small group, etc.] for encouragement and accountability.)
- Being transformed is often demanding and takes a long time, while conforming to what someone else is doing might take only a few minutes. What first transformation steps can we take today?

TALKING POINTS:

Share the following points with your students:

We all experience trouble

We all have trouble with spiritual transformation, but it doesn't mean we're unable to transform. We know we need to change, but it seems to be so difficult. The Bible says we can do it through Christ's power in us and through us.

Your transformation story

Share a personal story or illustration about conforming and transforming to open the discussion. Ask students to share examples of times they find it easier to conform (for example, in stressful situations, under peer pressure, etc.). Then ask for volunteers to share their steps in transformation.

Make a choice

In spite of how difficult it seems to choose to transform, we make difficult choices every day. It is well within our grasp to make the choice to transform. Every day we make choices when we exercise, study, hangout with friends, eat, learn to play an instrument, find entertainment, read, talk to others about others, relate to parents, and on and on. Our choices today determine what we'll be like tomorrow. But we don't have to go it alone. Christ is with us through the Holy Spirit to help us along the road to transformation.

REAL-LIFE CONNECTION: Blue or red?
Items needed:

- Computer to watch YouTube
- Red and blue M&Ms
- Paper
- Pens/pencils

Watch the "Blue Pill or Red Pill" (4:05) clip from *The Matrix*. Go to www.youtube.com and use the search words *matrix the pill*.

Afterward, give each student a red and a blue M&M. Tell them, if they choose the blue M&M they're choosing to wake up tomorrow, unchanged, as if nothing has happened today. They'll live life as they have been doing, but fail to understand the truth, about themselves, God, and the world. If they choose to eat the red M&M they'll be choosing to actively transform. They can't go back. From now on they're choosing to be open to the truth, to transform through God's power. Remind them they can only pick one.

Give students a blank piece of paper and a pen or pencil. Ask them to journal for five minutes about the choice they're about to make.

Ask them to choose. Close in prayer.

MEDIA: What will you choose?
See *The Matrix* video instructions (above in Real-life Connection).

Romans 13:1-7

TOPIC: I'm young, and I vote

OBJECTIVE: Students will know how a Christian is to support the government under which they live.

BACKGROUND/OVERVIEW: Paul wrote this letter instructing people to participate in the government and support the leaders even if they're not Christians. This passage is referred to often and is used to encourage people who are living under an oppressive government.

GAME/ICEBREAKER: Name that government leader
Make a PowerPoint show with photos of 10-20 elected national, state, and local government officials. If it's election season show all the candidates vying to be elected.

Conduct a written test to see if they can name the people they see on the screen. Go over the results and award a prize.

You could make this a team event with each team providing a competitor for each question. You ask a question such as, *Who is our national vice president?* and the first competitor to jump up and give the correct answer wins point for his or her team. Continue with new competitors for each question for a total of 10-20 questions about the identities of government officials.

ICEBREAKER QUESTIONS:

- Why do we have trouble identifying our government leaders?
- Who are your top three favorite government leaders? What do you like about them?
- What question would you ask any government leader of your choice?
- Do you see the government and our elected leaders as positive or negative? Explain.
- Which do you think is most effective in bringing change: Protesting against government leaders or praying for them? Explain.

SCRIPTURE: Romans 13:1-7
Have a student read the passage aloud from his Bible.

[1] Let everyone be subject to the governing authorities, for there is no authority except that which God has established. The authorities that

exist have been established by God. [2] Consequently, whoever rebels against the authority is rebelling against what God has instituted, and those who do so will bring judgment on themselves. [3] For rulers hold no terror for those who do right, but for those who do wrong. Do you want to be free from fear of the one in authority? Then do what is right and you will be commended. [4] For the one in authority is God's servant for your good. But if you do wrong, be afraid, for rulers do not bear the sword for no reason. They are God's servants, agents of wrath to bring punishment on the wrongdoer. [5] Therefore, it is necessary to submit to the authorities, not only because of possible punishment but also as a matter of conscience.

[6] This is also why you pay taxes, for the authorities are God's servants, who give their full time to governing. [7] Give to everyone what you owe: If you owe taxes, pay taxes; if revenue, then revenue; if respect, then respect; if honor, then honor.

STUDY QUESTIONS:

- What do you think about our government and how it serves the people?
- How is the legitimacy of any government connected to God?
- What should be a Christian's response to the laws and leadership of government?
- For what reason might a Christian disobey the laws of a government?
- What can Christians do to support the ruling government?

TALKING POINTS:
Share the following points with your students:

What is a responsible citizen?
The Romans 13 passage makes it clear Christians should pray for their government leaders, regardless of their laws and policies. We are to live upstanding lives, pay our taxes, and participate in the government system. Remember, this letter was written to people who lived under the oppressive Roman government—an absolute dictatorship. In a democracy Christians are to vote and express their political views as they have opportunity. They're to set a positive example for their nation.

Challenge government policy
The only time a Christian should disobey the laws of the government is when the human laws and authorities force a Christian to break God's laws.

Christians don't disobey the law as a matter of personal opinion, but only when they're forced by the government to go against what the Bible teaches—to violate or deny their faith. When they have reason to stand up to the government laws, they may suffer dire consequences—including being sent to prison. As Peter told the Roman officials, "We must obey God rather than human beings" (Acts 5:29). The focus should be put on lifting up Jesus Christ and obeying him.

Trust God

The confidence a Christian has about a bad government is that God is still in control and will still work through even the worst government to make his message of salvation, reconciliation, and eternal life known to everyone. God will bring judgment and punishment when it's necessary in his divine time plan. God will be with his minority and persecuted people. God will use even the most tragic events to reveal the truth to people.

REAL-LIFE CONNECTION: In God we trust

Items needed:

- Lists of government officials
- Paper
- Pens/pencils
- Envelopes

Distribute lists of government leaders and paper, pens, and envelopes. Tell the students to write at least one letter to a government leader. Suggest they express their faith and trust in God and in the government. They should tell the government leaders about their commitment to pray for them. They should also express how they feel about the status of the city, state, or nation. After everyone has finished, collect the letters. Be sure to mail them the next day.

MEDIA: Political campaign

Look for political campaign messages on www.youtube.com. Select a few your students would be most interested in and show them. (Make sure to select some with opposite viewpoints.) Ask students how the video campaign message affected them—did it change their mind or sway their vote? Ask what type of political video a Christian should produce or support.

Romans 14

TOPIC: The weak and the strong

OBJECTIVE: Students will begin to accept into their group Christians who may seem weak or different and will be aware of those with more sensitive consciences.

BACKGROUND/OVERVIEW: Nearing the end of his letter to the Christians in Rome, Paul talks about accepting and working with fellow believers. Some Christians thought food sacrificed to idols was totally evil and should not be eaten. Others found the meat to be in excellent shape and at a bargain price and so they bought it. Disagreements followed with one side accusing the other of not being spiritual. Paul pleads that these *minor* things should not divide the body of Christ.

GAME/ICEBREAKER: Artist or no artist
Items needed:
- Paper
- Art supplies
- Small prizes

Distribute 8.5x11" sheets of paper. Have a collection of pencils, pens, or crayons available. Get a volunteer leader to pose in front and have all the students draw a picture of the poser, concentrating only on the head. Give 5-10 minutes to complete these drawings. Collect the works of art and hang them up on a wall for all to see. Some of your kids are bound to have some pretty good talent while others would have a hard time drawing a stick figure. Decide by affirmation the best of show and the worst of show and give an equal prize to *both* students (candy bar, can of soda, CD, etc.).

ICEBREAKER QUESTIONS:
Hold the winning and losing portraits side by side. There will be a noticeable difference between them.

- **Why did you choose this winner and this loser? What was the basis of your decision?**
- **Is your decision objective or subjective? Explain.** (This question might lead into a brief discussion about opinions and perspectives. As the old saying goes, "One person's trash is another person's treasure." Go with this if you have time.)

- **Why don't you think less of the losing artist as a person because she could not draw as well as the winning artist?** (Note: Some will joke around, but the truth is they won't think less of the non-artist just because of her lack of talent.)

TRANSITION:

Say to your students—

The first Christians in Rome struggled with similar situations. Some believers did things other believers didn't do. Because of that, some thought they were stronger Christians and tended to look down on others as being weaker in the faith. Let's read Romans, chapter 14, to hear what Paul had to say about this matter.

SCRIPTURE: Romans 14

Have a series of students read the chapter aloud from their Bibles, with each student taking a paragraph—while everyone else follows along.

> [1] Accept those whose faith is weak, without quarreling over disputable matters. [2] One person's faith allows them to eat everything, but another person, whose faith is weak, eats only vegetables. [3] The one who eats everything must not treat with contempt the one who does not, and the one who does not eat everything must not judge the one who does, for God has accepted that person. [4] Who are you to judge someone else's servant? To their own master they stand or fall. And they will stand, for the Lord is able to make them stand.
>
> [5] Some consider one day more sacred than another; others consider every day alike. Everyone should be fully convinced in their own mind. [6] Those who regard one day as special do so to the Lord. Those who eat meat do so to the Lord, for they give thanks to God; and those who abstain do so to the Lord and give thanks to God. [7] For we do not live to ourselves alone and we do not die to ourselves alone. [8] If we live, we live to the Lord; and if we die, we die to the Lord. So, whether we live or die, we belong to the Lord. [9] For this very reason, Christ died and returned to life so that he might be the Lord of both the dead and the living.
>
> [10] You, then, why do you judge your brother or sister? Or why do you treat your brother or sister with contempt? For we will all stand before God's judgment seat. [11] It is written:
> "'As surely as I live,' says the Lord,
> 'every knee will bow before me; every tongue will confess to God.'"

[12] So then, we will all give an account of ourselves to God.

[13] Therefore let us stop passing judgment on one another. Instead, make up your mind not to put any stumbling block or obstacle in the way of a brother or sister. [14] I am convinced, being fully persuaded in the Lord Jesus, that nothing is unclean in itself. But if anyone regards something as unclean, then for that person it is unclean. [15] If your brother or sister is distressed because of what you eat, you are no longer acting in love. Do not by your eating destroy your brother or sister for whom Christ died. [16] Therefore do not let what you know is good be spoken of as evil. [17] For the kingdom of God is not a matter of eating and drinking, but of righteousness, peace and joy in the Holy Spirit, [18] because anyone who serves Christ in this way is pleasing to God and receives human approval.

[19] Let us therefore make every effort to do what leads to peace and to mutual edification. [20] Do not destroy the work of God for the sake of food. All food is clean, but it is wrong for a person to eat anything that causes someone else to stumble. [21] It is better not to eat meat or drink wine or to do anything else that will cause your brother or sister to fall.

[22] So whatever you believe about these things keep between yourself and God. Blessed are those who do not condemn themselves by what they approve. [23] But those who have doubts are condemned if they eat, because their eating is not from faith; and everything that does not come from faith is sin.

STUDY QUESTIONS:

- **What are some areas where Christians have differences in their faith or practices today?** (Answers: Attending church a different day of the week, using hymns instead of contemporary music, dressing differently, not using make-up, having different hairstyles, etc.)
- **What behaviors might be considered a "stumbling block or obstacle" (v. 13) in some Christian circles?** (Answers: Drinking alcoholic beverages, dancing, smoking, having tattoos or piercings, etc.)
- **What makes some Christians criticize or look down on other Christians or churches?**
- **Do you think Paul is legitimizing any type of behavior in verse 22?** (Answer: No. We must always consider all of Scripture. Paul isn't condoning sin. He doesn't mean if you believe in premarital sex it's okay for you. He's only referring to things not directly condemned in Scrip-

ture—like honoring a particular day of the week as holy, eating meat sacrificed to idols, etc.)

- How does a Christian decide what is an important rule that shouldn't be broken and what isn't important for other people who are Christians?

TALKING POINTS:
Share the following points:

One-on-one challenge
Michael Jordan was arguably the greatest talent to ever grace a basketball court. In addition to his ability to dunk like nobody else, he could also shoot from any distance and was a textbook example of a defensive player. No doubt Michael could play! If His Airness walked in this room and challenged you to a game of one-on-one, would you be up to the challenge? If he wanted to, he could probably hold you to zero points, but my guess is Michael would go fairly easy on you and probably let you drive past him and make a shot or two. Oh, he'd win, for sure, but you would both have some fun at it. Michael would not look down on you as a lesser human being because you can't play at his level. Jordan made many NBA players look like the last kid chosen at a playground basketball game. He'd realize you don't have the practice, knowledge, skills and abilities he does, but that wouldn't make you less of a person in his eyes.

Different opinions among Christians on non-biblical issues
The apostle Paul was a brilliant scholar. He could debate with the best of them and would often win his arguments—a couple times the losers were so sore they stoned Paul and drove him out of their towns. Yet Paul tells us to go easy on those who are not as strong in their faith as we might be.

Some Christians don't believe in dating. Instead, they think we're supposed to wait until that special someone appears and then get married—they court instead of date. Nothing is wrong with this approach. It works for some but not for others. However, Scripture does not explicitly dictate this type of romance as the only way to find your mate. As such, if you (and your parents) are in agreement that you may date people, that should be fine. But be careful not to think less of your friends who believe in courting as the only way. Respect their decision to go the non dating route.

It doesn't mean the person who believes in courting is any less of a Christian. That's not what Paul was saying. Some people firmly believe in a particular way of finding their spouse, and that's between them and God. If you don't believe that way, don't let that get between your friendships or relationships with fellow believers. They might think you are the weaker

Christian for entering the dating scene!

Dancing is another great divide between Christians. Some believe it's okay as long as it isn't suggestive and sexual in style. Others feel dancing is of the devil and should not be condoned at all. Don't let it bug you—it's a minor issue when you look at the big picture.

Be at peace with others

Paul basically says to make an effort to be at peace with those who don't believe exactly as you do (v. 19). We should not be in the practice of judging fellow believers in nonessential matters. The greater good of the body of Christ is at stake. How can we live in peace and love each other if we decide to ignore those who don't believe exactly as we do? We can agree to disagree and still be friends. Paul summed it up in his letter to the church at Ephesus when he said, "Make every effort to keep the unity of the Spirit through the bond of peace" (Ephesians 4:3).

REAL-LIFE CONNECTION: Christian brothers and sisters

Ask your students—

Think of anyone you may have looked down on because they may not believe as strongly as you do in some way. What attitude have you had toward them? Have you spoken negatively to others about them? What can you do to change your attitude?

Tell them—

Pray, asking God to forgive you for how you have treated other Christians. Go to Christians you have hurt, spoken negatively about, or ignored, and with humility explain what you have done and ask for their forgiveness. If possible, do something with that person during the next week to show your sincerity and start to build a friendship with them despite your differences.

MEDIA: We're Christians

Consider using one of the following videos from www.sermonspice.com. Search for the videos by the titles of the clips:

"A Body United" (3:29). This video talks about the divisions of church denominations and how we can come together as one.

"The Power of Unity" (1:25). This video illustrates unity using the process of making a cup of coffee.

"Road Music" (4:00). This humorous video highlights an argument over something as silly as music.

Romans 15:1-7

TOPIC: Friends beyond boundaries

OBJECTIVE: Students will decide to break out of exclusive groups of Christian friends and get to know someone new and different.

BACKGROUND/OVERVIEW: The gospel of Jesus Christ rearranged the social contacts of members of the new church in Rome. Believers became close friends with people from all races and all economic levels of society. The new church stood out like a bright light in an empire that treated people according to power, race, gender, and economics.

GAME/ICEBREAKER: Common Bonds
Distribute a sheet of Common Bond statements with pencils and have people get signatures of others to whom the statements apply. If your group is small, read the statements aloud and find out who has what in common.
Possible statements (add others):

- I share your birth month.
- I have the same hair color.
- I like the same music groups.
- I want to own the same type of car.
- I have the same first, middle, or last name.
- I like the same kind of dessert.
- I am in the same mood you are right now.

ICEBREAKER QUESTIONS:

- What month has the most birthdays in our group?
- What music group is most popular among people here?
- What new common interests did you find with people here today that surprised you?
- How would you describe our group based on this exercise—are we a lot like each other or very different from each other? Explain.

TRANSITION:
Say—
We are going to talk about a common tendency with many people. They like to hang out with people who are just like them. It's our nature

to become so comfortable with our group of friends that we give our time to being with them and make little effort to get to know other people, especially people different from us. Some people call this a clique—a tight friendship with an invisible wall that keeps others out. It happens in all cultures and countries, but God doesn't want people to live this way. Listen to how the Bible describes how we're to relate to other people.

SCRIPTURE: Romans 15:1-7

Have a student read the passage aloud from her Bible while everyone follows along.

[1] We who are strong ought to bear with the failings of the weak and not to please ourselves. [2] We should all please our neighbors for their good, to build them up. [3] For even Christ did not please himself but, as it is written: "The insults of those who insult you have fallen on me." [4] For everything that was written in the past was written to teach us, so that through the endurance taught in Scriptures and the encouragement they provide we might have hope.

[5] May the God who gives endurance and encouragement give you the same attitude of mind toward each other that Christ Jesus had, [6] so that with one mind and one voice you may glorify the God and Father of our Lord Jesus Christ.

[7] Accept one another, then, just as Christ accepted you, in order to bring praise to God.

STUDY QUESTIONS:

- What does this passage teach about relationships (see especially verses 1, 2, 5, and 7)?
- Verse 7 talks a lot about acceptance. What does it mean to accept another person or be accepted by someone else?
- What type of person do you find difficult to accept?
- How does God's acceptance of us influence and guide our acceptance of others?
- Is there anyone in your life you are friends with now whom you once thought would never be your friend? Who is it?
- What did both of you do to make that happen?
- When do you feel real unity with people in this group or with others in your school?

TALKING POINTS:
Share with your students:

Fear keeps us away from people who are different
We all grow up believing some stereotypes about people who are different from us. Most of those generalizations are not true, but we believe them because we don't have any personal experiences with those people. We are afraid of how they might treat us or what they think about us. Sometimes we feel superior to them. Sometimes we feel inferior. We can't believe we'd ever feel comfortable with them.

Christians don't tolerate other people—they accept them
Today we hear lots of talk about tolerating people who are different from us. God doesn't want us to be tolerant—he wants us to reach out and accept those people—because he created them in his image, he loves them, and Christ died for them. Acceptance means welcoming them into your life and into your group of friends. It requires time together and openness to new experiences and personal questions. People feel accepted when they know they can be honest and still be loved. They know their new friend is being honest with them even when they don't agree. The friendship grows strong as they support each other no matter what less-accepting people say about them.

Everybody has a story
Getting to know someone means knowing his story. Listening carefully and asking questions lets your personal connection grow deep. Knowing a story different from your story enriches your life and helps you understand the many experiences and concerns you have in common. A strong friendship keeps growing as the story keeps on happening and being shared. The best glue between friends is a shared faith in Jesus Christ. Learn each other's story about how you found Jesus, and encourage each other to keep growing in Christ. Christians who love and accept each other can look very different on the outside. Inside they share a deep love for Jesus.

REAL-LIFE CONNECTION: Friendship challenge
Challenge the group to each make one new friend this year with someone from a different race, culture, or school group. The goal is to get to know the person and build a real friendship. During the next month challenge the students to work on stretching their friendship circle by spending some good time together with their new friends when they can hear each other's stories. A big part of understanding someone is getting to know that person's family.

Suggest they invite their new friends to their homes for a regular meal. The idea is to let the new friend see the family in action.

MEDIA: Everyone needs somebody

Show the clip "Welcome" (2:46) from the movie *Antwone Fisher*. After Antwone finds his deceased father's family, they throw him a surprise welcome party to accept him into their family. This video clip shows the power of acceptance to someone who feels alone and rejected.

Show the clip "Wilson" (3:03) from the movie *Cast Away*. As Chuck sets out on his man-made raft, he loses his volleyball companion, Wilson. Chuck's relationship with Wilson is part harrowing and part humorous, but it shows how desperately we need a friend and companion.

Both of these clips are available from www.wingclips.com. Search for each one using the title of the clip.

Romans 16:1-16

TOPIC: The power of real friends

OBJECTIVE: Students will know being a disciple of Jesus Christ isn't a solitary experience but rather an expanding network of relationships built on love and commitment to bringing Christ to the world.

BACKGROUND/OVERVIEW: The apostle Paul wraps up this letter to the Romans with a long list of special people who give, sacrifice, help, and inspire him. Paul expresses his gratitude and appreciation to these people who have done so much for him.

GAME/ICEBREAKER: Friendship Skits

Break the group into teams with four people each and tell them they're to create and perform a skit or a mime depicting how people build strong friendships and how those friendships bring them happiness and satisfaction. Give each group four cards with a quality of real friendship written on each card. The group should incorporate the four qualities of friendship in their skit. Here are some suggested friendship qualities: Accepting, giving help, treating someone like a family member, sacrificing, loving, risking their life to save them, sharing similar beliefs, respecting each other, going through tough times together, visiting them when they're in trouble or discouraged, sharing what they have, encouraging, talking, and listening. So, for example, if one team was given the qualities of *respecting each other, visiting them when they're in trouble, giving help,* and *listening,* their task would be to create and perform a friendship skit based on those qualities.

Give the groups 10 minutes to prepare their skits. Call on groups to present their skits to the whole group.

ICEBREAKER QUESTIONS:

- What did you see in these skits that showed the real meaning of friendship?
- What is the difference between a person being someone you know and that person being a true friend?
- What could someone do that would make you want to be that person's friend?
- How many real friends do most people have?
- How many real friends do you want to have during your life?

SCRIPTURE: **Romans 16:1-16**

Distribute index cards and pens/pencils. Tell everyone to write all the names of people mentioned in the passage as you read the passage aloud.

[1] I commend to you our sister Phoebe, a deacon of the church in Cenchreae. [2] I ask you to receive her in the Lord in a way worthy of his people and to give her any help she may need from you, for she has been the benefactor of many people, including me.

[3] Greet Priscilla and Aquila, my co-workers in Christ Jesus. [4] They risked their lives for me. Not only I but all the churches of the Gentiles are grateful to them.
[5] Greet also the church that meets at their house.
Greet my dear friend Epenetus, who was the first convert to Christ in the province of Asia.

[6] Greet Mary, who worked very hard for you.

[7] Greet Andronicus and Junia, my fellow Jews who have been in prison with me. They are outstanding among the apostles, and they were in Christ before I was.

[8] Greet Ampliatus, my dear friend in the Lord.

[9] Greet Urbanus, our co-worker in Christ, and my dear friend Stachys.

[10] Greet Apelles, whose fidelity to Christ has stood the test.
Greet those who belong to the household of Aristobulus.

[11] Greet Herodion, my fellow Jew.
Greet those in the household of Narcissus who are in the Lord.

[12] Greet Tryphena and Tryphosa, those women who work hard in the Lord.
Greet my dear friend Persis, another woman who has worked very hard in the Lord.

[13] Greet Rufus, chosen in the Lord, and his mother, who has been a mother to me, too.

[14] Greet Asyncritus, Phlegon, Hermes, Patrobas, Hermas and the other brothers and sisters with them.

¹⁵ Greet Philologus, Julia, Nereus and his sister, and Olympas and all the Lord's people who are with them.

¹⁶ Greet one another with a holy kiss.

All the churches of Christ send greetings.

STUDY QUESTIONS:

- Of what value is this last chapter of Romans?
- What opinion do you form about the apostle Paul reading this chapter? What is he like?
- Help us make a list of what people did to help Paul and others. Whom did you have on your list?
- What actions can you remember that Paul is thanking them for doing?
- How did the actions of these people strengthen Paul's faith?
- Who has helped you and how did that person's actions strengthen your faith?

TALKING POINTS:

Have a conversation with your students using the following points as a guide:

God made us for relationships

This passage is the last chapter of Paul's letter to the Romans. Some people think it's a throwaway chapter filled with lots of strange names and personal comments. But don't overlook this chapter and what it's saying. It tells us how important relationships are to everyone who follows Jesus. God made us for relationships. The three-in-one God is a model of relationship. God wants to have relationship with us. Jesus died on the cross to reconcile us in our relationship with God. Jesus tells us many times to love one another. He says if we don't love each other, that's a sign we really don't know or love God.

We need each other

Romans 16 reminds us the apostle Paul did not live a solitary life. He was a mighty and courageous servant of God, but he did not do it alone. We read about all these people who helped him and encouraged him by their words and actions. Life is tough. God gives us resources and strength, often through the lives of special people around us. Even the strongest people need help and encouragement. Being connected to others keeps us active and growing. It helps us resist temptation and lets us feel loved. Love is just a theory until we live it out with other imperfect people. Experiencing that real love brings us genuine joy and satisfaction that can't be found in a solo lifestyle.

Express your love

A key part of relationship and life together is communication. God tell us how much he loves us, and encourages us to express those feelings to others. If you don't verbalize or act out love, people lack confidence and security. Chapter 16 shows Paul taking time to thank people for what they did for him and express his love and admiration for them and their faith. Some people live in good homes where no love is expressed; they have everything money can buy but feel hopeless and empty inside. We don't have to live like that—let's express our love and appreciation to the people around us.

REAL-LIFE CONNECTION: Let your praise be loud

Ask—

Who are the key people in your life? Think of people who have helped you, encouraged you, and stood by you when life was tough. When did you thank them recently? Write them a letter or an email telling how they helped you.

Say—

Let people know you're not taking on the world by yourself. Let your praise be loud and enthusiastic. Make a list and try not to leave anyone out. If someone on your list is here, before you leave tell that person how much you appreciate what she has done for you.

MEDIA: Thank you video

Get your students to form a media crew. Go on the street and ask people to name friends and others (outside their family) who they want to thank for helping them. Edit it and play it for the meeting.

Go to the group members prior to the meeting and film their answers to the question, To whom (outside your family) do you want to say thank you for helping you in your life? Say their name and briefly tell how they have helped you. Edit this and show it during the meeting.

GALATIANS

Galatians 1:11-24

TOPIC: What's your story?

OBJECTIVE: Students will be able to tell their story of coming to faith in Christ—how God became real to them.

BACKGROUND/OVERVIEW: Paul told his story to the Galatian church to establish his credibility with them as a trustworthy speaker for God's message. He spoke as to how the Gentile church was being pressured to adopt Jewish customs and rituals.

GAME/ICEBREAKER: What's my story?
This is a game show type experience. Beforehand, prepare a list of at least 10 celebrities. Include six to eight facts about each one's life (birth year, birthplace, first job, first famous moment, nickname, etc.—you can search Wikipedia for this information).

Select several student contestants to compete in this game. Have them come to the front and give a response sheet to everyone else. Divide the group by the number of contestants, and assign a contestant to each group section. The game begins with you revealing a fact about a specific celebrity and asking if any of the contestants would like to guess the identity of the person you're describing. If someone says yes, but guesses wrong, he's eliminated for that round. The groups watching participate by writing answers on the sheet or standing when they think they know the correct answer. Continue revealing facts until you have a winner. You can make your own rules. For example you could allow the contestant to yield to a member from his group who is standing to give the answer. This game is a trust and confidence test that involves the audience. Keep score and use a wide variety of celebrities.

ICEBREAKER QUESTIONS:

- Who is the most famous celebrity we used in this game?
- How much do we know about this celebrity?
- Why do we know so much about these celebrity personalities we have never met?
- If you could ask one of our celebrities a question, whom would you ask and what would you ask?
- What would you like to know about that person's spiritual life or relationship with God?
- What five facts would you like people to know about you and your life?

SCRIPTURE: Galatians 1:11-24

Hand out copies of the passage and pens/pencils. Tell everyone to follow along as you read. Instruct them to underline facts Paul reveals about himself.

[11] I want you to know, brothers and sisters, that the gospel I preached is not of human origin. [12] I did not receive it from any human source, nor was I taught it; rather, I received it by revelation from Jesus Christ.

[13] For you have heard of my previous way of life in Judaism, how intensely I persecuted the church of God and tried to destroy it. [14] I was advancing in Judaism beyond many of my own age among my people and was extremely zealous for the traditions of my fathers. [15] But when God, who set me apart from birth and called me by his grace, was pleased [16] to reveal his Son in me so that I might preach him among the Gentiles, my immediate response was not to consult any human being. [17] I did not go up to Jerusalem to see those who were apostles before I was, but I went into Arabia. Later I returned to Damascus.

[18] Then after three years, I went up to Jerusalem to get acquainted with Cephas and stayed with him fifteen days. [19] I saw none of the other apostles—only James, the Lord's brother. [20] I assure you before God that what I am writing you is no lie.

²¹ Then I went to Syria and Cilicia. ²² I was personally unknown to the churches of Judea that are in Christ. ²³ They only heard the report: "The man who formerly persecuted us is now preaching the faith he once tried to destroy." ²⁴ And they praised God because of me.

STUDY QUESTIONS:

- Early in Paul's life what was his religious activity like?
- What happened to Paul that changed his relationship with God and the whole direction of his life?
- What changes did God make in Paul's life?
- Why did Paul wait so long after his experience on the road to start preaching?
- What effect did Paul's story have on the people who heard it?
- What was Paul's reputation before and after his encounter with God?

TALKING POINTS:

Have a conversation with your students, using the following points as a guide:

Everyone has a unique story with God
Everybody has a story. God wants to be part of everyone's story, but for many people that hasn't happened yet. Perhaps they have never heard about how they could know God, or they haven't been interested because of their own religious upbringing. Some people have known God all their lives—or for as long as they can remember. Other people have a dramatic turnaround experience like the apostle Paul did.

Turn to someone right now and take three minutes to tell that person how you first found out about God and how you've responded to God since that time. Then let your partner tell you their response to the same question.

(Note: Be sure to build this six-minute discussion time into your meeting plan.)

Your story is powerful
What makes a story powerful or memorable? Dramatic stories with unusual events get most of the attention, but any story told honestly and with feeling connects with the person who hears it. Some people think because their story about God doesn't contain a dramatic turnaround they don't have a story. That's not true. God works in many different ways to accomplish the same result in all of us. When we come to know God—whether we're young or old, good or bad in behavior, slow or fast in response—our stories are powerful and memorable.

Turn back to your partner and in one minute tell them what you remember about her story that she just told you. What was amazing and memorable about that person's story?

(Note: Allow two to three minutes for this discussion time.)

Know and tell your story

People talked about the apostle Paul and his story because of how he changed so much after meeting God. That's what makes your story powerful. How have you changed since you met God? The change could have been long and slow or an immediate turnaround for you. Either way is just fine with God. Someone will identify with your story and be helped when hearing it.

Turn to your partner one more time and briefly explain how God changed you when you first came to know him. Also tell about a change in the past year God is helping you make.

(Note: Allow four to six minutes for this discussion and call out the time halfway through.)

This is your story

During the past 15-20 minutes you shared your story. It is powerful to hear how God is working in your life just like God worked in Paul. God prepared Paul to speak to a special group of people, and God is preparing you to talk to some people in your life. God will use your unique gifts and personality to tell your own special story. People will know God is real when they see your life and hear your story.

REAL-LIFE CONNECTION: Share your story

Share the following instructions with your students:

- Think about your story with God this week. Write down any additional parts of your story from your distant past or recent history.
- Talk about your story with someone this week.
- Ask someone about his story with God, listening carefully to learn about him.

MEDIA: Make a commitment to God

Show the clip "Future Yes Man" (1:09) from the movie *Yes Man*. Carl attends a seminar where he's pressured into making a commitment to say yes to everything. Use this video clip to compare pressuring someone about becoming a Christian in contrast to telling your story about God's work in your life.

This clip can be found on www.wingclips.com—search by the title of the clip.

Galatians 2:11-21

TOPIC: Walking the talk

OBJECTIVE: Students will learn saying one thing and doing another is wrong—no matter who does it. They'll also understand that Christ had to come because no one could be saved through the Old Testament law (or by any means other than through him).

BACKGROUND/OVERVIEW: Peter had come to the churches in Antioch for a visit and was having a great time of fellowship with the Gentile believers (Gentiles are those not of Jewish origin). As soon as some people from the church in Jerusalem (where James was the pastor) arrived, Peter began to pull away from his new friends and act in a more traditional way with his old friends. When Paul could no longer tolerate this blatant hypocrisy he reminded Peter in front of everyone both Jew and Gentile that Christ's sacrifice had done away with relying on the Old Testament law for salvation.

GAME/ICEBREAKER: **Hungry, hungry hypocrite**
Items needed:

  • Candy

   This small-group game is an amusing way to show just how much hypocrisy we have in our own lives. Give each student three or four pieces of candy they're not allowed to eat. Then ask a series of leading questions. Each time a student answers a question that contradicts an answer they have given to a previous question, take a piece of his candy. The game ends when only one student has candy left. That person wins by being the least hypocritical (or best liar). Now a kind leader would still give the students some candy when the game is over, of course.

   You could ask questions such as these: *Are you a Christian? Are you completely committed to Christ as Savior and Lord? Have you set aside time to pray this week? Have you read your Bible this week? Have you helped anyone this week? Have you sinned this week? etc.*

   Another line of questions could include these: *Do you consider yourself a good friend? Have you talked behind any of your friends' backs this week? Have you made fun of any of your friends this week? Did you drop what you had planned to do with a friend for a chance to do something better? Do you love your parents? etc.*

ICEBREAKER QUESTIONS:

- Define hypocrisy.
- How do you feel knowing of the hypocrisy in your life?
- How did it make you feel when that hypocrisy cost you something (candy, friendship, etc.)?
- Who are some obvious hypocrites (celebrity types) these days?
- Why is seeing hypocrisy in others easier than seeing it in ourselves?

SCRIPTURE: Galatians 2:11-21

Distribute copies of this passage and pencils/pens. Tell everyone to underline passages that relate to hypocrisy.

[11] When Cephas came to Antioch, I opposed him to his face, because he stood condemned. [12] For before certain people came from James, he used to eat with the Gentiles. But when they arrived, he began to draw back and separate himself from the Gentiles because he was afraid of those who belonged to the circumcision group. [13] The other Jews joined him in his hypocrisy, so that by their hypocrisy even Barnabas was led astray.

[14] When I saw that they were not acting in line with the truth of the gospel, I said to Cephas in front of them all, "You are a Jew, yet you live like a Gentile and not like a Jew. How is it, then, that you force Gentiles to follow Jewish customs?

[15] "We who are Jews by birth and not sinful Gentiles [16] know that a person is not justified by observing the law, but by faith in Jesus Christ. So we, too, have put our faith in Christ Jesus that we may be justified by faith in Christ and not by observing the law, because by observing the law no one will be justified.

[17] "But if, in seeking to be justified in Christ, we Jews find ourselves also among the sinners, doesn't that mean that Christ promotes sin? Absolutely not! [18] If I rebuild what I destroyed, then I really would be a lawbreaker.

[19] "For through the law I died to the law so that I might live for God. [20] I have been crucified with Christ and I no longer live, but Christ lives in me. The life I now live in the body, I live by faith in the Son of God, who loved me and gave himself for me. [21] I do not set aside the grace

of God, for if righteousness could be gained through the law, Christ died for nothing!"

STUDY QUESTIONS:

- What did you underline in the passage?
- What was Peter's hypocrisy?
- Why was Paul so upset by Peter's behavior?
- What does Paul mean when he writes, "By observing the law no one will be justified"?
- What does this mean: "If I rebuild what I destroyed, then I really would be a lawbreaker"?
- What was destroyed? How does rebuilding it prove Paul to be a lawbreaker?
- How does this story cause you to look at your own life? What might you need to change?

TALKING POINTS:
Try to make sure these specific points get talked about in the lesson:

No special treatment
Peter was one of the original 12 disciples of Jesus and one of the main guys in the original church, yet Paul had no problem letting him know when he was wrong. If Peter didn't get special treatment for his bad behavior, neither will we.

Rebuild what I destroyed
When Paul writes, "If I rebuild what I destroyed, then I really would be a lawbreaker," he's saying that when he accepted God's grace and put his faith in Jesus Christ for salvation, he destroyed his own reliance on following the Old Testament law for salvation. So if he were to begin again to rely on works for salvation, he'd be rebuilding what he had already destroyed (reliance on the law). In the process he'd prove, once again, he isn't good enough to get to God through the law (because he knows it's impossible to keep the whole law).

REAL-LIFE CONNECTION: Jesus can help you grow through your mistakes
Say to your students—

You may be thinking, *I have messed up a lot in my life and now I'm afraid if I try to talk about God to my friends, they'll think I'm a hypocrite.*

What should I do?

First: Everyone messes up. Be honest with your friends and let them know you're not perfect. Let them know that the fact that you're not perfect and *do* mess up is exactly why God makes his grace available to you every day.

Second: Make sure you continue to grow in your relationship with Christ. Hebrews 12:2 tells us to fix "our eyes on Jesus, the pioneer and *perfecter* of our faith," so it's a growth process. We'll always make mistakes, but hopefully we're letting Jesus help us to grow through our mistakes so we do not continue to make the same ones.

MEDIA: Different people, different cultures

Show the clip "Try to Understand" (1:23) from the movie *Lars and the Real Girl*. This clip is available on Wing Clips—search www.wingclips.com using the title of the clip.

Lars Lindstrom is a lovable introvert who has so much emotional baggage he can't have a relationship with a real person. He begins a *romance* with a life-sized doll named Bianca, whom he treats as though she were alive. In this scene Lars' family and some members of the community discuss if they should accept Lars and his new *girlfriend*. Compare this scene with Paul and Peter's disagreement. Paul was bringing people from outside the Jewish culture into faith in Christ. There was tension about non-Jewish people keeping the Jewish law. You can ask your students—how do you settle a disagreement between two well-meaning Christians?

Galatians 3:15-25

TOPIC: Is heaven for rule-keepers?

OBJECTIVE: Students will understand the difference between the Old Testament law and the promise of God.

BACKGROUND/OVERVIEW: The people in the Galatian churches were beginning to turn away from Paul's original teachings and add religious good works to the gospel because a group of people called *Judaizers* had infiltrated the churches and began bullying the Gentile Christians into doing things their way. Judaizers were Jewish Christians who taught that Gentile Christians still had to closely follow the Old Testament law. So Paul took this opportunity to explain the difference between the Old Testament law and the promise of salvation by grace from God.

GAME/ICEBREAKER: Red light, green light—one, two, three

This is a classic neighborhood game played by many kids. The key person, the Traffic Cop, stands with his back to the rest of the players, who are all standing a predetermined distance away. As the Traffic Cop calls out "red light, green light—one, two, three," all the other players are moving closer to the Traffic Cop's position. As soon as the Traffic Cop is finished calling out "red light, green light—one, two, three," and turns around, everyone must stop moving. If anyone is still moving they must go back to the starting point. Play continues until one of the players reaches and touches the Traffic Cop. The game then starts again with the winner as the new Traffic Cop.

ICEBREAKER QUESTIONS:

- Why is the Traffic Cop the one who gets to send players back to the beginning?
- How did you feel when the Traffic Cop busted you?
- In life, what are some of the ways you can get into trouble with a real Traffic Cop?
- People who get traffic tickets are guilty of breaking an earthly law—what is the penalty of breaking God's law?

SCRIPTURE: Galatians 3:15-25

Hand out copies of this passage. Have students read this silently, underlining every mention of *law* and circling every mention of *promise*.

[15] Brothers and sisters, let me take an example from everyday life. Just as no one can set aside or add to a human covenant that has been duly established, so it is in this case. [16] The promises were spoken to Abraham and to his seed. Scripture does not say "and to seeds," meaning many people, but "and to your seed," meaning one person, who is Christ. [17] What I mean is this: The law, introduced 430 years later, does not set aside the covenant previously established by God and thus do away with the promise. [18] For if the inheritance depends on the law, then it no longer depends on the promise; but God in his grace gave it to Abraham through a promise.

[19] What, then, was the purpose of the law? It was added because of transgressions until the Seed to whom the promise referred had come. The law was given through angels and entrusted to a mediator. [20] A mediator, however, implies more than one party; but God is one.

[21] Is the law, therefore, opposed to the promises of God? Absolutely not! For if a law had been given that could impart life, then righteousness would certainly have come by the law. [22] But Scripture has locked up everything under the control of sin, so that what was promised, being given through faith in Jesus Christ, might be given to those who believe.

[23] Before the coming of this faith, we were held in custody under the law, locked up until the faith that was to come would be revealed. [24] So the law was put in charge of us until Christ came that we might be justified by faith. [25] Now that this faith has come, we are no longer under the supervision of the law.

STUDY QUESTIONS:

- How many times is *law* mentioned? How about *promise*?
- How much should a follower of Jesus Christ be focused on following the commandments and rules of the Old Testament?
- How much of your Christian life-experience is based on keeping rules?
- What is God's promise (as opposed to the written laws of God)?
- Why does depending on the law (our works) mean we're no longer depending on God's promise?
- How is it we're held prisoners of the law?
- How has our faith in Jesus freed us from the constraints of the law?

TALKING POINTS:

Share the following points with your students:

What's God's promise?

The law equals works-based salvation: For the purposes of this discussion, it's important for us to realize when Paul mentions being under the law, he's talking about the Jews who feel salvation cannot possibly be as easy as God's grace through faith in Jesus, so they keep returning to trying to fulfill the Old Testament laws. For today's Christian that translates into what we call works-based religion. In other words, some people believe they need to be good, do good works, keep religious rituals, or do some other work to please God and get to heaven. But works-based doesn't work. God has given only one way to please him, and that way is through Jesus Christ.

What's God's promise? God had promised Abraham (Abram) in Genesis 12 that "all peoples on earth will be blessed through you." God had promised to bless the whole world through Abraham's seed (Jesus). The law was in place to set the people of God apart from the other nations until the seed of Abraham (Jesus) came to the earth.

God Keeps His Promise

Just as the prophets had predicted for hundreds of years, Jesus did come into the world. He came to lay down his life and pay for the sins of all people who put their trust in him. A Christian is justified and redeemed by God—not by his good works, but by his faith in Christ as his Savior. That's the gospel.

REAL-LIFE CONNECTION:

Live role-play and group interview

Set up an adult visitor to play the role. Have the visitor declare to the students: "I believe I am going to heaven because I am a good person. I stay out of trouble and help people many times a month. I am much better than 80 percent of the people I know. How can God or any of you judge me and tell me I am not going to heaven?"

Let the students interact with the role-playing guest, and finish the discussion emphasizing these points:

- Keep the focus on Jesus—who he was and why he came.
- Share why you believe in Jesus and what that means to you.
- Then ask your friend what he believes about Jesus and what that means to him.

Say—

If a person does not believe Jesus is the only way to get to heaven, you won't be judging that person and saying she isn't going to heaven. This conversation may be difficult, but if you love your friend, you need to have it.

It's not your job to save anyone—your only job is to love your friend and to tell her what the Bible says. Pray your friend will see the truth. The rest is up to God.

MEDIA: Grace

Show the "Grace" (2:18) clip from *The Case for Faith*. (This clip is available on Wing Clips—search www.wingclips.com using the words *case for faith*.)

You can also show the scene "His Name is Jesus" (1:55) from the movie *The Last Sin Eater*. (This clip is available at www.wingclips.com.) In 1850s Appalachia, 10-year-old Cadi Forbes is wracked with guilt over the death of her sister. She feels responsible for the loss and sets out to find a man known as the Sin Eater to take away her guilt. But while seeking redemption, Cadi learns a devastating secret that has the potential to tear apart her family and community. This film clip is a clear reminder our mistakes are paid for by the sacrificial, atoning death of Jesus Christ and not by our human effort to live a righteous life.

Galatians 4:8-20

TOPIC: No turning back

OBJECTIVE: Students will know and feel how foolish it would be to turn their back on their faith in Christ and return to their old ways of living.

BACKGROUND/OVERVIEW: The people in the Galatian churches were beginning to turn away from Paul's original teachings and add works to the gospel because the Judaizers had begun to stir things up. Paul views adding any sort of requirements to the gospel and to our faith as returning to the exact same situation we were in before we received Christ as our Savior—lost people trying to get to God through our own efforts. We'd be returning to being enslaved to these weak efforts that won't get us any closer to God anyway. Paul is trying to explain the foolishness of this to the Galatians.

GAME/ICEBREAKER: Wink

Have all the girls sit on chairs in a circle. Leave one chair empty and have all the boys each stand directly behind a chair. The boys should keep their heads down except the boy behind the empty chair. The game begins when the boy behind the empty chair winks at one of the girls who then has to try to get away from her chair before the boy behind her can reach out and stop her (by grabbing her shoulders). The boy must remain behind the chair at all times. After a while, switch and let the boys sit with the girls doing the winking. With an uneven amount of boys and girls, you could have a staff person sit with the girls or boys as needed.

ICEBREAKER QUESTIONS:

- What was the secret to making a quick getaway when someone in the game would wink at you?
- What are the positives and negatives for being the one who escapes and the one who tries to keep someone from escaping? Which role do you like better? Why?
- In what ways is this game like your relationship with your parents as you're growing up? What is *winking* at you—calling you to run away—and what do your parents do to try to keep you from running away from the values and beliefs of your family?
- In what ways is this game like our relationship with God? What *winks* at us and tempts us to run away from God?

SCRIPTURE: Galatians 4:8-20

Have students read this by themselves, silently.

[8] Formerly, when you did not know God, you were slaves to those who by nature are not gods. [9] But now that you know God—or rather are known by God—how is it that you are turning back to those weak and miserable forces? Do you wish to be enslaved by them all over again? [10] You are observing special days and months and seasons and years! [11] I fear for you, that somehow I have wasted my efforts on you.

[12] I plead with you, brothers and sisters, become like me, for I became like you. You have done me no wrong. [13] As you know, it was because of an illness that I first preached the gospel to you. [14] Even though my illness was a trial to you, you did not treat me with contempt or scorn. Instead, you welcomed me as if I were an angel of God, as if I were Christ Jesus himself. [15] What has happened to all your joy? I can testify that, if you could have done so, you would have torn out your eyes and given them to me. [16] Have I now become your enemy by telling you the truth?

[17] Those people are zealous to win you over, but for no good. What they want is to alienate you from us, so that you may have zeal for them. [18] It is fine to be zealous, provided the purpose is good, and to be so always, not just when I am with you. [19] My dear children, for whom I am again in the pains of childbirth until Christ is formed in you, [20] how I wish I could be with you now and change my tone, because I am perplexed about you!

STUDY QUESTIONS:

- Paul was concerned about these people turning away from their faith and trust in Christ Jesus. What makes Christians turn away from their faith?
- These people were going back to their old lifestyle. What are some of the "weak and miserable forces" and beliefs that pull people away from Christ?
- What does it mean to turn your back on God?
- What would you say to a friend who was losing the excitement and commitment to follow Jesus?
- What are some bad habits that are hard for you to break and stay away from?
- Who in your life is zealous to win you over to their way of doing

things (dressing, acting, cliques, and so forth) and why would that alienate you from God?

• Paul really cares about these people even when they're going the wrong direction. What can you do to show love and truth to people who have walked away from Jesus?

TALKING POINTS:
Use the following points as a guide for your conversation with your students:

Returning to slavery
Paul was writing to people who had given their lives to Christ and now were returning to their old habits and lifestyles. He said they were going back to slavery. Most of us focus on being free to do whatever we want to do and never consider ourselves slaves to anything. But we can be slaves to our own desires, slaves to what people think about us, slaves to fitting in, slaves to our addictions, and much more. What else could we put on that list? (Write a list from the suggestions given by the group).

Christ came to set us free from that kind of slavery
Christ freed us to love God, worship God, and glorify God in our lives. When we live with Christ in us, our lives are transformed to be like his. This doesn't mean we always do what is right and never feel the lure of temptations. We can still be tempted to return to the old sins and masters that used to run our lives. But we don't have to. Christ gives us the ability to choose to do what is right. Most of us were on a very slow but self-destructive path that would ruin our lives. Christ gave us total acceptance and forgiveness for our old lives and set us free.

Make sure you care about the right things
Paul talks about having zeal and concludes it's all right to care a lot about things and get fired up by them. But many people care a lot about the wrong kind of things. They get focused on their own desires and what is best for them, which is selfish. Many people care about the environment, or their favorite sports team. Nothing's wrong with that, but the main things we should care about and have a real zeal for are the very things that seem to get left out of our lives. It's okay to be fired up, but make sure it's about the right things: Loving God, loving people, and bringing glory to God's name.

REAL-LIFE CONNECTION: How would you respond?
Present this statement and ask your students to respond:

I would never turn my back on God—I just don't feel like doing church stuff or God stuff right now. It's just not relevant to my life. I still love God, but I do what I think is best for me.

After the students give their responses, you can add this:

As Christians, we don't just *do* God stuff. Our faith is who we are. It should flow through everything we do—even the everyday things. God isn't just a feel-good pill we use on Sundays. He's part of every aspect of our lives.

If you really feel as if God isn't relevant to your everyday life, you should probably take a good look at how you're living. The reason we soften our Christian beliefs and set them aside is because it's countercultural to believe what we believe—it goes against everything the world tells us is cool. It is what we do that shows others what we believe, not what we say. Only you and God know if you truly love him. No one else can judge you. Take an honest look at your life—how you spend your time, the things you do and dream about, the way you treat people created in God's image—and then you will know if you really love God.

MEDIA: What is important?

Make your own video interview of young adults talking about why their faith is less important to them than it was when they were in a high school youth group. Use the interviews to spark discussion.

You can also show a clip from *Star Wars* (original movie). After the Icebreaker play the clip where Han Solo takes off before the big battle. (Chapter 43—1:41:00.) Talk about his excuses for leaving ("I owe Jabba money," "It's not my fight," etc.). Later play the clip where Han Solo saves Luke and talks about what his actions really said to his friends.

Or play the song "Magnificent Obsession" from the *Declaration* album by Steven Curtis Chapman. Print and have your students review the words about making Jesus Christ first in our lives.

Galatians 5:16-24

TOPIC: Life by the Spirit

OBJECTIVE: Students will understand how the fruit of the Spirit is developed in them as they walk with Christ.

BACKGROUND/OVERVIEW: Paul wrote this passage to Christians to remind them that when they're in a relationship with God, people will see the evidence.

GAME/ICEBREAKER: The banana pass game
Items needed:

• Bananas

This can be a messy relay race. The *baton* is a fresh banana. The challenge of the game is players must only use their feet to pass it. So it's best played outdoors.

Players lie down on the grass, head to toe in a straight line with each person's toes about two feet away from the next teammate's head. When the game begins, the first person in line grabs hold of the banana with her feet and swivels around on her back (like a crane) to pass it to the next person's feet. The next person receives the banana with his feet and swivels on his back and passes again until the entire team is done. Do the relay with one to three bananas. When the bananas have been passed to the last person, this person runs with the fruit to the front of the line where the team is now standing and waiting. As a team they have to eat all the fruit to win the relay.

ICEBREAKER QUESTIONS:

- What was the most difficult part of this relay?
- What thoughts did you have about eating bananas that had been *foot-handled*?
- How do you know if fruit is going to be good to eat (not spoiled) when you peel it?
- When fruit goes bad, how can you make it good to eat again?
- What bad character traits in a person spoil them like bad fruit?
- If you could change one personality trait in yourself, what would you change?

SCRIPTURE: Galatians 5:16-24

Copy this passage on a sheet of paper. Pass it around and have kids read the verses aloud, one person per verse.

[16] So I say, walk by the Spirit, and you will not gratify the desires of the sinful nature. [17] For the sinful nature desires what is contrary to the Spirit, and the Spirit what is contrary to the sinful nature. They are in conflict with each other, so that you are not to do whatever you want. [18] But if you are led by the Spirit, you are not under the law.

[19] The acts of the sinful nature are obvious: sexual immorality, impurity and debauchery; [20] idolatry and witchcraft; hatred, discord, jealousy, fits of rage, selfish ambition, dissensions, factions [21] and envy; drunkenness, orgies, and the like. I warn you, as I did before, that those who live like this will not inherit the kingdom of God.

[22] But the fruit of the Spirit is love, joy, peace, patience, kindness, goodness, faithfulness, [23] gentleness and self-control. Against such things there is no law. [24] Those who belong to Christ Jesus have crucified the sinful nature with its passions and desires.

STUDY QUESTIONS:

- This passage lays out two contrasting lists of bad and good behavior. From where do these contrasting behaviors come?
- What is the conflict between sinful nature and the Holy Spirit?
- What are some of the acts of sinful nature that are really prevalent today? Which of those are most accepted and encouraged?
- What acts of the sinful nature tend to entangle you?
- Which characteristic of the fruit of the Spirit do you find most difficult to express?
- How do you see the character of the Holy Spirit growing in your life?

TALKING POINTS:

Share the following points with your students:

The two forces within us

When we have a relationship with God, we have two forces within us: The Holy Spirit and our own sinful nature. When we operate from our sinful nature, we desire to satisfy our flesh. The lure of sin can lead to the acts

Paul listed in Galatians 5. When we follow the Holy Spirit, those acts are not nearly as attractive because of the strength we find through God.

Who wins?

In this constant battle between following our sinful nature and the Holy Spirit, we ultimately decide who wins. We make choices every hour of the day, and those choices reflect whether we're trying to please God or simply conforming to our own selfish desires or the ways of the world. When we commit our lives to Christ, the Holy Spirit takes up residence in us and begins to help us fight the cravings of our sinful nature. We have to yield to God and the Holy Spirit, saying yes to godly actions and no to sinful temptations.

How do we recognize which one is winning? That is determined by what we show on the outside. The kind of fruit that grows on the outside of a tree reflects the nature of the tree. Apples grow on apple trees; tomato plants produce tomatoes. And the fruit you show on the outside is a reflection of what is going on inside you.

What is the fruit of the Spirit?

The fruit of the Spirit is a collection of nine visible attributes of a Christian—how she walks, talks, and acts. The goal of a Christian is to become like Christ and be transformed by the renewing of our minds. When we abide in Christ and obey his Word, the fruit of the Spirit starts showing up in our lives.

Fruit delivery service

God does not give us the patience, joy, self-control, or any other fruit in a wrapped box. We have to ask for these fruits and commit to practice them when opportunities arise. When you pray a prayer such as "Lord, please give me more patience," God will give you opportunities to develop and practice patience instead of simply granting you patience. You will find out how much God wants to change the way you think, speak, and act. Be patient and be obedient to God's Word and to the Holy Spirit prompting you about what you should say and do. When that happens, the fruit is growing.

REAL-LIFE CONNECTION: What fruit do you have?

Give the following instructions to your students:

Partner with someone you know (same gender) and tell them how you see God working in them and changing them recently. Give them examples of choices you saw them make. Give them encouragement.

Stay with the same partner and tell them about one or more of the fruit of the Spirit where you have made bad choices and need improvement.

After sharing, read the list of the fruit of the Spirit aloud (Galatians 5:22-23) and pray together.

MEDIA: Which fruit are you?

Visit the Web site www.quizilla.com. In the search box, type *fruit of the Spirit*. This is a fun Web site to share with your students at the end of the lesson. It features a fun quiz they can take to find out which fruit of the Spirit is strong in them.

Galatians 6:1-5

TOPIC: We need each other

OBJECTIVE: Students will know the importance of helping one another through difficult times. They'll also learn to be responsible for their own actions.

BACKGROUND/OVERVIEW: Paul taught that believers should carry each other's burdens and help each other with personal struggles. He also encouraged believers to be their best and to be proud of who they are—they should not compare themselves with others.

GAME/ICEBREAKER: **Fruit punch chug relay**
Items needed:

- Two jugs of fruit punch (clear jugs work best)
- Straws (enough for two per student)
- Drop cloth (if indoors—the game can get a little messy).

Divide into two teams. Give each student a straw (giving two straws to each student will make the game go a little faster if you're crunched for time). At the other end of the room have a one-gallon jug of fruit punch or other drink of your choice (you can put the drop cloth down under the jug of juice for minor spills). Tell the students that on "Go!" they're to run in pairs (three people can go at once if there's a time crunch) to the fruit punch. They're to stick their straws into the jug and take a big gulp. Then they're to run back to their team to tag the next pair to do the same. This will continue until the drink is almost finished. Then, when you see the juice is at the lowest point they can reach, give one person permission to run down, pick up the jug, and drink the rest of the punch. The team to drink all the fruit punch first wins. Until you give the word, students cannot touch the jug while drinking. As the juice gets lower and lower encourage students to *work together* to come up with a strategy on how to reach the juice halfway down (putting two straws together, etc.).

ICEBREAKER QUESTIONS:

- When was this game easy? At what point did it become difficult?
- What was the winning strategy?
- In what ways are Christians a team?
- In the Christian life, when is teamwork necessary?

- How should you help a friend who is struggling with something with which you're struggling as well?

SCRIPTURE: Galatians 6:1-5
Have a student read the passage aloud from her Bible.

[1] Brothers and sisters, if someone is caught in a sin, you who live by the Spirit should restore that person gently. But watch yourselves, or you also may be tempted. [2] Carry each other's burdens, and in this way you will fulfill the law of Christ. [3] If any of you think you are something when you are nothing, you deceive yourselves. [4] Each of you should test your own actions. Then you can take pride in yourself, without comparing yourself to somebody else, [5] for each of you should carry your own load.

STUDY QUESTIONS:

- What is the best approach to helping a fellow believer caught in sin?
- How can you share the burden of someone else?
- What responsibility do Christians have toward each other?
- What does it mean to carry your own load if you're also instructed to carry each other's burdens?

TALKING POINTS:
Use the following points to guide the discussion with your students:

No solo Christians
None of us is called to live our Christian life alone. God gives us one another to work together (as in our game) and to help in our struggles and when we need encouragement. Here Paul says we should help others when they're caught in sin. He explains we need to be careful in two ways here. First, we need to be gentle, and humble. If we're not, we could look like we think we're better than they are. Second, we need to guard ourselves, making sure helping this person won't tempt us as well. If we're struggling with the same issue it's probably best to include another helper. The church functions best when believers glorify Christ by reaching out and helping each other.

The helper needs help, too
Paul also tells believers to watch their actions to make sure they're doing what is right in every situation. What he means by saying we can take pride

in ourselves is we're allowed to feel good about ourselves, but we can get caught up in comparing ourselves with others. Sometimes in order to make ourselves feel better, we look at others and focus on their weaknesses and point out everything they do wrong. But Paul says we should do the opposite. If we work our hardest and do our best, we can be proud of our work. God gives each of us different talents and skills, and we should each use well what God has given us.

Help and be helped

Paul's two points go together. If we try to be our very best in everything we do, we'll feel good about ourselves and the work we're doing. If we feel good about ourselves, we'll want to help others feel good about themselves as well. Then we can help each other and truly be the body of Christ!

REAL-LIFE CONNECTION: Reach out and help someone

Share with your students—

John 13:34 tells us Jesus made a new commandment, which is to love one another, just as he loves us.

- Do you know someone who needs to be loved? Who?
- Do you know someone who needs help? Who?

We can go through life and not be aware of the needs around us. Make yourself comfortable and take a few minutes to ask God to show you people close to you who may need your help. Then listen. Let God speak to you and show you who needs your help. Make it a point this week to reach out to those people in some way:

- Pray for them, and tell them you prayed for them.
- Invite them out with you and some friends.
- Invite them out to lunch or dinner—just the two of you.
- Invite them to your youth group or church if they do not already go.
- Ask how they're doing, and really listen.

MEDIA: Working together

Show the clip "Assistant Coach" (1:03) from the movie *We Are Marshall*. This clip is available from Wing Clips. (Go to www.wingclips.com and type the title of the clip in the search box.) You can use this clip to show how working together can be better for everyone. We can use the strength of one another to bring out the best in those around us.

EPHESIANS

Ephesians 1:15-21

TOPIC: No more kiddie prayers

OBJECTIVE: Students will start praying daily to get to know God more deeply.

BACKGROUND/OVERVIEW: In Ephesians 1, the apostle Paul laid a foundation of who God is, what God has done, and how God wants people to know him. The first three chapters of Ephesians tell the story of how much God loves us. The last three chapters list the practical application of how to live when we understand God's love.

GAME/ICEBREAKER: Text-message prayers
Items needed:

- Cell phones
- Signs with leaders' cell phone numbers printed on them
- Small pieces of paper
- Pens/pencils

Ask everyone to turn *on* his cell phone. Position two leaders at the front of the room and have them hold big signs with their cell phone numbers printed on them. Instruct the students to text a prayer to God using normal texting language. They should then send it to the phone of the leader standing on their side of the room. Instruct students to make their prayer a typical one they'd say or quietly think to God. They should keep the prayers short—within one screen limit on their phone (160 characters). Give students without cell phones a piece of paper on which to write their message (they also must stay within the 160-character limit).

After four to five minutes of texting time, quiet the room and let the leaders take turns reading the prayers they received (they should not reveal who wrote them.) Leaders should quietly read the entire prayer before reading it aloud so they can skip over any specific names or situations that involve personal or negative subject matter.

Do a second round of texting prayers, and this time have students answer a question from God: *What do you want?* Give students two to three minutes to respond and once again read the responses (using the same guidelines).

ICEBREAKER QUESTIONS:

- How would you describe the way we pray to God?
- In the first prayers, what was on our minds and what did we communicate to God?
- What comments reflected appreciation, thanks, or praise to God?
- How much of our prayers were about us or what we needed?
- What questions did we bring to God?
- In the second prayers responding to God, what did we want from God?

SCRIPTURE: Ephesians 1:15-21
Have students silently read this from their Bibles.

> [15] For this reason, ever since I heard about your faith in the Lord Jesus and your love for all his people, [16] I have not stopped giving thanks for you, remembering you in my prayers. [17] I keep asking that the God of our Lord Jesus Christ, the glorious Father, may give you the Spirit of wisdom and revelation, so that you may know him better. [18] I pray that the eyes of your heart may be enlightened in order that you may know the hope to which he has called you, the riches of his glorious inheritance in his people, [19] and his incomparably great power for us who believe. That power is the same as the mighty strength [20] he exerted when he raised Christ from the dead and seated him at his right hand in the heavenly realms, [21] far above all rule and authority,

power and dominion, and every name that can be invoked, not only in the present age but also in the one to come.

STUDY QUESTIONS:

- In what ways is Paul's prayer different from our prayers?
- What can we learn about prayer from reading Paul's prayer?
- How many of us prayed (as Paul did) we'd get to know God better?
- How often is that something you want from God—to get to know him better?
- What is it about God most of us don't know enough about?
- Paul wants us to know the hope God has called us to—what is that?
- What do you know about the great power God wants to give us?
- What do you need to do to improve your prayer life?

TALKING POINTS:

Have a conversation with your students using the following points as a guide:

Our stunted prayer life

When did you start learning to pray? How have your prayers changed as you have grown and gotten older? Many people in the church are still praying like they did when they were children. They ask God for things they want and need. God does tell us to ask, but if our prayer life is just a heavenly home-shopping network, maybe we're missing what God really wants to give us.

God says, *Get to know me*

Our relationship with God is more important than any tangible object he could give us. God created us to have a relationship with him. How would you describe your relationship with God? If I asked you what you learned about him in the last month, what would you tell me? How would that answer compare with what you learned about your friends this past month? Of course it's easier to have a relationship with other humans, but that's why Paul is praying "for God to give us the Sprit of wisdom and revelation, so we can know him better." Paul also prays that we know the hope God has called us to possess and that we experience the power of God that raised Jesus from the dead. How real is that hope and power in your life?

Time to grow up in God

Being a Christian isn't the result of a one-time prayer where we pray to be forgiven and then we get to go to heaven. From the time we meet God, we're to keep growing in knowledge and faith in God. Acting like a baby when we're living in an adult body wouldn't be healthy. We grow in God by building our relationship with him and obeying what he directs us to do. Our faith grows each time we see God's way is best. But growing requires focused attention—that means putting God first in our lives. The whole letter Paul wrote to the Ephesians is a blueprint for healthy Christian living. The first three chapters are the foundation of who God is and what he has done for us. The last three chapters give specific practical instructions about how to live God's way. We need to study and apply everything we read in Ephesians so we can grow up in God.

REAL-LIFE CONNECTION: Move it and grow it
Say to your students—

Take out your cell phones again. Let's finish this meeting by texting another prayer to God. Use what you learned tonight to make this prayer come from your heart and your deepest desires. You can text it to a friend who is here with you or to one of the two numbers we called earlier in the meeting (put up the signs again). Let's take a few minutes of silence and either send our prayers by text, or by writing them on paper.

During this next week write a text or handwritten prayer every day. Send it to a friend or to the numbers of these leaders. You will be praying all your life—this week is intended to get your prayer life moving and growing.

MEDIA: Build a relationship through prayer
Show the video clip "Prayer—The Struggle of Faith, Hope, and …." This edgy video expresses some of the questions people have about prayer. It is well-done and open-ended for a good discussion about how prayer is part of a growing relationship with God. It's available for purchase from www.sermonspice.com. Use the search words *prayer struggle faith hope*.

Ephesians 2:1-10

TOPIC: Grace that works

OBJECTIVE: Students will understand salvation is free—a gift, and they'll understand the role of works in the lives of Christ-followers.

BACKGROUND/OVERVIEW: In Ephesians 2 Paul reminded the church of their past. He did this not to condemn them, but to give them a greater understanding and appreciation of the work of God in Christ Jesus. He reminded them God has brought them together and unified them so he could live among them (vv. 20-22). They should live in grace, knowing they have been freed and forgiven through what Christ did on the cross. And in response they should complete their unique work in the world to help fulfill God's purpose of being seen and glorified.

GAME/ICEBREAKER: Help wanted

Items needed:

- *Help Wanted* newspaper ads
- Paper
- Pens/pencils

This activity will get your group thinking about the kind of people God is looking for.

Read aloud a sampling from your newspaper's *Help Wanted* section. Then have kids write their own help-wanted ads as if they were written by God and run in the local newspaper. The ads could be titled *Help Wanted* or *Position Available* and contain a description of the kind of person God wants. Here's a sample ad:

Help Wanted: Need believers who are responsible, loving, under-standing, willing to sacrifice themselves for others. False pretenses are not welcome. Applicant must be loyal, faithful. Great benefits. Life insurance paid in full. Please call me at B-I-B-L-E anytime—I'm always there. An equal opportunity employer.

When ads are completed, have kids turn over their papers and write their résumés to qualify for the job. Or post all the ads on a bulletin board and have kids write a reply to the one that most appeals to them—make sure they include a note to God explaining why they're qualified for the job. Invite volunteers to read the ads and replies to the group, or collect the ads and replies and read them aloud to the group.

ICEBREAKER QUESTIONS:

- The word *saved* is used to refer to people who are a part of God's family. If you believe you're saved, what have you done to be accepted by God?
- If you're not sure whether or not you're saved, or think you might not be saved, what do you think you need to do *to be* saved?
- What makes someone saved or unsaved? How do you know if you are or are not?

TRANSITION:

Say to your students—

Today we're going to talk about how God accepts us and how that changes what we do and don't do. How does God's acceptance of us into his family change how we act?

SCRIPTURE: Ephesians 2:1-10

Have someone read aloud the entire passage, Ephesians 2:1-10. Then you read aloud verses 8-10 again—for emphasis.

[1] As for you, you were dead in your transgressions and sins, [2] in which you used to live when you followed the ways of this world and of the ruler of the kingdom of the air, the spirit who is now at work in those who are disobedient. [3] All of us also lived among them at one time, gratifying the cravings of our sinful nature and following its desires and thoughts. Like the rest, we were by nature deserving of wrath. [4] But because of his great love for us, God, who is rich in mercy, [5] made us alive with Christ even when we were dead in transgressions—it is by grace you have been saved. [6] And God raised us up with Christ and seated us with him in the heavenly realms in Christ Jesus, [7] in order that in the coming ages he might show the incomparable riches of his grace, expressed in his kindness to us in Christ Jesus. [8] For it is by grace you have been saved, through faith—and this is not from yourselves, it is the gift of God— [9] not by works, so that no one can boast. [10] For we are God's handiwork, created in Christ Jesus to do good works, which God prepared in advance for us to do.

STUDY QUESTIONS:

- What is this *grace* that saves us?
- Tell about a time you personally experienced grace—or a situation in which you saw grace in action.
- How would you feel if you went to great lengths to show someone the extent of your love for them, only to have them walk away without even saying "thank you"?
- If grace saves us, what is the point of being *good*?

TALKING POINTS:

Share the following points with your students:

You can't buy it

Paul reminds us we have not *earned* our standing with God. Salvation is available only because of God's grace provided by the death of Jesus on the cross. It is entirely initiated and freely given by God alone. Grace is a gift, and a gift, by definition, is free—it cannot be bought or earned, only accepted. Grace is best understood as unearned, undeserved favor. As with any gift given to us, our job is simply to receive it.

But you can show it

While salvation is about God's work and not ours, it doesn't mean the way we live our new life in Christ is unimportant. A change of attitude and behavior is hugely important in the lives of Christ-followers. We need to understand that our new Christ-like behavior is part of our secure acceptance as part of God's family. Good behavior doesn't save us—it's the sign that we recognize God's grace to us. Saving us is *God's* work. He had Christ die on the cross to pay the penalty for all our sins. Our new behavior (what the Bible calls *works*) shows our love for God and our gratitude for the grace he freely gives to us.

Faith's feet

Paul says, "We are God's handiwork, created in Christ Jesus to do good works, which God prepared in advance for us to do" (v. 10). The phrase "for us to do" means believing is just the first step of our new life in Christ. Too many believers in Jesus mentally agree with certain historical statements about God. They often point to John 3:16 and other passages, which state that believing is what being a Christian is all about. Believing the facts about Jesus is very important, but those facts are not an end in themselves. Belief is a starting point for action. Jesus clearly taught if we really believe who he is and what he taught, we'll do what he said (Matthew 7:21; 12:50).

How are you showing your gratitude?
Do your attitude and actions show others how much you thank God for his gift of salvation to you? God has called you, forgiven you, gifted you, and positioned you to be his hands, feet, and mouth in this world. How can you influence the people around you and make them hungry to know God's grace and new life?

REAL-LIFE CONNECTION: Grace thank-you
Ask your students—
- How could misunderstanding God's grace mislead you as a Christ-follower?
- What personal beliefs do you need to change about what saves you and makes you part of God's family or how God wants you to live as one of his children?
- What are you discovering about the "good works God has prepared for you to do?"

Say—
Let's write God a thank-you letter, poem, or song for his grace to us.

Finish by saying—
Make a list of what you want to do for God this next month.

MEDIA: Gifts and grace
Show a short clip about the nature of *grace*—"That's Why They Call It Grace" (1:53). This video can be purchased at www.sermonspice.com—use the search words *why amazing*.

You could also take a look at the Discovering Spiritual Gifts Curriculum: *Congratulations ... You're Gifted!* by Doug Fields and Eric Rees (Youth Specialties, 2008). Through interactive exercises and questions students learn more about their God-given gifts and how they can partner with God to make a difference in the world.

Ephesians 3:14-19

TOPIC: Filled up with something

OBJECTIVE: Once students realize what fills their lives, they'll learn to fill them with Christ, instead.

BACKGROUND/OVERVIEW: Ephesians 3 is the wrap-up of three chapters focused on God's love and plan for the world. In chapter 4 Paul begins describing the specific lifestyle changes God wants his followers to make. Those changes will be difficult at best without understanding God's tremendous love for us and utilizing the power he gives to everyone who follows Jesus Christ.

GAME/ICEBREAKER: Fill it up challenge
Choose one or two of these games with a *fill it up* theme:

Relay: Put a container (you decide the size) on one side of the room and have several teams compete to fill the container to a certain level. Students can use anything from cups to straws to carry water from a bucket to the container.

Sprint: Have two or three students compete. At one end of the room, place five clear glasses or cups (for each competitor) on a table. These cups should be marked with pieces of colored tape to indicate water levels (have different levels for each of the five cups). Then give each competitor a container of water and have him stand at the other end of the room. At your signal, the competitors should run race to the table and fill each cup (to the exact level marked) and then finish by drinking all the water remaining in the original container. The first one to finish and have each glass filled correctly wins.

Target Filling: Choose three students to compete to see who can fill a plastic cup to the very top with one continuous pour—without any spilling over the top. Provide a pitcher of colored water, and have them pour one person at a time. Only one continuous pour is allowed. When they stop pouring the water, they're finished. If the water goes over the top, the student is automatically disqualified. After all three students have poured, compare the cups to see which one is fullest.

ICEBREAKER QUESTIONS:

- What was difficult about the *fill it* up task? What was easy?
- In everyday life, when would we be frustrated with something that wasn't being filled to the top? (Possible answers: Drinking glass at a restaurant, gas tank, popcorn bag at a movie, water bottle, book [with half the pages blank], a Christmas stocking, etc.)
- How would you react if you went to a restaurant and the server brought a drink that was only half full?
- What would you say if the store started selling bottled drinks that were half full?
- With what do most people fill their lives?
- The Bible says we're to be filled up with God. Why is that important? How does that happen?

SCRIPTURE: Ephesians 3:14-19

Have a staff member read the following passage aloud.

[14] For this reason I kneel before the Father, [15] from whom every family in heaven and on earth derives its name. [16] I pray that out of his glorious riches he may strengthen you with power through his Spirit in your inner being, [17] so that Christ may dwell in your hearts through faith. And I pray that you, being rooted and established in love, [18] may have power, together with all the Lord's people, to grasp how wide and long and high and deep is the love of Christ, [19] and to know this love that surpasses knowledge—that you may be filled to the measure of all the fullness of God.

STUDY QUESTIONS:

- What does Paul want us to understand and experience with God?
- How does Christ live in the heart of someone who believes in him?
- Describe how much God loves you and how you experience that love?
- What kind of power does God give to people who believe in Jesus?
- What does it mean to be filled to the top with the fullness of God?
- In what experiences have you known for sure God was in your life?
- How would you get God filling up your life? What do you have to do?

TALKING POINTS:
Share the following points with your students:

We'll be full of something
No one has a spiritual part that is empty. We can't seal our mind, heart, and soul to keep everything out—something is always in us. So it's never a question of whether we'll be full—the question is what will fill us. Look around at people to see what fills them. Some are consumed with sports—some with friends—others with money—still others with a special person. All of these have one common denominator: The focus is on the self. Being filled with thoughts about what is best for us comes naturally: Do we have what we want, what makes us feel good, and what other people have? The biggest competitor to us worshipping God is our self-centeredness and our self-worship. Let's face it: We live to please ourselves.

Be full of God
In the Ephesians 3 passage we read, that Paul prayed we'd be filled to the top with the fullness of God. It doesn't mean we'll comprehend God completely or we'll have all of him neatly packaged in our minds—that would be impossible. Instead, it means God has all of us. And if God had all of us, his Spirit would permeate our mind, heart, and soul like water flowing in and covering everything. God's Spirit would dominate our mind and desires. Jesus said, "For whoever wants to save their life will lose it, but whoever loses their life for me and for the gospel will save it" (Mark 8:35). The best choices you will make and the most fulfilling life you can experience come from filling your life with God. Only then will you find your truest and best self.

Full of God means...
This process starts with the desire that something be better—like looking at a messy, dirty room and deciding it's time for a change. A lot of junk needs to get tossed out. That junk is taking up valuable space in our mind. Get rid of what wastes your time, and begin to focus on God's best for you. Paul prays (v. 17) that Christ may dwell in your heart through faith. This means Jesus Christ lives in us when we invite him in. Verse 18 says when we get a taste of Christ's genuine love, we'll want it to fill every nook and cranny of our lives. This is a daily process of surrendering to him, opening new doors so his love can become the dominant influence in everything we think, say, and do. Worldly forces and attitudes are always present and ready to rush into any available open spaces in us. When Paul writes about this experience in Romans 12:1-2, he says it's like being a "living sacrifice." In other words, we must continually choose to die to self and live for Christ,

giving him control over what we think, say, and do. Yielding our lives to God fills us beyond anything we could ever dream or hope. We are truly alive when Christ is filling us.

REAL-LIFE CONNECTION: Filled up with God
Items needed:

- Paper
- Pens/pencils

Distribute paper and pencils/pens. Tell everyone to draw a big glass or clear container on the paper to represent their life. Next, they should draw in the container what currently is filling that space. What do they think about? How do they spend their time? What do they love the most? Whom do they spend time with? They also should consider the place of God in their lives.

After a few minutes, ask volunteers to share their containers and contents with the group. Using your personal experience explain what you have found being *filled* with God means—what gets tossed out, what stays, and how God changes your activities and relationships.

Next, ask students to draw what changes they want to make to be filled by God. End in prayer—ask God to *fill* each person in the group.

MEDIA: Christ's Home
My Heart, Christ's Home by Robert Munger (InterVarsity Press, 1986) is a classic story picturing a person's life as a house where Christ comes to live. The story clearly shows how Christ wants to be Lord of *all* of a person's life and how the process happens over a period of time. This booklet is well worth the modest expense and would be a great handout to students after this meeting.

Ephesians 4:17-24

TOPIC: Living as children of light

OBJECTIVE: Students will know God's plan to change their lives from old to new. They'll understand their responsibility to make choices each day to leave the old life and to live in the new life Christ provides for them.

BACKGROUND/OVERVIEW: Becoming a Christian begins a lifetime of change and transformation from old habits, attitudes, and lifestyle to new ones as a person becomes like Jesus Christ. The young church at Ephesus lived in a very secular, cosmopolitan society. They felt the pressure to be like the people around them. The apostle Paul reminded them their new, changed lives in Christ would bear strong witness to the power of the gospel.

GAME/ICEBREAKER: Clothes-pinning
Items needed:

- Clothespins (six per student)

This wild game is simple, yet fun to play with any size group. Give everyone in the group six clothespins. On a signal each player should try to pin the clothespins on other players' clothing. Each of the six pins must be hung on six different players. No one is allowed to remove any clothespins that have been attached to him. While trying to hang his pins on others, a player must also keep moving to avoid having clothespins hung on him. When a player is rid of all six of his clothespins, he must remain in the game and try to avoid having more pins hung on him. At the end of a time limit, the person with the least amount of clothespins hanging on him is the winner, and the person with the most is the loser. Another way to play this is to divide the group into pairs and give each person six clothespins. Each person then tries to hang all her pins on her partner. The winners then pair off again, and so on until there is a champion *clothes-pinner*.

ICEBREAKER QUESTIONS:

- **What's the most annoying part of that clothes-pinning game?**
- **In what ways is that game like your life?** (Possible answer: "I feel like everyone is blaming me for stuff—trying to pin things on me", or I feel that way because I have so much to do!")

- What are people trying to *pin* on you?
- What kinds of *pins* or labels do you have because you're a Christian? (Possible answers: Jesus freak, nun, holy roller, goodie-two-shoes, etc.)
- How might those affect your friendships?

SCRIPTURE: Ephesians 4:17-24

Have everyone read this passage from her Bible, silently.

[17] So I tell you this, and insist on it in the Lord, that you must no longer live as the Gentiles do, in the futility of their thinking. [18] They are darkened in their understanding and separated from the life of God because of the ignorance that is in them due to the hardening of their hearts. [19] Having lost all sensitivity, they have given themselves over to sensuality so as to indulge in every kind of impurity, and they are full of greed.

[20] That, however, is not the way of life you learned [21] when you heard about Christ and were taught in him in accordance with the truth that is in Jesus. [22] You were taught, with regard to your former way of life, to put off your old self, which is being corrupted by its deceitful desires; [23] to be made new in the attitude of your minds; [24] and to put on the new self, created to be like God in true righteousness and holiness.

STUDY QUESTIONS:

- In what ways does God want a Christian's life to change?
- How do people act and live when they don't know God?
- What are some of the specific differences you see between a person's old life and his new life in Christ?
- How does a person get a new attitude and a new self created to be like God?
- Some people think they'll wait until they're old to become Christians. What's flawed about that way of thinking? (Possible answers: They may die before they get the chance, they miss out on all that Christ brings to life, they can become set in their ways and never follow Christ, etc.)
- Why is becoming a follower of Christ as a young person a good decision? (Possible answers: You will have a whole life of experiencing God's amazing work in and through you; when you're old, you will be able to look back on your life with no regrets, etc.)

- How would you explain your decision to follow Christ to someone who thinks you're missing out on lots of wild fun you're supposed to have when you're young?

TALKING POINTS:
Make sure you share the following points with your students:

The old way of life destroys people
When we don't understand God, we think life is all about making us happy. We destroy ourselves and hurt other people. Ephesians 4 says we don't understand because we can't see the truth—we don't know God's plan for us. Our hearts are hardened and resistant to change. When we mistakenly think life is all about us having a good time, we can base our relationships on things such as sex and sensual physical pleasure. We can define love by how much we get from other people and how good we feel. And we can follow the rest of the world believing life is all about having the most toys. We get greedy and fill our lives up with material possessions looking for satisfaction they can't deliver. This leads to a dead end.

God gives us a new life
As Paul told the Ephesians, because of Jesus Christ we can change and leave the old, dead-end life of sin behind. We can open our eyes and embrace the new life God offers us. We can change. The change isn't automatic—there's no easy button to push. Changing to live a Christ-like life is an ongoing process filled with daily choices and decisions. A person doesn't immediately think all good thoughts and make all good choices the moment he becomes a Christian. But if we keep listening to God, we'll begin to look more like Christ and act more like Christ every day. We still need to make conscious decisions each day to cling to the new life we have found. The Holy Spirit, now living in us, gives us a new way of thinking and the help we need to live for Christ.

Living in the light
Sometimes we may be tempted to return to our old ways of thinking and living. We may get discouraged following Christ. Some days we find living like Jesus difficult and reverting to our old self-centered ways easy. Paul told the Ephesians to remember where they came from and how much better it is to live in the light—to have a new life in Christ. We get to decide every day whom we'll serve—Christ, or ourselves—and where we'll live—in the darkness or in the light. Paul urges us to make the right choice—following our Lord and Savior Jesus Christ.

REAL-LIFE CONNECTION: Vital signs

Give the following instructions to your students:

- Draw a simple picture of yourself from head to feet. Do your own spiritual CAT scan looking for signs of your new life and your old life before you knew Jesus Christ.
- Mark on the picture of yourself an *NL* where you see evidence of your new life in Christ. (For example, you could either put an *NL* on your mouth because the words you now speak are different, or an *NL* on your hands because you help people more now and are less selfish.)
- On this picture of yourself, mark an *OL* where you're still struggling with old habits and attitudes you know Christ wants to change in you.
- Write a prescription for yourself about what you need to do (with God's help) to remove the *OL* (old life) and start building the *NL* (new life) in you.
- Share your picture and prescription with someone before you leave this meeting. Ask them to pray with you right now and during this next week.

MEDIA: Before and after

Clip advertisements from magazines, or record TV commercials about weight-loss products or beauty care products with *before* and *after* photos. Together, look at the photos and try to decide if this advertisement is a true story of a real person. Can people expect this kind of change? Talk about why these advertisements are so effective.

Ask your students—

If God were to run a *before* and *after* advertisement about the people who follow Jesus Christ, what would it say or show? Write and design your own ad for God's changing power in your life. What is your story?

Ephesians 5:15-16

TOPIC: Make your life count

OBJECTIVE: Students will know how to productively use the time given them.

BACKGROUND/OVERVIEW: Ephesians 5 contains a descriptive list of Christ-like behaviors on a wide range of subjects. Ephesians 1-3 tells how much God loves us and what he has done for us. Ephesians 4-6 tells how to live in response to God's life-transforming love. Use of our time and the focus of life is part of how we use what God gives us.

GAME/ICEBREAKER: Ready for success?

This is an indoor scavenger hunt. Divide into teams of four or five. Explain that you'll call out the name of an item, and the first person to stand with that item and hold it high will win the round for her team. Keep score and give a prize to the winning team. Here are some items to call out:

Goal-related items to call (Note: If someone holds up an electronic device with the item on it, that item must be visible on the screen to win):
- Calendar
- Watch
- Task to-do list
- Appointment date on calendar
- College logo or symbol
- Bank receipt for a deposit (not withdrawal)
- Grade report, map
- Anything related to dieting
- Any measuring device
- Paycheck stub
- Health club membership
- Running shoes
- Class schedule
- Stand and say date of next SAT exam
- Educational podcast on iPod

Non-goal items to call
- 37 cents
- Shoestring out of shoe
- iPod song (name a popular song) playing on screen
- Photo of you and two friends
- Photo of you sleeping

Some of the items won't be present with any groups (that's part of the point of the meeting), so you will need to mix in some common items to keep the game moving and make the point about what we focus on instead of goals that advance us.

ICEBREAKER QUESTIONS:

- Which items in our game had something to do with goals?
- How would you describe those who have goals for the future? What do they do that makes you think they're aiming toward future goals and can achieve them?
- Why do some people have few or no goals?
- What would you like to do or accomplish during your lifetime?

SCRIPTURE: Ephesians 5:15-16

Have a volunteer read the passage aloud—twice.

[15] Be very careful, then, how you live—not as unwise but as wise, [16] making the most of every opportunity, because the days are evil.

STUDY QUESTIONS

- When God tells us to be careful how we live, what does he want us to do and to avoid?
- Describe and compare how an unwise person lives versus a wise person.
- How will what you're doing now determine what you will do and accomplish as an adult?
- What do you do with your time that is positive and productive? What is negative and a waste of time?
- What do your parents want you to do with your time? What do you want to do?
- What do you think God wants you to do in the future? What about right now?

TALKING POINTS:

Share the following points with your students:

God gave you one life

You only have one life, and no one knows how long you will live. You only get one chance to live each day. Have you heard adults talk about how they'd live differently if they had another chance? What you decide and do when you're young is strongly connected to what you will do as an adult. God gave you your life. How often do you think about what he wants you to do both in the future and each day this week?

God guides us to our life goals

Loving, serving, and pleasing God should control our decisions and goal-setting. Jesus tells us to focus on what is most important (Matthew 6:33), and that people are more important than possessions (Matthew 8:28-34). God gave each person special gifts to develop and special opportunities to use them. We find fulfillment when we spend most of our time doing what God created us to do.

God helps us work hard to achieve goals

We need to set goals that help us be balanced people mentally, physically, socially, and spiritually—like Jesus (see Luke 2:52). God gives us strength to give extra effort to achieve excellence in whatever we do (Philippians 4:13). God tells us to use our time wisely. If we waste our time, we'll never reach our goals. Popular culture tells us (if we're young) that now is the time to have fun because you will have to work all during your adult life. God wants young people to use their energy and enthusiasm developing their gifts working and serving others. You will find your future in what you're doing now as a young person.

REAL-LIFE CONNECTION: Future goals

Say—

Let's identify our future goals and do something to advance them this month.

Hand out a sheet with 12 general goal areas listed. Leave space with each goal for personal notes:

Goals for Life—I will make the next 12 months the best year of my life by adopting the following goals:

- Doing my best in school.
- More involvement in this youth program.
- More involvement in positive school activities.
- Positive and active social life.
- More spiritual growth—reading the Bible, praying, serving others, and learning at church.
- Working part-time and saving money.

- Investing time in friendships and showing Christ to my friends.
- More time and loving relationships with my family.
- Working on my physical fitness.
- Learning a new skill.
- Volunteering my time to help others.

Say to your students—

Looking over this list of goals, mark a maximum of five categories where you want to work and see improvement.

Next to the goals you marked write a few specific steps you will take to improve this area of your life.

Let students work on their sheets for five minutes, have several people share one goal and what they hope to do. Then close in prayer—asking God to help them be wise with their time to achieve these goals.

MEDIA: Don't have regrets

Show a clip from the movie *On the Waterfront* (1954) starring Marlon Brando as a young man who gives up his goal of being a boxer to be a longshoreman. In the most famous scene he says to the man who influenced him, "I could have been somebody, instead of a bum like I have become." You can get this clip on www.youtube.com—search words: *on the waterfront famous scene*. This is a powerful illustration of someone who wishes he had reached his goals.

Ephesians 6:10-20

TOPIC: In a bind

OBJECTIVE: Students will learn God has equipped them with the tools to withstand difficulties and sin in their lives. They'll be able to list the *armor of God* from Ephesians 6 and will create reminders for themselves regarding the lesson.

BACKGROUND/OVERVIEW: Paul reminds the people in the Ephesian church of God's strength and power to provide for them in difficult times. He uses an analogy of armor to show not only that God protects us, but that we also must actively *put on* his protection.

GAME/ICEBREAKER: Caught in a trap

Items needed:

- Balls of yarn (one for every five to eight students)

In groups of five to eight, have students form a tight close circle with one student standing in the middle. Take a ball of yarn and give it to one of the students in the circle. Have that first person hold tightly to one end of the yarn and pass the ball of yarn to the student across the circle from them. Each subsequent person should tightly hold the portion of string they're passed as they hand the ball to the next person. The student in the middle should never touch the ball of yarn, but the students passing the ball of yarn back and forth across the circle are to make it go through or around his head, arms, and legs. Remind students to pass the yarn over heads, under arms, through legs—anywhere they can get it through. Pretty soon a web of yarn should trap the student in the center of the circle. At this point he should try to get out—it should be virtually impossible.

ICEBREAKER QUESTIONS:

- What sins start out small but quickly can grow?
- Committing a seemingly *small sin* (like a white lie) is like standing in the middle of that circle. Every time you tell a lie, another string holds you in, until it's impossible to get out. When did you do something *small* that got you in trouble in a big way?
- How did it feel to be trapped in the middle of a huge web of yarn? How does it feel to be trapped in the middle of a sin?

SCRIPTURE: Ephesians 6:10-20

Play this passage from *The Bible Experience* CD while students follow along.

[10] Finally, be strong in the Lord and in his mighty power. [11] Put on the full armor of God, so that you can take your stand against the devil's schemes. [12] For our struggle is not against flesh and blood, but against the rulers, against the authorities, against the powers of this dark world and against the spiritual forces of evil in the heavenly realms. [13] Therefore put on the full armor of God, so that when the day of evil comes, you may be able to stand your ground, and after you have done everything, to stand. [14] Stand firm then, with the belt of truth buckled around your waist, with the breastplate of righteousness in place, [15] and with your feet fitted with the readiness that comes from the gospel of peace. [16] In addition to all this, take up the shield of faith, with which you can extinguish all the flaming arrows of the evil one. [17] Take the helmet of salvation and the sword of the Spirit, which is the word of God.

[18] And pray in the Spirit on all occasions with all kinds of prayers and requests. With this in mind, be alert and always keep on praying for all the Lord's people. [19] Pray also for me, that whenever I speak, words may be given me so that I will fearlessly make known the mystery of the gospel, [20] for which I am an ambassador in chains. Pray that I may declare it fearlessly, as I should.

STUDY QUESTIONS:

- Paul lists *truth, righteousness, peace, faith,* and *salvation* as weapons God has issued us. What importance does each have against the sins we face?
- Paul lists *God's Word* as another weapon God gives us. In what ways does Scripture help us in our everyday lives? How did it help Jesus through tough times?
- Prayer is also something Paul mentions as a spiritual weapon. How have you seen prayer work in your life or the lives of others?
- Something can be said for preparation. On a scale of 1 (weakest) to 10 (strongest), how spiritually prepared do you feel to face everyday battles and difficulties?

TALKING POINTS:
Share the following with your students:

Arm yourself
Items needed:

- Easel or whiteboard
- Markers
- List of the armor of God

We live in a dangerous and sinful world that is trying to corrupt and control us. Think of all the things you see that are bad for you and could hurt or destroy your life.

We are not alone during difficult times, whether we're dealing with a little white lie snowballing into a giant web of lies or a family hardship. God has equipped us to face problems and conflicts head on.

You need the armor
Ask students to call out difficulties or sins they struggle with (for example, anger, drugs, arguments, alcohol, stress, parents' divorce, etc.). Write them in a vertical column on an easel or board where students can see the list.

Write *truth*, *righteousness*, *peace*, *faith*, *salvation*, *Scripture*, and *prayer* in a vertical column on the same easel sheet or board. Ask students to call out what they think can help them with the difficulties they just listed. Draw lines to connect the listed difficulties with the armor that God supplies.

Hand out a pre-printed list of the *Armor of God* listing each item and the spiritual purpose. Review the list with them and ask—

- Do you have on the full armor of God?
- Which areas of your spiritual life are you leaving exposed?

REAL-LIFE CONNECTION: Armor reminders
Items needed:

- Index cards pre-punched with two holes on one end of the card (seven cards per student)
- Pens/pencils

Pass out index cards—seven cards to each student, if possible—each pre-punched with two holes on one end of the card. Have students take a moment and write each weapon/virtue listed in Ephesians 6. On the flip side of the cards ask them to write a short prayer asking God to help them put on this armor to face a situation or challenge in their daily life. For example: Lying—*Dear God, help me to remember I am to be righteous in all that I do. Give me strength to speak the truth.* Cut up pieces of the yarn used in the icebreaker and have students string up the seven cards into small booklets as reminders of the lesson.

MEDIA: The battle

Sermonspice (www.sermonspice.com) has a large selection of videos on the Armor of God from which to review and select something appropriate for your group. One very helpful video from their listing is "Battle—Extra Footage Testimonies," which features students talking about the battles they're fighting and how God is helping them. Use the search words: *armor of God.*

PHILIPPIANS

Philippians 1:27-30

TOPIC: United and working together

OBJECTIVE: Students will understand that working together as a group and supporting one another is a dynamic response to persecution and opposition.

BACKGROUND/OVERVIEW: Paul instructed the Philippians to stand together, united, when they faced problems and persecutions.

GAME/ICEBREAKER: Hula Hoop lift
Put six to 12 students around a Hula Hoop. Instruct them to rest it on their two index fingers at a waist-high level. As a group they're to lower the Hula Hoop from waist-level to the floor without anyone in the circle losing finger contact with the hoop. Keep the instructions minimal, but enforce the rules. Let the group work out the strategy and cooperation needed to complete the exercise.

ICEBREAKER QUESTIONS:

- What is the secret to making the Hula Hoop exercise work?
- What were the challenges of working as a group?
- What is energizing and helpful when you work with a group? What is frustrating?

SCRIPTURE: Philippians 1:27-30
Have a student read this passage aloud from her Bible.

[27] Whatever happens, as citizens of heaven live in a manner worthy of the gospel of Christ. Then, whether I come and see you or only hear about you in my absence, I will know that you stand firm in the one Spirit, striving together with one accord for the faith of the gospel [28] without being frightened in any way by those who oppose you. This is a sign to them that they will be destroyed, but that you will be saved—and that by God. [29] For it has been granted to you on behalf of Christ not only to believe on him, but also to suffer for him, [30] since you are going through the same struggle you saw I had, and now hear that I still have.

STUDY QUESTIONS:

- How did Paul instruct people to respond to persecution and opposition?
- What message will be sent to the world when Christians stand together?
- How can being part of a group help you face problems better than you would handle them as an individual?

TALKING POINTS:
Share the following points with your students:

Life is filled with challenges
Regardless of how you feel right now or how things are working out for you, the fact is that life is filled with challenges, conflicts, and pain. Sooner or later you will meet a challenge that can potentially damage your faith and destroy your life. You may be tempted to try to go it alone, but that would be disastrous.

We need community
Back at creation, God said is wasn't good for the man to be alone (Genesis 2:18). The fact is that we need others—relationships. God created us to live in community, not isolated from others. Solomon highlights this truth when he explains how two are so much better than one, and three, together, are better yet (Ecclesiastes 4:12). And the New Testament emphasizes the importance of the church, the body of Christ (Ephesians 4:1-16).

The enemy is looking for an opportunity to attack
The Bible depicts our enemy the devil as a lion prowling for isolated, weak victims to attack (1 Peter 5:8-9). He does this through doubt (wondering if the Bible is true and/or faith real), delay (putting off doing what we know we should), discouragement (feeling like quitting when the going gets tough—depression can set in, too), and defeat (giving in to temptation). When we're isolated, on our own, we're much more vulnerable to his attacks.

Believers must work together
In this Philippians passage Paul urges believers to work together so people who persecute them because of their faith won't frighten them. God wants us to work together to rescue and protect individuals who are attacked by others. Together we can support, encourage, and affirm each other—while holding each other accountable. We can create a safe place where people are accepted and loved, and we can send a message to the watching world about how Christians love each other.

REAL-LIFE CONNECTION: Protect and serve
Ask your students—

- What pressures and persecution are hurting people around us?
- What can our group do to help rescue and protect others who need help?
- How can we act as a group to show people our love is real?

After discussing these questions and brainstorming ideas for working together, give the group one or two of the following assignments:

- Establish a *prayer partner* program for the group. Form groups of three who will get together once a week to pray. Between those times, you will communicate regularly (text message, phone call, email, etc.) to check in with each other.
- List five kids at school who are hurting and make an effort to reach out to them during the next three weeks.
- Establish a small *task force* to redesign the youth group to enhance community.
- Choose an *advisory group* to consult with leaders to think of ways the youth group can show the world their love is real.

MEDIA: **Work together**

Show the YouTube video "Battle at Kruger." This video captures an unusual turn of events at a game park reserve in South Africa. When lions attack a buffalo calf, the herd of buffalo surrounds the lions and rescues the calf. A great visual illustration of how working together can send a predator/enemy running. There are many versions of this episode. The best version is 8:23 long. You will see it and the others listed on www.youtube.com.

Philippians 2:12-18

TOPIC: Shining as stars

OBJECTIVE: Students will know God wants them to be like Christ and stand out among their peers as an example of God's love and life-changing power. They'll know how complaining and arguing can be the start of a spiritual decline, and they'll be motivated to live for Christ even when their adult leaders are not present.

BACKGROUND/OVERVIEW: Paul started the church at Philippi on his second missionary journey. He wrote this letter from prison to remind them true joy comes from following and serving Jesus.

GAME/ICEBREAKER: American Idol unplugged
Items needed:

- MP3 player with a short playlist
- Lyrics to the songs on the playlist
- Headphones
- (Optional) Video camera

Select five people to play this one. You should start with the youth leader or a student with a strong outgoing personality who can take some ridicule. This activity will bring out some laughs. Take all the participants out of the room and bring them in one at a time to sing. Play a popular song through headphones to the chosen student so only the participant can hear the music. Give the student the lyrics and tell him or her to sing along with the song. The audience won't hear the music—just the tone-deaf singing of the youth leader or student. Play the song one minute or less for their *American Idol* audition moment. Have the rest of the group vote on who is good enough to *go to Hollywood*. For extra fun, videotape the singers and play all the performances when everyone has finished. Be sure to give the singers lots of love and applause. This could be a challenge to a person's self-esteem.

ICEBREAKER QUESTIONS:

- (Ask the participants): **How did it feel standing alone singing to the whole group?**
- (Ask the participants): **How much did the response of the audience affect how you felt while you were singing?**

- What is so scary about singing in front of other people?
- What other situations have you had in your life where you were ridiculed or criticized because you got involved and did something?
- How did you feel when you heard other people complaining or criticizing while they did nothing?

SCRIPTURE: Philippians 2:12-18

Beforehand, write a letter similar to this passage in which a youth minister is writing to a former member of his youth group who has just begun college. Have an adult volunteer read your letter aloud. Explain how it relates to this passage, then read the passage aloud.

[12] Therefore, my dear friends, as you have always obeyed—not only in my presence, but now much more in my absence—continue to work out your salvation with fear and trembling, [13] for it is God who works in you to will and to act in order to fulfill his good purpose.

[14] Do everything without grumbling or arguing, [15] so that you may become blameless and pure, "children of God without fault in a warped and crooked generation." Then you will shine among them like stars in the sky [16] as you hold firmly to the word of life. And then I will be able to boast on the day of Christ that I did not run or labor in vain. [17] But even if I am being poured out like a drink offering on the sacrifice and service coming from your faith, I am glad and rejoice with all of you. [18] So you too should be glad and rejoice with me.

STUDY QUESTIONS:

- Why do you think I wrote that first letter the way I did?
- Why would the Philippian believers find it fairly easy to obey God when Paul was with them? Why would that be more difficult in his absence?
- It sounds as if these Christians were going through hard times. What do you think was happening that was discouraging them about following Christ?
- What do your friends complain about most? What do you complain about most?
- What does Paul tell them that will make them shine like stars?
- How does "shining like stars" when your adult leaders aren't around encourage your school friends to believe Jesus is real?

- In what ways is the world you live in "a warped and crooked generation"?
- What makes living like a child of God in this world so difficult?
- Why was Paul (the writer who started this church) so intensely focused on helping these people shine like stars?

TALKING POINTS:

Have a conversation with your students using the following points as a guide:

You know the truth—don't slip

Paul had been with the believers in Philippi a long time—teaching them about Jesus and encouraging them to follow Christ. That would be similar to our youth group and how we get together to learn, have fun, and encourage each other. But Paul had left them to minister to others. So, out of concern they could slip back into their old attitudes and habits, he wrote them this letter.

It starts with complaining

Paul didn't rant to these young Christ-followers about sex, drugs, and rock and roll. Instead he focused on complaining, grumbling, and arguing. We might consider these small, unimportant temptations, but they're very important. Slipping away from God starts with forgetting to be thankful for what God has done for you and what he has given you. It gets worse when we have unresolved disputes with other Christians. Our ongoing arguments divide us and destroy the love Christ gave us. If nonbelievers look at Christians and see gossip and arguments, they'll get a false impression of who Jesus really is. Instead, we're to be full of peace, patience, and purity so we stand out from the rest of this dark world—"shining like stars."

Shine like stars

Paul encouraged this church to keep obeying God despite the fact that Paul was no longer with them. He wanted them to kick it up a notch and really tap into the joy of following Jesus, giving thanks in all situations and loving each other unselfishly. He told them to do everything cheerfully, without bickering. Paul wanted to see them grow and be lights to the world because then people would get to see God working in ordinary people. In the same way we must be careful how we live when our Christian leaders aren't around. We should focus on being thankful for what Christ did for us, and we should live in love and peace with each other so we won't be sidetracked.

REAL-LIFE CONNECTION: **Pray to shine**

Items needed:

- Paper
- Pens/pencils
- Markers

Give the following instructions to your students:

- On a piece of paper write, in big letters, two or three things you complain or argue about with your family or friends.
- Turn to someone near you and show them what you wrote and explain each item.
- Next, on the top of the paper write *shine like the stars.*
- With a marker or pen write a circle with a slash over top each of your complaints (like the *No Smoking* or *No Crossing* signs).
- Draw a big star in the middle of the paper (over the top all you have already written) and write some of the godly qualities you want in your life.
- Show your paper (or send it) to a Christian leader who has personally invested in your growth as a follower of Christ. Ask that person to pray for you to "shine like a star" for God's kingdom.

MEDIA: **Shine**

Play and discuss the Matt Redman song "Shine" from his album, *Beautiful.* You can view it on YouTube, too. (Search www.youtube.com using the search words *shine Matt Redman.*) Get the lyrics on the Internet and print them for the group.

Philippians 3:12-14

TOPIC: Reaching for the goal

BACKGROUND/OVERVIEW: Students will understand what it means to have Christ as the prize of their lives and what it takes to attain that prize.

GAME/ICEBREAKER: Bat-spin relay race
Items needed:

- Two to four Wiffle bats

Divide into even teams. Have each team member spin around 10 times with his or her forehead on a Wiffle bat. When they're done spinning, they must race to the end of the room and back to tag the next team member. Continue until the whole team has gone. The first team to finish wins. Be sure to have some adult leaders positioned to help the dizzy runners returning to the team. Don't let them crash into something and get hurt.

ICEBREAKER QUESTIONS:

- How did it feel to race when you were dizzy?
- What made getting back to your team so difficult?
- What would have made this race easier?
- In what ways might this game picture how some people live?
- What big goals do you see adults pursuing with passion and commitment?
- What goals are you trying to reach that are difficult to attain?

SCRIPTURE: Philippians 3:12-14
Have someone read this with feeling aloud from his Bible.

12 Not that I have already obtained all this, or have already arrived at my goal, but I press on to take hold of that for which Christ Jesus took hold of me. 13 Brothers and sisters, I do not consider myself yet to have taken hold of it. But one thing I do: Forgetting what is behind and straining toward what is ahead, 14 I press on toward the goal to win the prize for which God has called me heavenward in Christ Jesus.

STUDY QUESTIONS:

- In what competition have you participated recently in which you wanted badly to win?
- What was the prize for winning?
- What happened?
- In this passage what prize is Paul talking about?
- What does Paul mean when he says, "Forgetting what is behind and straining toward what is ahead..."?

TALKING POINTS:
Share the following points with your students:

A life full of ups and downs
Our lives are filled with unusual, sometimes tragic, events. At times our spiritual journey feels like a roller coaster ride—ups and downs, fun times and scary times. Paul's life must have been like that, too. He was quick to admit he doesn't have it all together—he hasn't arrived yet. That is a relief to hear. If this great man of God can admit this, then it must be okay for us to be in that place, too. However, Paul didn't want to stay in this place of imperfection.

Paul's plan of action
To receive the prize Paul dedicated his life to two actions: First he committed to forget what was behind him—what in your past do you need to forget? Maybe it's a sin for which you can't forgive yourself. Maybe you need to forget what seems to be a character flaw or weakness. Maybe your family history makes you feel trapped. Whatever it is, Paul said, "I am forgetting all that is behind me."

The second action Paul took as he strained and pressed toward the prize was focusing completely on Jesus Christ. We must keep our eyes on the prize if we want to receive it. Looking to our past problems, temptations, or anything else will hinder us from reaching our goal.

The finish line
Sprinters have a fundamental rule: Always keep your head forward looking only at the finish line from start to finish. Never look around, especially at any of your competitors. Why? Because the minute you take your eyes off of the goal, you immediately slow down. You may not intend to do it, but your body will automatically slow down to decrease chance of injury.

Paul said no matter what was going on in his life, Jesus is the prize—so he'd focus completely on reaching his goal.

REAL-LIFE CONNECTION: The grand prize

Share the following with your students:

Paul called Jesus the *prize*. He's the prize Paul would do anything to attain. He'd not let his past or any obstacle stop him from going after Jesus. Is Jesus your prize? Do you want him more than anything else? This means giving him the most important place in your life.

If Jesus is your prize, what hinders you from reaching him? Let go of the past—shake off whatever is slowing you down and strain toward the end of the race. You may need to ask God for forgiveness and also forgive yourself. Focus all your attention on Jesus. Isn't he worth it?

What are some changes you could make in your life this week that would show other people how important Jesus is to you?

MEDIA: Keep your eye on the prize

Show the clip "Cut It Off" (1:41) from the movie *Men of Honor*. After a tragic accident, Carl recommends the doctors cut off his leg so he can continue diving and realize his dream of becoming a Master Chief Diver. You can obtain this clip from a rented video or through www.wingclips.com—search by the title of the clip. Show this clip early on, and use the following as one of your talking points:

Can you imagine having the kind of dedication demonstrated in this film? This man injures his leg but that does not stop him from reaching his goal of being Master Chief Diver. He's so dedicated to reaching his goal he willingly loses his leg. His dedication demonstrates the importance of keeping our eyes on the prize if we want to receive it. When you watch the rest of this film, you see he does exactly what he proposes here. In 12 weeks he proves he can continue, and eventually he reaches his goal.

Philippians 4:4-7

TOPIC: Ultimate joy and peace

OBJECTIVE: Students will learn that even when things don't seem to be going well in our lives, God wants us to rejoice, pray, and trust him.

BACKGROUND/OVERVIEW: When Paul wrote this letter to the Philippians, he was sitting in prison. Paul was instructing all Christians to rejoice in all situations, no matter how bad. In every situation we should pray and afterward rest in the "peace of God."

GAME/ICEBREAKER: American laugher

Items needed:

- Small prizes for the winners of the contest

Choose students to compete in a contest of skill, imagination, and creativity (don't reveal what they'll be doing). Be sure to choose competitors who will ham it up. Explain that you want to have a laughing contest, to choose the *Great American Laugher*. Set this up like *American Idol*, with three *celebrity* judges (from your staff). After each contestant, the judges will rate the performance on a 10-point scale and make evaluative comments about the performance. Keep the totals so you can determine a winner.

Have all the contestants stand side by side in front of the room, facing the group, with the judges seated to the side on an angle so they can see the contestants and the group. For the first round, ask the contestants to laugh as though they had just heard a joke from a friend. The joke wasn't very funny, but they don't want to offend her.

For round two, have them laugh as though they're being tickled.

For round three, have them laugh with delight after being reunited with an old friend.

For round four, have them laugh as though they have just seen the most hilarious scene in a movie.

Total the points, announce a winner, and award a prize.

ICEBREAKER QUESTIONS:

- What's the funniest movie scene you have ever seen? What makes it so funny?

- When do you find laughing difficult?
- What people always smile and laugh—they seem to find fun in every situation?
- When did you find yourself smiling on the outside but crying on the inside?
- What's the difference between *happiness* and *joy*?
- The Bible tells us to "rejoice always"—how is that possible?

SCRIPTURE: Philippians 4:4-7

Have your winning competitor read this passage aloud from her Bible—with feeling.

> [4] Rejoice in the Lord always. I will say it again: Rejoice! [5] Let your gentleness be evident to all. The Lord is near. [6] Do not be anxious about anything, but in every situation, by prayer and petition, with thanksgiving, present your requests to God. [7] And the peace of God, which transcends all understanding, will guard your hearts and your minds in Christ Jesus.

STUDY QUESTIONS:

- Share your most joyous moment or occasion. What made you so happy?
- When have you been *happy* but not *joyful*? When have you been *joyful* but not *happy*?
- When has joy been difficult to find?
- What other emotions tend to push joy out of your life? Why are anger, fear, and other emotions often stronger than joy in us?
- What does Paul present in this passage as the secrets to having joy?
- How are *joy* and *peace* related?

TALKING POINTS:

Share the following points with your students:

It's about our attitude

It's human nature to just feel in the moment. When we're happy, we laugh and smile. When we're sad, we cry. So how can we "rejoice" always when not every moment of our lives is great? Paul wrote this letter while in prison: "Rejoice in the Lord always. I will say it again: Rejoice!" Paul probably had no reason to rejoice while being incarcerated. But he chose to control his attitude and rejoice in the situation he found himself in.

How do we control our attitudes?

Controlling our attitudes isn't easy. We naturally get discouraged when we experience hard times. So we have to be determined to make ourselves "rejoice." This doesn't mean acting fake and saying life is great when it isn't. It means understanding we aren't alone—that Jesus is with us through everything. We find true joy in God. When we focus on Jesus and not on our situations, we find hope to get through it, and find joy.

Don't be anxious

This is easier said than done! But when we present all of our needs and situations to God through prayer, we can stop stressing out. We don't need to feel anxious with trying to find a way to fix things. When we start to worry, we just need to stop and pray and trust God.

Ultimate peace

God promises that when we pray and tell him everything we're anxious about, he'll give us peace—a peace that "transcends all understanding" and will "guard your hearts and your minds in Christ." Ultimate joy and peace come from Christ being in us and knowing he's always with us.

REAL-LIFE CONNECTION: Prayer requests

Hand out paper and pens to students. Ask them to write down the situations in their lives they're most anxious about. Lead them in prayer. Have them present their requests to God and let go of the anxiety over them. Pray for God's peace and the protection of their hearts and minds.

MEDIA: What happens without peace

Show the clip "Turning into the Hulk" (1:04) from the movie *The Hulk*. It's available from www.wingclips.com (use the search words *turning into hulk*). You may want to play this near the beginning of the meeting. Tie it into the discussion by saying that when we're anxious and stressed out in our lives, we feel like we're going crazy and sometimes turn into *monsters* to others.

Colossians 1:9-14

TOPIC: Finding God's will

OBJECTIVE: Students will understand how to determine God's will.

BACKGROUND/OVERVIEW: Paul's letter to the Colossians is filled with answers to the Gnostic assertion that it took special knowledge to be accepted by God. Paul reminds believers the goal of life isn't knowledge, but knowing God can give them the knowledge they need. God wants people to know his will so they can act with confidence and help other people.

GAME/ICEBREAKER: **Dear God, I need to know!**
Items needed:

- Index cards (three per student)
- Pens/pencils

Give each student three index cards and a pencil. Tell everyone to write one question they have about God's will for their lives on each card (e.g., *Whom should I marry? Where should I go to college? Should I work on the weekends?* etc.). Collect and shuffle the cards. Divide into groups of three and distribute the cards evenly among the groups. Ask each group to determine how a person could find God's answer to each question. Students should discuss the responses but not write them down. Afterward bring the large group back together and let the small groups share the questions and their responses to each.

ICEBREAKER QUESTIONS

- What are most of our questions to God about?
- Ideally, how would you like God to communicate with you (audible voice, letter, etc.)? How would you like to communicate with him?
- Tell us about a time you're sure God sent you a message or an answer to something?
- What do you tell a person who says God doesn't answer prayers or tell a person what to do in life?

SCRIPTURE: Colossians 1:9-14

Read the passage aloud while everyone follows along in their Bibles. Tell them to listen for statements that relate to finding God's will.

9 For this reason, since the day we heard about you, we have not stopped praying for you. We continually ask God to fill you with the knowledge of his will through all the wisdom and understanding that the Spirit gives, 10 so that you may live a life worthy of the Lord and please him in every way: bearing fruit in every good work, growing in the knowledge of God, 11 being strengthened with all power according to his glorious might so that you may have great endurance and patience, 12 and giving joyful thanks to the Father, who has qualified you to share in the inheritance of his people in the kingdom of light. 13 For he has rescued us from the dominion of darkness and brought us into the kingdom of the Son he loves, 14 in whom we have redemption, the forgiveness of sins.

STUDY QUESTIONS:

- What did you hear in the passage about how to determine God's will?
- Describe what you're thinking and how you're feeling about your future plans.
- Why should you be concerned about knowing what God wants you to do?
- What does the phrase "wisdom and understanding that the Spirit gives" mean?

- How can we get that "wisdom and understanding"?
- How can a person "life a life worthy of the Lord"?
- For what decisions in your life do you need God's answer or approval?
- For what decisions or choices do you need God's help and guidance?

TALKING POINTS:

Have a conversation with your students using the following points as a guide:

God has already told you

God has already given us clear direction about some of our choices in his Word. Here are three examples:

1. Should I be sexually active outside marriage? Read 1 Thessalonians 4:3.
2. Is it okay to get drunk once in a while? Read Ephesians 5:18.
3. Is there anything wrong with marrying a person who isn't a Christian? Read 2 Corinthians 6:14-16.

Ask God about what isn't already answered

If the situation you're facing isn't clearly stated in the Bible, you need to pray and ask God to show you what to do. If you're invited by some school friends to go to Mexico with them for spring break, how do you know if the trip is God's will for you? How will God let you know his answer to your prayers?

Too many good choices

What if you're faced with two equally good choices? You have read your Bible and prayed about your decision. How do you decide?

Five Cs for finding God's will

Circumstances—Inspect every aspect of why this opportunity exists for you.

Counsel—Get wise advice from mature Christians.

Common Sense—Use your God-given ability to think out the possible results of your choice.

Compulsion—Think about whether God has given you an inner feeling about which choice is right for you.

Contentment—Consider how you feel. Finding God's will usually brings a feeling of deep inner peace.

REAL-LIFE CONNECTION: Listening for God's will

Say to your students—

Think about the choices and decisions you're facing right now. Apply what we have learned in this meeting. Which of the five Cs will help you know what to do? How does this help you move toward a decision? Talk this over with a friend or leader this week.

God doesn't always say yes, so be willing to receive an answer you might not want or an answer that might ask you to wait for a future time of opportunity. Be honest with God and want his will more than your own will. God will bless you for listening to him.

MEDIA: Answering God's call

Show the trailer for the movie *Evan Almighty* (2:52). It's available on you-tube.com (search using the words *Evan Almighty trailer*) and www.wingclips.com (search for *Evan almighty*). God calls newly elected Congressman Evan Baxter to pursue a greater calling and build an ark. This illustrates God communicating his will to a man in a humorous way—similar to how Noah might have responded to God's plans for his life.

Colossians 2:6-8

TOPIC: Don't be deceived

OBJECTIVE: Students will know specific reasons why some students walk away from Christ when they leave high school, and they'll learn what they can do to strengthen their faith in Christ.

BACKGROUND/OVERVIEW: The Colossian church was under attack by the people who didn't believe in God or Jesus Christ. People in the church were being misled to believe other ideas about God and were turning away from Christ. Paul urged believers to put their focus on Jesus Christ and to reject all false teachings and teachers.

GAME/ICEBREAKER: Clothespin attack

Items needed:

- 60 colored clothespins—20 red and 40 blue (or any other contrasting colors you can find)

You need three volunteers for this game. Give each person 20 clothespins of the same color so one person will have all the red clothespins and the other two people will split the blue clothespins. They should clip all of them somewhere on their clothes. Draw a small circle around the three people. They must stay inside the circle during the game. From the time you start they have 60 seconds to get their clothespins off their clothes and onto the person with different colored clothespins. It is two people against one—the two are trying to get the 20 red pins off the person and their 40 blue ones on that person. At the end of 60 seconds, count the number of pins on them and count the difference between the colors. Which color clothespins are winning? Play several times with different people.

ICEBREAKER QUESTIONS:

- Which color clothespins won the game? How did having two-on-one affect the outcome?
- What strategy would best help you keep the right pins on you and the wrong pins off you?
- How is this game like what happens to a Christian when they're at school or work?
- How do you get bad stuff stuck on you?

SCRIPTURE: Colossians 2:6-8

Have a volunteer read the passage aloud from his Bible.

> [6] So then, just as you received Christ Jesus as Lord, continue to live your lives in him, [7] rooted and built up in him, strengthened in the faith as you were taught, and overflowing with thankfulness.
>
> [8] See to it that no one takes you captive through hollow and deceptive philosophy, which depends on human tradition and the elemental spiritual forces of this world rather than on Christ.

STUDY QUESTIONS:

- Give me a number from your observation. What do you think is the percentage of young people who go to church in high school who walk away from Christ by the time they're 25 years old?
- What makes them do that?
- What is present in their life as a young adult that contributes to a loss of faith?
- What does Paul say in Colossians about how to keep your faith strong?
- How could not being thankful cause a loss of faith or turning away from God?
- How does expressing your thankfulness to God keep your faith growing and strong?

TALKING POINTS:

Share the following points with your students:

Why do young people turn away from Christ?

Surveys show more than 50 percent of young adults who went to church as young teens leave that faith after high school. Some surveys put the number at 70-80 percent. If this is true how would our group look in five years? Let's count off by 10. Numbers one, five, and nine stand up while the rest of you stay seated. This is 30 percent of us staying strong in our faith and 70 percent deciding to discard our faith in Christ. Let's sit down now and talk about how to keep our faith strong and growing.

What factors diminish our faith in Christ?

We just talked about this question—what do you think are the most powerful reasons people leave their faith? (Review your discussion from the study questions section.)

Here are a few key decisions young people make that diminish or destroy their faith:

- Choosing not to seek out and join Christians in a new location (college, or military, or job).
- Getting into a romantic relationship with a non-Christian.
- Consistently disobeying God's commands.
- Deciding not to maintain a personal time with God (including prayer and Bible reading).
- Hanging out with non-Christian friends more than Christian friends and church activities.
- Blaming God for something bad that happened (for causing it or not stopping it).
- Not seeking answers to questions raised by non-Christian teachers or friends.

What other reasons or factors would you add to these?

Get rooted to God and grow

Keeping your faith isn't just about saying no to the temptations of the world and relationships with non-Christians. Paul told the Colossian believers that just as they trusted Christ to save them when they were younger, they needed to trust him every day with all their problems. They needed to keep growing from having a childish faith to having an adult faith that can stay strong even when life is tough and discouraging.

Paul said to get "rooted and built up" in Christ. Without roots no plant grows. Underground and out of sight, roots keep growing and seeking from the soil water and nutrients they send to the fruit or flower above the ground. The spiritual disciplines of prayer and reading as well as seeking encouragement from other Christians are what make us strong inside so we can say no to temptations and make decisions about relationships and behavior that would turn us away from Christ.

Who loves you most?

Paul made a special point telling us to overflow with thankfulness. When we get down and depressed about what's happening or not happening in our lives, we can forget what God has done, is doing, and will do for us. When we lose our thankfulness, we start craving the cheap substitutes the world offers in place of knowing Christ and living for God. When we stop being thankful, self-centeredness and selfishness move in. We start looking at everything thinking about what is best for us. God takes second place in life—or third place—or fourth place—and becomes less important to us. Many times life isn't fair, and we get knocked down for doing good and trying hard. Instead of blaming God we need to remember who loves us most and who gave everything for us—Jesus. He suffered for us—we can suffer a bit as we follow him. In fact during those toughest times is when we learn the most and when God's love means the most to us.

REAL-LIFE CONNECTION: Whom are you trying to please?

Items needed:

- Paper
- Pens/pencils

Give everyone a full sheet of blank paper and a pencil. Have them divide the paper into four equal-size quadrants. Have them label the four sections: *Family, Friends, Personal Feelings, Work/School*. Then say—

If you have other significant sections of your life, you can create a box for them and label them. Now look at each box and make an honest evaluation of how you feel about these parts of your life—write either *unhappy* or *thankful*.

Next look at the boxes again, thinking about whom you're honestly trying to please and write *self, friends,* or *God*.

Look at your own paper. Which way are you leaning in your outlook about life? Are you in a danger zone with your mind and heart drifting away from God and feeling unhappy?

If you see the danger signs, talk to a leader or a strong Christian friend about changing your direction and attitude.

MEDIA: Remember to say thanks

Show "Be Thankful" (1:29), a short video about young people complaining about their problems when they appear to be living comfortable lives. It's available for purchase from www.sermonspice.com—use the search words *thankful baked pickles*.

Colossians 3:1-11

TOPIC: Smashing old walls

OBJECTIVE: Students will know God wants to immerse them in godly values—not the values of the world.

BACKGROUND/OVERVIEW: False teachers and worldly philosophies were misleading the Colossian church. In this letter Paul urged believers to focus on Christ as the one, true God and to make their lives more Christ-like.

GAME/ICEBREAKER: Makeover madness

There are several options depending on the resources available.

Professional Makeover: Bring in a professional hairdresser, makeup artist, or fashion consultant. Let this expert talk about what she does to change the appearance of individuals. Have this person demonstrate on you or on selected students.

Gender Makeover:
Items needed:

- A selection of beauty products (blush, eye shadow, mascara, lipstick, etc.)
- Girls' clothing that will fit the guys in your group

Have some girls make over some guys. If it isn't offensive to your group, have them dress the guys as girls.

Comic Makeover:
Items needed:

- A variety of colors of washable stage paint

Have your students make up themselves as clowns.

Watch the time because each of these options could take 20-40 minutes.

ICEBREAKER QUESTIONS:

- If you were given a free makeover, what would you want to change about your outward appearance?
- In what ways would changing your outward appearance change how you feel about yourself?
- What kind of makeover does God offer us?
- How does God change people from the inside out?
- What changes would you like God to make in you?

SCRIPTURE: Colossians 3:1-11

Distribute copies of the passage and have everyone read it and underline everything dealing with God's *makeover*.

[1] Since, then, you have been raised with Christ, set your hearts on things above, where Christ is seated at the right hand of God. [2] Set your minds on things above, not on earthly things. [3] For you died, and your life is now hidden with Christ in God. [4] When Christ, who is your life, appears, then you also will appear with him in glory.

[5] Put to death, therefore, whatever belongs to your earthly nature: sexual immorality, impurity, lust, evil desires and greed, which is idolatry. [6] Because of these, the wrath of God is coming. [7] You used to walk in these ways, in the life you once lived. [8] But now you must also rid yourselves of all such things as these: anger, rage, malice, slander, and filthy language from your lips. [9] Do not lie to each other, since you have taken off your old self with its practices [10] and have put on the new self, which is being renewed in knowledge in the image of its Creator. [11] Here there is no Gentile or Jew, circumcised or uncircumcised, barbarian, Scythian, slave or free, but Christ is all, and is in all.

STUDY QUESTIONS:

- What did you underline as relating to God's makeover? (Let students share, and don't comment on what they say.)
- The world isn't the way God wants it to be. What's wrong with the world?
- We are not the way God wants us to be. What's wrong with us?
- What does this passage tell us to put off from our lives?
- What does this passage tell us to put on new in our lives? (See also Galatians 5:22-23.)

- What change does God want to make in how we treat other people?

TALKING POINTS:
Share the following with your students:

Let God give you a real makeover
We are worried about what we look like on the outside, but God is most concerned about what we are on the inside. We've got it all backwards. The gospel of Jesus Christ isn't only about being given eternal life by God's grace; it's also about life transformation. God's plan is to make us more like Jesus Christ and his character. After you ask Christ to be your Savior, every day of the rest of your life on earth is all about becoming more like Jesus. That's an extreme, total makeover you have been looking for.

Don't find your significance by comparing
Unfortunately, instead of measuring our lives by what's important to God, we compare ourselves with others. Our looks versus theirs…our talent versus theirs…our wealth versus theirs…it goes on and on. People at the very top of our celebrity culture are scared to death about not being good enough. Comparing ourselves with others is a never-ending struggle.

Find your new identity in Christ
We discover our true value and significance when we come to know Jesus Christ. Paul said, "It's not who I am but who Christ is in me (vv. 9-11)." We are created by God and made in his image. We find fulfillment and satisfaction when we obey God. Our security and peace come from God's promise to us, not our personal achievements or acceptance by others.

Find new friendships
This new life in Christ smashes the old wall of separation. The early church confounded the watching world as Jew, Gentile, slave, free, men, and women treated each other as equals in Christ. When Christ is all and in all, a new glue that holds friends and the family of God together is released. This is the answer to the toughest, ongoing human problems of the world. When followers of Jesus put on the character of Christ, society starts changing for the better. You have the opportunity to be part of it. Don't miss it.

REAL-LIFE CONNECTION: Put on—put off
Use a prepared card with two columns of words. One column is a list of what

we're commanded to put off in our lives. The other column is a list of what we're commanded to put on in our lives.

Put Off:	Put On:
Sexual immorality	Purity
Impurity	Fruit of the Spirit
Lust	(Galatians 5:22-23)
Evil desires	Love
Greed	Joy
Anger	Peace
Rage	Patience
Malice	Kindness
Slander	Goodness
Filthy language	Faithfulness
	Gentleness
	Self-control

Distribute the cards and give these instructions:

- Put your name on the card and circle one to three words/phrases in each column according to how you want God to change your life.
- Make your choices and give your card to an adult leader.
- Talk together about how Christ can change specific attitudes and behavior in your life.

MEDIA: Choose what is right

Show one of these video clips. Both illustrate a person making the choice to change to do what is right.

Antwone Fisher—"I Owe You" (2:01). Through Dr. Davenport's counseling, Antwone is able to confront and forgive his mother. Antwone also helps Dr. Davenport. Search www.wingclips.com using the words owe you.

The Devil Wears Prada—"Necessary Choices" (2:34). When Andy realizes she's becoming more like her ruthless boss Miranda, she makes the decision to leave her position and maintain her dignity. Search www.wingclips. com using the words *necessary choices*.

Colossians 4:2-4

TOPIC: How should we pray?

OBJECTIVE: Students will know the basics about prayer and how important prayer is to their relationship with God.

BACKGROUND/OVERVIEW: Life for the early Christians wasn't comfortable. The Colossian believers were under pressure to survive, make a living, and keep their faith in Christ. After giving several instructions, Paul reminded them they could get the help they needed by praying to God. He gave them some key points about staying faithful and thankful as they pray.

GAME/ICEBREAKER: This is a fork

Items needed:

- Forks and spoons (one for every 10-12 students)

Put the group in circles of 10-12 students. Give one student a fork and a spoon. This student will turn to the person on her left and say, "This is a fork," and hand it to him. The person receiving the fork should say, "A what?" The first student repeats, "A fork." Then the second person turns to the left and says to a third person, "This is a fork," and hands it to him. The third person should say, "A what?" Then the second person turns back to the first person and repeats the question, "A what?" The first person repeats, "A fork." The second person turns to the third person and repeats, "A fork." The third person continues this with the next person on the left and repeats the same conversation. This goes all the way around the circle. Each time the question and answer have to go all the way back to the first person. Do a practice round with just one fork. Then add the spoon going the opposite way around the circle with the same dialogue. The confusion really starts when the fork and spoon cross in the circle. It requires a lot of concentration to remember which direction your questions and answers are going. You might have to try several people as the number one person holding the fork and spoon. That person needs strong concentration and confidence. Usually there is lots of laughter when this gets crazy. See how far around the circle the group can go.

ICEBREAKER QUESTIONS:

- At what point in this game did you get confused?
- What part of the instructions was most important for you to know to be successful in this game?
- What do you have to do well to make this work? (Answer: Concentrate.)
- How might this apply to prayer?
- How do people get confused about important matters in their life?
- What instructions does God give us about life? How do we misunderstand them?
- What do you try to remember every day that helps you be successful?

SCRIPTURE: Colossians 4:2-4

Have three students read this short passage aloud from their Bibles, one after the other.

> [2] Devote yourselves to prayer, being watchful and thankful. [3] And pray for us, too, that God may open a door for our message, so that we may proclaim the mystery of Christ, for which I am in chains. [4] Pray that I may proclaim it clearly, as I should.

STUDY QUESTIONS:

- Why is prayer so important?
- What difference does it make in your daily life if you pray or don't pray?
- What is difficult for you when you pray or try to pray?
- What would make you pray more?
- What convinced you that prayer does or doesn't work?
- How does God want us to pray?

TALKING POINTS:

Share the following points with your students:

What is prayer?

Prayer is simply talking to God about what is going on in our lives. Prayer provides the opportunity to give thanks to God and praise him for his greatness and goodness. Prayer also lets us confess our sins and mistakes to God. Prayer can mean asking God for what we want and what we need the most.

Prayer also means being quiet and listening to God. Sometimes we use words from a formal prayer like the Lord's Prayer. We repeat these words and make them our words.

God wants us to ask

God delights in giving us what we need. God says: "Call on me in the day of trouble; I will deliver you, and you will honor me" (Psalm 50:15). Jesus says, "And I will do whatever you ask in my name, so the Father may be glorified in the son" (John 14:13). God wants us to pray and ask with confidence and commitment. He doesn't always give us what we ask for or when we want it, but he does answer all our prayers in his time, and he knows what is best for us.

Make prayer a big part of your life

Six times in the New Testament we're told to "devote ourselves to prayer," including this passage in Colossians. God wants us to pray often and to make prayer part of daily life. We should keep at it and work against distractions and hindrances that keep us from talking to God. A good prayer life includes both focused times when we go deep, as well as lots of short prayers and quick words and thoughts all day long when we're on the go. Prayer can be like breathing—inhaling God's Word and exhaling our thoughts and feelings to God.

Get started

Start where you are. Find a comfortable way to pray. Be yourself and talk to God about what is on your mind. Don't wait to pray perfect prayers—they don't exist. Get started where you are. Find a friend or leader and pray with her several times a week in addition to your own private prayers. Write your prayers in a notebook, speak to God, sing to God, think about God. God is listening.

REAL-LIFE CONNECTION: Your appointment with God

Say to your students—

Make three appointments with God this week. Be specific about date, time, and place. Shut off all the distractions and get quiet. Ask God to meet you. Read something from the Bible and think about it as though God is speaking to you. Spend time thanking God, confessing your sins, and asking him for what you need. Be silent for several minutes and enjoy your time with him. Talk to a leader or friend about your time with God. He can help you learn more about God and be more comfortable praying.

MEDIA: Ask for what you need

Show the clip "Praying For Friends" (1:53) from the film *Because of Winn-Dixie*. After moving to a new town, Opal is having difficulties fitting in with the other children, so she prays to God for true friendship. The clip is available on DVD or at www.wingclips.com. Search for this video by the title of the clip.

1 TIMOTHY

1 Timothy 1:12-17

TOPIC: God's grace and our new lives

OBJECTIVE: Students will know God forgives our sins and uses people with sinful pasts to share his love and message with the world.

BACKGROUND/OVERVIEW: Paul was writing to his young friend and protégé Timothy about leading a church. He reminded Timothy to never forget what God had done for him.

GAME/ICEBREAKER: Attribute ads
Items needed:

- A selection of common objects (e.g., light bulb, roll of tape, ruler, iPod, hat, etc.)

This exercise will stir the creative juices of your group. Divide into teams of three. Give each team a common object. Ask the teams to compose a one-line slogan that describes how God is like the object. If it's a light bulb the team could say, "God lights up the darkness," or for a roll of tape, "God holds the world together." Give the teams time to compose and write their slogans. Have the teams share their objects and slogans with the whole group.

ICEBREAKER QUESTIONS:

- With all these creative slogans we're reminded to look for God every day in the simple things of life. What were some of your favorite slogans?
- What simple objects did Jesus use to describe God and the kingdom of God?
- What objects, places, people, or activities remind you to think about God?
- When you think about what God has done for you, what comes to mind?

SCRIPTURE: 1 Timothy 1:12-17
Read the following passage aloud to your students.

[12] I thank Christ Jesus our Lord, who has given me strength, that he considered me faithful, appointing me to his service. [13] Even though I was once a blasphemer and a persecutor and a violent man, I was shown mercy because I acted in ignorance and unbelief. [14] The grace of our Lord was poured out on me abundantly, along with the faith and love that are in Christ Jesus.

[15] Here is a trustworthy saying that deserves full acceptance: Christ Jesus came into the world to save sinners—of whom I am the worst. [16] But for that very reason I was shown mercy so that in me, the worst of sinners, Christ Jesus might display his unlimited patience as an example for those who would believe on him and receive eternal life. [17] Now to the King eternal, immortal, invisible, the only God, be honor and glory for ever and ever. Amen.

STUDY QUESTIONS:

- What did Paul do when he was against Christ?
- God could have punished and destroyed Paul for his actions. What did God do instead?
- Why does God show mercy and patience to people who oppose him?
- Why did Christ come into the world?
- Why doesn't God give up on really bad people who are against Christ?

TALKING POINTS:

Have a conversation with your students using the following points as a guide:

God forgives people

The apostle Paul couldn't stop thanking God for his all-encompassing forgiveness and acceptance. Paul admitted he used to curse Jesus and hunt down Jesus' followers. He had beaten them and had participated in killing some of them, including Stephen. He used to be ignorant and hardened toward Jesus. Paul was amazed that Jesus would forgive him and now send him out to tell others about him. Paul was completely forgiven.

Some people think they can never come to God because of something they have done in the past. God forgives the worst sinners who come to him confessing and repenting.

God changes people

Paul wasn't the man he used to be. He used to be the worst kind of sinner, but he had been changed to one who was completely focused on pleasing and serving Jesus. The new Paul saw the real Jesus. His goal was to become like Jesus.

Christ changes everyone who comes to him and surrenders his life. Some changes are quick—some are slow. But God never stops working in our lives to make us like Jesus in how we think, talk, act, and love others.

God uses people

As unbelievable as it seems, God uses people like Paul (whom many would consider the least likely candidate) to share the message of forgiveness and redemption. God seems to find great joy in letting ordinary people deliver the news from heaven to us. Paul wrote that he was a perfect example of God's unlimited patience as he calls people to give their lives to him.

God will use the events and experiences of your life to connect with people who need him. How would your life show people about the greatness and love of God?

Never forget what Jesus did for you

Paul could never forget. When we understand how far God came to rescue us and how much he paid for our forgiveness, the praise and appreciation flows out of us. When we face challenges we don't give up because God never gave up on us. When we struggle, we remember Jesus' promise to never leave us or forsake us.

REAL-LIFE CONNECTION: Gone in a flash of grace

Item needed:

- Magician's flash paper from a novelty store (enough for all students to have a small piece)

At the end of the lesson distribute the magician's flash paper to the students. (Don't say anything about it being special paper.) Instruct students to write down their worst sin(s) on the paper (similar to the way Paul described himself as the worst sinner). Make sure no one puts any names on the papers. After a couple of minutes collect the papers and put them in a metal coffee can or metal cooking pan with high sides. Gather everyone to stand around you and the container. With all the papers in the pan, instruct the students to think of their sin and say together with you, one phrase at a time:

- Here is a trustworthy saying that deserves full acceptance:
- Christ Jesus came into the world to save sinners
- Of whom I am the worst.
- God forgive me for my sins.
- Use me and my story to bring people to you.
- I put my trust in you.

Light a match and drop it on the papers. They'll go *poof* and be completely gone. Close with a prayer of thanksgiving.

MEDIA: Lord, forgive me

Show the clip "Will God Forgive Us?" (1:05) from the movie *The Family That Preys*. It's available from Wing Clips. (Search www.wingclips.com using the words *will God forgive*.) Charlotte asks her friend Alice if God will forgive her for all of her past sins.

1 Timothy 2:1-8

TOPIC: Prayer for everyone

OBJECTIVE: Students will understand the importance of prayer and will commit to praying daily for others.

BACKGROUND/OVERVIEW: Paul was giving Timothy instructions on worship for the church in Ephesus. Recognizing that prayer is a vital part of a healthy church, Paul urged the church to pray for everyone in general and leaders specifically. He underscores the impact of prayer on our daily lives and on others.

GAME/ICEBREAKER: Prayer survey

You can do this as a secret exercise—the whole group voting individually with their heads down and eyes closed. Or you can have students express their answers openly for all to see. Explain that in a couple of minutes you'll read a series of statements. After each statement you'll give them the opportunity to vote, and they should raise a hand at the appropriate time. Remind students this survey has no right or wrong answers, and assure them they can be honest in this safe environment. Read each statement, asking students to raise their hands for each number so you can see where they are in terms of their overall beliefs about prayer. Note: As they're voting, have a helper total the number of votes for each option and be prepared to share the results at the end.

After each statement, ask students to give their answers according to the following 5-point scale: I totally disagree; I somewhat disagree; I don't disagree or agree; I somewhat agree; I totally agree.

So you would say something like this:

I believe there is a God, but I question whether he's personally interested in people. If I don't see an obvious answer, I begin to wonder if God answers at all.

How many of you totally disagree? Somewhat disagree? Neither disagree nor agree? Somewhat agree? Totally agree?

Try to get through all the statements, but be ready to eliminate some of them if this is taking too long. At the end have your helper give the totals for each statement.

Negative:

1. I believe there is a God, but I question whether he's personally interested in people. If I don't see an obvious answer, I begin to wonder if God answers at all.
2. I treat God like a Santa Claus—give me this, give me that.
3. I can hardly accept a no answer.
4. In my book answered prayer is just a coincidence.
5. I prayed once and God never answered, so I don't pray anymore.
6. Days go by, and I never pray.
7. If I don't feel like praying, then I don't.
8. I won't pray in public.
9. I've almost buried my prayer life.

Positive:

1. I believe beyond a shadow of a doubt that God answers prayer. I don't always know how God answers prayers, but I always have faith he will.
2. I often praise and thank God as well as ask him for things.
3. When God answers no, I feel it's for my own good.
4. When God answers a prayer, my faith is strengthened.
5. If God says, "Wait awhile", I accept his timing without reservation.
6. I find myself praying all during the day.
7. When I don't feel like praying, that's when I pray the hardest.
8. I feel as comfortable praying in public as I do alone.
9. I feel that my prayer life is really growing.

ICEBREAKER QUESTIONS:

- Which statement(s) bothered you the most—that is, which ones did you have the most difficulty figuring out?
- What is the purpose of prayer?
- Why might God answer no to a prayer?
- For whom should we pray?

TRANSITION:

Share with your students—

Prayer is our way of sharing with God what is on our hearts. Today we're going to deepen our understanding of prayer by looking at something Paul told Timothy that applies to all of us as followers of Jesus.

SCRIPTURE: 1 Timothy 2:1-8
Read the passage aloud while the group follows along in their Bibles.

[1] I urge, then, first of all, that petitions, prayers, intercession and thanksgiving be made for everyone— [2] for kings and all those in authority, that we may live peaceful and quiet lives in all godliness and holiness. [3] This is good, and pleases God our Savior, [4] who wants all people to be saved and to come to a knowledge of the truth. [5] For there is one God and one mediator between God and human beings, Christ Jesus, himself human, [6] who gave himself as a ransom for all people. This has now been witnessed to at the proper time. [7] And for this purpose I was appointed a herald and an apostle—I am telling the truth, I am not lying—and a true and faithful teacher of the Gentiles.

[8] Therefore I want the men everywhere to pray, lifting up holy hands without anger or disputing.

STUDY QUESTIONS:

- For whom does Paul say we should pray and why?
- What is the connection between prayer and how we live?
- What is the connection between how we live and others being saved?

TALKING POINTS:
Share the following points with your students:

Four aspects of prayer
Paul begins this section of his letter to Timothy with an invitation to prayer. He lists four aspects of prayer that we'd do well to ensure are a part of our prayer lives as well. The differences among the first three can be seen as splitting hairs—not really necessary. Nevertheless, their subtle differences affirm the richness of the practice of prayer, so we'll just note them briefly:

Petitions: These are requests made to God by which one recognizes their need and humbly asks him for help.

Prayers: The word used here is a general word for prayer. It helps us see prayer as an act of worship.

Intercession: The word translated *intercession* is another word for making a request, but it's specifically used of a request to a superior. The concept of intercession throughout both the Old and New Testaments involves standing in the gap on behalf of someone else. Paul doesn't mention this specifically; we can see the concept implied when Paul says our prayers should be humbly brought before God on the behalf of others.

Thanksgiving: Finally Paul reminds us prayer must be done with an attitude of gratitude. For what should we be thankful? We should be thankful God hears us, knows all things, is in control, is able, and is trustworthy.

Prayer pointed outward
Being self-centered is in our nature, and we experience this often in prayer. Paul knew this was a tendency all humans have, so he urged believers to pray for everyone generally and for leaders specifically. Prayer isn't to be a selfish activity confined to our own interests. Our prayers should be focused outward. We're to pray for others and, in keeping with the heart and teachings of Jesus, not just for friends and family, but also for strangers and even our enemies.

Paul specifically mentions we should pray for our leaders who rule over us and who are in places of importance and influence (whom we sometimes see as our enemies). Why? Perhaps it's because Paul knew our human tendency to forget these people in prayer, especially when we don't like them. We must remember praying for our leaders—political leaders, teachers, spiritual leaders, and even parents—isn't based on whether we care for (like) them or on whether we agree with their stances on issues. And we shouldn't limit those prayers for times of crisis. Our prayers for our leaders must be done consistently out of obedience to Christ.

Prayer leads to peace and proper living
When we live prayerfully, our lives will be marked by peace and calm—a stillness that isn't shaken when the world seems to be crumbling. Our quiet stability during chaos will show our devotion to the Lord and our trust in him as the Source and Sustainer of life. When we pray our lives will begin to reflect God's heart and character. We'll be known for our respect, honesty, and integrity. Prayer leads to peace and proper living.

Prayer is the foundation for salvation
As people see how we live, they'll be confronted with a choice. Paul says God wants all people to be saved, but he'll not force them to embrace him

as Savior and Lord—that choice is up to the individual. When people see our dependence on the Lord that all begins with prayer, and when our lives reflect the presence of Jesus, the Prince of Peace, we'll play an important role in convincing people of their need for Christ as well. Prayerful living is one way we can actively point people to Jesus.

REAL-LIFE CONNECTION: Prayer connection
Ask—

- For what can we thank God in prayer?
- In what specific ways does prayer change your perspective and affect your daily actions?
- Paul says prayer should impact how we live. He then seems to suggest that how we live plays a role in others accepting him. How have you seen that work in your life?

MEDIA: Healing prayer
Show the Sermonspice video "Healing of the Blind Man" (2:55). (Go to www. sermonspice.com and use the search words *healing of the blind man people*.) This video looks at the encounter of Bartimaeus with Jesus in a modern-day setting.

You could also show the clip "Talk to God" (2:11) from the movie *Saving God*. Convicted felon Reverend Armstrong returns to his neighborhood a changed man looking to take over his father's old church, which is in a neighborhood littered with drugs and gangs. In this scene Reverend Armstrong challenges a young man to pray—he explains what prayer is and how it works. This clip is available at www.wingclips.com—search by the title of the clip.

1 Timothy 3:1-7

TOPIC: Prepare to lead

OBJECTIVE: Students will know the standards required of a church leader, and they'll begin developing godly character now in preparation for their future service for Christ.

BACKGROUND/OVERVIEW: Paul was giving his young protégé, Timothy, specific instructions about the qualifications for a church leader, pastor, or overseer.

GAME/ICEBREAKER: **Are you qualified?**
Items needed:

- Worksheets (see below)
- Pens/pencils

Hand out copies of the following worksheet (be sure to leave space for answers after each listed occupation). Tell everyone to fill it out honestly and not to put a name on the paper.

For each of the following jobs, please list two or three of your most important qualifications. This does not mean you want any of these careers—only that you might be qualified for them.

- Dogcatcher
- Garbage collector
- Flight attendant
- Driver's Ed. instructor
- Coach
- Brain surgeon
- Youth leader
- Disk jockey
- Horse jockey
- Model
- Sales rep
- Pastor

Collect the papers and give them to a staff person. Then explain the following statements were found on real résumés and cover letters for people seeking employment. Read some of them aloud.

- "I have lurnt Word Perfect 6.0 computor and spreasheet progroms. Am a perfectionist and rarely if if ever forget details."
- "Let's meet, so you can 'ooh' and 'aah' over my experience."
- "You will want me to be Head Honcho in no time."
- "I procrastinate, especially when the task is unpleasant."
- "Note: Please don't misconstrue my 14 jobs as 'job-hopping.' I have never quit a job."
- "Reason for leaving last job: They insisted that all employees get to work by 8:45 AM every morning. I couldn't work under those conditions."
- "References: none. I've left a path of destruction behind me."

From the July 21, 1997, issue of *Fortune* magazine.

Then have your staff person read a selection of qualifications from the worksheets—one occupation at a time. But he shouldn't read the qualifications for pastor.

ICEBREAKER QUESTIONS:

- What makes a person qualified for one type of job and not another?
- If you were the person doing the hiring, what would you look for in a personal résumé? How about in the interview?
- What do most employers look for when they interview job candidates?
- How can you make a good impression on a potential employer?

Have a staff person read the qualifications listed on the sheet for pastor. Then ask what they think of those qualifications.

SCRIPTURE: 1 Timothy 3:1-7

Redistribute the worksheets and pens/pencils, and tell everyone to use the blank side and to write the qualifications of a church leader as you read this passage aloud. They should write these qualifications in their own words and not just repeat what the verses say.

[1] Here is a trustworthy saying: Whoever aspires to be an overseer desires a noble task. [2] Now the overseer is to be above reproach, faithful to his wife, temperate, self-controlled, respectable, hospitable, able to teach, [3] not given to drunkenness, not violent but gentle,

not quarrelsome, not a lover of money. ⁴ He must manage his own family well and see that his children obey him, and he must do so in a manner worthy of full respect. ⁵ (If anyone does not know how to manage his own family, how can he take care of God's church?) ⁶ He must not be a recent convert, or he may become conceited and fall under the same judgment as the devil. ⁷ He must also have a good reputation with outsiders, so that he will not fall into disgrace and into the devil's trap.

STUDY QUESTIONS:

- What did you have on your list? (Put them on a whiteboard or piece of posterboard.)
- What are they supposed to do? What are they told not to do?
- Which of these requirements are about a person's character and apply to lifestyle and actions all the time? Which ones are limited to what this person does when on the job, working in the church?
- Which of these job requirements are most important for a leader in the church?
- Which would be the most difficult for you to fulfill as a leader? (Let's assume you're married and have children.)
- What happens to a church when the pastor or leaders ignore or break these leadership rules?
- In what ways would following these rules help you regardless of your future occupation?

TALKING POINTS:

Share the following points with your students:

Build your resume to work for God

God doesn't want leaders selected on the basis of popularity, physical appearance, or power—God is looking for a person whose heart is fully committed to loving and serving him and the people who need him. God is interested in what a person believes and how that person lives. The standards are high for leaders because they're expected to be examples and role models, not of perfection but of heart-driven commitment to doing what is right.

Leader standards are important

We can find many examples of leaders in government, business, and the church who have disappointed and hurt the people they were supposed to serve. Can you name a few of them? God is using Paul to tell Timothy (a young leader and pastor) the standards he requires from leaders:

- Set a good example.
- Be self-controlled in all activities and behaviors.
- Give generously and serve others.
- Be a good leader in your family.
- Be mature in your faith in Christ and have a humble attitude.
- Have a good reputation with others inside and outside the church.

Start preparing now

Start preparing for your adult job and responsibility right now. Start building your character and reputation this week. Your character and qualifications are not the words you write on a paper when you need a job—they are how you live every day, starting today. Popular culture encourages young people to go crazy now and then shape up later, but the habits you establish now stay with you into your young adult and adult life. If you're selfish now, or lazy, or lack self-discipline, you can't flip a switch when you graduate or get a job. Your attitude and habits stick with you and can take a long time to change. Take responsibility now and live for Christ when you're young. You'll learn so much more and be known by others for your reliability and enthusiasm. Your life and work tomorrow starts today. Be the leader God wants you to be. Start today.

REAL-LIFE CONNECTION: Invisible CEO

Give your students the following instructions:

This week I want you to live as though you're being watched at home and school by the CEO of a company you would love to work for and where you could earn good money when you get out of school. This CEO is going to see your attitude and work habits, hear your words, and watch your interaction with people and how well you learn and follow instructions. Pretend this CEO is sitting in your classes, eating at your table, and talking to your parents and friends. What would he think about you by the end of the week?

At the end of the week remind yourself a person's character is what we do when we think no one is watching. The CEO wasn't there last week and won't be there this week, but you'll be there. Every hour and every day is an opportunity for you to develop the skills and gifts God has given you. What you work on developing this week and this year will be what God uses in the future.

MEDIA: Bad examples

Search for *job interviews* or *bad job interviews* on www.youtube.com to find a wide variety of funny job interviews. (Be sure to preview them for inappropriate language or content.)

1 Timothy 4:12-16

TOPIC: Leading by example

OBJECTIVE: Students will understand how the way they live influences others, and they'll choose to take steps toward living exemplary Christian lives.

BACKGROUND/OVERVIEW: Paul wrote this letter to Timothy, a young pastor whom he had placed in charge of his work in the city of Ephesus. Paul considered young Timothy to be like a son. Evidently some in the church at Ephesus were having a problem with Timothy's relatively young age. So Paul wrote to affirm Timothy and encourage him to faithfully carry out his leadership responsibilities, regardless of his age.

GAME/ICEBREAKER: **Paul's dilemma**
Use this as a dramatized role-play. Beforehand choose eight actors and give each one a note card you have prepared with the description of what they say to Paul (see below). The actors don't have to memorize what's on their cards—instead each should use the card as a prompter for what to say. Seat Paul in the center of the room. Then have each character come to him to speak. A few props for the different characters will make it more memorable.

Set up the play by explaining the following:

Paul is a junior in high school. He's relatively well accepted by his friends. He makes average grades and is a member of several school organizations: choir, the track team, and student council. He has been friends with one group of five guys through most of his junior high and high school years. His parents are respectable members of the community. His father is a lawyer, and his mother is the secretary of a popular civic organization. The whole family is active in a local church where his father and mother hold leadership positions. Paul's problem is that he has been close with this group of five guys for a long time, and their values have always been quite similar. But lately the guys have been messing with drugs and alcohol. At first Paul was with them, but now he's beginning to feel more and more uncomfortable. He discussed the problem with his buddies, but they don't see anything wrong with what they're doing. If Paul decides to stop going along with the group, it may cost him his relationship with the guys. He approaches a number of acquaintances seeking advice.

Youth Group Volunteer Leader: I'm concerned you may get sucked into the habits of your buddies. My advice is to break the relationship.

Jesus never allowed relationships to get in the way of his convictions. Take Martin Luther—he did what he knew was right regardless of the circumstances.

Paul's Uncle: I'm your favorite uncle and a lawyer. You tell me you don't see what is so wrong with all of partying and the drugs and alcohol. You just don't feel right about it. I can tell you with statistics the dangers of marijuana and alcohol. Let me tell you abstinence is the only logical and safe choice. Don't do it ever.

Sunday School Teacher: Paul, I have been your Sunday school teacher for many years. You're either with Christ or against him. You either are committed or not committed. What is at stake is behaving like a Christian should and renouncing every appearance of evil or being worldly and sold out to sin.

Youth Director: Paul, I had a close friend who was bothered by the direction his friends were going but didn't have enough courage to stand for his conviction. As a result he became heavily involved in drugs, disgraced his family and friends, and eventually committed suicide. You have great potential, Paul, to influence hundreds of young people—in fact I was just going to ask you to take a leadership position in the youth group.

A Neighbor (who is also a policeman): Paul, I saw a report at work with the names of some of your friends who are on the brink of getting into trouble with drugs. I'm concerned you understand the legal implications of your friends' behavior. I counsel you to stay away or you and your friends will get busted. I personally don't see what's wrong with a kid experimenting with marijuana, but we must all obey the laws or there would be total chaos. Laws are there for our protection and we must follow them.

The Pastor: Paul, the church has always spoken out against non-Christian behavior. Ever since the church was founded such things weren't acceptable for church members. The purity of the church, whether it's a local body of believers or the church universal, has always been a focal point for our doctrine.

The Girlfriend: Paul, regardless of what anyone else says, you need to do what's right. If you make the wrong choice, you'll never be able to live with yourself. If your parents knew you're experimenting with marijuana and alcohol, your mother would be crushed, and your father would be humiliated. Besides, what about me and our relationship? You know what I think of your group of friends and their actions. If I meant very much to you, you would think carefully about what you're doing.

Paul's Older Brother: I think you're making a big issue out of nothing. What you're feeling is false guilt produced by the old-fashioned values of our parents. I regularly smoke pot and drink and I still maintain a high grade point average and hold down a good job. Paul, don't get involved in heavy drugs or excessive drinking, but don't sacrifice your good friendships for a nonissue.

ICEBREAKER QUESTIONS:

- What were the strongest, most convincing statements given to Paul?
- Which arguments were the weakest and least convincing?
- With which person do you most agree? Why? Least agree? Why?
- What answer would you have given Paul?
- If you were in Paul's situation, to whom would you listen? What would you do?

TRANSITION:

Say—

A young person's life is filled with choices. Someone has said that who we are is the sum of our choices. But our choices do not just affect us. Our choices and our lifestyles directly impact others. God wants us to live in a way that positively impacts others. You can make decisions about how to live that will cause you to grow in Christ and also enable you to influence others for him. Let's check out what another Paul had to say about this to his young friend.

SCRIPTURE: 1 Timothy 4:12-16

Have a young man read the passage aloud from his Bible.

[12] Don't let anyone look down on you because you are young, but set an example for the believers in speech, in conduct, in love, in faith and in purity. [13] Until I come, devote yourself to the public reading of Scripture, to preaching and to teaching. [14] Do not neglect your gift, which was given you through prophecy when the body of elders laid their hands on you.

[15] Be diligent in these matters; give yourself wholly to them, so that everyone may see your progress. [16] Watch your life and doctrine closely. Persevere in them, because if you do, you will save both yourself and your hearers.

STUDY QUESTIONS:

- What is Paul's main message to Timothy?
- Why is he telling him this?
- When have you had something important to say but felt as though older people weren't taking you seriously because you were young?
- What does it mean to set an example?
- When have you been told you're an example? What difference did that statement make to you?
- Who has been the most influential, positive example in your life?

TALKING POINTS:

Share the following points with your students:

You can be young and be a leader

Timothy was called by God and sent by Paul to be a leader in the city of Ephesus. A relatively young man, Timothy no doubt had his critics—mostly, it would seem, older people. For older people to be instructed by younger isn't the way it usually works. Paul wrote, "Do not let anyone look down on you because you are young." This could be translated something like: *Don't you dare let anyone give you a hard time just because they're older!* He told Timothy he had the authority to do the work of a leader.

Leadership isn't age or power

Paul didn't tell Timothy to call a meeting to hammer his opponents or use his title to verbally put them in their place—he wrote that Timothy's authority should lead through his example, the quality of his life. Authority has little to nothing to do with age, and everything to do with maturity. Paul told Timothy to let his life do the talking.

Lead by example

Paul identified five areas of life where Timothy was to be an example:

1. <u>Speech</u>: We must give careful attention to the things we say in public and private. Whether in group discussions, private phone calls, on the Internet, or in text messages, the exemplary leader ensures

their words are not slanderous or gossip-filled, but life-giving and seasoned with salt (Colossians 4:6; James 3:1-12).

2. <u>Conduct</u>: We must also be conscious of how we're living and ensure our behavior is honoring to Christ. Whatever situation or environment we find ourselves in, we must be the salt and light Christ desires us to be (Matthew 5:13-15).

3. <u>Love</u>: This is agape love—sacrificial, serving love that always seeks the good of others, no matter the cost. Love is the mark of Christ and the goal of every Christ-follower (1 Timothy 1:5).

4. <u>Faith</u>: Exemplary leaders must also be known for their reliability, trustworthiness, and loyalty. We must be known as steadfast in our commitment to Christ and dependable in the work of advancing his kingdom.

5. <u>Purity</u>: Finally we must set a pattern for others to follow in the areas of chastity and modesty. We must be committed to God's Word, maintaining blameless thought lives and living with godly, biblical relational standards. We need to view others with respect and purity (1 Timothy 5:2). We need to weigh carefully the motives and the messages behind such things as what we wear (or don't wear), what we talk about, how we talk about it, and the effect our behavior in this respect will have on others.

Watch your life

Paul urged Timothy to watch his life and doctrine closely (v. 4:16). Before he could help anyone else, he must first help himself. Jesus taught, "Love your neighbor as yourself" (Matthew 22:39). He also said, "Out of the overflow of the heart, the mouth speaks" (Matthew 12:34). What's inside us will eventually come out—what we do flows out of who we are. Therefore caring for our own souls is of primary importance if we're to be people who influence others through our example.

REAL-LIFE CONNECTION: Circle of influence

Ask your students—

• Who are the people in your circle of influence? You influence upward to parents, older siblings, teachers, politicians. You influence downward to younger students at school and younger siblings. You influence outward to your peers.

- What messages are you communicating to others through your example in each of the areas Paul mentions?
- What areas do you need to improve in? How can you do that?

Give them the following assignment:

Pick one area to work on during the next month. What is one way you'll try to set a better example in that area? Commit to doing it for one month. After a month come back and share with the group how you're doing.

MEDIA: Lessons in prayer

Show the Sermonspice video "1 Timothy 4:12" (1:16). This clip can be purchased from www.sermonspice.com (search using the words *visual scripture Timothy*). This is a visual presentation of 1 Timothy 4:12 with music.

You can also show the Sermonspice video "Christianity Lite" (1:18). Lite on prayer? Lite on Bible reading? Lite on compassion? No problem! Christianity Lite, the new, less filling, less commitment, sport drink is your beverage of choice. Very refreshing! This short, humorous, commercial is a great way to broach the subject of the cost and commitment involved in following Christ.

1 Timothy 5:1-8

TOPIC: Practical care for the elderly

OBJECTIVE: Students will organize an outreach to give help and encouragement to widows and senior citizens in their community.

BACKGROUND/OVERVIEW: Paul, the older, experienced church leader, was explaining to Timothy, the young pastor, the complicated needs of the church with its different age groups and relational challenges. He gives specific instructions about caring for the older widows in the church.

GAME/ICEBREAKER: Don't be afraid of wrinkles

Dress up one of the youth leaders as a senior citizen. Pretend she's the oldest person in the area. Introduce that person as a special guest and interview her about old age. Ask about the person's past experiences, present life, and what she thinks about young people. Make it funny. Let the students ask questions and interact with the guest.

If you've taken the Media suggestion (see page 364), show the video made by the youth group team about local senior citizens.

ICEBREAKER QUESTIONS:

- At what age do people become old? (If it's not age, what is it that makes someone old?)
- Who is your favorite older person? What do you really like about that person and other senior citizens?
- What makes you uncomfortable being around older people?
- How many older people in the church do you know by name?
- What responsibility do Christians have for older believers?
- How have you seen that carried out in your family, in the church, and elsewhere?
- What could you do that would help an older widow or senior citizen?

SCRIPTURE: 1 Timothy 5:1-8

Ask the youngest person in the room to read this aloud as everyone follows along in their Bibles.

> [1] Do not rebuke an older man harshly, but exhort him as if he were your father. Treat younger men as brothers, [2] older women as

mothers, and younger women as sisters, with absolute purity.

[3] Give proper recognition to those widows who are really in need. [4] But if a widow has children or grandchildren, these should learn first of all to put their religion into practice by caring for their own family and so repaying their parents and grandparents, for this is pleasing to God. [5] The widow who is really in need and left all alone puts her hope in God and continues night and day to pray and to ask God for help. [6] But the widow who lives for pleasure is dead even while she lives. [7] Give the people these instructions, so that no one may be open to blame. [8] Anyone who does not provide for their relatives, and especially for their own household, has denied the faith and is worse than an unbeliever.

STUDY QUESTIONS:

- Why is Paul giving these instructions to Timothy? (Answer: Timothy is the pastor, the leader; older people were powerless and often poor—they needed help.)
- In what ways is the church supposed to be like a family?
- How does seeing and treating other people in the church like members of your family help everyone in the church?
- How much help is the church supposed to give to younger and older widows?
- What have you done in the past to help a widow or senior citizen in the church?
- Why do so many senior citizens feel lonely and unhappy?
- What older people in your family do you help care for?
- Why do many younger people find it difficult to give time to help older people?

TALKING POINTS:

Share the following with your students:

Caring for lonely people—getting involved

Don't put up a social wall that isolates you from other believers, regardless of their age. Get involved and let your faith bring hope and help to lonely and needy people. Paul told Timothy to get active helping widows in his church. The Bible says the religion God accepts as pure and faultless is looking after orphans and widows in their distress (James 1:27).

It would be great to go on a mission trip to another city or country for a week. But we have year-round opportunities for mission service very close to home. Our church and community have many elderly people who need our help more than one week a year.

Getting others involved

Paul told Timothy he wasn't responsible for everyone. Many people have family and friends who can help them, but for some reason they aren't involved. Paul told Timothy to start by setting a good example for everyone; his example would give him the opportunity to talk to others who need to help their own family members. The best way to show love to the widows is by giving them time, attention, and physical help with their homes. God will reward people for what they do and use it to prepare them for other opportunities.

Reverse adoption

Paul commands Timothy to treat people in the church as though they were part of the family. This means treating them with respect and patience. Look at the older people in the church as though they're your grandparents, aunts, or uncles. Help them with their housework, errands, and special projects (e.g., snow removal, leaf-raking, painting, etc.). Give them time and attention because so many of them feel lonely and forgotten. Learn from them by asking questions about their lives and faith in God. Tell them about your needs and ask them to pray for you. Give them special reason to live because you love them and need their prayers.

REAL-LIFE CONNECTION: Senior connection

Build off this meeting with an action plan to connect students to senior citizens. Let students be part of the planning. Select an appropriate number of senior citizens in the church according to the size of your group and start a home action project led by students.

Start with several short, one-day projects, but be sure to include interaction time among students and seniors. You want to build a relationship that bridges the age gap and allows both groups of people to identify each other and speak to each other at church.

Look for other small projects where students can take something to the seniors or where students can sit and talk with them. Give students assignments and topics to share with the seniors and have them report to the youth leaders. Organize a dinner, a game night, or a dance and participate with the seniors as well as serve them.

At the end of this meeting ask students to sign up to be part of a special project with local senior citizens.

MEDIA: Senior interviews

Prior to the meeting send a video crew to two or three senior citizen homes and interview a number of seniors about their lives. Be creative and split the interview time between describing who they are as individual people and what life is like for them now. Get your student teams to prepare some great questions before the interview (asking about their fears, hopes, accomplishments, happiness, etc.).

The video team could also go to a senior citizen event in the church or community to conduct some video interviews. Edit the video and show it to the group.

1 Timothy 6:6-10, 17-19

TOPIC: Gotta have stuff

OBJECTIVE: Students will learn material wealth and possessions do not provide true happiness.

BACKGROUND/OVERVIEW: First Timothy is a letter to a young pastor from Paul, his mentor and role model. Paul gave Timothy guidance and teaching about what is important in life and what could destroy his life.

GAME/ICEBREAKER: I'd say that
Place a sign on the wall of the meeting room. Write on it I'D SAY THAT. On the opposite wall place a sign that says I WOULDN'T SAY THAT. Explain that you'll be reading real statements from students. When they hear the quotation, they must decide how much they agree or disagree with the statement. Where they stand in the room between the signs shows how much or how little they agree or disagree with the statement. After each statement and movement by the group you can discuss (as they're standing in place) how they feel about the statement.

Statements by Students:
- Money controls everything. With money, you have somebody with you at all times. You have power. You have a say in government. You have lots of friends.
- Sometimes you have money, but you don't have happiness, so your life becomes an empty space.
- Earning my own money has changed my attitude. I used to go out and I would bug my mom to buy me this or buy me that. But now I say, "Whoa, look at the price of those sneakers. It took me 12 hours of work to pay for that."
- I love money. I see a lot of poor people and everything; but if I was like that, I don't know if I could survive. It's important to me to have a lot of the good stuff, like nice clothes.
- Money is everything. It feels good to have it. I want to make a lot of money. I don't know how but I will. Whoever said money couldn't buy happiness didn't know where to shop.
- To me having a lot of money isn't important. But if you don't have money, most people think you don't have a real life.

ICEBREAKER QUESTIONS:

- What possessions matter most to you?
- How would you react if you lost those possessions? Be specific.

SCRIPTURE: 1 Timothy 6:6-10, 17-19
Read the passage aloud while everyone follows along in his Bible.

[6] But godliness with contentment is great gain. [7] For we brought nothing into the world, and we can take nothing out of it. [8] But if we have food and clothing, we will be content with that. [9] Those who want to get rich fall into temptation and a trap and into many foolish and harmful desires that plunge people into ruin and destruction. [10] For the love of money is a root of all kinds of evil. Some people, eager for money, have wandered from the faith and pierced themselves with many griefs.

[17] Command those who are rich in this present world not to be arrogant nor to put their hope in wealth, which is so uncertain, but to put their hope in God, who richly provides us with everything for our enjoyment. [18] Command them to do good, to be rich in good deeds, and to be generous and willing to share. [19] In this way they will lay up treasure for themselves as a firm foundation for the coming age, so that they may take hold of the life that is truly life.

STUDY QUESTIONS:

- How much money would you like to have? How much do you need?
- When you had more money than you normally have, how did it make you feel?
- The Bible doesn't say money is evil, but the love of money is the root of all evil. In what ways does loving money bring more trouble into your life?
- What does Paul warn Timothy can happen to people with money? What do they become?
- What does God think is better for us than more money?
- How does God want people with money to use it?

TALKING POINTS
Share the following points with your students:

Money is dangerous

The Bible says it can make you arrogant. You might start thinking you're better than people without money or that you don't need anyone else because you can buy whatever you need. The Bible says money leads people into temptation more easily. Having money can create a desire for more things we really don't need. It can cause us to wander away from God because we think we have everything we need. It can make us pray less. In reality some rich people are unhappier than most poor people. Can you think how that would happen? The major danger of money is it would cause you to be satisfied with what you have.

Money is potentially good

Money can have some powerful, positive effects. It can be used to help people with basic needs, medical help, and education. Money can do many good deeds helping encourage God's people, building God's kingdom, providing help to less fortunate families, and sharing God's good news. People who use money for good know the money doesn't belong to them forever. At any time their lives could end or they could lose all they have. That realization helps them hold their money loosely. It is a gift from God to be used for God's work. The best potential of money is the freedom to be generous with what you have.

REAL-LIFE CONNECTION: Possession confession

Have students think back to the most prized possession they mentioned earlier in the meeting. Pass out copies of a *Possession Confession* (prepare these ahead of time) and a pen or pencil. Challenge them to fill out the sheet and sign it agreeing to live a week without their prized possession to loosen its grip on them.

Possession Confession:

I, _____, really like my (name of possession), but I know I'll never find true happiness with this. As an exercise of submission to God and a reflection of his ownership of everything I have, I will go one week without using this possession.

Signed_____ Date_____

MEDIA: Money, money, money...

Play the song "For the Love of Money" by the O'Jays. You can find the song on iTunes and on youtube.com. This song from the 1970s is lively and fun. You can use this during the meeting when students are making their possession confession or play a clip of the song every time you make a transition in the meeting. Give some of your high-tech young people the song and ask them to make a video or slide show for this meeting.

2 TIMOTHY

2 Timothy 1:7-10

TOPIC: A life of power and purpose

OBJECTIVE: Students will know they're able to live lives of power and of purpose through God.

BACKGROUND/OVERVIEW: Timothy was a young pastor in Ephesus and was Paul's protégé—like a son to him. Knowing Timothy could become discouraged in the ministry, Paul encouraged Timothy by reminding him of the power God gave to him and the purpose to which God had called him—to live a holy life.

GAME/ICEBREAKER: Build it better
Items needed:

- Building materials (e.g., Legos, blocks, or a small, cheap model car kit. Small wooden projects can be purchased at a craft supply store for about a dollar.)

Divide the group into two teams. Give each team a building project to be made from materials you choose to give them. Tell them they're responsible for building a certain project. Separate the teams so they can't see or hear what the other is doing. Give one team directions (or set instructions) on how to build the project. Let them freely interact and talk together. Give the other team nothing and tell them they're not allowed to talk about or discuss what they're building. Set a time frame, and let them work it out. At the end of the time, show the students a model of what they should have built.

ICEBREAKER QUESTIONS:

- How did each team figure out what they were supposed to be building?
- Which team had it easier? Why?
- Why was it better to have instructions and be able to communicate with your team members?
- In what other areas of life does this lesson apply?
- In what ways does the Bible give us instructions?

SCRIPTURE: 2 Timothy 1:7-10

Have someone read the passage aloud from her Bible.

[7] For the Spirit God gave us does not make us timid, but gives us power, love and self-discipline. [8] So do not be ashamed of the testimony about our Lord or of me his prisoner. But join with me in suffering for the gospel, by the power of God, [9] who has saved us and called us to a holy life—not because of anything we have done but because of his own purpose and grace. This grace was given us in Christ Jesus before the beginning of time, [10] but it has now been revealed through the appearing of our Savior, Christ Jesus, who has destroyed death and has brought life and immortality to light through the gospel.

STUDY QUESTIONS:

- What kind of life has God called us to?
- What do you think are God's purposes for us?
- What instructions does God give us for receiving his power and achieving his purposes?
- What resources does God give us for doing the job? (See verse 7.)
- What are we supposed to do with those resources?

TALKING POINTS:
Have a conversation with your students using the following points as a guide:

What is your purpose in life?
You get up every day, go to school, do your homework, and hang out with your friends. You spend hours watching television, playing video games and talking to your friends through IM. Do you ever get to the point where you wonder about your purpose in life? Ephesians 2:10 says, "For we are God's handiwork, created in Christ Jesus to do good works." First Timothy 1:9 reminds us God has called us to live a holy life because of his purpose.

So your purpose is to live a holy life, but how do you do that?
If you know God and live close to him, you know he has a purpose for your life. By reading the Bible, you'll be able to see God wants you to love others and to point them to Christ. Many things can keep us from spreading God's love. Often we know what God wants us to do, but we don't follow through because, like Timothy, we're timid. Paul knew a spirit of timidity was one of the main things that could keep Timothy from living out God's purpose for his life.

Timid no more, embracing the spirit of power
Sometimes it just takes a reminder. This is what Paul did for Timothy when he told him, "The Spirit God gave us does not make us timid, but gives us power, love and self-discipline." Sometimes we need to be reminded we have nothing to fear because God is with us, for us, and in us. His Spirit gives power, love, and discipline to do his work. Ephesians 1:19-20 explains that the power God gives us is the same power he used to raise Christ from the dead. Remembering we have this power makes it much easier to boldly share the love of Christ with anyone.

REAL-LIFE CONNECTION: Life purpose
Ask your students—

Are you living a life of purpose and power? If not, what do you need to change to live the life God has given?

Say—

In the next 24 hours set aside an hour to either be alone for reflection or to talk deeply with a very close, trusted friend. During that hour, talk about and write down what you're learning about the purpose of your life.

- What is happening this year that is a hint to you about your life purpose?

- How is God showing you anything that gives you a direction or plan for your life?
- What needs to happen for you to fulfill your purpose? What changes do you need to make?
- What reminder do you need from God to actively pursue his purpose for you?

MEDIA: Find your purpose

Show the clip "An Ark to Build" (00:57) from the movie *Evan Almighty*. (Search www.wingclips.com using the title of the clip.) God appears to Evan and reveals he knows very personal information about him and he wants him to build an ark. Use this clip to open a discussion about finding our purpose in life and God's will for our futures.

2 Timothy 2:19-22

TOPIC: Cleaning house

OBJECTIVE: Students will identify some of the things in their lives that need to be cleaned out so God may use the students to do his will.

BACKGROUND/OVERVIEW: Paul encourages Timothy to be a workman who is approved by God. In order to do this, certain things need to be cleaned out of his life. Timothy is encouraged to flee his evil desires and embrace Godly character in order to be used by God.

GAME/ICEBREAKER: Treasure in the trash
Items needed:

- Trash treasures (see below)

Fill a garbage can with random bits of *clean* trash that could possibly be mistaken for something good (e.g., an empty candy-bar wrapper, an empty potato-chip bag, a small ball with a hole in it, etc.), as well as a variety of *good* items (e.g., candy bar, ping pong ball, pack of gum—anything that can be labeled and collected apart from the trash).

Divide students into teams and have them line up on one end of the room. Explain that this is a relay race and the first team to finish will receive 5,000 points, the second team 4,000, the third team 3,000, etc. (Note: If you only have two teams, begin at 2,000 points). But they'll be able to get bonus points as well. One at a time they'll race to the garbage can where they'll reach in and pull out two items, trying to pick up one piece of trash and one good item. They'll then bring both items back to the line, where they'll discard the trash, and keep the good item. Each good item is worth 100 bonus points. (The competitors must decide whether to go quickly or carefully, adding to the tension.) Give the signal to begin the race. At the end total the points, and the team with the most points wins.

ICEBREAKER QUESTIONS:

- Why was it important to get rid of the trash when looking for the good items?
- What's the problem with keeping the trash and good items together?
- Why did you have difficulty deciding what was trash and what was good?
- What do we have in our lives that could be considered trash? Why do we need to get rid of it?

- Many people today, even many church people, think it's all right to have trash in their lives. What would you say to them?

SCRIPTURE: 1 Timothy 2:19-22
Read the passage aloud.

[19] Nevertheless, God's solid foundation stands firm, sealed with this inscription: "The Lord knows those who are his," and, "Everyone who confesses the name of the Lord must turn away from wickedness."

[20] In a large house there are articles not only of gold and silver, but also of wood and clay; some are for noble purposes and some for disposal of refuse. [21] Those who cleanse themselves from the latter will be instruments for noble purposes, made holy, useful to the Master and prepared to do any good work.

[22] Flee the evil desires of youth and pursue righteousness, faith, love and peace, along with those who call on the Lord out of a pure heart.

STUDY QUESTIONS:

- Describe God's foundation. What is it?
- What's essential for a Christian to do concerning wickedness? How do you know what is wicked and what isn't?
- Paul calls some bad things for disposal of refuse, or not noble. What is he referring to? What happens when a person cleans out everything in his life that is not noble?
- What are we supposed to pursue when we clean up our lives?

TALKING POINTS:
Share the following points with your students:

What kind of garbage are you living with?
Let's be honest. From the outside, we're all pretty good-looking people. But in God's eyes just having a good-looking exterior doesn't cut it. First Samuel 16:7 records God telling Samuel he doesn't look at what humans look at—he looks at our hearts. If people were to truly see what's on the inside, what would they see? They'd see some of the good things, that's for sure. But what about all the garbage we hide in our lives? Think about it for a moment. What kinds of nasty junk do you have in your life you would never want other people to see?

Cleaning house

God doesn't want us to hide the garbage in our lives. No—he wants us to get rid of it. Picture yourself actually living in the middle of a garbage dumpster. No matter how much good stuff you had with you, the garbage would still infect it. Think back to the game. Would you eat candy that had been lying on top of rotting garbage? After a while, the garbage can over-power the good in our lives. That's why God commands us to clean house and get rid of the garbage in our lives.

Out with the old, in with the new

Once we clean out the garbage, God tells us we need to run as fast as we can away from it, from those evil desires. Sometimes cleaning out the garbage means literally throwing away trash reading material. But it also can mean taking steps to not go to certain Internet sites, TV programs, and movies. For some it will mean stopping destructive habits. When we get rid of the garbage, we need to pursue godly characteristics, including righteousness, faith, love, and peace. Not only should we pursue these characteristics individually, but we also should get help and encourage-ment from other believers.

REAL-LIFE CONNECTION: Sin garbage

Item needed:

- A bag of *real* garbage

Before you end the meeting, put a real bag of nasty garbage (rotting food, like day-old fish or salad) in the middle of the group. Open the bag so everyone gets a whiff of what is in it. Ask them who will take this bag home and put it in his room for a week.

Say—

Living with sin in our life is like living with garbage. Maybe you have got-ten used to the smell of sin and are not in a hurry to get rid of it. But it still stinks, and it's contagious. What do you need to clean out of your life? How is the garbage hindering how God might be able to use you?

Share one thing with a friend or leader that you want to clean out of your life. Ask them to keep you accountable to this goal.

MEDIA: Who I've been...

Print out the words and play the Relient K song "Who I Am Hates Who I've Been" from the album *MMHMM*. Look for the video version on www.youtube.com.

2 Timothy 3:12-17

TOPIC: No matter what

OBJECTIVE: Students will know and acknowledge that the Christian life comes with obstacles they can overcome with a solid knowledge of the Bible.

BACKGROUND/OVERVIEW: As Paul sits in prison, awaiting execution, he encourages Timothy, his son in the faith and ministry protégé, and tells him how to persevere through persecution. Timothy is a second-generation believer, having heard the gospel through his mother. Paul also emphasizes the importance of Scripture as Timothy's foundation.

GAME/ICEBREAKER: Good, old-fashioned dodgeball
Item needed:

- A ball (soft enough to throw at people)

For this version of dodgeball you only need one ball. The goal is for one person to use the ball to get everyone else out. Only one person can have the ball at a time, and when that person has the ball, he cannot move. The person with the ball throws the ball at other people to get them out. Any person who gets hit with the ball is out and has to stand off to the side as the game continues. A person can reenter the game if a ball then hits the person who hit him or her. For instance, if John throws the ball and hits Ryan and Katie, and then Phil throws the ball and hits John, then Ryan and Katie reenter the game. The game ends when one person uses the dodgeball to get everyone else out.

ICEBREAKER QUESTIONS:

- What makes this type of dodgeball difficult to play?
- What makes you lose interest in this game (or other games)? What makes you feel like quitting?
- What games or life situations have tested your commitment to keep going?
- What lessons have you learned through these experiences?

SCRIPTURE: 1 Timothy 3:12-17
Ask someone to read this passage aloud from his Bible.

[12] In fact, everyone who wants to live a godly life in Christ Jesus will be persecuted, [13] while evildoers and impostors will go from bad to worse, deceiving and being deceived. [14] But as for you, continue in what you have learned and have become convinced of, because you know those from whom you learned it, [15] and how from infancy you have known the Holy Scriptures, which are able to make you wise for salvation through faith in Christ Jesus. [16] All Scripture is God-breathed and is useful for teaching, rebuking, correcting and training in righteousness, [17] so that all God's people may be thoroughly equipped for every good work.

STUDY QUESTIONS:

- Why do you think Paul was writing to Timothy about these issues? (Answers: Paul is about to die, and he wanted Timothy to be prepared, ready for anything in ministry; Paul knew persecution was inevitable for Timothy.)
- What is the cost of living a godly life?
- What kinds of persecutions do Christians around the world face today?
- What kind of persecutions have you experienced?
- What is the key help available to Christians to combat the persecution?
- What do these verses say about the Bible and its purpose?

TALKING POINTS:

Share the following with your students:

What is the cost?

Everything costs something. The Bible says living a godly life in Christ Jesus also has a cost. Christians throughout the world are paying the price. Some may be experiencing ridicule. Others may pay with their lives. (Briefly tell the story of a persecuted Christian. You can find many stories from *Jesus Freaks* [Tulsa, OK: Albury Press, 1999], *Extreme Devotion* [Nashville, TN: Word Publishing, 2002], or another Voice of the Martyrs resource.)

Who will help you through?

No matter the cost, God provides ways to stay strong in your faith. For Timothy it was remembering "those from whom you learned." Who taught you about the Bible and the truth of salvation? How do their lives inspire you to continue regardless of what comes your way? God never meant for our walk of faith to be a solo experience. Most important is God's strength and encouragement. In addition to God's help and encouragement is the face-to-face encouragement we get from our brothers and sisters in Christ.

The Bible: God-breathed

When we go through trials or persecutions we need to know the Bible. Paul reminds Timothy (and all of us) the Bible is God's instruction book, life-guide, and encouragement to us. When we read and understand the Bible, we'll be equipped and ready for every good work. We need to be prepared for any task in life, whether it's physical training for a sport or simply using gloves when working outdoors. These preparations prepare us for those experiences. When you look at your Christian life, you should know persecutions and trials will come. Prepare yourself by knowing God's Word.

REAL-LIFE CONNECTION: The problem of persecution
Ask—

- What kind of persecution would it take to intimidate you and keep you silent about Jesus?
- What would break your faith or cause you to deny being a follower of Jesus?
- Have you ever been made fun of for believing in God? Have you been teased or harassed?
- If the fear of this happening keeps you from even opening your mouth about your faith, you need to ask God for strength and courage.
- God wants you to be aware and to be prepared. How are you preparing to face the persecutions that may come your way?
- How much of God's Word do you know and use? How many Bible verses do you have memorized? In what ways do these verses help you battle temptation and persecution?

Talk this over with a trusted friend or youth leader. Ask this person to help you prepare for persecution. Learn several Bible verses each month for the entire year.

MEDIA: Prepare for persecution

Show the scene "He Didn't Spear Back" (1:19) from the movie *End of the Spear.* (This clip is available at www.wingclips.com—search using the title of the clip.) When the widows of the slain missionaries go to live in the village of the people who killed their husbands, the natives express their surprise and amazement that the men did not fight back when attacked. This movie clip can be used as an example of Christian character being demonstrated even when personal loss is great. The love and forgiveness the women demonstrated brought many in that village to faith in Jesus Christ.

2 Timothy 4:7-8

TOPIC: The big picture

OBJECTIVE: Students will see how their lives fit into God's big picture and plan, and they'll know the rewards God promises to those who persevere.

BACKGROUND/OVERVIEW: Paul was sitting in prison, awaiting execution, so this book contains his last words to his beloved friend and son in the faith, Timothy. He closed by encouraging him and reminding him he was on the way toward the all-important goal of fulfilling God's purposes for his life.

GAME/ICEBREAKER: Photo scavenger hunt
Items needed:

- Close-up photographs taken of objects and locations within your church
- Small items to use as a marker (small Post-it, checker, etc.)

This game takes a little preparation but is a lot of fun. Find a variety of objects and specific locations within your church or meeting place and take close-up pictures. At each location, leave a defining marker, like a small Post-it note, a checkers piece, or anything that would designate that location. Using a PowerPoint presentation or developed pictures, divide students into teams and send them out with the goal of finding the locations that were photographed. The photo should show a small area of the bigger location. When they find a correct object or location, they should note it on their sheet of pictures. The students will know they've found the right location, as they'll find the marker letting them know they're right. The game ends when all photo locations are found.

ICEBREAKER QUESTIONS:

- How easy is it to find something when you can only see a small part of what you're looking for?
- What benefit is there in seeing the bigger picture?
- When did you have difficulty finding something that was nearby but you couldn't see it?
- What do we miss when we focus exclusively on what is directly in front of us?

- How does this apply to the direction of our lives?
- On what bigger picture should we be focused?

SCRIPTURE: 2 Timothy 4:7-8

Have three students read this aloud—one after the other, in three different translations, ending with this one (TNIV).

> [7] I have fought the good fight, I have finished the race, I have kept the faith. [8] Now there is in store for me the crown of righteousness, which the Lord, the righteous Judge, will award to me on that day—and not only to me, but also to all who have longed for his appearing.

STUDY QUESTIONS:

- What projects or endeavor have you started that have been hard to finish?
- What keeps you from finishing those projects? Why is that frustrating?
- In what ways is life like a race? What keeps someone from finishing a race?
- What reward awaits those who finish the race God has given them?
- Why do people who start following Jesus drop out and stop living their faith?
- Why is it important to know God rewards us for running well as we follow Jesus, especially when life is really hard and we want to quit?

TALKING POINTS:

Share the following points with your students:

The fight, the finish, the faith

This is a beautiful, compact look at the essentials of our Christian life. First Paul portrays it as a fight—a good fight, but still a fight. Christianity is opposed to everything in the world contrary to God and his Word, and there is no shortage of ideas and actions to oppose God. This fight isn't always easy, but it's worthwhile. Paul also compares the Christian life to a race. God has a future prepared for us more wonderful than we can ever imagine. Without faith, nothing we do truly matters. Our faith makes the effort, the fight, and the finishing complete.

Looking at the bigger picture

No matter how big life or its issues seem, a bigger picture exists. We're not always able to see that picture, but that's why we put our faith in the One who sees everything. God sees the bigger picture. God knows how it will all work out. He has a plan. When we realize our lives are just a blip on the big screen of history and what we do in that blip is what matters in the end, we'll begin to see God's bigger picture.

Reward zone

In this passage we see that the bigger picture includes our goal—the end to the race—and rewards for those who finish the race. Thanks to the grace of God and Christ's gift of salvation, that includes all who believe in Christ. Remember, the things we do on earth are seen by God. God loves us as his children, and he wants us to have what's best for us. God delights in rewarding his children for their faithfulness. This in itself should motivate and encourage us to do his will, to live his way.

REAL-LIFE CONNECTION: Don't be a quitter
Ask—

What are you thinking about quitting this week? Maybe you shouldn't quit, even if it isn't related to God. Finishing what we start and keeping our promises is a good character trait.

If you're battling with following Jesus and keeping your faith, ask God to help you persevere this week. The end is in sight. God wants us to "fight the good fight, finish the race, and keep the faith." He delights in rewarding his children and promises to do so. No matter how tough things may get, or how hard it is to do what's right, this goal is worth shooting for, and one that God will help us complete.

MEDIA: The bigger picture
Play these songs: "Meant to Live" from *The Beautiful Letdown* album by Switchfoot and "Deathbed" from *Five Score and Seven Years Ago* by Relient K. Use the lyrics or show the video found on youtube.com. Discuss how this music talks about finding our purpose in life even when events are extreme.

Titus 1:10-16

TOPIC: Flush out the church-wreckers

OBJECTIVE: As a result of this lesson students will know the characteristics of false teachers, and students will know their responsibility to stay away from these deceptive leaders.

BACKGROUND/OVERVIEW: The island of Crete was filled with many false teachers who were leading people away from the gospel and the church. Paul instructed Titus to know the truth and to refute these deceptive leaders. Paul laid out his objections to these false teachers with straightforward descriptions of what they do.

GAME/ICEBREAKER: Bible true or false

Type the series of true/false questions below (without the answers). Distribute copies and use it as a quiz or hold a team competition and read the questions below, awarding points for every correct true or false answer and bonus points for whoever knows the reason the statement is true or false. The correct answers—and reasons—are in parentheses.

BIBLE TRUE OR FALSE

1. T/F   The book of Hezekiah comes after the book of Proverbs in the Bible. (False: The Bible has no book of Hezekiah.)

2. T/F   A familiar Bible proverb says, "God helps those who help themselves." (False: Ben Franklin said that.)

3. T/F   According to the Bible, three kings visited the baby Jesus at the stable. (False: They're called "wise men" or "magi," not kings. No number of wise men is given, and they saw the child Jesus in a house, not the stable.)

4. T/F   The oldest man in the Bible lived 969 years but died before his father. (True: Methuselah lived to be 969, but his father, Enoch, was taken to be with God without dying—Genesis 5:21-27.)

5. T/F   According to Jewish law it's illegal for a man to marry his widow's sister. (False: The law doesn't mention it, but it would be impossible because the man would be dead if he had a widow.)

6. T/F   Jesus said he was and is the only way to God. (True: Check out John 14:6 and other passages.)

7. T/F   God changed the apostle's name from Saul to Paul. (False: "Saul" is simply the Hebrew version of the Greek "Paul.")

8. T/F   Moses was born at home because he wanted to be close to his mother. (False)

9. T/F   John the Baptist and Jesus were cousins. (True)

10. T/F   Nehemiah (Knee-high-miah) was the shortest man in the Bible. (False)

Determine your winner and award the prize(s).

ICEBREAKER QUESTIONS:

- Which true/false answers surprised you?
- For which questions did you think you knew the correct answers for sure but turned out to be wrong?
- Would most of your friends at school do very well on that test or very poorly? Why?
- What statements have you heard at school, on TV, in movies, etc., that supposedly come from the Bible but don't?
- What's the best way to determine what's true and what's false when it comes to Bible teaching?

SCRIPTURE: Titus 1:10-16
Explain the background to the passage; then read the passage aloud.

¹⁰ For there are many rebellious people, full of meaningless talk and deception, especially those of the circumcision group. ¹¹ They must be silenced, because they are disrupting whole households by teaching things they ought not to teach—and that for the sake of dishonest gain. ¹² One of Crete's own prophets has said it: "Cretans are always liars, evil brutes, lazy gluttons." ¹³ He has surely told the truth! Therefore rebuke them sharply, so that they will be sound in the faith ¹⁴ and will pay no attention to Jewish myths or to the merely human commands of those who reject the truth. ¹⁵ To the pure, all things are pure, but to those who are corrupted and do not believe, nothing is pure. In fact, both their minds and consciences are corrupted. ¹⁶ They claim to know God, but by their actions they deny him. They are detestable, disobedient and unfit for doing anything good.

STUDY QUESTIONS:

- How did Paul feel about those who were "teaching things they ought not to teach" (v. 11)?
- What were the false teachers (rebellious people) doing that Paul so strongly condemned?
- What do rebellious people in the church do that hurts the church?
- What do a leader's actions reveal about his relationship with God?
- How did Paul want Titus to respond to these false teachers?
- What are the signs a church or leader is teaching something that isn't true?

TALKING POINTS:
Have a conversation with your students, using the following points as a guide:

Sneak attack on the church
In certain places in the world Christian churches are under attack by enemies from outside the church. Their goal is to destroy the church, and their attacks are obvious. In Western Christianity churches are often under attack from the inside, where false teachers and immoral leaders are destroying the reputation of the church. It's subtle and insidious.

Counterfeit alert
We're not launching an investigation of any particular church or pastor. The

point of this lesson is to alert us and to prepare us, just as Paul was alerting and preparing Titus to discern and identify counterfeit leaders, teachers, and pastors. You'll need to know how to find a good church in the future. When you talk to friends about their church experiences, you'll need to know what Paul taught Titus about these leaders who are wrecking the church. Sadly they're out there deceiving and corrupting many unknowing people.

Telltale signs
Here's what to watch for:

Watch Their Talk: What they say and teach.

Does their teaching really come from Scripture and match with what the Bible teaches? Do they tell the truth in big and small matters? Does their speech deceive people about what really happened? Do you trust them?

Who gets the credit? Do they exalt God and Jesus Christ or themselves? Are they humble or full of pride?

Are they more critical of others than they are of themselves? Do they judge others by their own extra laws beyond the Bible?

Are they smooth talkers who sound good but do not use the Bible or quote it accurately?

Watch Their Tactics: How they get things done and achieve their goals.

Do they teach and lead for financial reward? How important are money and compensation to them? How does that influence their motivation?

Are they rebellious? Do they work cooperatively with other pastors, leaders, and churches? Whom do they follow? Who gives them direction?

Do they teach for fame? Are they adding their own extra requirements to the gospel? Are they teaching myths and adding stories to the Bible stories?

Watch Their Lives: Has the gospel made a distinct difference in their behavior, conversation, desires, and the way they treat others?

Do they demonstrate humility and service or pride and selfishness?

Avoidance
Paul wrapped up his instructions to Titus with these words: "They claim to know God, but by their actions they deny him. They're detestable, disobedient and unfit for doing anything good." When you see a leader, spiritual teacher, or pastor like this, stay away.

REAL-LIFE CONNECTION: **Put your faith in the real Jesus**

Take time to discuss these questions with the group:

- What real experiences have you had with Christian leaders or pastors who have led people astray or deceived people?
- How have those disappointing situations or people influenced your faith for good or bad?

Wrap up the lesson with this reminder:

Whenever there's something real and valuable there will always be counterfeits who try to fool people. Nobody counterfeits Monopoly money. The Christian faith is real. False teachers who use it to deceive people are real, but their despicable behavior does not discredit the real Jesus Christ. Put your faith in him.

MEDIA: **False teachers**

Go to www.youtube.com and check out "Mark Driscoll on Using Words to Confront False Teachers" (5:58)—use the search words *Mark Driscoll on using words*. This is a powerful interview from the 2008 Desiring God Conference.

Titus 2:11-15

TOPIC: The power of grace

OBJECTIVE: Students will know the meaning of grace and how grace motivates Christians to live a holy life.

OVERVIEW/BACKGROUND:

Paul told Titus, a young pastor in Crete, to keep his focus on God's grace because it was most important for his ministry with the church. Without God's grace Titus had no life-changing message. Paul also exhorted Titus to teach and remind his people about the reality of God's grace and its importance to them.

GAME/ICEBREAKER: **Grace is...**

Items needed:

- Worksheet (see below)
- Pens/pencils

Beforehand type the following worksheet. Distribute copies and pens/pencils. Explain the students should fill out the sheets quickly and anonymously.

Grace is...
What would grace be to each of these people?

1. To a child caught with his hand in the cookie jar—
2. To a driver pulled over for speeding—
3. To a young person who is caught illegally copying DVDs and music—
4. To a person bad-mouthing a friend and overheard by that friend—
5. To a student who forgot to turn in his term paper—
6. To a convicted felon—
7. To an athlete who blows it in the big game—
8. To someone who breaks a friend's prize possession—
9. To an angry spouse who made regrettable statements in a marital conflict—
10. To a parent who wrongly punishes a child—
11. To someone who treats a date poorly—
12. To a worker who gets caught loafing on the job—
13. To a sibling who misuses a sibling's stuff—
14. To a student who gets caught cheating—

After they've finished, tell them to circle the statements that apply to them. In other words, in which of these situations have they been the person needing grace?

Collect all the sheets and have a helper total how many students circled each statement.

ICEBREAKER QUESTIONS:

- We hear the word *grace* a lot in Christian circles—what does it mean? (Answer: Undeserved favor.)
- When have you been the obvious recipient of grace in a situation similar to the ones on the worksheet? What happened, and how did you feel?

Take the worksheets from your helper with the totals and read a selection of what group members wrote for each situation, noting each time how many had circled that number.

- When have you given grace to someone?
- When you received grace from someone, and how did that affect your relationship with that person? Take situations five and 14, for example: How do you think the student's relationship with the teacher might change? Or how about the athlete's relationship with his or her coach (No. 7)?
- In what ways have you experienced grace from God?
- What difference has that made in your relationship with him?

SCRIPTURE: Titus 2:11-15

Read the passage aloud.

[11] For the grace of God has appeared that offers salvation to all people. [12] It teaches us to say "No" to ungodliness and worldly passions, and to live self-controlled, upright and godly lives in this present age, [13] while we wait for the blessed hope—the appearing of the glory of our great God and Savior, Jesus Christ, [14] who gave himself for us to redeem us from all wickedness and to purify for himself a people that are his very own, eager to do what is good.

[15] These, then, are the things you should teach. Encourage and rebuke with all authority. Do not let anyone despise you.

STUDY QUESTIONS:

- According to this passage, what does God's grace bring to us? (Answer: Salvation; the power to say no to wrong living and to live right, to have hope.)
- What motivation do recipients of grace have to live righteous lives?
- Why is it so important to teach all Christians about grace?
- What are you learning about God's grace as you're growing up?
- How has God's grace affected your choices and actions?

TALKING POINTS:
Share the following points with your students:

Transformed by grace
Knowing God's grace is the most beautiful human experience. Someone once said GRACE simply stands for God's Riches At Christ's Expense. In other words, through grace God gives us his gift of salvation. We can't do anything to earn forgiveness, salvation, or eternal life. In fact we're totally undeserving in every way. Yet God loved us so much he sent Jesus to pay the penalty for sin so through faith in him we can be forgiven. Only by grace can we be saved from our sin—its power and penalty.

Paul told Titus this grace of God had "appeared." How? It appeared in Christ Jesus—through his birth, ministry, and atoning death. Paul reminded Titus that Christ "gave himself for us" (v. 14) and took our place on the cross. Jesus suffered the wrath of God as he carried the guilt of our sins. This is what Christ did for us on the cross. We have a huge debt because of sin, a debt we're unable to pay. But Christ took it upon himself to pay that debt for us.

What grace does for us
Through God's grace we're redeemed (v. 14). This word means "to set free by a ransom." With his blood, Christ ransoms us from sin, Satan, and evil. Because of sin we're enslaved by the power of darkness, but Christ paid the ransom that sets us free.

Through God's grace in Christ we're also purified (v. 14) to be God's people. Purify means "to cleanse or wash." By Christ's blood we're washed of the filth and pollution of sin—made fit to come to God in Christ.

How we respond to grace
As redeemed and purified recipients of grace, we're "to live self-controlled, upright and godly lives" (v. 12).

Going back to our previous discussion, we agreed a recipient of grace will feel closer to the grace-giver—it will change their relationship. The athlete will work harder for the grace-giving coach. The student will feel closer and do her best for the grace-giving teacher. So knowing we have been forgiven totally and freely given eternal life, we should love God even more and want to obey him.

We are to be "self-controlled" (v. 12). This should describe our personal ethics and behavior. Self-control is what a drunk intoxicated on alcohol does not show. In this present world everyone is in danger of becoming intoxicated by the things of this world—alcohol, popularity, money, sex, and material wealth. The grace of God teaches us to be self-controlled.

Second, we're called to live "upright" lives (v. 12). "Upright" describes how we behave in relation to our neighbor. It means we love our neighbor in the same way and to the same intensity as we love ourselves. It means we show mercy and work for justice. It means we forgive even as God has forgiven us.

Third, we're called to live a "godly" life (v. 12). This deals with our relationship to God. It means we love and serve him in all of life. It means our relationship to him is the dearest thing we have.

Last, we say no to "ungodliness and worldly passions" (v. 12). We reject, deny, and refuse all ungodly temptations and thoughts. We don't willingly break any of God's commandments. We don't love the worldly passions, lusts, and covetousness that stand opposed to God.

REAL-LIFE CONNECTION: Ode to God's grace

Give the following instructions to your students:

During this coming week write a song, poem, or short essay about your experience with God's grace. Add new thoughts and verses to it every day. Bring it to our next meeting. Share it with us to remind us why grace is the center of Christian life.

MEDIA: How sweet the sound

Watch the trailer for the movie *Amazing Grace* (2:51) (available on www. wingclips.com—use the search terms *amazing grace—trailer*). This film depicts William Wilberforce maneuvering his way through Parliament in 18th century England as he endeavors to end slavery in the empire.

Have the words and music for "Amazing Grace" available and sing it together.

Titus 3:1-8

TOPIC: Let Jesus shine through

OBJECTIVE: Students will know how to live like Christ in their school and with their friends.

BACKGROUND/OVERVIEW: Paul was exhorting Titus, his Greek protégé and young pastor on Crete, and the whole church to live for Christ in a very immoral society.

GAME/ICEBREAKER: This Little Light of Mine
Explain you want to take your group back to their childhood. Lead everyone in the children's chorus "This Little Light of Mine" complete with hand motions. Instruct them to hold their right index finger in the air as their light and make a horizontal circle in the air when they sing "let it shine," yell "no" at the appropriate moment, etc. (Note: If you're afraid your kids are too cool and won't participate willingly, find a rocking version on YouTube and play it as they sing along, as suggested in "Media.")

ICEBREAKER QUESTIONS:

- What Bible passage inspired this song? (Answer: Matthew 5:14-16—read it aloud.)
- What does it mean?
- Why is light used as a metaphor for Christian living? (Answer: Light illuminates, leads, pushes away darkness, gives hope, etc.)
- What can believers do to "let their lights shine"?

SCRIPTURE: Titus 3:1-8
Have a student volunteer read the passage aloud from her Bible.

[1] Remind the people to be subject to rulers and authorities, to be obedient, to be ready to do whatever is good, [2] to slander no one, to be peaceable and considerate, and always to be gentle toward everyone.

[3] At one time we too were foolish, disobedient, deceived and enslaved by all kinds of passions and pleasures. We lived in malice and envy, being hated and hating one another. [4] But when the kindness

and love of God our Savior appeared, [5] he saved us, not because of righteous things we had done, but because of his mercy. He saved us through the washing of rebirth and renewal by the Holy Spirit, [6] whom he poured out on us generously through Jesus Christ our Savior, [7] so that, having been justified by his grace, we might become heirs having the hope of eternal life. [8] This is a trustworthy saying. And I want you to stress these things, so that those who have trusted in God may be careful to devote themselves to doing what is good. These things are excellent and profitable for everyone.

STUDY QUESTIONS:

- What drastic changes have happened in the lives of people in the Crete church?
- How does the way Christians live influence what nonbelievers think about Jesus Christ?
- What specific instructions does Paul give Titus and the people about how to live out their commitment to Christ?
- What will people in Crete think about the message and claims of Christ when they meet and interact with the Christians from the church where Titus is the pastor?
- According to this passage (in that world and in ours), what can Christians do to let their lives shine out in the darkness?
- Why might someone say those actions are "countercultural"? (Answer: They're opposite of how most people act and react.)

TALKING POINTS:

Share the following with your students:

Your life is your light

The words Paul wrote to Titus apply to us right now. Paul wanted the church to show the whole city how real Jesus Christ is by the way they lived their lives. Let's update this and let Paul's exhortation be for us as we go to school every day.

These countercultural actions exhorted by Paul can be light in the darkness. Think what would happen in your school if you seriously acted this way:

- Be subject to rulers and authorities: You cooperate with the principals and teachers.
- Be obedient: You be the best at following the rules.

- Be ready to do whatever is good: You look for opportunities to help people every day.
- Slander no one: You don't insult or gossip and only speak positively about others.
- Be peaceable: You refuse to quarrel or fight and let the other person win the argument or dispute.
- Be considerate: You're generous with your kindness and time, doing for others what you would like done for you.
- Be gentle toward everyone: You're ready to yield your rights and desires to help others.

REAL-LIFE CONNECTION: Live a believer's life

Ask—

Do you really want to let your school and your friends know Jesus changes people's lives? Take these exhortations seriously. Think about your motivation and source of strength.

Question: Why do I make this major change in your attitude and lifestyle?
Answer: The kindness I give to others comes from the kindness God has given to me.

Question: How can I do this?
Answer: I can do this only by the power of the Holy Spirit living and working in me.

If you want your school to know the real Jesus, show them with your life. Let your light shine.

MEDIA: Rockin' Little Light of Mine

Go on www.youtube.com and find a great version of a choir singing "This Little Light of Mine" (a number of great ones are available). Play it for everyone at the close of the lesson.

PHILEMON

Philemon 4-6

TOPIC: Lifestyle evangelism

OBJECTIVE:
Students will understand that God wants to use them to share the message of his love with others. They'll consider the opportunities before them daily and discover how they can share their faith in Christ in those situations.

BACKGROUND/OVERVIEW:
The book of Philemon is a short letter written by Paul to a fellow Christian named Philemon. After a few words of greeting and thanksgiving, Paul wrote a prayer that expressed his heart's desire for Philemon. His prayer has echoed throughout history and is applicable to our lives today.

GAME/ICEBREAKER: Communication game
Items needed:

- Three pieces of paper with shapes drawn on them (see below)
- Paper
- Pens/pencils

Choose a volunteer. Explain that on a piece of paper you have drawn a circle, a square, and a triangle. These three figures are all in a certain relationship to each other.

Everyone else should have a piece of paper and pencil and be ready to draw. Without showing the picture to the rest of the group, the volunteer is to look at the drawing and describe it to the others as effectively as possible, so the rest of the group can reproduce it correctly on paper. Have your volunteer stand with her back to the audience and describe the figures using only words, no gestures.

In a few minutes, compare drawings—there will be quite a variation.

Choose another volunteer to do the same thing with a new set of figures, only this person may face the audience and use his hands in describing what is on the paper. Once again the audience should write down what the second person has described. When you compare the pictures with the original, there still will be many differences.

Choose a third person to repeat the process. This time the person may face the audience, use her hands, and answer questions. The audience should draw their interpretations again. This time almost everyone's drawings will be correct.

ICEBREAKER QUESTIONS:

- What was frustrating about trying to create what was being described when you only heard a voice or saw only hand motions?
- What was the key to being able to reproduce the drawing accurately?
- How does this game compare with sharing our faith with people?

TRANSITION:
Say to your students—
Communication is about more than just words. For communication to be successful, it must be personal. Today we'll discover how we can actively and successful communicate God's love to others.

SCRIPTURE: Philemon 4-6
Read this passage aloud.

> [4] I always thank my God as I remember you in my prayers, [5] because I hear about your love for all his people and your faith in the Lord Jesus. [6] I pray that your partnership with us in the faith may be effective in deepening your understanding of every good thing we share for the sake of Christ."

STUDY QUESTIONS:

- What are some other words for the word *active*?
- What does the phrase "sharing your faith" mean?
- What comes to your mind when you think of evangelism? Where did you get that idea?
- Paul writes that when we share our faith, we'll gain a deeper understanding of what we have in Christ. What are some of the good things we have in Christ?
- How does sharing our faith deepen our understanding of these things?

TALKING POINTS:

Share the following with your students:

Me...evangelism? No way!

For many people the idea of sharing their faith (evangelism) is scary. This is often the case because their image of evangelism is narrowly defined. They may picture the funny-looking guy they saw at the beach wearing a fanny pack and short shorts passing out tracts, or the strange person on the street corner carrying a big sign and yelling, "Turn or burn!" That kind of evangelism is intimidating, and frequently the intimidated people are Christians who think, *If that's evangelism, I'm out!*

Sharing your life

Paul's words to Philemon are a great encouragement. The good news is God desires our participation in communicating the message of his love to the world. He could've just snapped his fingers and made the world believe in him, but he has chosen us, you and me, to be his partners. The comforting news is God doesn't force us all to do it the same way because he has uniquely created each person. God will stretch us and call us out of our comfort zones, certainly; but if we're open, he'll show us how to communicate his love in a way consistent with our personalities and wiring. The word Paul uses for "sharing" is the Greek word koinonia, which means partnership, communion, fellowship. It's where we get the idea of communication—sharing thoughts and ideas, and community—sharing life. Paul is exhorting Philemon to share his life with others. Paul said to the Thessalonians, "We loved you so much, we were delighted to share with you not only the gospel of God but our lives as well" (1 Thessalonians 2:8). Evangelism has something to do with what we say, but on a deeper level it's about the message we communicate through our lives. St. Francis of Assisi said, "Preach the gospel always, if necessary use words." Our challenge is to identify the opportunities we have each and every day and how we can be agents of God's love in those situations through our words and actions.

Focus on giving, not getting
As we begin to step out and share our faith, something special begins to happen—not just in others, but also in us. We must remember that just as God loved us freely and selflessly, we also must be obedient to share our faith, not for what we'll get out of it, but because of the hope we can give others. Our focus in sharing our faith should always be on giving, not on getting—on others, not on ourselves. Nevertheless, Paul points out the reality that as we give, we'll grow. As we do our work, we'll have a better understanding of how God works and the blessings we have as a result of Christ's work. (See Colossians 1:9-10.) Our participation doesn't produce profit (benefits) or position (acceptance); it produces perception (understanding) of that which we already have in Christ (possessions).

REAL-LIFE CONNECTION: How do you evangelize?
Ask your students—

- What are some of your fears when it comes to sharing your faith with others?
- Would you define your evangelism as passive or active? Why?
- What are some of the opportunities you have on a daily basis to share your faith?
- What are some simple and creative things we can do to share our faith individually and as a group?
- What should our motive be in sharing our faith?

MEDIA: Share your faith
Show the Sermonspice video "Evangelism Linebacker" (3:52). This clip may be purchased from www.sermonspice.com—search using the words *evangelism linebacker no excuses*.) This funny video shows someone who won't accept excuses from those who don't share their faith.

Or you can show the Sermonspice video "Neal" (2:38). This may also be purchased from www.sermonspice.com—search using the word *Neal*. This funny video shows an overenthusiastic Christian who finds an opportunity to preach a message of fire and brimstone.

And check out "Bullhorn" from NOOMA (www.nooma.com). This video features a man standing on a corner and preaching from a bullhorn and handing out flyers. Rob Bell comments on this and other approaches to evangelism.

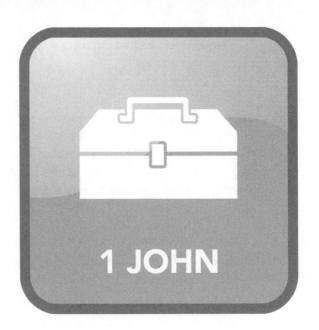

1 JOHN

TOPIC: Don't turn off the light

OBJECTIVE:
Students will confess their sins and receive God's forgiveness.

BACKGROUND/OVERVIEW:
John explains the power and work of Jesus as light in a dark world. He challenges those who believe in Jesus to live in the light and avoid the darkness.

GAME/ICEBREAKER: Eye-lympics
Items needed:

- Two blindfolds
- Posterboard
- Markers

Get four student competitors for this series of tasks. Securely blindfold two of them so they can't see anything. Have the four (two with blindfolds and two without) do the same tasks. Give them a task that requires sight and light to complete well. Have them draw a picture or a face on a posterboard with a magic marker. After each instruction (e.g., draw the eyes, the nose, the ears, the hair, etc.) completely turn the blindfolded participants around twice to disorient them. The blind portraits will be very disjointed if they're being spun around and not being helped to find what they previously drew. (You could also ask them to write their name one letter at a time.) Afterward, vote on the best picture of the blindfolded competitors and award a prize.

ICEBREAKER QUESTIONS
Say—

First of all let's be clear we're not mocking anyone who is visually impaired. People with a visual disability lead very productive lives and amaze us with how they get around and do the tasks a sighted person struggles to do. Our point today is that being able to see is a special gift; and if God gives us two good eyes, we should use them for good. The major point we want to make is about the spiritual light and blindness that afflicts everyone.

Ask—

- If you lost your physical sight, what would you miss being able to see?
- What would be harder for you to do if you could not see?
- What is spiritual blindness? How does that mess up a person's life?

SCRIPTURE: 1 John 1:5-10
Have a staff member read aloud verses 5-7, followed by another staff person reading aloud verses 8-10.

[5] This is the message we have heard from him and declare to you: God is light; in him there is no darkness at all. [6] If we claim to have fellowship with him and yet walk in the darkness, we lie and do not live out the truth. [7] But if we walk in the light, as he is in the light, we have fellowship with one another, and the blood of Jesus, his Son, purifies us from all sin.

[8] If we claim to be without sin, we deceive ourselves and the truth is not in us. [9] If we confess our sins, he is faithful and just and will forgive us our sins and purify us from all unrighteousness. [10] If we claim we have not sinned, we make him out to be a liar and his word is not in us.

STUDY QUESTIONS:

- What strong point is John making when he says "God is light" as opposed to him saying "God is darkness"?
- What you think it means to walk in the darkness or walk in the light?

- What does the daily life look like of a person who spiritually walks in the light?
- What is so bad about living in the darkness? What does the daily life of a person who spiritually walks in the light look like?
- What are the two responses we can have to the sin in our life?
- How does God respond to us when we confess our sins?
- Who should confess their sins? How often should they confess them?

TALKING POINTS:

Have a conversation with your students using the following points as a guide:

Light is life

Try to imagine living in total darkness. What would you be missing? We'd miss color. Black is a popular color for clothes, but could you live in a completely dark world? (Note: We are not using the color black as a racial term. In reality no one has skin that is completely white or black. This isn't a condemnation of anyone's skin color.)

We'd miss beauty. What is most beautiful to you? Without light you would never see it. We'd miss life and growth. Light is the source of energy that makes so many things grow. John says God is light and in him is no darkness. God is the source of all that is good and true.

Walk in light, not darkness

We are enticed to darkness and the desires of the world, which is the opposite of what God wants. Darkness destroys relationship with God. When we're in the darkness, we can't see life and the world the way God sees it. In the light we see reality, and our eyes and brain are ignited by the beauty we see everywhere. The light helps us find what is best. Light is full of joy, hope, and freedom. Darkness is full of threat and danger.

Don't close your eyes

God gave us the ability to close our eyes. They need rest every day. Also, in a symbolic way, we should close our eyes to those ugly, nasty sights created by our sinful world that repulse us. We need to learn to close our eyes to evil and hate and sin but to open our eyes to God's beautiful creation and the people around us. The idea is to see the world the way Jesus sees it, looking at people as unique creations made in God's image, hating sin but loving sinners, looking for opportunities to serve and love. Some people do just the opposite and foolishly close their eyes to what God wants them to see. They can't see the reality of what they do that hurts others and themselves.

See what God sees
We build a relationship with God by agreeing with him. John's statement to confess our sins means we should agree with God and see ourselves and the world the way God sees them. When we agree with God and confess our sins, he forgives us and begins correcting our vision. We start loving and desiring what God says is good instead of the world's evil darkness. We live and move in the light.

REAL-LIFE CONNECTION: Light in the darkness
Items needed:

- Blindfolds or big paper towels
- Matches
- Candle

To close the meeting darken the room as much as possible. Pass out blindfolds or big paper towels to everyone. Ask everyone to cover their eyes and sit in the darkness for a minute. Ask each person to think about something in their life they're keeping in the dark so God or others won't see it. Suggest they imagine God's light shining on that dark part of their life. Talk about the light of God bringing peace to their fears and forgiveness to their mistakes.

Read aloud 1 John 1:5 and strike a match and light a candle at the end of that verse. Tell the group to open their eyes and see the new light in the room. Read the rest of the Scripture passage again. Ask them to silently confess that darkness in their lives. Explain the forgiveness of God and the freedom of walking in the light. Close the meeting by turning on all the lights.

MEDIA: In the Light
Watch the YouTube video of DC Talk "In the Light"—a live performance. This old song has strong music and perfect lyrics for this lesson. (Search for the clip on www.youtube.com by the words *in the light DC Talk.*

1 John 2:15-17

TOPIC: Love the world or love God

OBJECTIVE: Students will know what it means to love the world and why loving God is the better choice.

BACKGROUND/OVERVIEW: The culture of the first century was basically like the world in which we live. People were focused on sex, materialism, pride, and power. Not much has changed. People wanted God and *all* the world's pleasures, but John said you can't have both. Make a choice— one way leads to destruction and the other to life.

GAME/ICEBREAKER: Temptation Hunt

Items needed:

- A selection of popular magazines and recent newspapers

Divide the group into teams of four. Give each team a stack of newspapers and magazines. Explain that this will be a scavenger hunt competition. You'll call out a topic, item, or category, and they should tear out something from their magazines or newspapers that fits your description and hold it up. The first team to do so wins that round. Any section of the magazine or newspaper is fair game. Note: Be sure to collect the winning pictures/stories. Then read from the following list. (Add others as appropriate, especially relating to breaking news).

- A picture of someone smoking
- A story about political corruption
- Something to do with illegal drugs (steroids count)
- A sex scandal
- Money
- Power
- An ad about looking amazingly good
- An offer that seems too good to be true
- Chocolate
- Etc.

Total the points and announce the winning team.

ICEBREAKER QUESTIONS:

Display the winning pictures and stories. Then ask what they had in common. (Answer: Temptation). You may want to explain how each picture/story relates to temptation.

- Which of these temptations are the most powerful and alluring to you? How would you summarize the major temptations we face in this world during our lifetimes?
- What temptations were strongest to the females? How was it different for the males?
- What temptations would be strongest for a person who is 40 years old? 70 years old? A teenager?
- What do many men love more than God? What do women often love more than God?
- What is the most tempting desire for you that would go against your love of God?

SCRIPTURE: 1 John 2:15-17

Read this aloud, repeating verse 16.

[15] Do not love the world or anything in the world. If you love the world, love for the Father is not in you. [16] For everything in the world—the cravings of sinful people, the lust of their eyes and their boasting about what they have and do—comes not from the Father but from the world. [17] The world and its desires pass away, but whoever does the will of God lives forever.

STUDY QUESTIONS:

- What's your opinion about a person who (romantically) loves two different people at the same time when they're not married? What about when they're married to someone else?
- What three big sins did John mention that keep people away from God?
- What does the "the cravings of sinful people" mean?
- Is "lust of their eyes" about sex, materialism, greed, or something else?
- John says you can't love these sins and love God. Explain why you agree or disagree.
- Some people list these sins as "money, sex, and power." How have desires for these worldly sins destroyed government leaders, pastors, and athletes?

- How will these sins destroy the life of a young person? What's wrong with sampling a little of these temptations or experimenting with them while you're young?
- Why does John say it's more important (and smarter) to love God?

TALKING POINTS:
Share the following:

No two-timing God
You can't have it both ways. A lot of people try to compartmentalize their faith in God. They love God on Sundays and when they're with church people, but they love these sins of the world when they want to have fun. God says either you love the world or you love me. Jesus said no one can serve two masters: Either you'll love one and hate the other or you'll hate one and love the other (Matthew 6:24). The world isn't about God. It pushes God out and cannot coexist with love for God.

Going...going...gone
Would you buy stock in a company that's going bankrupt? John says loving the world is a lost cause. It's going to pass away into nothing. If you love the world you'll lose everything. Some people think death is the end, so why not eat, drink, and live it up because we're going to die soon anyway. Jesus came to tell us we'll live forever—either with God, or alone and separated from God forever. Whom are you going to believe?

To live forever
John lays it out clearly: "The world and its desires pass away, but whoever does the will of God lives forever" (v. 17). Living forever is God's gift to everyone who loves and obeys God. John reported what Jesus said about genuine love for God: "If you love me, keep my commands" (John 14:15), and "This is love for God: to keep his commands" (1 John 5:3).

Most important
It comes down to what's real and what's going to last. Everything is garbage compared with the value of knowing Jesus Christ. If your love for Christ is cooling down, that's probably because the world and its desires are taking over your heart and slowly killing your love for God. Every heart loves something. What do you want most?

REAL-LIFE CONNECTION: Who are you gonna serve?

Items needed:

- Posterboard, whiteboard, or flipchart
- Markers

Use a posterboard or flipchart to finish the lesson. On the left side write the three desires for loving the world, and on the right side write how to redirect those desires toward loving God.

Loving the World	Loving God
Desire for what we don't have	Desire for what God can give you
Pride in what you possess	Possess God and be an heir with Christ
Passion for pleasure	Passion to love and serve others with God's love

Ask students to identify where their desires are right now. Invite them to move from the desires on the left side to pursuing and loving God on the right side. Give them a few moments of quiet to think about crossing over from left to right. Then play the suggested media clip "You Gotta Serve Somebody" to close the meeting.

MEDIA: Gotta Serve Somebody

Show the www.youtube.com video "Gotta Serve Somebody" (from the *Slow Train Coming* album) by Bob Dylan.

1 John 3:10-18

TOPIC: The heart of the gospel

OBJECTIVE: As a result of this lesson the students will know the best definition of real love from 1 John 3:16.

BACKGROUND/OVERVIEW: John's three years with Jesus taught him love is the most powerful force in the world. John wanted everyone to know how much Jesus showed God's love and begin showing that kind of love to each other.

GAME/ICEBREAKER: Love, love, love
You can refer to this as a competition between teams or as an elimination tournament. The goal is to make the other person—the other competitor—smile. Choose two competitors and have them stand and face each other. One at a time they'll repeat expressions of love to each other in an attempt to make the other person smile without smiling himself. In a tournament the first person in a pair to smile is eliminated. In team competition award points and bring up the next couple. Here are some lines to use:

- I love the way your eyes sparkle in the moonlight.
- I love you, not for who you are, but for who I am when I'm with you.
- My little love puppy—you're so adorable!
- Oh look at those precious cheeks. I just want to squeeze them!
- Your lips are so supple.
- Remember that walk on the beach when you took me by the hand and whispered in my ear you'd never leave me?
- Of all the boyfriends/girlfriends I've ever had, you're certainly one of them.
- Your teeth are like stars—they come out at night.
- Your lips are like petals—bicycle pedals!
- I remember when you rolled your eyes at me. I picked them up and rolled them right back.
- Ooooooo—I just want to hug and kiss you!
- Etc.

ICEBREAKER QUESTIONS:

- Who's the hardest person to get to smile or laugh?
- Who's the easiest person?
- How often do people tell you they love you? How does it make you feel?
- Some people grow up in homes where their father or mother has never said "I love you." What impact would that have on a person

not hearing that from a parent?
• How can you tell if a person really loves someone?

SCRIPTURE: 1 John 3:10-18

Have students read this passage silently from their Bibles. Then have a student volunteer read verses 16-18 aloud.

[10] This is how we know who the children of God are and who the children of the devil are: Those who do not do what is right are not God's children; nor are those who do not love their brothers and sisters.

[11] For this is the message you heard from the beginning: We should love one another. [12] Do not be like Cain, who belonged to the evil one and murdered his brother. And why did he murder him? Because his own actions were evil and his brother's were righteous. [13] Do not be surprised, my brothers and sisters, if the world hates you. [14] We know that we have passed from death to life, because we love each other. Anyone who does not love remains in death. [15] Anyone who hates a fellow believer is a murderer, and you know that no murderers have eternal life in them. [16] This is how we know what love is: Jesus Christ laid down his life for us. And we ought to lay down our lives for one another. [17] If any one of you has material possessions and sees a brother or sister in need but has no pity on them, how can the love of God be in you? [18] Dear children, let us not love with words or tongue but with actions and in truth.

STUDY QUESTIONS:

• What is the best test to see if a person really knows and loves God?
• Why did Cain murder his brother?
• According to John, how are we like Cain when we hate someone?
• How do we know what real love is?
• What does it mean to love one's brother or sister?
• What is hard about sharing our material possessions with others in need?
• How do you show your true love for other people?

TALKING POINTS:

Share the following points with your students:

The heart of the gospel

Love is a worn-out word in our culture, but true love is still rare. Everyone talks about love, but few people can explain what real love really is. John tells us God expects us to have real love for each other. Love is the best test of a person really having new life in Christ—it's the heart of the gospel.

Contrasting examples
John tells us about Cain killing his brother Abel (in Genesis 4) because he was jealous of how Abel's sacrifice pleased God. Instead of seeking to please God, Cain aligned himself in rebellion against God and did the opposite of what God wanted. Jesus did what God the Father told him to do. He laid down his life voluntarily as a sacrifice for the sins of the world. He asked his Father for another way, but he did what his Father directed him to do because he loved God and all the people of the world.

The greatest sacrifice
John gives the clearest definition of real love in verse 16: "This is how we know what love is: Jesus Christ laid down his life for us. And we ought to lay down our lives for one another." Jesus sacrificed his well-being and submitted to the most terrible physical and emotional pain for the eternal good of others. He gave the most precious possession he had—his life. It was (and still is) the greatest expression of love.

Practical not theoretical
Christians find their own greatest joy in actively working for the good of others—even when it requires self-sacrifice. Love is more than words. John says we show Christ's love when we see need and respond with what God has given us. We discover it's really more blessed to give than to receive. We give glory to God by loving others with our time, possessions, and money.

REAL-LIFE CONNECTION: Practical love
Give the following instructions to your students:

Let's make love real in our life. It has to be more than just talk. Let's follow the example of Jesus and give something valuable to someone in need. It could be money or a material possession or our time and energy.

Spend this week looking for someone who needs some practical love. Take action this week. Come back next meeting and tell us what you did and what happened.

MEDIA: Why didn't he fight back?
Watch the clip "He Didn't Spear Back" (1:19) from the film *End of the Spear*. When the widowed wives of the American missionaries approach the Waodani about Jesus, one of the tribesmen wonders why their husbands never fought back. This clip is available on www.wingclips.com—search using the words *he didn't spear back*.

1 John 4:7-8

TOPIC: God's love is contagious

OBJECTIVE: Students will be challenged to love others the way God loves them.

BACKGROUND/OVERVIEW: John teaches that love is the dominant message and action of God and that Jesus' followers need to follow his example loving others.

GAME/ICEBREAKER: The greatest form of flattery

This icebreaker features a couple of sets of imitations. Recruit five or six students to do each set.

Set One: Imitating Famous People. Have students do imitations of famous people (no vulgar language or actions).

- Do a round of physical imitations (walking, hand gestures, facial gestures).
- Do a round of verbal imitations.

Set Two: Imitating Youth Leaders.

- Do a round of physical imitations (walking, hand gestures, facial gestures).
- Do a round of verbal imitations.

ICEBREAKER QUESTIONS:

- Which were the best imitations?
- When is imitating someone a put down? When is it a compliment?
- Whom have you positively imitated or copied in your life?
- Who is a person you're a lot like?
- Who do you wish you were like in speech or action?
- If someone told you to act or talk like God, what would you do?

SCRIPTURE:1 John 4:7-8

If possible have staff or students read this passage aloud in different languages (e.g., Spanish, French, German, Arabic, etc.). See if students can interpret—that is, ask if they can figure out what the passage is about. (Answer: Love.)

[7] Dear friends, let us love one another, for love comes from God. Everyone who loves has been born of God and knows God. [8] Whoever does not love does not know God, because God is love.

STUDY QUESTIONS:

- What does John encourage everyone to do?
- What is the relationship between knowing God and loving God?
- What example has Jesus set for us to follow?
- What would be the best imitation we could do of God?
- What are some of the situations in your life where you find it difficult to love others?
- What can you do to learn how to love others?

TALKING POINTS:

Share the following with your students:

God is love

Our world talks about love constantly but misunderstands love and its source. God is the source of love. Explaining love as a physical or emotional feeling is popular, but not true. God defines love as an intentional choice to do what is best for someone else. *Love* is more of a verb than a noun, involving *doing, giving,* and *serving.* God sets the standard for love by giving his Son to live on earth and die to pay for our sins. Everything Jesus did in his life is an example of love.

Know God; know love

John says the way to know real love is to know God. We can know God by reading the Bible to learn his story. We can know God by praying and listening to God. We can know God by looking closely at Jesus and seeing the choices he made and how he lived.

Do what God does

God gave us clear examples of love so we can imitate him. We cannot give our lives as a sacrifice for sin, but we can follow Jesus' example and be willing to give what we have to help someone. Love is doing what's best for others, even when it's difficult. God loves people who don't love him, and he does good things for them so they'll see his generous grace. God wants us to do the same. God sets an example we can follow.

REAL-LIFE CONNECTION: **Take risks**

Ask—

- What sacrifice are you willing to make to show love to someone? Think of a real person. What love does this person need?
- Think of what Jesus did for us and how uncomfortable it was for him to come into our world. He was born in a barn and laid in a rough wood crib complete with splinters and plenty of dirt. He took the risk of being a baby in a tough world.
- What risks and hardships are you willing to take to show love to the person in your life you identified?

MEDIA: **How deep?**

Go to www.youtube.com and type the song title "How Deep the Father's Love." Several different artists' versions of this very powerful song are available. Select the video clip that best fits your group.

1 John 5:6-13

TOPIC: What's more important than eternal life?

OBJECTIVE: Students will know they can have eternal life if they believe in God's Son.

BACKGROUND/OVERVIEW: No one can escape death, but we can prepare for it. Through John, God tells us how to have eternal life.

GAME/ICEBREAKER: Ten minutes to eternity
Items needed:

- Chairs
- Snacks
- Paper
- Pens/pencils
- Flashlights

Set up the room like a commercial airplane. You can have one aisle or two depending on the size of your group. Have a first-class section and an open cockpit. Set up some of your leaders to be flight attendants. Start the meeting as though you're leaving on a flight. Check in everyone and seat them in the plane. Do the normal safety announcements in a humorous way. After takeoff start a beverage and snack service, but interrupt it with an urgent message from the captain about engine failure and the 100 percent chance the plane will crash in 10 minutes. Tell them to prepare for the crash. Have a flight attendant direct them to get a sheet of paper and pencil (either handed out or preplaced under the chairs). Tell them to write a quick letter describing how they are feeling right now and sending the most important messages to the people in their lives. With one minute to go collect all the letters. Get everyone into crash position, count down to the crash, and turn off the lights in the room at impact. Turn on several flashlights held by leaders and with the group completely silent, read several of the letters written by the students.

ICEBREAKER QUESTIONS:
Say—

That reenactment of a plane crash is very sobering. I hope we didn't scare you too much. None of us know when life will end or how it will end.

All we can do is be ready. Maybe this experience will help us get ready.

- If you were in a real death situation, how do you think you would react to it?
- Whom would you be thinking the most about?
- What would you be thinking, doing, saying to God or about God?
- What can you do to be prepared to die?
- What help does God give us to prepare us for what will happen to us after we die?

SCRIPTURE: 1 John 5:6-13

Distribute copies of the passage and have students read it silently, thinking of how it relates to the previous discussion.

> [6] This is the one who came by water and blood—Jesus Christ. He did not come by water only, but by water and blood. And it is the Spirit who testifies, because the Spirit is the truth. [7] For there are three that testify: [8] the Spirit, the water and the blood; and the three are in agreement. [9] We accept human testimony, but God's testimony is greater because it is the testimony of God, which he has given about his Son. [10] Whoever believes in the Son of God accepts this testimony. Whoever does not believe God has made him out to be a liar, because they have not believed the testimony God has given about his Son. [11] And this is the testimony: God has given us eternal life, and this life is in his Son. [12] Whoever has the Son has life; whoever does not have the Son of God does not have life.
>
> [13] I write these things to you who believe in the name of the Son of God so that you may know that you have eternal life.

STUDY QUESTIONS:

- Where does John say we can find eternal life?
- How do we get eternal life?
- Why is John wrapping up his letter to this church talking about death and eternal life?
- What do you need to do to be sure you're a child of God?
- How would you respond to those who profess to want to have eternal life but will wait until they know they're dying to get the Son of God in their lives?
- Why would a person want to go to heaven at death, yet not want Jesus in his or her life while alive on earth?

- How does knowing you have eternal life help you on days when you aren't in a near-death situation?

TALKING POINTS:
Share with your students:

Most important
In the last 10 minutes of your life, the kind of car you own and how much money you have in the bank is irrelevant. None of the material things we desire so much and work so hard to get means anything when our heart starts skipping beats. When we dramatized the plane crash, what jumped to the top of your list as important? If you lived every day as though it was your last, how would your life be different? Would you focus on yourself and your personal pleasure, or would you give your attention to other people you love and to God who gave you your life? In reality you'll be seeing God very soon after your life on earth is over. It would be smart to be ready to talk to him. Why wait until the last minutes of life to get a cram course in knowing God? Start today and you'll be ready when your final day comes.

God's offer
God loves us and doesn't want us to die alone. He gives us free will and doesn't force us. We get to decide if we'll worship God and receive the gift of eternal life he has provided for us. He made a way for us to live forever with him. He sent his Son Jesus to pay the price for our sins against God. Jesus said, "I have come that [you] might have life" (John 10:10).

Getting the Son
To get the Son you must believe and trust in him. We can be forgiven if we believe and trust Jesus to be our Savior and rescue us from eternal separation from God. If you were in legal trouble you'd retain a lawyer—someone to stand with you and represent you before the judge. If you were drowning you'd call out to the lifeguard for rescue. You would let the lifeguard pull you out the danger and resuscitate you.

Don't let your pride keep you from asking God for the help you need—you can't do this yourself. Don't let your shame block your path to God. His love and forgiveness are greater than anything you have done to hurt him or others. He wants to give you freedom from your guilt and a fresh start. Bow your heart before God and acknowledge his power, wisdom, and love. If you humble yourself before God, he'll lift you up.

REAL-LIFE CONNECTION: Choose what's important

Say to your students—

You didn't die tonight. I am thankful for that, and I know you are, too. Earlier, when we were frightened, we wrote letters. What did you write? Perhaps you wrote what's really important to you. What needs to change in your life? Now is the time. If you know you need God, don't wait another minute. Pray with one of the leaders and tell God you want the Son.

MEDIA: Don't die alone

Show the clip "Die Alone" (1:26) from the movie *Bucket List*. Carter secretly sets up a meeting between Edward and his estranged daughter. They argue about Edward reconciling with his daughter before he dies of his terminal illness. Edward rejects the attempted reconciliation and says he wants to die alone. This clip is available on www.wingclips.com—search using the words *die alone*. This highlights the reality of death and the different ways people approach dying. Ask why dying alone would be so bad.

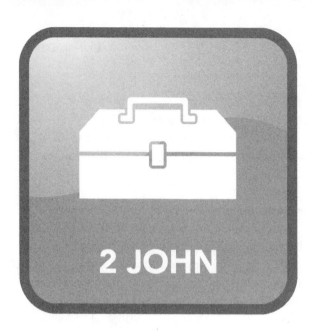

2 JOHN

2 John 4-11

TOPIC: Right beliefs plus right actions

OBJECTIVE:
Students will read the Bible accounts of Jesus teaching on love and his claims to be the Son of God.

BACKGROUND/OVERVIEW:
John addresses the never-ending problem of false teaching about Jesus by reminding his readers of the truth. He should know—he was as an eyewitness to Jesus' life.

GAME/ICEBREAKER: Snopes test
In this activity students decide if a story is true or false. Go online to www.snopes.com or www.truthorfiction.com where you'll see a long list of messages, stories, and urban legends widely distributed on the Internet and by word of mouth. Select five to 10 stories (e.g., Bill Gates and Microsoft will pay you $100 if you forward a message to 100 friends) and present them to the group. Read the stories one at a time and ask who thinks the story is true and who thinks it's false. Use a mixture of true and false stories. For the voting you can have students move to one side of the room or the other to show if they believe a story is true or false before you reveal the correct answer.

Another fun possibility is to get two of your adult volunteers or expressive student leaders to present each story. Have one enthusiastically endorse the story as true and the other argue against it as false. Then have the students vote by going to stand with the person they believe. The more energy the person who presents the story uses, the better. You'll see how much persuasion and peer pressure influence what students think is true. Be sure to read to the whole group the *Snopes* or *Truth or Fiction* findings about what's true before moving to the next story.

ICEBREAKER QUESTIONS:

- What stories completely fooled you?
- What did you learn tonight that you have wrongly believed? How long have you been wrong about this?
- What makes so many people believe what they read or hear even when it's clearly wrong?
- How do you decide if something is true or false?
- What are some things people believe about Jesus that aren't true?
- What's the danger to a Christian of believing false teaching about Jesus?

SCRIPTURE: 2 John 4-11

Read the passage aloud as students follow along in their Bibles.

[4] It has given me great joy to find some of your children walking in the truth, just as the Father commanded us. [5] And now, dear lady, I am not writing you a new command but one we have had from the beginning. I ask that we love one another. [6] And this is love: that we walk in obedience to his commands. As you have heard from the beginning, his command is that you walk in love.

[7] Many deceivers, who do not acknowledge Jesus Christ as coming in the flesh, have gone out into the world. Any such person is the deceiver and the antichrist. [8] Watch out that you do not lose what we have worked for, but that you may be rewarded fully. [9] Anyone who runs ahead and does not continue in the teaching of Christ does not have God; whoever continues in the teaching has both the Father and the Son. [10] If anyone comes to you and does not bring this teaching, do not take them into your house or welcome them. [11] Anyone who welcomes them shares in their wicked work.

STUDY QUESTIONS:

- What is God's command for the people who follow him?
- What does "walking in love" look like in daily life? What does God want to see?
- What are some of the ideas people teach about Jesus that contradict what the Bible says?
- How do you know what is true about Jesus Christ?
- How does John want the church to treat people who are teaching false information about Jesus?
- If someone told you the Bible doesn't teach that Jesus is the Messiah, the Son of God, or the only way to heaven, how would you respond to him? What could you tell that person from the Bible to support your argument?

TALKING POINTS:

Share the following points with your students:

Love others

One way to tell real Christians from phony ones is their love for others. Real Christians love others because they're following Jesus and doing what he did. This is an old command that goes back to Moses and the books of the Law, or the Pentateuch (the first five books of the Bible). Jesus brought this commandment out of the law books and showed people how it looks and works in real life—accepting others, helping people in need, forgiving enemies, giving time and attention to the unpopular people of society, serving others, not condemning people, and much more. True Christ-followers obey Jesus' commands and love others.

Know the truth

Jesus is the most truly unique person in history. He's fully God and fully human. He was conceived by the Holy Spirit and born of a woman. Jesus experienced all human temptations, yet he never gave in to do evil or disobey God. His claims to be the Son of God and Lord and Savior of the whole world still cause controversy and debate. If Jesus is who he says he is, then the whole history and future of the world is forever changed. If he isn't, Jesus is just another beloved religious leader.

Don't mess with Jesus

Anyone who wants to challenge or change the Christian faith must challenge or change what he believes about Jesus. From the early days of the new church certain people were twisting and changing the story of Jesus. Some said he didn't have a real body or didn't really die. John warns us not to believe these false teachings about Jesus because he and the other disciples had been eyewitnesses and had written the truth about Jesus' life, death, and resurrection. John says to keep our focus and faith on the real Jesus—don't be fooled by false teachers.

Reject the false teachers

People are still questioning and doubting the real Jesus. Some say Jesus isn't fully God or he wasn't fully human. Both of these ideas dangerously distort the truth. The best-selling book The DaVinci Code, for example, tells a fictional story about how Jesus didn't actually die on the cross, but married Mary Magdalene and moved to France where they had a baby. In other words Jesus was just another religious man with no sinless life, death, or resurrection. That makes Christianity just another human-made religion. (And it's a pack of lies.) Whether you're a Christian or not, the biggest question you need to answer in your life is, Who is Jesus Christ? And how will you know? Read the biblical eyewitness accounts and believe in the One who was sent to earth by God. Let's face it: John, a first-century eyewitness, is much more credible than popular 20th-century sources. The Jesus John knew is the source of truth and love, and Jesus wants everyone to know him.

REAL-LIFE CONNECTION: The most important assignment

Say—

Here's an important homework assignment for you this week: Don't just go through life believing what someone else told you about Jesus. Examine what Jesus said about himself. Jesus made some strong claims about being the Son of God, the Messiah, the One with authority to forgive, the Lord and Savior.

Here is a list of gospel accounts that record the words of Jesus. (Distribute a list of "The Claims of Christ." These can be found in The Life Application Study Bible notes in John 6 or as a heading in other study Bibles or books.)

John wants these young followers of Jesus to know real love—that includes you.

Here is a listing of what Jesus said about love. (Distribute a list of "What Jesus Said about Love." These can be found in the Life Application Study Bible notes in Mark 12 or in other study Bibles or books.)

To know the real Jesus and the real love Christians talk about you need to examine the real evidence. Know what is true so you can identify and reject what is false.

(Note: Set up a time to follow up this assignment. Discuss the readings and how the Bible accounts of Jesus contrast with what false teachers were and are telling people.)

MEDIA: Who is Jesus?

Show the Sermonspice video clip "Jesus Is" (1:31). The world offers a wide range of mixed answers to this simple question. Was he simply a good man or was he the Son of God? This video examines what people think about him. It is available at www.sermonspice.com—search using the words *who is Jesus eleven72*.

The *Life Application Study Bible* is a rich resource of study notes and topical listings on the life of Jesus. Give your students an introduction to this rich biblical resource as you do an in-depth follow-up study.

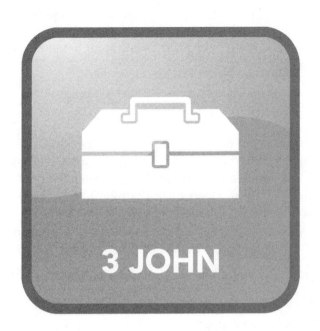

3 JOHN

3 John 1-12

TOPIC: What are you known for?

OBJECTIVE: Students will decide to build a positive, Christ-honoring reputation.

BACKGROUND/OVERVIEW: The apostle John wrote this short letter to commend Gaius, a prominent Christian in one of the churches, and to encourage him in his Christian life.

GAME/ICEBREAKER: Celebrity reps

Print a sheet or prepare a PowerPoint presentation that lists five to 10 celebrities in one column and a list of character or physical traits (positive and negative) that the celebrities are known for (e.g., adopting children, using steroids, fighting disease). The goal is to match up the traits with the correct celebrity.

Youth leader reps:

Follow the contest with this activity.

Shoot a local video asking students in the youth group to describe in two words what comes to mind when you name a specific youth leader from your group. You can do this with several youth leaders. Edit the answers into a fast-moving video. Keep it positive and upbeat when showing anything about local people.

ICEBREAKER QUESTIONS:

- How does a person get a reputation, good or bad?
- Who is a person with a good reputation whom you admire?
- What would you like people to think about you when you graduate from high school? Don't say it doesn't matter, because people will think something. What would you like it to be?

SCRIPTURE: 3 John 1-12
Read this aloud to your students as they follow along in their Bibles.

[1] The elder,
   To my dear friend Gaius, whom I love in the truth.

[2] Dear friend, I pray that you may enjoy good health and that all may go well with you, even as your soul is getting along well. [3] It gave me great joy to have some believers come and testify to your faithfulness to the truth, telling how you continue to walk in it. [4] I have no greater joy than to hear that my children are walking in the truth.

[5] Dear friend, you are faithful in what you are doing for the brothers and sisters, even though they are strangers to you. [6] They have told the church about your love. You will do well to send them on their way in a manner worthy of God. [7] It was for the sake of the Name that they went out, receiving no help from the pagans. [8] We ought therefore to show hospitality to such people so that we may work together for the truth.

[9] I wrote to the church, but Diotrephes, who loves to be first, will have nothing to do with us. [10] So when I come, I will call attention to what he is doing, spreading malicious nonsense about us. Not satisfied with that, he refuses to welcome other believers. He also stops those who want to do so and puts them out of the church.

[11] Dear friend, do not imitate what is evil but what is good. Anyone who does what is good is from God. Anyone who does what is evil has not seen God. [12] Demetrius is well spoken of by everyone—and even by the truth itself. We also speak well of him, and you know that our testimony is true.

STUDY QUESTIONS:

- What does John commend Gaius for being and doing?
- How did Gaius get this reputation?
- What does John think about Diotrephes and his relationship with people?
- In what area of your life is it difficult to love and help people?
- In what situations do we love to be first, like Diotrephes?
- Where do many of us need to do better imitating good rather than evil?

TALKING POINTS:

Share the following information with your students:

Your contact with people is important

Three questions to start our talk:

- How many people do you see (and people see you) on an average day?
- To how many people do you talk each day?
- What do you do with these people that impacts them positively?

Think about it. History is made every day by ordinary people doing ordinary things with other people. What we do and say impacts their lives and our lives as well. Being with people at school, work, or home isn't wasted time—it's life. Whether it's good or bad can be up to us and what we do.

Small acts of help are big

Most of us think about the big things we hope we'll do some day in the future that will make a significant difference and change the world. You don't have to wait for a special day in the future to do something big. Gaius and Demetrius did small, ordinary acts of kindness and service for people many days of their lives. They were careful to say what was true and helpful. The sum total of what they did and said added up to a huge reputation of being faithful friends to people who needed them. You and I can make the same impact by doing something kind and thoughtful for someone in our lives every day.

Stay humble and serve people

John calls out Diotrephes for his self-centered personal agenda. He was full of himself. He wanted to be big so bad he spread malicious rumors about John and other believers. Opening his home and being hospitable was an inconvenience to his self-centered life. In contrast Gaius and Demetrius had opposite reputations. People spoke well of them because they cared about people and because they lived it out every day. What reputation do you want? God loves humble people who spend their lives serving others.

You know people who need the help you can give them. Serve people and be humble. God will smile as he watches.

REAL-LIFE CONNECTION: Start small

Say to your students—

Before we dismiss the meeting, turn to a person next to you and tell them two positive qualities you see in them and how they live. After both of you have spoken, tell about two people you think God wants you to help this week. Pray for each other and encourage each other to be known for doing something small for God every day.

MEDIA:

What path will you walk?

Play the DVD clip "The Right Path" (1:37) from the movie *A Perfect Day*. You can access it at www.wingclips.com (search using the words *right path*). Michael appears to Rob and encourages him to seek the right path for the remainder of his short life. Rob has lived a very self-centered life and now is confronted with the end of his life and what he has done to his family and friends.

Jude 3-7

TOPIC: Who's telling the truth?

OBJECTIVE:
Students will know how to identity false teaching about Jesus and why it's important to compare what they see, hear, and read with the Bible.

BACKGROUND/OVERVIEW:
The first-century world (after Jesus' life) was filled with false teaching about God, Jesus, and the gospel message. Jude and all of Jesus' disciples were constantly warning people about these false teachers who were driven by fame, ego, and money. In 2,000 years not much has changed. Truth is always under attack. The modern media outlets are loaded with false teaching that leads many people away from what the Bible teaches.

GAME/ICEBREAKER: Hearing the truth
Items needed:

- Prizes (candy, books, money, hug)
- Penalties (pie in the face)
- Towel for cleanup
- Blindfold

Choose volunteers who want the chance to win a nice prize. Send them out of the room with a staff person. While they're out of the room, choose one wall of the room and place a truth-teller in the corner at one end and a liar in the corner at the other end (these people should have been chosen and briefed beforehand). Have the staff person (out of the room) blindfold the first volunteer, bring him back into the room, and place him at the middle of one wall. Explain that in both corners along the wall stand people who will be trying to convince the volunteer to walk to them. One is trustworthy and will be telling the truth. This person will have a prize. The other person, however, is untrustworthy and will be lying. He will have a penalty. As soon as the volunteer crosses a masking tape line on the floor in front of a person, he will receive the penalty or prize.

After the first participant is placed at the wall, give the signal to begin. Only the truth-teller and liar should speak to try to convince the person to move in his direction. They'll make statements like, "You can trust me, honest! I have a wonderful surprise for you. Have I ever misled you? Don't listen to him—he's lying!" and so forth. If the participant moves toward the liar, as soon as he crosses the line, the liar should push a whipped cream pie in his face. Conversely, as soon as the participant crosses the line in front of the truth-teller, he should receive the prize.

Repeat with the other volunteers.

ICEBREAKER QUESTIONS:

- (To the participants): **What influenced you the most in trying to determine who was telling the truth?**
- (To the participants): **How did you feel when you received your penalty or prize?**
- (To the whole group): **What have you read on the Internet or heard from someone that you now know isn't true (e.g., an urban legend)?**
- **How do you feel when you find out something you thought was true is actually a hoax or a false rumor?**
- **What's the danger of hearing and believing something about Jesus that isn't true?**
- **If you followed a false teacher for 10 years and found out what you were being taught wasn't true, what damage would it do to your life?**
- **How do you decide who is telling you the truth about Jesus and being a Christian, and who is misleading people with false teaching?**

SCRIPTURE: Jude 3-7

Make sure everyone has a Bible, and have them look up Jude and, then, read the passage.

³ Dear friends, although I was very eager to write to you about the salvation we share, I felt compelled to write and urge you to contend for the faith that the Lord has once for all entrusted to us, his people. ⁴ For certain individuals whose condemnation was written about long ago have secretly slipped in among you. They are ungodly people, who pervert the grace of our God into a license for immorality and deny Jesus Christ our only Sovereign and Lord.

⁵ Though you already know all this, I want to remind you that the Lord at one time delivered his people out of Egypt, but later destroyed those who did not believe. ⁶ And the angels who did not keep their positions of authority but abandoned their proper dwelling—these he has kept in darkness, bound with everlasting chains for judgment on the great Day. ⁷ In a similar way, Sodom and Gomorrah and the surrounding towns gave themselves up to sexual immorality and perversion. They serve as an example of those who suffer the punishment of eternal fire.

STUDY QUESTIONS

- Why would Jude spend so much time warning people about false teachers and false beliefs?
- What makes a false teacher so believable and so successful? (Possible answers: Many followers, fame, and financial success.)
- With so many different and opposing messages in the media outlets today about Jesus and the true way to find salvation, how do you figure out what is true and what is false?
- What have you seen, heard, and read this past year that is giving people wrong ideas about Jesus and what it means to be a Christian?

TALKING POINTS:

Share the following points with your students:

Important to know the truth

Jude wrote to remind these people about the true message of Jesus Christ and warn them about the false teachers who were twisting the facts about God's commands and plan of salvation. Can you explain what you believe and why it's true? It's easy to let what you learn at church school or in the church membership classes go in one ear and out the other. It doesn't seem important at the time. But not knowing what you believe about God and Jesus Christ is dangerous. The person who believes in nothing or doesn't know what she believes often falls for the message of a false teacher.

Believing what is wrong is dangerous

False teachers usually have a motive. Either they want your money or they want to control you and use you for their own wicked purposes. In both cases they draw you into a belief system that leads you away from the real Jesus. The choices you make under their control or using their twisted values can wreck your life.

Make the Bible your standard of truth

The U.S. Treasury Department trains agents to find counterfeit money by having them study the real U.S. currency. When they know the real thing well, they can spot the phony money. The best way to know the authentic Christian faith is to diligently read and study the Bible. Test what you hear and read. Does it match what the Bible says? Does it agree with historic Christian beliefs about Jesus and the gospel message?

Don't be fooled

Many false teachers use the Bible as their source. They often claim new revelations or inside information that no one has ever known. Treat all new teachings with caution. Talk about it with an experienced pastor and read from historic Christian writings on the subject. Be as careful with spiritual teaching as you are with the food you eat. You don't want to ingest anything that will make you sick.

REAL-LIFE CONNECTION: Take-home sheet: Truth in Media survey

Hand out a take-home sheet that has three columns:

- Source: Web site, Movie, TV Show, Magazine, or Book. (List where you saw it or heard it.)
- Who Said What? (List the person and what they said that you question is true.)
- Contradicts the Bible? (Describe what you think goes against what the Bible says.)

Tell everyone to watch and listen during the week with attentive eyes and ears, trying to find at least five examples of people saying something that disagrees with the Bible about God, Jesus, the purpose of life, how to get to heaven, the Bible, or being a Christian. Have them write a brief report on the sheet and bring it back to the next meeting.

MEDIA: What's true?

Teach your students how to research if a story or message on the Internet is true or false. This will teach them not to believe everything they hear or read about Jesus and the Christian faith.

Demonstrate (on a large screen) how to visit Web sites that research the truthfulness of the rumors that are prevalent on the Internet. Select a popular story that most people believe and visit a site like www.snopes.com or www. truthorfiction.com during the Game/Icebreaker section of the meeting. Students will be surprised by how much of what they read on the Internet or hear from others isn't true.

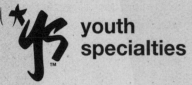

youth specialties

All About Youth Ministry

RESOURCES FOR YOUR MINISTRY,
YOUR S   OUL

The complete
NEW
TESTAMENT
resource for
YOUTH
WORKERS

Jack Crabtree, Editor

Curriculum

FOREWORD BY CHAP CLARK

FOLLOWIN
ESUS into colle
and beyo

Jeff Bax

Books for
Students

Check out all our resources at **www.youthspecialties.com.**